SCOTLAND'S GA
SCHEME 2018 GI

Printed by Belmont Press. Cover image Wormistoune, Fife
Maps produced by Alan Palfreyman Graphics @APalfreyman Contains OS data © Crown copyright MiniScale 2015

Scotland's Gardens Scheme, 2nd Floor, 23 Castle Street, Edinburgh EH2 3DN
T: 0131 226 3714 E: info@scotlandsgardens.org W: www.scotlandsgardens.org
Scottish Charity Number SC011337
ISSN: 2054-3301   ISBN: 978-0-901549-33-4

CHAIRMAN'S MESSAGE

In life we often find ourselves in situations we never expected and for myself this is one of them. Looking back over my forty years in horticulture I never thought, when I began my career as an apprentice at Maxwelton House, Moniaive, that I would one day be writing the Chairman's Message for Scotland's Gardens Scheme. I am honoured to have taken on this role and look forward to working with you further as we endeavour to improve the quality of life for individuals and communities across Scotland.

I would like to thank Mark Hedderwick especially for his kindness and guidance in the past few years. I am also grateful to the other Trustees for all the support they have provided in helping to build a strong foundation for the charity's future.

However, it is Volunteers and Garden Openers, District Organisers and Treasurers that are the lifeblood of the charity; selflessly committing time, effort and enthusiasm to raise funds. Always keen to hear their views, following a series of Regional Meetings around the country, the Trustees agreed to change the 60/40 split of garden gate funds raised in favour of the gardens owners chosen charity. It is hoped that this will encourage even more gardens to open. They also made the decision to revert back to our old name 'Scotland's Gardens Scheme' something that I know will please many.

Looking ahead to 2018 I hope that we can use it to grow our volunteer force among young people especially. As well as developing stronger partnerships which will improve horticultural training opportunities and, where possible, nurture and support horticultural therapy activities.

Hopefully the weather in 2018 will be kinder towards gardeners, but undoubtedly nature will have her say. However, I know that she will also reward in so many unimaginable ways. Whatever you are doing, be it planting, sowing, grass cutting or weeding or simply taking time to enjoy the horticultural efforts of others, thank you for your support. Remember, no matter what your age gardening changes lives for the better, please work with us to help others make that discovery.

David R Mitchell
Chairman

As the President of Scotland's Garden Scheme, I am delighted to hear that in 2018 we will be helping to celebrate VisitScotland's Year of Young People. Children of all ages love to have a patch of garden of their own and once they discover of the magic of gardening, it will, I am sure, lead to a life-long passion for many of them.

In September my husband and I visited Netherthird Community Garden, in East Ayrshire. This lovely garden, crammed full of flowers and vegetables, is host to a plethora of community groups. It introduces children to the pleasure of tending plants together and offers grownups a chance to learn many new skills. It even doubles-up as an outdoor classroom for the primary school children next door… This unique garden opened for the first time to the public in 2017 as part of the Scotland's Gardens Scheme.

All over Scotland, 2017 has been a good year (despite the weather!) for visiting gardens. More than 500 owners, from East Lothian to Orkney, threw open their gates to welcome visitors. As ever, I would like to thank every volunteer, organiser and garden owner for all the hard work that makes the Scotland's Garden Scheme possible.

I wish you all good gardening and good weather for 2018!

Camilla

WHO'S WHO IN SCOTLAND'S GARDENS SCHEME

Scotland's Gardens Scheme is supported by Trustees and Staff in the Head Office, each of whom bring their own expertise to the table. At the heart of the charity are our Volunteers, without whom there would be no gardens to visit. The Trustees and Staff are devoted to the charity. As keen garden lovers themselves, we asked them to share their favourite plant.

David Mitchell
Chairman

My favourite plant is Eucalyptus gunii, specifically the one at Inverewe gardens. It is an old childhood friend which I revisited this year.

Sarah Landale
Deputy Chairman

My favourite plants are sweet peas! They smell so wonderful, keep producing and remind me of sunshine (lacking in Dumfriesshire).

Peter Yellowlees
Treasurer

I like Hellebores. They add a splash of winter colour and don't take too much looking after. Ideal plants for me.

Trish Kennedy
Trustee

Primula – so varied and diverse: vulgaris, wanda, denticulata, alpicola, secunda, vialii, pulverulenta, to name but a few!

Richard Burns
Trustee

My favourite plant is the iceberg rose, which we enjoy at the house we visit in France, and soon at our home in the Scottish Lowlands!

Catherine Erskine
Trustee

The snowdrop. Why? Because my passion for snowdrops has introduced me to so many people.

Minette Struthers
Trustee

Eucryphia is my favourite plant just now. Of the 7 species, 5 grow well in our mild and damp west, to give late autumn colour.

Max Ward
Trustee

My favourite plant is a hyacinth, as it is one of the few I can recognize!

OUR PRESIDENT

Scotland's Gardens Scheme is delighted to have HRH The Duchess of Rothesay as our President.

PRESIDENT
HRH The Duchess of Rothesay

HEAD OFFICE

Charlotte Hunt
Trustee

My favourite plant is the lily of the valley. I also like to have plenty of autumn colour: foliage or berries!

Terrill Dobson
National Organiser

Borage is a fantastic plant, for courage, its beautiful blue and for all the bees it brings to the garden.

Hazel Reid
Office Manager

I love meconopisis. They're just a big burst of blue in the garden and look so special.

We also have many fantastic organiser Volunteers, whose hard work we could not do without. They are listed under our Districts.

Imogen McCaw
Marketing Officer

I'm a big fan of cowparsley, even if it is considered a weed. I love the delicate flowers and it's great for pollinators!

Lisa Pettersson
Graphic Design

My favorite plant is the birch tree, it reminds me of Sweden where its foilage is used for festive occations throughout the summer.

Growing something.

It doesn't happen overnight.

It takes time.

But don't hesitate.

Learn about the environment.

Ground yourself, but don't tie yourself down.

After all, circumstances can change in an instant.

But if you understand all the elements, that idea you planted won't just flourish, it will thrive.

Offices at: Bath Belfast Birmingham Bournemouth Cheltenham Edinburgh Exeter Glasgow Guildford Leeds Liverpool London Manchester Reigate Sheffield

At Investec Wealth & Investment we understand the potential of growth, that's why we've been sponsoring Scotland's Gardens Scheme, a source of beauty and inspiration, since 2009.

While we have over 15 offices across the UK, including Edinburgh and Glasgow, we like to invest in opportunities that are local. Whether that's helping individuals and businesses grow their portfolio or ensuring charities meet their goals, our investment managers are committed to securing prosperous futures for everyone we work with.

Please bear in mind that the value of investments and the income derived from them can go down as well as up and that you might not get back the amount that you have put in.

Find out more at investecwin.co.uk

or contact our Scottish Offices:
Edinburgh – 0131 226 5000
Glasgow – 0141 333 9323

WHAT HAPPENS TO THE MONEY RAISED?

Through our garden openings, Scotland's Gardens Scheme supports over 250 different charities each year. Beginning in 2018, our Garden Openers may choose a charity(s) to receive up to 60% of their open days takings. Many of these charities are small and local. We hope that this increase, from 40% in past years, will have a positive impact on our local communities and the charities close to our Garden Owners' hearts. The net remaining 40% of funds raised at our openings is distributed to Scotland's Gardens Scheme's beneficiaries.

Scottish Spca · Macmillan Cancer Support · Newburgh Cub Scouts · Buccleuch And Queensberry Caledonia Pipe Band

Appin Parish Church · Fobp · Scottish Autism · Feedback Madagascar · **Acting For Others** · Lynton Day Centre · Coldstream Gateway Association · The Dalhousie Centre Day Care For The Elderly · Hessilhead Wildlife Rescue · Church Of The Holy Name Oakley · **Accord Hospice** · **Children First** · **Beatson West Of Scotland Cancer Centre** · Highland Hospice · **Ben Walton Trust** · Fingask Follies · Girlguiding Dundee · Forgan Arts Centre Scio · **Abernethy In Bloom** · Blairgowrie Black Watch Army Cadet Force · **Fresh Start** · Inach Parish Church · **Alvo Rural South Lanarkshire** · **Aberdeen Royal Infirmary Roof Garden** · Brooke Action For Working Horses And Donkeys · Bumblebee Conservation Trust · **Black Isle Bee Gardens** · Fauna And Flora International · Plant Heritage · Mamie Martin Fund · Lothian Cat Rescue · **Cancer Research Uk** · **The Bread Maker** · **Alzheimer Scotland** · Ellon Men's Shed · **Abf The Soldiers' Charity** · Ahf · Elvanfoot Trust · **Perennial** · Royal Blind · Home Start Stonehaven · Sands · **Aberlemno Parish Church Of Scotland** · Fife Voluntary Action · Girl Guiding Montrose · **Alzheimer's Research Uk** · **Maggies Centre** · **Befriend A Child Ltd** · **Artlink Central Ltd** · Mary's Meals · Chest Heart And Stroke Scotland · **Alyn Hospital Jerusalem** · **St James The Great Scottish Episcopal Church Dollar** · **The Queen's Nursing Institute Scotland** · Rda · Nas · Lupus Uk · **Argyll Animal Aid** · **British Heart Foundation** · Loch Arthur · Arbroath St Vigeans Church Of Scotland · Soul Soup · Blebo Craigs Village Hall Trust · **The National Trust For Scotland** · Ifdas · Sarda · **All Saints Church Glencarse** · **Save Bellfield Campaign** · **Abdie And Dunbog Parish Church Of Scotland** · Pcds · **Amnesty International** · **Save Bellfield** · Lamancha Hub · Help For Heroes · Cheviot Churches Church Of Scotland · **Feis Na H'apainne** · **Nspcc** · Horatio's Garden · **Girlguiding Ayrshire North** · Crail Preservation Society · Friends Of Anchor · Ms Centre · Coronation Hall Muckhart · Enf En Foundation · Send A Cow · Port Logan Hall · **Glen Art** · **Rnli** · Colinsburgh Galloway Library · **Leuchie** · Dr Neils Garden Trust · **Bennachie Guides** · Erskine Hospital · Fortingall Parish Church · Haemophilia Scotland · Start Wigtownshire · **Home** · **Mind** · **Host** · **Japes** · Pituitary Foundation · Coulter Public Library Trust · Crossroads Care Skye And Lochalsh · Dalbeattie Community Initiative · **Dorward House** · Earl Haig Fund Poppy Scotland · **Dogs Trust** · Edinburgh Young Carers Project · **Dogs For Good** · Dementia Research Uk · Cruickshank Botanic Gardens · Craigentinny Telferton Allotments · **Clic Sargent** · **Cldf** · **Hope** · **Christ Church** · **Blesma** · Children's Hospice Association Scotland · **Diabetes Uk** · Cowal Elderly Befrienders Scio · **Dumfries Music Club** · Friends Of St Madan's Rosneath

Our Charity Tree, 2018

WHO ARE SCOTLAND'S GARDENS SCHEME'S BENEFICIARIES?

We also raise funds for our four beneficiaries: The Queen's Nursing Institute Scotland, Maggie's Centres, The National Trust for Scotland's Garden Fund and Perennial. Read more about them in the following pages.

INTRODUCTION TO THE GUIDEBOOK

We're thrilled about this year's fresh new guidebook look. We've made some changes to our format: adding a fold out map and key information at the back, and rearranging our Districts listings back to alphabetical order, both which we hope will make your guidebook easier to use.

As always, the pages are packed with gardens to visit, about 500 this year with some 60 new gardens. There's a wide variety of gardens choosing to open with us for charity. Long past are the days of primarily stately home openings. There are now many more village openings, allotments and a growing number of urban gardens. Community gardens are also on the rise, as enjoyed by our President, HRH The Duchess of Rothesay, with her visit to Netherthird Community Garden. Gardens with areas devoted to wildlife are also popular as well as woodlands.

Many of our gardens boast scenic views including coastal gardens and those on the islands of Arran, Skye and Shetland. Despite Scotland's very rural complexion, more than a quarter of our gardens can be reached with public transportation with the crème de la crème being Attadale Gardens with its own train station!

And if you're a dog lover, almost half of our gardens welcome dogs, on leads of course. We hope you've been following Mr Lowry's blog on our website. In fact he's made appearances in this year's guidebook - have you spotted him?

Learn the traditional skills of growing and drying flowers at Priorwood Garden or hear talks about beekeeping at Merchinston Cottage. Or perhaps you're a history buff. A number of our gardens are registered Designed Landscapes and many are steeped in history.

We're pleased to celebrate VisitScotland's Year of Young People for 2018. All of our private gardens will offer free admission to accompanied children to encourage families to explore our gardens and many will offer children's activities. Hunt for fairies from Culter Allers (Lanarkshire) to Balmeanach House (Skye), make a willow crown at the Cambo Spring Plant Sale or follow the Gruffalo Trail at Ardkinglas Woodland Garden.

The lore and legends behind many gardens make them the ideal background for our new "Growing Stories" venture teaming up with The Scottish Storytelling Centre to bring stories into our gardens.

Whether its wildflowers or roses, bogs or water features, leaf through these pages and find inspiring gardens to visit. If you need convincing, keep in mind that most of our openings offer homemade teas. And just think of all those charities that will benefit from your visits. What could be better!

Terrill Dobson
National Organiser

Find your way through cancer

Come to Maggie's

Maggie's provides free practical, emotional and social support for people with cancer and their family and friends.

Built in the grounds of NHS hospitals, our network of Centres across the UK are warm and welcoming places, with professional staff on hand to offer the support you need to find your way through cancer.

Maggie's Centres are open Monday to Friday, 9am – 5pm, and no referral is required.

Maggie's Centres across Scotland receive vital funds from every garden opening. Our heartfelt thanks go to everyone who supports Scotland's Gardens Scheme by opening their garden, volunteering or visiting a garden.

www.maggiescentres.org

Scotland's
GARDENS
Scheme
OPEN FOR CHARITY

MAGGIE'S

Everyone's home of cancer care

BENEFICIARY MESSAGES

MAGGIE'S
Everyone's home of cancer care

Here in Scotland it's sometimes easy to take the outstanding natural beauty of our landscape for granted, from the resilient heathers growing wild in our Highlands to the delicate bluebells that form a spectacular carpet in our woodlands each spring.

In the face of such natural beauty, one might ask how gardeners are to compete! Yet Scottish gardeners are made of stern stuff, embracing the challenges of our climate to produce stunning gardens of grand and modest proportions in equal measure. Scotland's Gardens Scheme does a marvellous job of reminding us of what glorious gardens are in our midst, in spite of the challenges our climate presents, and a stroll around one of the garden openings brings an inner calm and respite from the busy schedule of our daily lives.

At Maggie's we recognise that being in a natural environment can have a positive effect on wellbeing, improving mindfulness and reducing stress levels. Run by experienced gardeners, our therapeutic gardening groups are open to anyone with cancer, their family and friends, and offer the chance to enjoy the gardens at Maggie's and take part in a creative activity with other people who are going through a similar experience.

I would like to take this opportunity to thank you all for your most welcome support of Maggie's in Scotland again this year. All of our Centres benefit from Scotland's Gardens Scheme donations and from every garden opening, for which we are enormously grateful.

Happy gardening!

Laura Lee
Chief Executive
Maggie's

Maggie's Glasgow Gartnavel
Architect: OMA
Garden design: Lily Jencks
Photography © Nick Turner

Thank you to all the supporters of Scotland's Gardens Scheme who continue to help fund our Queen's Nurse programme - allowing us to make a real difference to the health and wellbeing of people in communities across Scotland.

www.qnis.org.uk   @QNI_Scotland

QNIS is a Scottish Charitable Incorporated Organisation, SC005751

BENEFICIARY MESSAGES

THE QUEEN'S NURSING INSTITUTE SCOTLAND

In 1931, Scotland's Gardens Scheme was created to raise money for the Queen's Nurses before the NHS was established. The Institute has been generously supported by garden owners and visitors ever since.

Last year a new and important chapter in the long history between the Queen's Nursing Institute Scotland (QNIS) and Scotland's Gardens Scheme got under way as the Queen's Nurse title was awarded in Scotland for the first time in 50 years. The move saw 20 outstanding community nurses selected to take part in a nine-month development programme funded directly by Scotland's Gardens Scheme.

The programme promotes excellent community nursing practice. Each participant is at the heart of bringing compassionate, person-centred, community-based health and care to the people they work with. The course is designed to enable each practitioner to be the best they can be, acting as role models for others. It includes a residential course, follow up workshops and monthly telephone coaching to support the personal and professional development of the individual. During the programme each candidate works on a key issue for their community to improve the quality of care and enhance the wellbeing of patients.

The new Queen's Nurses are employed by the voluntary and independent sectors, as well as the NHS. Their day-to-day roles vary from being the only healthcare professional on a small and remote island, to being a midwife caring for asylum seeking mothers in Glasgow or being the nurse in charge of caring for people who find themselves in police custody. We have a wide range of roles performed by our first cohort – there are also health visitors, a care home nurse, practice and district nurses, school nurses and a Parish nurse. As Queen's Nurses they are following in the footsteps of the previous generation as they share an absolute commitment to promoting excellent care within their community.

As well as running the new Queen's Nurse programme, we also provide funding to nurse-led community projects aimed at reducing health inequalities. In 2017, we funded seven projects under the Catalysts for Change scheme – with the money going directly to making a difference to the community. Those selected include a group who will run nature walks to improve wellbeing, and an inner-city partnership that will find and refurbish premises to set up a men's shed – a meeting place for men to share and learn new skills.

We continue to provide support to more than 400 retired Queen's Nurses in Scotland and beyond. We have a committed network of retired Queen's Nurses who volunteer to visit other retired community nurses in their own homes, to bring companionship and look out for their welfare. The retired Queen's Nurses have regular gatherings where they remain connected and enjoy fellowship.

We are proud to maintain our status as a Beneficiary Charity of Scotland's Gardens Scheme and are immensely grateful to all those who open their gardens and to the garden visitors who continue to support our work.

It is an exciting time for QNIS and we are delighted that the decades-long support of Scotland's Gardens Scheme continues as another group of community nurses work towards becoming the second cohort to receive the Queen's Nurse title in 2018.

Clare Cable
Chief Executive and Nurse Director, QNIS

NATIONAL TRUST *for* SCOTLAND

Spectacular

SEASONAL GARDENS

OPEN
ALL YEAR

nts.org.uk

The National Trust for Scotland is a Scottish charity, SC007410

BENEFICIARY MESSAGES

NATIONAL TRUST *for* **SCOTLAND**

On behalf of the National Trust for Scotland, I would like to thank all of Scotland's Gardens Scheme owners and volunteers for their ongoing support and commitment to the National Trust for Scotland's heritage gardens. Your financial support, and assistance in many other ways, is particularly appreciated by our staff at our participating gardens as it directly benefits their daily work.

Our organisations have developed in parallel over many years, with Scotland's Gardens Scheme becoming an important pillar for the continued growth of the National Trust for Scotland's gardens. Together we share a deep love of gardens and gardening, and recognise their value for the people of Scotland and beyond.

You support us in our most important aims – to protect and care for our heritage and to encourage opportunities for people to experience it. In 2017, through our 42 Scotland's Gardens Scheme events, we engaged with many visitors by holding sales of rare and garden plants, giving demonstrations, providing fun quizzes and crafts for children, organising specialist walks and talks, hosting cookery demonstrations and creating some unique evening-access experiences.

In 2017 we also undertook a review of our gardens, led by our new Head of Heritage Gardening, Ann Steele. In addition to recognising the gardens' importance for plant and garden conservation and access and enjoyment by a wide range of people, our review highlighted the growing shortage of professional gardeners with the skills to manage complicated heritage sites. You already help us through your direct support of a student at our School of Heritage Gardening, and we aim to do more in the future to grow the next generation of great gardeners in Scotland.

Simon Skinner
Chief Executive

Branklyn, Perth & Kinross

Pitmedden, Aberdeenshire

Threave, Kirkcudbrightshire

PERENNIAL

GARDENERS' ROYAL BENEVOLENT SOCIETY

Helping Horticulturists In Need Since 1839

Helping people in desperate need

We need you

Our world depends on the generosity of others and we can only continue to provide life changing services for people facing considerable hardship with your help.

Your visits to gardens open through Scotland's Gardens Scheme help Perennial throughout the year.

If you would like to contribute further to our work, please consider making a personal donation or find out more about how you can support us.

perennial.org.uk/support

If you know someone who may need help, please pass on our details.

General advice: 0800 093 8543

Debt advice: 0800 093 8546

perennial.org.uk/help

Donations: 0800 093 8510

Perennial, 115-117 Kingston Road, Leatherhead, Surrey, KT22 7SU.

Perennial has been supporting gardeners and wider horticulturists in need for over 175 years.

Our UK wide team of caseworkers and debt advisers see the difficulties that people face daily to survive, particularly when things go wrong through illness, financial hardship, old age and any other of life's many challenges. In a profession that is generally low-paid, prone to job insecurity and which often carries considerable risk of injury, Perennial helps with financial advice, emotional support and practical guidance when there is no one else.

Thanks to all those who visited gardens open under Scotland's Gardens Scheme, the organisation donated a record £37,000 to Perennial in 2017. This covered 45% of the charity's costs in Scotland, including paying a dedicated senior caseworker.

On behalf of everyone at Perennial, thank you.

Dougal Philip
Owner, New Hopetoun Gardens, Edinburgh
Chairman of Perennial Trustees

"Thank you to the hundreds of volunteers who open their glorious gardens to raise money for the charities supported by Scotland's Gardens Scheme. Most people come to Perennial as a last port of call, but we want everyone in the industry to know that Perennial is here for as long as it takes if they should ever need help. This partnership is a crucial part of spreading that message in Scotland."

Carole Baxter,
Beechgrove Garden
presenter &
Perennial Trustee

Martin's Story

When Martin was struck down with Guillain-Barré syndrome, a rare auto-immune disease, he was signed off work for three years. Barely able to walk, he could only watch as the family landscaping business, which he ran with his mother Morven, went under.

When his mother came across Perennial's stand at Gardening Scotland a few years ago, their luck began to turn around.

Martin says:

"I had never been out of work, but when I became ill it never even occurred to me that I would get more than two or three days' sick pay. The Perennial caseworker was amazing and her input made all the difference in the world. She helped sort out my Disability Living Allowance and other benefits to help keep the family afloat until I recovered and could return to work. Without her help, we would have been destitute."

Martin now teaches horticulture at Argyll College, part of the University of the Highlands and Islands.

He and his wife Amber also run a successful design and landscaping business.

They are committed to helping Perennial spread the word about its life-changing services in Scotland.

Martin and Amber share their story and talk more about how Perennial helped them in a short film on the charity's website.

perennial.org.uk/martin

Find everyday greetings cards online year-round

Our beautiful range of everyday and seasonal greetings cards can be purchased online.

Every sale helps Perennial support more people in need.

Shop our full range of cards, gifts and garden and home essentials at perennial.org.uk/shop

GROWING STORIES: STORYTELLING FOR ALL

Hear about long lost villages, hidden from sight. Listen to stories about the maiden voyage of Britain's first steamboat. Hear tales of the Bronze age hoard in Duddingston Loch below Dr Neil's garden.

Once upon a time...

Scotland's Gardens Scheme has teamed up with The Scottish International Storytelling Festival, to share the stories of our gardens. Gardens are places of stories, each with their distinctive 'storybank', from the secrets they hold, to the plants they nurture. We will be co-hosting "Growing Stories", fantastic storytelling events at our special gardens across Scotland in 2018. A perfect family friendly day out; so throw on your coats and don your wellies, there's lots in store!

Storytelling is the sharing of experiences, memories, gossip and compelling yarns. But live storytelling is something more specific. It is carefully chosen and crafted stories, presented with enthusiasm, to stir curiosity, imagination and learning. This sense of storytelling is based on centuries of older human culture, when what was shared through the spoken word, and held in the memory, was fundamental, in the absence of books and ipads!

However, live storytelling has come back into its own in the digital age, as people come more and more to value direct human exchange and contact. Stories that are shared directly between people are almost as important as the content of the story being told.

Every garden has a story to tell

Ken Shapley shares Nature Tales at the Royal Botanic Gardens
© Solen Collet

Storyteller David Campbell and young nature fans © Colin Hattersley

There is a treasure trove of stories in gardens: from the lores, tradition and botanical history behind the plants and trees, to the harvest and seasonal festivals. There might be tales behind the garden's location and relationship with the surroundings, as well as the creation and history. And behind it all is the great backdrop; the drama of nature herself. Gardens are private worlds for animals and birdlife, and play an important setting for their perennial activities. How was the garden, its inhabitants and plants affected by the changing weather and it's inimitable climatic events? What old weather lore has been passed down through the garden's generations of carers?

Harnessing these stories involves looking back, by reaching into the store of memory. A memory comprised of the stories and skills that are involved in tending a garden. To grow a garden, people grow and care for plants and trees, and in turn the plants nurture people and grow their knowledge and skills. These intrinsic experiences and stories also lead to questions about the future. What hopes and dreams do our gardens inspire? What does the future hold for these gardens and gardens in general?

"Everything you look at can become a fairytale, and you can get a story from everything you touch"

Hans Christian Andersen

Today many schools have gardening projects, but at least a couple of previous generations missed out, leaving a generation gap in the lives of gardens. Community garden projects are reaching out across the generations and Scotland's Gardens Scheme is playing its own part. By looking at 'Growing Stories' The Scottish International Storytelling Festival and Scotland's Gardens Scheme hope to reach out to new audiences, and draw people of all ages into the wonderful experience of gardens and gardening.

So it becomes a story of welcome and sharing; to share the life of gardens and the stories of our gardens with the wider community. A wonderful aim for Scotland's Gardens Scheme and The Scottish International Storytelling Festival to strive towards in 'Growing Stories'. We hope you will explore these gardens with us!

Donald Smith
Director of The Scottish Storytelling Centre

Creating an inspiring, rewarding and enjoyable experience for volunteers and visitors alike

PARTICIPATING GARDENS

PARTICIPATING GARDENS	DATE
Culzean Castle, Ayrshire & Arran	Monday 7 May
Dr Neil's Garden, Edinburgh, Midlothian & West Lothian	Monday 7 May
Inverewe Garden & Estate, Inverness, Ross, Cromarty & Skye	Saturday 12 May
Tyninghame House and The Walled Garden, East Lothian	Sunday 13 May
Fingask Castle, Perth & Kinross	Thursday 11 October
Dalswinton, Dumfriesshire	Sunday 21 October

Tiny Tales in Nature with Jane Mather © The Scottish Storytelling Centre

DIANA MACNAB AWARD
FOR OUTSTANDING SERVICE

The Diana Macnab Award, presented annually at our Conference, is granted to someone who has given outstanding service to Scotland's Gardens Scheme. In 2017 the recipient was Lucy Lister-Kaye, our District Organiser for Inverness, Ross, Cromarty & Skye.

No one in the Highlands will be the least surprised that Lucy Lister-Kaye is this year's recipient of The Diana McNab Award. Lucy has been a diligent ambassador for Scotland's Gardens Scheme for more years than she is prepared to admit. Not only has she always opened her own garden, but she has administered the Highlands' gardens programme with diplomacy, tact and a special brand of persuasiveness, all of which has maintained a high level of participation and a continuously solid contribution to owners' own charities and those the scheme supports.

Lucy's District stretches from the Monadliaths to Morayshire, from Inverness to Skye and the Western Isles. She has made a point of visiting the gardens herself whenever she can, and always pays to enter, an exemplary dedication to the overarching aims of the scheme.

In her own garden at the House of Aigas, she has not only completely created the garden from scratch 30 years ago, but, assisted by Highland Hospice volunteers, has provided sumptuous teas for hundreds of visitors every open day each summer. The garden continues to grow and delight, almost all done by herself. She is a passionate gardener, achieving remarkable results even in the Highlands' unpredictable climate. Her skill at blending foliage colours is legendary - some wag once accused her of 'Fifty Shades of Green'. Her herbaceous borders burst with lilies, hydrangeas, roses, rudbeckias, salvias, geraniums, geums, digitalis and clematis right through the summer and on into autumn. This year for the first time she included a spectacular roundel of annual wildflowers.

When friends ask her husband 'How is Lucy?' his answer is 'No improvement! She shows no sign of slowing down.' When they ask 'Where is she?' he answers 'God only knows - out there somewhere!'

MAGICAL GARDENS: ACTIVITIES FOR YOUNG GARDEN EXPLORERS

Scotland's Gardens Scheme is thrilled to be celebrating VisitScotland's 'Year of Young People' in 2018. Many of our garden openings will be hosting children's activities throughout the year.

Gardens can be inspirational spaces for younger visitors and make wonderful family days out. From garden exploration and delicious teas to garden quizzes and hands-on activities, our garden owners have fantastic activites in store. Here's inspiration for what you can do in *your own* green space:

LEAF COLLAGE

Whether you design an abstract piece or collage a hedgehog, these autumnal artworks are a great decorations for the kitchen fridge. Keep a look out for friendly insects that make their homes in leaf piles!

PAPER DAFFODILS

What signals spring better than the yellow trumpets of daffodils? These paper daffodils are super easy to make at home. Why not create a bunch and pop them in a vase for long-lasting enjoyment? Watch out for sticky, glue covered fingers though!

BIRD FEEDER

Create your own bird feeder to keep the birds well fed in the winter! These feeders are super cool because they decompose afterwards.

INGREDIENTS:

Bird seeds

Pine Cone

String

Lard

Method: Dip the pine cone into the softened lard, so that the lard oozes into all the gaps. Next, roll the lard covered pine cone in the seeds, so that it is fully covered. Leave it to harden. Then, with some string (and some adult help) tie the newly created bird feeder into the trees! Good job feeding all the birds!

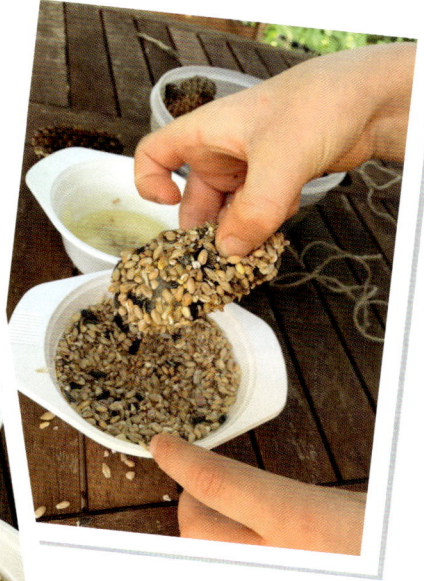

"For children, most importantly, being in the garden is something magical"

Fritjof Capra

BARK RUBBING

This simple activity is a great way to compare the differences in tree bark, and admire the patterns! As it only requires a bit of paper and a crayon (or two!) it's easy to do at home or try this in one of our gardens.

This icon (found on our garden listings) means the garden hosts family friendly children's activities, so find out what's on near you! Open the garden door, and explore the magic within!

A GARDEN FOR ALL: NETHERTHIRD COMMUNITY GARDEN

Netherthird Community Garden, Ayrshire was set up in 2010 by Margaret Campbell. The garden is a wonderful resource to the local community and is used for a range of activities: from an outside classroom for the Primary School to a site for adult education and further training.

The garden has transformed the lives of local residents and this was recognised in September 2017. The garden extended an invite to Their Royal Highnesses The Duke and Duchess of Rothesay for a special Scotland's Gardens Scheme opening. It was a great day for all, despite the traditional Scottish weather!

Maggie Campbell founded the garden in 2010 as a space for all and it has reshaped the lives of many of the local residents.
Photo: David Blatchford

Quirky metal sculptures, donated to community garden by artist Brian Maxwell.
Photo: David Blatchford

Inside the polytunnel, vegetables and hanging baskets ready for sale on the open day.
Photo: Robert Davis

The garden was built on a piece of unused scrub of land on a 30 year lease from East Ayrshire Council.
Photo: David Blatchford

Gorgeous wooden gazebos, funded by the Prince's Foundation, are the central features of the garden.
Photo: David Blatchford

Our District Organisers Rose-Ann Cuninghame and Kim Donald.
Photo: David Blatchford

Visitors to the garden didn't leave empty handed!
Photo: Robert Davis

Garden produce and cut flowers from the garden presented to Their Royal Highnesses.
Photo: Robert Davis

Wildflower garden with a children's hideaway hut.
Photo: Robert Davis

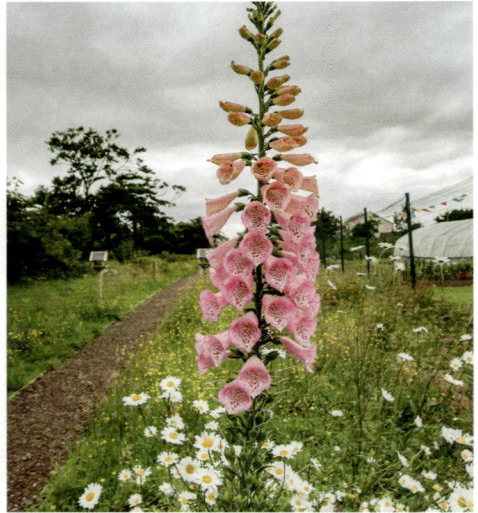

The inner formal garden is surrounded by a wildflower and wildlife garden.
Photo: Robert Davis

Our President, The Duchess of Rothesay, The Duke of Rothesay and local primary school children.
Photo: Robert Davis

The garden opened for Scotland's Gardens Scheme for the first time on the 24th June 2017

NEW GARDENS FOR 2018

Scotland's Gardens Scheme welcomes all sorts of gardens, big and small, ornamental or vegetable. This year Scotland's Gardens Scheme is delighted to welcome over 50 new gardens into the fold. From Liggat Cheek Cottage in Wigtownshire to Shanvall in the Highlands, all unique and well worth exploring. We hope you'll show your support by visiting them in person!

ABERDEENSHIRE

105 Inchgarth Road
Parkvilla
Three Hidden Gardens

ANGUS & DUNDEE

Dunvorist Cottage
Melgund Castle
The Gardens of Brechin

ARGYLL & LOCHABER

Baile Geamhraidh
Inveryne Woodland Garden
Oakfield
Ormsary House

AYRSHIRE & ARRAN

Clover Park
Glendoune House Walled Garden
Townend of Kirkwood

BERWICKSHIRE

Coldstream Open Gardens
Marlfield and Ruthven Gardens

CAITHNESS, SUTHERLAND, ORKNEY & SHETLAND

The Gardens of Dornoch

The Gardens of Dornoch, Caithness, Sutherland, Orkney & Shetland

Dunvorist Cottage Garden, Angus & Dundee

DUMFRIESSHIRE

Crawick Multiverse
Dalswinton Mill
Kirkcaldy House

EAST LOTHIAN

Eastfield and Redcliff Gardens

EDINBURGH, MIDLOTHIAN & WEST LOTHIAN

Belgrave Crescent Gardens
Open Gardens of the Lower New Town
Whitburgh House Walled Garden

FIFE

Fife Spring Trail
Hidden Gardens of Newburgh
Lathrisk Gardens
Lucklaw House

GLASGOW & DISTRICT

The Good Life Gardens

INVERNESS, ROSS, CROMARTY & SKYE

5 Knott
Kilcoy Castle
Kiltarlity Gardens
Shanvall

KIRKCUDBRIGHTSHIRE

Barwhinnock House
Dalbeattie Community Allotments Association
Linden Lea
Luckie Harg's

Viewpark Allotments, Lanarkshire

LANARKSHIRE

5 Fergus Gardens
Symington House
Viewpark Allotments and Gardens

MORAY & NAIRN

Gordon Castle Walled Garden
Logie House

PERTH & KINROSS

5 Sutherland Crescent
Eastbank Cottage
Errol Park

RENFREWSHIRE

Bravehound - Erskine Hospital

ROXBURGHSHIRE

Stable House
Thirlestane
West Summerfield

STIRLINGSHIRE

Kippen Village
The Japanese Garden at Cowden

WIGTOWNSHIRE

Liggat Cheek Cottage

Easter Ord, Aberdeenshire

Thinking of opening your garden? We're here to help

Shanvall, Inverness, Ross, Cromarty & Skye

SGS PLANT SALES

Local SGS plants sales are a great place to buy plants for your garden. You'll find a large selection of locally grown plants tried and tested in your climate.

- You can seek advice from the plant sellers about where and when to plant.

- Good quality plants and good quality prices.

- You get the pleasure of taking home an abundance of lovely new plants, knowing that the proceeds go to charity.

- And don't forget that many of our garden openings also offer plants for sale. Look for the flower icon next to the listing.

DONATE YOUR PLANTS

FIND PLANTS THAT WILL FLOURISH IN YOUR GARDEN

Overstuffed herbaceous borders? Copious cuttings? Superfluous seedlings? Why not donate plants to a local plant stall, or run one yourself? It's a great way to clear some space, share some horticultural knowledge and help support a local charity.

Bruckhills Croft, Aberdeenshire

PLANT SALES 2018

FIFE

Cambo Gardens Spring Plant Sale, Kingsbarns

Sunday 15 April
11:30am - 3:30pm

RENFREWSHIRE

Kilmacolm Plant Sale, Outside Kilmacolm Library,
Lochwinnoch Road, Kilmacolm

Saturday 28 April
10:00am - 12:00pm

PERTH & KINROSS

NEW Pitcurran House, Abernethy

Sunday 20 May
12:00pm - 5:00pm

PEEBLESSHIRE & TWEEDDALE

8 Halmyre Mains, West Linton

Sunday 10 June
10:00am - 12:00pm

ANGUS & DUNDEE

Angus Plant Sale, Logie Walled Garden

Saturday 1 September
11:30am - 2:00pm

DUNBARTONSHIRE

Hill House Plant Sale, Helensburgh

Sunday 2 September
11:30am - 4:00pm

FIFE

Hill of Tarvit Plant Sale & Autumn Fair, Cupar

Sunday 30 September
10:30am - 3:00pm

Money may not buy happiness, but it can buy plants for your garden.

SNOWDROP OPENINGS

SCOTTISH SNOWDROP FESTIVAL
SATURDAY 27 JAN – SUNDAY 11 MARCH

Celebrate the first signs of spring by exploring our beautiful Snowdrop Gardens.

Scotland's Gardens Scheme, Discover Scottish Gardens and VisitScotland work together to support the popular Scottish Snowdrop Festival and promote this very special time of year for visiting gardens.

The following gardens will be opening for charity under Scotland's Gardens Scheme for the 2017 Scottish Snowdrop Festival:

ABERDEENSHIRE
Bruckhills Croft

ANGUS & DUNDEE
Dunninald Castle
Langley Park Garden
Lawton House

ARGYLL & LOCHABER
Ardmaddy Castle
Maolachy's Garden

AYRSHIRE & ARRAN
Blair House, Blair Estate
Craufurdland Estate

DUMFRIESSHIRE
Craig

EAST LOTHIAN
Shepherd House

FIFE
Lindores House

INVERNESS, ROSS, CROMARTY & SKYE
Abriachan Garden Nursery

KINCARDINE & DEESIDE
Ecclesgreig Castle

KIRKCUDBRIGHTSHIRE
Barwhinnock House
Brooklands
Danevale Park

LANARKSHIRE
Cleghorn

MORAY & NAIRN
10 Pilmuir Road West

PEEBLESSHIRE & TWEEDDALE
Kailzie Gardens

PERTH & KINROSS
Braco Castle
Fingask Castle
Kilgraston School

STIRLINGSHIRE
Duntreath Castle
Gargunnock House Garden

WIGTOWNSHIRE
Castle Kennedy and Gardens
Craichlaw

The common snowdrop's latin name Galanthus nivalis means Milk Flower of the Snow.

Visit some of the most magical swathes of snowdrops in gardens and woodlands of Scotland. These dainty flowers are a wonderful sight on a brisk winters walk through native woodland or on a garden stroll.

DID YOU KNOW?
Old Scottish lore dictates that it is bad luck to bring snowdrops indoors.

GET IN TOUCH IF YOU HAVE SOME LOVELY SNOWDROPS
We would love to feature your garden in 2019!

" Lone flower, hemmed in with snows, and white as they
But hardier far, once more I see thee bend
Thy forehead as if fearful to offend,
Like an unbidden guest"

from 'To A Snowdrop' by William Wordsworth

'Wendy's Gold', Bruckhills Croft, Aberdeenshire

LONG SERVICE AWARDS

Scotland's Gardens Scheme likes to celebrate milestone anniversaries. In 2018, five gardens will receive Long Service Awards.

As any gardener will know it takes time and commitment to keep a garden. Our Garden Owners go above and beyond in their generosity of time to, not only their garden, but in hosting visitors and promoting their openings. All this commitment comes with knowledge of their gardens and plants. This knowledge makes Garden Owners an excellent resource. Our garden owners love to share their knowledge, so if you've got a burning question – ask it!

We are thankful for the commitment these gardens show to our charity and their dedication to such a worthy cause. Why not congratulate them in person by visiting during their opening?

75 Castle Kennedy
(Wigtownshire)

50 Glendoick
(Perth & Kinross)

25 Crinan Hotel
(Argyll & Lochaber)

Inveresk Lodge Garden
(East Lothian)

Kirklands
(Fife)

Castle Kennedy, Wigtownshire, Stair family and gardening team © Phil Rigby/Dumfries & Galloway Life Magazine

Inveresk Lodge Garden, East Lothian

Glendoick, Perth & Kinross

Crinan Hotel, Argyll & Lochaber © Liam Anderstrem

Kirklands, Fife

"We are delighted to be celebrating the 75th anniversary of the opening of Castle Kennedy Gardens with Scotland's Garden Scheme in 2018. This represents the involvement of four generations of the Stair family, including both our children, and we hope it will include many more".

Emily, Lady Stair

OVER 500 GARDENS OPEN WITH US ANNUALLY

NATIONAL PLANT COLLECTIONS

National Plant Collections aim to preserve and develop a comprehensive collection of one group of plants in trust for the future. These gardens do a wonderful job at safeguarding plant species, some of which might otherwise be lost to future generations.

For more information about plant collections, see The Plant Heritage website (www.nccpg.com)

ANGUS & DUNDEE

3 Balfour Cottages
Primula auricula (alpine)

ARGYLL & LOCHABER

Benmore Botanic Garden
Abies, South American Temperate Conifers, *Picea*

Crarae Garden
Nothofagus

AYRSHIRE & ARRAN

Brodick Castle & Country Park
Rhododendron (subsect *Grandia,* subsect *Falconera,* and subsect *Maddenia*)

DUMFRIESSHIRE

Newtonairds Lodge
Hosta plantaginea cvs. and hybrids

FIFE

Backhouse at Rossie Estate
Narcissus (Backhouse cvs.)

Cambo
Galanthus

GLASGOW & DISTRICT

Greenbank Garden
Bergenia cvs. & spp.

INVERNESS, ROSS, CROMARTY & SKYE

Inverewe Garden and Estate
Olearia, *Rhododendron* (subsect. *Barbata*, subsect. *Glischra*, subsect. *Maculifera*).

GROWING FOR THE FUTURE

Primula auricula. 3 Balfour Cottages, Angus & Dundee

KINCARDINE & DEESIDE

Crathes Castle Garden
Dianthus (Malmaison)

MORAY & NARIN

Brodie Castle
Narcissus (Brodie cvs.)

PEEBLESSHIRE & TWEEDDALE

Dawyck Botanic Garden
Larix spp. and *Tsuga* spp.

PERTH & KINROSS

Branklyn Garden
Cassiope, *Meconopsis* (large flowered blue spp. &
cvs.) and *Rhododendron* (subsect. *Taliense*)

Explorers Garden
Meconopsis (large blue flowered spp. & cvs.)

Glendoick
Rhododendron(sect. *Pogonanthum*, subsect.
Uniflora, subsect. *Campylogyna* & subsect. *Glauca*
and Cox hybrids)

Parkhead House
Lilium (Mylnefield lilies)

WIGTOWNSHIRE

Logan Botanic Garden
Gunnera, *Leptospermum* spp., and *Griselinia* spp.,
Clianthus and *Sutherlandia*.

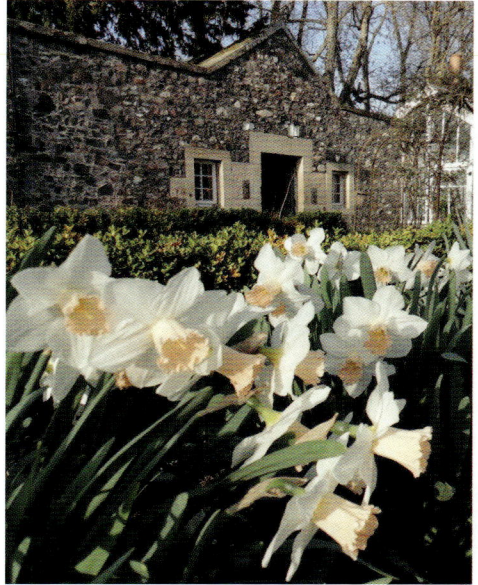

Daffodils, Rofsie Arts Garden, Fife

Hosta, Newtonairds Lodge, Dumfriesshire

Meconopsis, Explorer's Garden, Perth & Kinross

CHAMPION TREES

Champion Trees are trees of notable status listed on the UK Tree Register. These trees are recorded due to outstanding size and growth, their unique characteristics, rarity or historical significance. Below are some of our gardens with Champion Trees, which will you visit? For more information see The Tree Register website (www.treeregister.org).

ABERDEENSHIRE

Cruickshank Botanic Gardens
Quercus ilex, *Acer griseum* and a tri-stemmed *Nothofagus obliqua*

ARGYLL & LOCHABER

Ardkinglas Woodland Garden
'Grand Fir' tallest tree in Britain and others

Arduaine Garden
Nine, including *Gevuina avellana*

Crarae Garden
Abies, Acer and *Chamaecyparis*

AYRSHIRE & ARRAN

Brodick Castle & Country Park
Several

EAST LOTHIAN

Tyninghame House
Two British and seven Scottish

FIFE

Falkland Palace and Garden
Acer platanoides 'Crimson King'

INVERNESS, ROSS, CROMARTY & SKYE

Dundonnell House
Yew and Holly

Red squirrel, Caithness

House of Aigas and Field Centre
Douglas fir, Atlas cedar and *Sequoiadendron giganteum*

Inverewe Garden and Estate
Over 20

Old Allangrange
Yew

KINCARDINE & DEESIDE

Crathes Castle Garden
Four champions including *Zelkova* x *verschaffeltii*

PEEBLESHIRE & TWEEDDALE

Dawyck Botanic Garden
Numerous

Kailzie Gardens
Larch planted 1725

PERTH & KINROSS

Branklyn Garden
Pinus sylvestris 'Globosa'

Fingask Castle
Bhutan Pine

ROXBURGHSHIRE

Yetholm Village Gardens
The Old Yew Tree in Yew Tree Lane

WIGTOWNSHIRE

Castle Kennedy and Gardens
6 British, 11 Scottish and 25 for Dumfries and Galloway

Logan Botanic Garden
Polylepis and *Eucalyptus*

Logan House Gardens
7 UK and 11 Scottish

Ardinklas, Argyll & Lochaber, Mightiest Conifer in Europe

Bhutan Pine, Fingask Castle, Perth & Kinross

FIFE SPRING TRAIL

Running over the spring this year in April and May, the Fife Gardeners are offering an opportunity to visit 12 privately owned gardens across Central and East Fife.

This offers a very flexible way to keep up your weekly dose of beautiful gardens, and excellent value for money. Fife can look quite bleak in March, with brown arable fields and fringed by a cold North Sea, but by April, the countryside is starting to burst into verdant colours, and our gardens are also starting to bloom. A wide variety of gardens are on offer, from bluebell and daffodil woodlands, through natural style plantings of rhododendrons and other spring flowering shrubs, to more formal garden settings in some of Fife's most notable gardens, large and small.

A ticket for the Fife Spring Trail makes a perfect gift – and do treat yourself as well!

Wemyss Castle, Coaltown of Wemyss

Wormistoune, Crail

THE GARDENS

Cambo Plant Fair
Kingsbarns KY16 8QD

Craigfoodie
Dairsie KY15 4RU

Crail Gardens
2 Castle Street, Crail KY10 3SQ
17 Marketgate, Crail KY19 3TL

Kenlygreen House
Boarhills, St Andrews KY16 8PT

Myres Castle
Auchtermuchty KY14 7EW

South Flisk
Blebo Craigs, Cupar KY15 5UQ

Straiton Farmhouse
Straiton Farm, Balmullo KY16 0BN

The Murrel
Aberdour KY3 0RN

The Tower
1 Northview Terrace, Wormit DD6 8PP

Wemyss Castle
Coaltown of Wemyss KY1 4TE

Wormistoune
Crail KY10 3XH

CHARITIES

40% net of the proceeds goes to Scotland's Gardens Scheme's beneficiary charities. The remainder will be split equally between RHET Fife Countryside Initiative and Riding for the Disabled Fife.

ADMISSION

£25 for entrance to all gardens. Accompanied children free. Pre-sales tickets available only online at Eventbrite (browse 'SGS Fife Spring Trail'). Tickets otherwise available on the day at the gardens. Gardens can also be visited individually for £5.00 each.

OPENING TIMES

SUNDAY PLANT SALE		
Cambo Plant Fair	11:30am – 3:30pm	15 April

TUESDAYS		
Crail Gardens	1pm-4pm	10, 17, 24 April & 1 May
Kenlygreen	10am-1pm	17, 24 April & 1 May
Wormistoune	2pm-4pm	10, 17, 24 April & 1 May

WEDNESDAYS		
Craigfoodie	10am-4pm	11 April & 16, 23 May
Straiton Farmhouse	1pm-4pm	11 April & 16, 23 May
The Murrel	2:30pm – 4:30pm	11, 18, 25 April
Wemyss Castle	1pm-4pm	11, 18, 25 April

THURSDAYS		
Myres Castle	2pm-5pm	12, 19, 26 April & 3 May
South Flisk	1pm-5pm	12, 19, 26 April & 3 May
The Tower	2pm-5pm	19, 26 April & 3, 10 May

Straiton Farmhouse, Balmullo

ABERDEENSHIRE

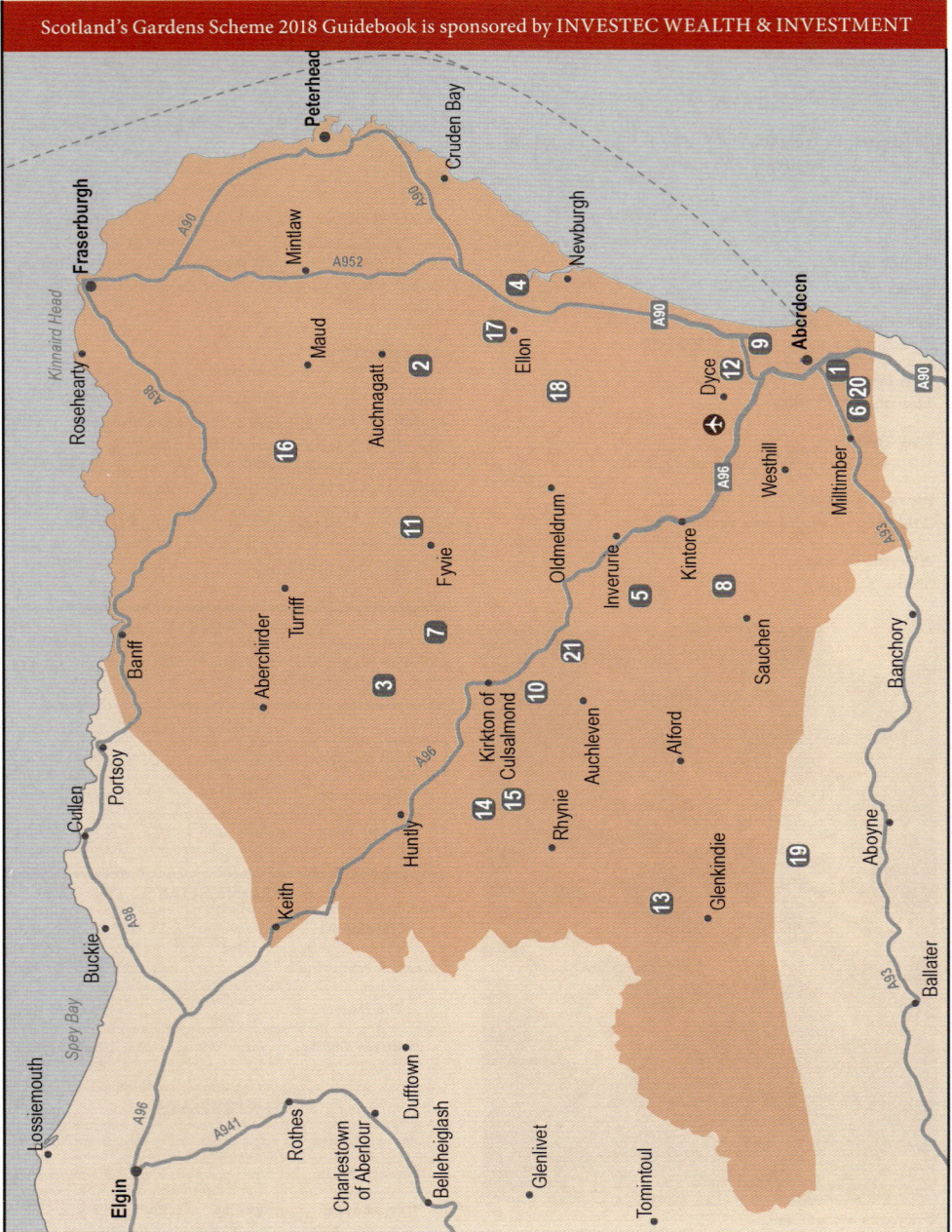

ABERDEENSHIRE

OUR VOLUNTEER ORGANISERS

District Organiser:	Verity Walters	Tillychetly, Alford, AB33 8HQ
		E: aberdeenshire@scotlandsgardens.org
Area Organisers:	Linda Colquhoun	Hillview, Rothienorman, Inverurie, AB51 8YL
	Gill Cook	Old Semeil, Strathdon, AB36 8XJ
	Jennie Gibson	6 The Chanonry, Old Aberdeen, Aberdeen, AB24 1RP
	Anne Lawson	Asloun, Alford, AB33 8NR
	Penny Orpwood	Middle Cairncake, Cuminestown, Turriff, AB53 5YS
	Helen Rushton	Bruckhills Croft, Rothienorman, Inverurie, AB51 8YB
Treasurer:	Tony Coleman	Templeton House, Arbroath, DD11 4QP

GARDENS OPEN ON A SPECIFIC DATE

Auchmacoy, Ellon	Sunday, 15 April
Westhall Castle, Oyne, Inverurie	Sunday, 22 April
Castle Fraser Garden, Sauchen, Inverurie	Saturday/Sunday, 5/6 May
Airdlin Croft, Ythanbank, Ellon	Friday/Saturday, 25/26 May
Leith Hall Garden, Huntly	Saturday, 26 May
Kildrummy Castle Gardens, Alford	Sunday, 3 June
Three Hidden Gardens, Blairs, Westhill and Banchory-Devenick	Sunday, 10 June
Birken Cottage, Burnhervie, Inverurie	Sunday, 17 June
Airdlin Croft, Ythanbank, Ellon	Friday/Saturday, 22/23 June
Bruckhills Croft, Rothienorman, Inverurie	Sunday - Thursday, 24-28 June
Leith Hall Garden, Huntly	Thursday, 28 June
Farkvilla, 47 Schoolhill, Ellon	Saturday/Sunday, 30/1 June/July
Cruickshank Botanic Gardens, 23 St Machar Drive, Aberdeen	Wednesday, 11 July
Drumrossie Mansion House, Insch	Sunday, 15 July
Middle Cairncake, Cuminestown, Turriff	Saturday/Sunday, 21/22 July
Leith Hall Garden, Huntly	Thursday, 26 July
Middle Cairncake, Cuminestown, Turriff	Sunday, 5 August
Middle Cairncake, Cuminestown, Turriff	Sunday, 12 August
Pitmedden Garden, Ellon	Sunday, 12 August
Leith Hall Garden, Huntly	Saturday, 25 August
Tarland Community Garden, Aboyne	Saturday, 29 September
Kildrummy Castle Gardens, Alford	Sunday, 30 September

GARDENS OPEN REGULARLY

Fyvie Castle, Fyvie, Turriff	5 January - 22 December

Aberdeenshire

GARDENS OPEN BY ARRANGEMENT

Laundry Cottage, Culdrain, Gartly, Huntly	On request
Bruckhills Croft, Rothienorman, Inverurie	11 February - 11 March
Grandhome, Danestone, Aberdeen	1 April - 31 October
105 Inchgarth Road, Pitfodels, Cults, Aberdeen	1 May - 30 June
Birken Cottage, Burnhervie, Inverurie	13 May - 31 July
An Teallach, Largue, Huntly	1 June - 31 August
Middle Cairncake, Cuminestown, Turriff	1 June - 31 August
Blairwood House, South Deeside Road, Blairs	17 June - 26 August

KEY TO SYMBOLS

NEW New garden	Full wheelchair access	Dogs on leads
Basic teas	Partial wheelchair access	**NPC** National plant collection
H Homemade teas	Plants for sale	Champion trees
C Cream teas	Children's activities	Designed landscape
Refreshments	Accessible by public transport	Snowdrop opening

All our gardens open to raise money for charity. Each opening may nominate a charity(s) to receive up to 60% of the takings and these are included with each listing. The net remaining raised supports our core beneficiaries. Information about our core beneficiaries can be found in the front section of the book. More information about our charity scheme and our symbols can be found in the back foldout section of the book under 'Tips for Using Your Guidebook'.

Aberdeenshire

1

105 INCHGARTH ROAD
Pitfodels, Cults, Aberdeen AB15 9NX
Mr and Mrs W. McGregor
T: 01224 861090 E: wahmcgregor@me.com
....

Informal cottage style garden situated in one third of an acre featuring azaleas, rhododendrons, orchids, peonies and a selection of alpines.

Open: Open by arrangement 1 May - 30 June, admission £4.00, children free.

Directions: From North Deeside Road, turn off along Station Road, Pitfodels. Access and parking along back lane.

H 🚌 NEW

· *The Archie Foundation & Aberdeen Royal Infirmary Roof Garden*

2

AIRDLIN CROFT
Ythanbank, Ellon AB41 7TS
Richard and Ellen Firmin
T: 01358 761491 E: rsf@airdlin.com
....

A large woodland garden, eventually destined to fill our five acre croft, features species of rhododendrons, hydrangeas, viburnums, ferns, hostas and other shade tolerant plants. A sheltered, sunny terrace hosts some tender exotics. One of two polytunnels houses the 'library collection' of container grown hosta cultivars. We go out of our way to attract wildlife - 100 bird species recorded here since 1983.

Open: Friday/Saturday, 25/26 May, 10am - 4pm. Also open Friday/Saturday, 22/23 June, 10am - 4pm. Admission £4.00, children free. Disabled access to plant sale only. Teas available at Haddo House or Formartine's, about five miles away.

Directions: From the A948, three miles north of Ellon, take the left turn towards Drumwhindle. After another couple of miles take the second left towards Cairnorrie. Proceed for nearly a mile, ignoring the first Airdlin Croft at Coalmoss, and turn left at the first bend, go down our 300 metre track, parking is in the field at the bottom.

🌷 ♿

· *Fauna & Flora International*

3

AN TEALLACH
Largue, Huntly AB54 6HS
Gary and Victoria Morrison
T: 01464 871471 E: gary.k.morrison@gmail.com
....

This young cottage garden of approximately one acre (and growing) was created in 2013 and has become established in a remarkably short time. Surrounded by uninterrupted views of rolling hills and farmland, the garden includes a charming variety of colourful herbaceous, mixed borders, a terraced woodland bank, rose garden, fruit and vegetable beds, and an (as yet) untamed quarry area. The growing collection of plants and flowers provides interest from May to October.

Open: Open by arrangement 1 June - 31 August, admission £4.00, children free.

Directions: Leaving Largue on the B9001, head towards Rothienorman. An Teallach is the first track on the left, after the national speed limit sign.

· *Dogs Trust*

Aberdeenshire

4

AUCHMACOY
Ellon AB41 8RB
Mr and Mrs Charles Buchan
....

Auchmacoy House's attractive policies feature spectacular displays of thousands of daffodils.

Open: Sunday 15 April, 1pm - 4pm, admission £3.00, children free. Concessions £2.50. Soup available.

Directions: A90 from Aberdeen. Turn right to Auchmacoy/Collieston.

· *The Royal British Legion: Ellon Branch*

5

BIRKEN COTTAGE
Burnhervie, Inverurie AB51 5JR
Clare and Ian Alexander
T: 01467 623013 E: i.alexander@abdn.ac.uk
....

This steeply sloping garden of just under one acre is packed with plants. It rises from a wet streamside gully and woodland, past sunny terraces and a small parterre, to dry flowery banks.

Open: Sunday 17 June, 2pm - 5pm. Also open by arrangement 13 May - 31 July. Admission £4.00, children free.

Directions: Burnhervie is about three miles west of Inverurie. Leave Inverurie by the B9170 (Blackhall Road) or B993 (St James' Place).

· *Friends Of Anchor*

Creating an inspiring, rewarding and enjoyable experience for volunteers and visitors alike

Blairwood House

6

BLAIRWOOD HOUSE
South Deeside Road, Blairs AB12 5YQ
Ilse Elders
T: 01224 868301 M:07732 532276 E: ilse.elders@yahoo.co.uk
....

A mature, densely planted, one acre garden full of flowering shrubs, herbaceous perennials and bulbs. The garden is laid out in naturally curving lines to harmonise with the surrounding fields. It includes a pond, a small but beautifully designed vegetable garden, a herb garden and a sunken patio. A lovely short walk leads to the river and back.

Aberdeenshire

Open: Open by arrangement 17 June - 26 August, admission £4.00, children free. Also open with Three Hidden Gardens on 10 June, see entry for details.

Directions: Please do not use SatNav to find this garden. From Bridge of Dee roundabout take the South Deeside road for approx. four minutes until you see the road sign *Riverside of Blairs*. Almost immediately you will see a large electricity pylon on your right and an electronic speed sign on your left. Entrance is opposite the speed sign. Coming from Milltimber Bridge, turn left towards Aberdeen. Follow the South Deeside road for a few minutes until you see Copland Motors Garage on your left. Entrance is about 100 metres beyond.

· *Elvanfoot Trust*

7 BRUCKHILLS CROFT
Rothienorman, Inverurie AB51 8YB
Paul and Helen Rushton
T: 01651 821596 E: helenrushton1@aol.com
....

An informal country cottage garden extending to ¾ acre with a further acre as wildflower meadow and pond. The pond has been extensively replanted with primulas and irises for 2018. Themed borders include a White Border, a Butterfly Alley and a Blue and Yellow Border. We specialise in rabbit proof planting. Relax on one of the many seats in the garden, enjoy a cuppa and homebake in the pavilion, and children can follow the treasure trail. Our snowdrops featured on the *Beechgrove Garden* in 2017.

Open: Open by arrangement 11 February - 11 March for the Snowdrop Festival. Also open Sunday 24-29 June 2pm - 5pm. Admission £4.00, children free.

Directions: At Rothienorman take the B9001 north, just after Badenscoth Nursing Home turn left, in one mile you will be directed where to park depending if it is the winter or summer opening.

· *Befriend A Child Ltd*

8 CASTLE FRASER GARDEN
Sauchen, Inverurie AB51 7LD
The National Trust for Scotland
T: 01330 833463 E: www.nts.org.uk/castlefraser
W: www.nts.org.uk
....

Castle Fraser's designed landscape and parkland are the work of Thomas White dating from 1794. Castle Fraser, one of the most spectacular of the Castles of Mar, has a traditional walled garden of trees, shrubs and herbaceous plantings, a medicinal and culinary border and organically grown fruit and vegetables. You can stroll through the woodland garden with its azaleas and rhododendrons or take the young at heart to the Woodland Secrets adventure playground and trails.

Open: Saturday/Sunday, 5/6 May, 11am - 4pm, admission details can be found on the garden's website.

Directions: Near Kemnay, off the A944.

· *Donation to SGS Beneficiaries*

Aberdeenshire

9

CRUICKSHANK BOTANIC GARDENS
23 St Machar Drive, Aberdeen AB24 3UU
Cruickshank Botanic Garden Trust, Aberdeen University
W: www.abdn.ac.uk/botanic-garden/

An evening tour with the Curator, Mark Paterson and Head Gardener, Richard Walker. The garden comprises a sunken garden with alpine lawn, a rock garden built in the 1960s complete with cascading water and pond system, a long double sided herbaceous border, a formal rose garden with drystone walling, and an arboretum. It has a large collection of flowering bulbs and rhododendrons, and many unusual shrubs and trees. It is sometimes known as The Secret Garden of Old Aberdeen.
Champion Trees: *Quercus ilex, Acer griseum* and a tri-stemmed *Nothofagus obliqua*.

Open: Wednesday 11 July, 6:30pm - 8:30pm, admission £5.00, children free. Admission price includes tea/coffee and biscuits.

Directions: Come down St Machar Drive over the mini roundabout, just before the first set of traffic lights turn left into the Cruickshank Garden car park. The pedestrian garden entrance is off The Chanonry.

· *Cruickshank Botanic Gardens*

10

DRUMROSSIE MANSION HOUSE
Insch AB52 6LJ
Mr and Mrs Hugh Robertson

The property, which can be traced back to the Crusades, is surrounded by three acres of landscaped lawns, formal walled garden, veg and greenhouse area and a newly planted orchard. There are 27 acres of wooded walks, paddocks and a large wildlife pond. Vegetables are grown in raised beds. The walled garden is laid out in lawns of a very high standard, with herbaceous borders and fruit trees on the south facing wall. There is a large collection of hostas and alstroemerias, as well as herbaceous plants, heathers and azaleas, a productive vegetable garden, plant raising area and polytunnel for early veg and flowers, a large glasshouse for tomatoes and a sunken greenhouse which provides over wintering heat for tender plants. A main feature is the well which in days gone by provided the water supply to the house.

Open: Sunday 15 July, 1pm - 5pm, admission £4.00, children free.

Directions: Enter drive from Drumrossie Street off the crossroads in centre of village. The drive is through trees at the back of the Costcutter Supermarket. Do not follow SatNav.

· *Insch Parish Church: Restoration Fund*

11

FYVIE CASTLE
Fyvie, Turriff AB53 8JS
The National Trust for Scotland
T: 01651 891363 / 891266 E: gthomson@nts.org.uk
W: www.nts.org.uk/Property/Fyvie-Castle/

An 18th century walled garden developed as a garden of Scottish fruits and vegetables. There is also the American garden, Rhymer's Haugh woodland garden, a loch and parkland to visit. Expert staff are always on hand to answer any questions. Learn about the collection of Scottish fruits and their cultivation, and exciting projects for the future. Check the Fyvie Castle Facebook page for up to date information on fruit and vegetable availability.

Aberdeenshire

Open: 5 January - 22 December, 9am - Dusk, admission details can be found on the garden's website.

Directions: Off the A947 eight miles south east of Turriff and 25 miles north west of Aberdeen.

· *Donation to SGS Beneficiaries*

12 GRANDHOME
Danestone, Aberdeen AB22 8AR
Mr and Mrs D R Paton
T: 01224 722202 E: davidpaton@btconnect.com

Eighteenth century walled garden, incorporating rose garden (replanted 2010); policies with daffodils, tulips, rhododendrons, azaleas, mature trees and shrubs.

Open: Open by arrangement 1 April - 31 October, admission £4.00, children free.

Directions: From the north end of North Anderson Drive, continue on the A90 over Persley Bridge, turning left at the Tesco roundabout. 1¾ miles on the left, through the pillars on a left hand bend.

· *Children 1st*

13 KILDRUMMY CASTLE GARDENS
Alford AB33 8RA
Kildrummy Garden Trust
W: www.kildrummy-castle-gardens.co.uk

These gardens were created in the ancient quarry below the Castle. The bridge spanning the garden is a copy of famous brig o' Balgownie and reflects beautifully on the largest of the four ponds which plays host to a wide range of water plants. Rhododendrons and azaleas feature from April (frost permitting). In June the lovely blue of the meconopsis can be enjoyed and September/October bring colchicums and brilliant colour with acers, fothergillas and viburnums.

Open: Sunday 3 June, 12pm - 5pm. Also open Sunday 30 September, 12pm - 5pm. Admission £5.00, children free. Concessions £4.00.

Directions: On the A97, 10 miles from Alford, 17miles from Huntly. Car park free inside the hotel main entrance. Coaches park up at the hotel delivery entrance.

· *Multiple Sclerosis Society: Aberdeen Branch*

Encouraging, promoting and supporting garden opening since 1931

Aberdeenshire

14 **LAUNDRY COTTAGE**
Culdrain, Gartly, Huntly AB54 4PY
Judith McPhun
T: 01466 720768 E: simon.mcphun@btinternet.com

The garden takes its cues from the surrounding Strathbogie landscape of rolling, tree and heather-clad hills. Divided by undulating hedges, the various parts of the garden are planted in an informal, cottage garden style and contain a mixture of the common place and many unusual plants. Grass paths lead from one section to another, and although the area around the cottage is level, there are also flower meadows on steep banks (not suitable for wheelchairs), leading down to the river Bogie. An organic vegetable garden lies behind one of the mixed borders and elsewhere there is a small orchard.

Open: Open by arrangement, admission £4.00, children free.

Directions: Four miles south of Huntly on the A97.

· **Amnesty International (UK Section) Charitable Trust**

15 **LEITH HALL GARDEN**
Huntly AB54 4NQ
The National Trust for Scotland
T: 01464 831148 E: www.nts.org.uk/leithhall
W: www.nts.org.uk

The west garden was made by Charles and Henrietta Leith-Hay around the beginning of the 20th century. In summer the magnificent zigzag herbaceous and serpentine catmint borders provide a dazzling display. A lot of project work has been ongoing in the garden, including a rose catenary along with large borders which have been redeveloped in a Gertrude Jekyll style and a laburnum archway with spring interest borders. The carefully reconstructed rock garden is a work in progress with new planting being added throughout the season.

Open: A series of guided tours by the Head Gardener. Saturday 26 May & Saturday 25 August, starting at 10am. Also on Thursday 28 June & Thursday 26 July, starting at 7pm. Cost of tour is £5.00, children free. Booking essential for the tours, email Sarah Ramsay (sramsay@nts.org.uk).

Directions: On the B9002 one mile west of Kennethmont.

· **All proceeds to SGS Beneficiaries**

16 **MIDDLE CAIRNCAKE**
Cuminestown, Turriff AB53 5YS
Nick and Penny Orpwood
T: 01888 544432 E: orpwood@hotmail.com

The shape of our property has determined our garden plan of a series of areas with different plantings. Our prime aim has been to make a garden which appeals to the senses: roses selected for their scent, planting generally to please the eye. The kitchen garden with polytunnel creates self-sufficiency and the pond adds interest. Sustainability, wildlife and recycling are priorities. The garden has views over the surrounding countryside. A winter garden is our next project.

Open: Saturday/Sunday, 21/22 July, 12pm - 5pm. Also open Sunday 5 August & Sunday 12 August, 2pm - 5pm. And open by arrangement 1 June - 31 August. Admission £4.00, children free. Overflow parking 100m.

Aberdeenshire

Directions: Middle Cairncake is on the A9170 between New Deer and Cuminestown. It is clearly signposted.

[icons]

· *Parkinsons UK*

Parkvilla

17

PARKVILLA
47 Schoolhill, Ellon AB41 9AJ
Andy and Kim Leonard

A south facing Victorian Walled Garden, lovingly developed from a design started in 1990, for colour and interest all year. Enjoy densely planted herbaceous borders, pause under the pergola clothed in clematis, honeysuckle and rambling roses, continue on to the bottom of the garden where three ponds and a wild flower bed reflect a strong focus on wildlife. A hidden gem of a garden that has won awards including Ellon Best Garden, and includes plants rarely seen in NE Scotland.

Open: Saturday 30 June & Sunday 1 July, 2pm - 5pm, admission £4.00, children free.

Directions: From centre of Ellon head north towards Auchnagatt. Schoolhill is third left. From Auchnagatt head into Ellon along Golf Road, Schoolhill is first right after the Golf Course. Limited on-street parking, car parks in Ellon (five minutes walk) and Caroline Well Wood.

[icons]

· *St Mary On The Rock Episcopal Church Ellon, Alzheimer Scotland & Ellon Men's Shed*

Aberdeenshire

18

PITMEDDEN GARDEN
Ellon AB41 7PD
The National Trust for Scotland
T: 01651 842352 E: sburgess@nts.org.uk
W: www.nts.org.uk/Property/Pitmedden-Garden/

Pitmedden is a seventeenth century walled garden on two levels. Original garden pavilions with ogival roofs look down on an elaborate spectacle of four rectangular boxwood parterres flanked by fine herbaceous borders and espalier trained apple trees on south and west facing granite walls. An avenue of yew obelisks runs from east to west and up to 30,000 bedding plants add to the wow factor of this immaculately kept formal garden.

Open: Sunday 12 August, 6:30pm - 8:30pm, admission £10.00, children free. Head Gardener's evening guided walk, with refreshments included.

Directions: On the A920, one mile west of Pitmedden Village and 14 miles north of Aberdeen.

· *Donation to SGS Beneficiaries*

19

TARLAND COMMUNITY GARDEN
Aboyne AB34 4ZQ
The Gardeners of Tarland

Tarland Community Gardens opened in 2013 and is a Tarland Development Group project. It provides an inclusive and accessible community growing space for local residents. It has indoor (polytunnel) and outdoor raised beds for rent plus communal planting areas including a soft fruit cage, fruit trees, and a herb garden. The community bee group also manages a hive at the site. It is a place for members to grow produce, learn, share and have fun.

Open: Saturday 29 September, 12pm - 4pm, admission £3.00, children free. Activities at the garden as part of the Tarland Food and Music Festival.

Directions: Take the B9094 from Aboyne or the A96 and B9119 from Aberdeen. Arriving at the village square the gardens will be clearly signposted.

· *Tarland Development Group*

20

THREE HIDDEN GARDENS
Blairs, Westhill and Banchory-Devenick AB12 5YQ
Ilse Elders, Catherine Fowler and Angela Townsley

Blairwood House South Deeside Road, Blairs AB12 5YQ: A mature, densely planted, one acre garden full of flowering shrubs, herbaceous perennials and bulbs. The garden is laid out in naturally curving lines to harmonise with the surrounding fields. It includes a pond, a small but beautifully designed vegetable garden, a herb garden and a sunken patio. A lovely short walk leads to the river and back. No disabled access.
Easter Ord Farm Easter Ord, Skene, Westhill AB32 6SG: The house has open views towards Lochnagar and is surrounded by mixed herbaceous borders divided into a series of 'rooms'. There is a vegetable garden, a small orchard set in a wildflower area and a wildlife pond.
Pinetrees Cottage Banchory-Devenick AB12 5XR: A mature cottage garden set in ¾ acre captures the imagination with a wide range of hardy plants, which include acer, rhododendrons, azaleas, topiary, roses and rock plants. Set in a backdrop of mature pine trees to the north and open fields to the south.

Open: Sunday 10 June, 2pm - 5pm, admission £7.00, children free. Teas available at Blairwood House from 1-4pm and at Easter Ord Farm from 11am-1pm. Light refreshments available from Pinetrees Cottage. Tickets available from all three gardens.

Aberdeenshire

Directions: Blairwood House: See Blairwood guidebook entry above.
Easter Ord Farm: Easter Ord Farm as follows: Two miles from Westhill. Use SatNav with full postcode. 100 metres from Beechgove Garden. From Aberdeen - take A944 towards Westhill. At the traffic lights before Westhill take the slip road on to the B9119 then immediately left again towards Brotherfield.   After one mile turn right at T junction, and after 0.2 miles garden is on your left.
Pinetrees Cottage: Banchory-Devenick is four miles from Bridge of Dee. Turn off B9077 at Banchory-Devenick church. Follow to T-junction, turn right. Next right is Butterywells Steading. From there follow yellow signs.

· *The Archie Foundation & Aberdeen Royal Infirmary Roof Garden*

21

WESTHALL CASTLE
Oyne, Inverurie AB52 6RW
Mr Gavin Farquhar and Mrs Pam Burney
T: 01224 214301 E: enquiries@ecclesgreig.com

Set in an ancient landscape in the foothills of the impressive foreboding hill of Bennachie. A circular walk through glorious daffodils with outstanding views. Interesting garden in early stages of restoration, with large groupings of rhododendrons and specimen trees. Westhall Castle is a 16th century tower house, incorporating a 13th century building of the bishops of Aberdeen. There were additions in the 17th, 18th and 19th centuries. The castle is semi-derelict, but stabilised from total dereliction. A fascinating house encompassing 600 years of alteration and additions.

Open: Sunday 22 April, 1pm - 4pm, admission £4.00, children free.

Directions: Marked from the A96 at Old Rayne and from Oyne Village.

· *Bennachie Guides*

Pinetrees, Three Hidden Gardens

ANGUS & DUNDEE

Scotland's Gardens Scheme 2018 Guidebook is sponsored by INVESTEC WEALTH & INVESTMENT

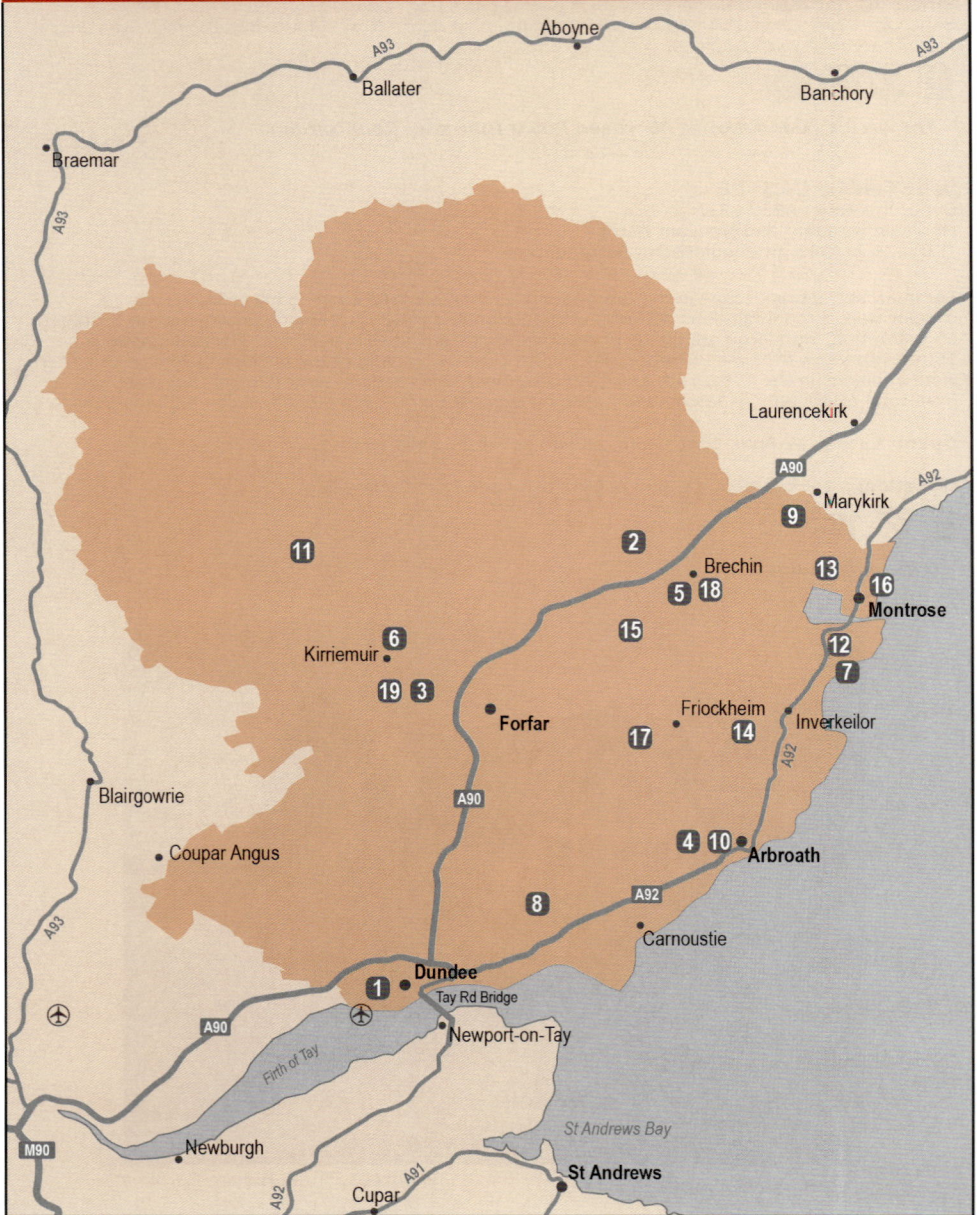

ANGUS & DUNDEE

OUR VOLUNTEER ORGANISERS

District Organisers:	Terrill Dobson	Logie House, Kirriemuir, DD8 5PN
	Jan Oag	Lower Duncraig, 2 Castle Street, Brechin, DD9 6JN
		E: angus@scotlandsgardens.org
Area Organisers:	Pippa Clegg	Easter Derry, Kilry, Blairgowrie, PH11 8JA
	Moira Coleman	Templeton House, Arbroath, DD11 4QP
	Frances Dent	12 Glamis Drive, Dundee, DD2 1QL
	John Dent	12 Glamis Drive, Dundee, DD2 1QL
	Mary Gifford	Kinnordy House, Kinnordy, Kirriemuir, DD8 5ER
	Jeanette Ogilvie	House of Pitmuies, Guthrie, DD8 2SN
	Sue Smith	Balintore House, Balintore, by Kirriemuir, DD8 5JS
	Mary Stansfeld	Dunninald Castle, By Montrose, DD10 9TD
	Gladys Stewart	Ugie-Bank, Ramsay Street, Edzell, Brechin, DD9 7TT
	Claire Tinsley	Ethie Mains, Ethie, DD11 5SN
Treasurer:	James Welsh	Dalfruin, Kirtonhill Road, Kirriemuir, DD8 4HU

GARDENS OPEN ON A SPECIFIC DATE

Dunninald Castle, Montrose	Saturday/Sunday, 24/25 February
Langley Park Gardens, Montrose	Sunday, 25 February
Dunninald Castle, Montrose	Saturday/Sunday, 3/4 March
Lawton House, Inverkeilor, by Arbroath	Sunday, 4 March
3 Balfour Cottages, Menmuir	Saturday, 5 May
Brechin Castle, Brechin	Sunday, 6 May
Inchmill Cottage, Glenprosen, nr Kirriemuir	Thursday, 10 May
Dalfruin, Kirtonhill Road, Kirriemuir	Sunday, 13 May
Inchmill Cottage, Glenprosen, nr Kirriemuir	Thursday, 24 May
Gallery Walled Garden, Gallery, by Montrose	Saturday/Sunday, 26/27 May
Inchmill Cottage, Glenprosen, nr Kirriemuir	Thursday, 7 June
Inchmill Cottage, Glenprosen, nr Kirriemuir	Thursday, 21 June
Arbroath Collection of Gardens, Locations across Arbroath	Saturday, 23 June
Inchmill Cottage, Glenprosen, nr Kirriemuir	Thursday, 5 July
Hospitalfield Gardens, Hospitalfield House, Westway, Arbroath	Saturday, 7 July
Melgund Castle, Melgund, Aberlemno, Brechin	Sunday, 15 July
Inchmill Cottage, Glenprosen, nr Kirriemuir	Thursday, 19 July
Gallery Walled Garden, Gallery, by Montrose	Saturday/Sunday, 21/22 July
The Gardens of Brechin, Locations across Brechin	Sunday, 22 July
The Herbalist's Garden at Logie, Logie House, Kirriemuir	Saturday/Sunday, 28/29 July
Montrose Gardens, Montrose	Sunday, 5 August
Inchmill Cottage, Glenprosen, nr Kirriemuir	Thursday, 9 August
12 Glamis Drive, Dundee	Saturday/Sunday, 18/19 August
Inchmill Cottage, Glenprosen, nr Kirriemuir	Thursday, 23 August
Angus Plant Sale, Logie Walled Garden, Logie	Saturday, 1 September
Inchmill Cottage, Glenprosen, nr Kirriemuir	Thursday, 6 September
Inchmill Cottage, Glenprosen, nr Kirriemuir	Thursday, 20 September

Angus & Dundee

GARDENS OPEN REGULARLY

Pitmuies Gardens, Guthrie, By Forfar	1 April - 31 October
Dunninald Castle, Montrose	15 May - 31 August
Dunvorist Cottage, Drumsturdy Road, Kingdennie, Dundee	1 - 30 June & 1 - 31 August (Mondays only)
Gallery Walled Garden, Gallery, by Montrose	1 June - 31 August (Tuesdays only)

GARDENS OPEN BY ARRANGEMENT

Kirkton House, Kirkton of Craig, Montrose	1 May - 30 September
Gallery Walled Garden, Gallery, by Montrose	1 June - 31 August

KEY TO SYMBOLS

NEW New garden	Full wheelchair access	Dogs on leads
Basic teas	Partial wheelchair access	NPC National plant collection
H Homemade teas	Plants for sale	Champion trees
C Cream teas	Children's activities	Designed landscape
Refreshments	Accessible by public transport	Snowdrop opening

All our gardens open to raise money for charity. Each opening may nominate a charity(s) to receive up to 60% of the takings and these are included with each listing. The net remaining raised supports our core beneficiaries. Information about our core beneficiaries can be found in the front section of the book. More information about our charity scheme and our symbols can be found in the back foldout section of the book under 'Tips for Using Your Guidebook'.

Angus & Dundee

1 12 GLAMIS DRIVE
Dundee DD2 1QL
John and Frances Dent

This established garden with mature trees occupies a half acre south facing site overlooking the River Tay and Fife hills. The tennis court lawn has herbaceous borders. The woodland area includes hidden features, garden ornaments and a miniature topiary garden and bower.   A small rose garden and fountain and two oriental themed water gardens complete the tour in time for tea in the marquee.

Open: Saturday/Sunday, 18/19 August, 2pm - 5pm, admission £4.00, children free. Musical performance.

Directions: Buses 22, 73 or 5 from Dundee city centre. Please note there is no roadside parking on Glamis Drive. Limited disabled parking available at the house.

· Girlguiding Dundee: Outdoor Centre & Dundee: Logie & St John's (Cross) Parish Church of Scotland

12 Glamis Drive

2 3 BALFOUR COTTAGES
Menmuir DD9 7RN
Dr Alison Goldie and Mark A Hutson
T: 01356 660280 E: alisongoldie@btinternet.com
W: www.angusplants.co.uk

Small cottage garden packed with rare and unusual plants. It comprises various 'rooms', containing myriad plants from potted herbs, spring bulbs and alpines in a raised bed, to a 'jungle' with a range of bamboos. Many other interesting plants include primula, hosta, meconopsis, fritillaria, trillium, allium, a large display of bonsai and auriculas.
National Plant Collection: *Primula auricula* (alpine).

Open: Saturday 5 May, 12pm - 4pm, admission £3.00, children free.

Directions: Leave the A90 two miles south of Brechin and take the road to Menmuir (3½ miles). At the T-junction turn right and it is in the first group of cottages on your left (175 yards).

· Earl Haig Fund Poppy Scotland

Angus & Dundee

ANGUS PLANT SALE
3
Logie Walled Garden, Logie DD8 5PN
SGS Angus & Dundee Organisers
E: pippaclegg@hotmail.com

Following the success of our first plant sale held in May 2017, the next one will be September 2018 to allow for preparation of a wider variety of plants. We will offer a good, interesting selection, sourced from private gardens and with some donations from local nurseries. Advisable to come early and bring boxes and trays. Donations of plants either before or during sales very welcome.

Open: Saturday 1 September, 11:30am - 2pm, admission £3.00, children free. Price includes soup and tea/coffee. Garden will also be open.

Directions: From the A90, take A926 towards Kirriemuir.   Just after *Welcome to Kirriemuir* take sharp left on to single track road, or from Kirriemuir take A926 towards Forfar and fork right on to single track road at Beechwood Place. Then take first left onto drive and follow signs. Bus 20 getting off at the Vet's.

· All proceeds to SGS Beneficiaries

ARBROATH COLLECTION OF GARDENS
4
Locations across Arbroath DD11 3BU
Gardeners of Arbroath

An interesting collection - two small gardens, three allotments and a nursery garden centre. The garden at St Vigeans is a charming cottage garden featuring ferns and acers, the garden in the Lochlands area, a small walled garden, a little gem with a collection of 70 clematis and interesting perennials. The St Vigeans Church will also be open. Arbroath Garden Allotment Association will open their two sites, Brechin Road and Ernest Street. Loads of interest in all sites for plants, fruit, vegetables and creative sheds and shelters. HOPE, an organic fruit and vegetable garden, which provides training and work experience for adults with learning and/or physical disabilities will also be supporting the afternoon. Ashbrook Nursery and Garden Centre will combine their open day with the Collection and run tours of the nursery throughout the afternoon.

10 George Street DD11 3BU (Wilma Simpson)
Arbroath Allotment Association Brechin Road, DD11 4AH and Ernest Street, DD11 1TZ.
Ashbrook Nursery Forfar Road, DD11 3RB (Anne Webster)
HOPE Organic Garden Westway, DD11 2NH (The HOPE Trustees)
Kirkstyle St Vigeans, DD11 4RR (Angela Nixon)

Open: Saturday 23 June, 1pm - 5pm, admission £5.00, children free. Tickets and maps from Ashbrook Nursery from 1 April, or on the day at the various gardens. Teas will be served at St Vigeans Hall (DD11 4ED).

Directions: Directions to individual gardens will be listed on the tickets and maps.

· Arbroath St Vigeans Church of Scotland: Church and Hall Fund

Angus & Dundee

5

BRECHIN CASTLE

Brechin DD9 6SG
The Earl and Countess of Dalhousie
T: 01356 624566 E: mandyferries@dalhousieestates.co.uk
W: www.dalhousieestates.co.uk
....

The uniquely curving walls of the garden at Brechin Castle are just the first of many delightful surprises in store. The luxurious blend of ancient and modern plantings is the second. Find charm and splendour in the wide gravelled walks, secluded small paths and corners. May sees the rhododendrons and azaleas hit the peak of their flowering to wonderful effect, with complementary underplanting and a framework of great and beautiful trees set the collection in the landscape. This is a lovely garden at any time of year and a knockout in the spring.

Open: Sunday 6 May, 2pm - 5pm, admission £5.00, children free.

Directions: A90 southernmost exit to Brechin, one mile past Brechin Castle Centre, Castle gates are on the right.

· *Unicorn Preservation Society & The Dalhousie Centre Day Care For The Elderly*

**Creating an inspiring,
rewarding and enjoyable
experience for volunteers
and visitors alike**

6

DALFRUIN

Kirktonhill Road, Kirriemuir DD8 4HU
Mr and Mrs James A Welsh
....

A well stocked connoisseur's garden of about a third of an acre situated at the end of a short cul-de-sac.   There are many less common plants like varieties of trilliums, meconopsis (blue poppies), tree peonies (descendants of ones collected by George Sherriff and grown at Ascreavie), dactylorhiza and codonopsis.   There is a scree and collection of ferns.   The vigorous climbing rose Paul's Himalayan Musk grows over a pergola. Interconnected ponds encourage wildlife.

Open: Sunday 13 May, 2pm - 5pm, admission £4.00, children free. Good plant stall with many unusual plants including trilliums, meconopsis, tree peonies and three year old monkey puzzle saplings. Teas served at St Mary's Episcopal Church.

Directions: From the centre of Kirriemuir turn left up Roods.   Kirktonhill Road is on the left near top of the hill. Park on Roods or at St Mary's Episcopal Church.   Disabled parking only in Kirktonhill Road. Bus 20 getting off at either stop on the Roods.

· *St Marys Episcopal Church & The Glens and Kirriemuir Old Parish Church of Scotland: Thrums Tots & Messy Church*

Angus & Dundee

7 DUNNINALD CASTLE

Montrose DD10 9TD
The Stansfeld Family
T: 01674 672031 E: estateoffice@dunninald.com
W: www.dunninald.com

....

We welcome our visitors to explore our 100 acres of woods, wild garden, policies and a walled
garden. From January to May the main interest is the wild garden and policies where snowdrops
in January are followed by daffodils and finally bluebells in May. In June the emphasis turns to
the walled garden; rich in interest and colour throughout the summer. Situated at the bottom
of the beech avenue, the walled garden is planted with rose borders, traditional mixed borders,
vegetables, herbs, soft fruits, fruit trees and a greenhouse.

Open: Saturday/Sunday, 24/25 February & Saturday/Sunday, 3/4 March, 1pm - 5pm for the
Snowdrop Festival. Also open 15 May - 31 August, 1pm - 5pm. Admission £4.00, children free.
Castle tours: 30 June - 29 July (closed Mondays) 1-5pm (last entry 4:30pm).

Directions: Three miles south of Montrose, ten miles north of Arbroath, signposted from the A92.

· *Donation to SGS Beneficiaries*

**Scotland's Gardens Scheme
welcomes all varieties of
gardens**

8 DUNVORIST COTTAGE

Drumsturdy Road, Kingdennie, Dundee DD5 3RE
Karen Fraser
T: 07854 167717 E: specialkfraser@hotmail.co.uk

....

Dunvorist Cottage is a small rural garden with all year colour and interest. The garden has an
open sunny aspect and includes a white rear garden with rural views, raised herbaceous borders,
a small wildlife pond, golden border, a rose gardens patio, herb garden, heuchera shady garden,
quirky garden pod, vegetable garden and a wildflower corner.

Open: 1 June - 30 June (Mondays only) & 1 August - 31 August (Mondays only), 10am - 4pm,
admission £4.00, children free.

Directions: On the B961 (Drumsturdy Road), ¼ mile west of Newbigging and about ½ mile east
of Kingennie. Opposite the Laws. Look out for greenhouse behind hedge and gated entrance.

· *Parkinsons UK: Dundee Group*

Angus & Dundee

9

GALLERY WALLED GARDEN
Gallery, by Montrose DD10 9LA
Mr John Simson
T: 01674 840550 E: galleryhf@googlemail.com

The redesign and replanting of this historic garden have preserved and extended its traditional framework of holly, privet and box. A grassed central alley, embellished with circles, links themed gardens, including the recently replanted gold garden and hot border, with the fine collection of old roses and the fountain and pond of the formal white garden. A walk through the woodland garden, home to rare breed sheep, with its extensive border of mixed heathers, leads to the River North Esk. From there rough paths lead both ways along the bank. This very special garden has been featured in the March 2015 edition of *Homes & Gardens*, the December 2017 edition of *English Garden* and later in 2018 in *Country Life* .

Open: Saturday/Sunday, 26/27 May, 2pm - 5pm. Also open Saturday/Sunday, 21/22 July, 2pm - 5pm. And open 1 June - 31 August (Tuesdays only), 1pm - 5pm. And open by arrangement 1 June - 31 August. Admission £5.00, children free.

Directions: From the A90 south of Northwater Bridge take the exit to Hillside and next left to Gallery and Marykirk. From the A937 west of rail underpass follow signs to Gallery and Northwater Bridge.

· *Perennial*

Gallery Walled Garden

Angus & Dundee

10 HOSPITALFIELD GARDENS
Hospitalfield House, Westway, Arbroath DD11 2NH
Hospitalfield Arts
E: info@hospitalfield.org.uk
W: www.hospitalfield.org.uk

At Hospitalfield in Arbroath the artist Patrick Allan-Fraser (1813-1890) remodelled a 13th century hospital to create his 19th century Arts and Crafts home. The walled gardens have been cultivated from the early medieval period, from the medicinal and the orchard to the Victorian passion for collecting ferns. This lovely flower and vegetable garden, set against the red sandstone neo Gothic architecture is maintained by a part time Gardener and a team of volunteers through their Garden Club. They run an international cultural programme rooted in the contemporary visual arts, inspired by the long and extraordinary heritage of the site.

Open: Saturday 7 July, 12pm - 4pm, admission £4.00, children free.

Directions: See website for directions.

· *The Hospitalfield Trust*

11 INCHMILL COTTAGE
Glenprosen, nr Kirriemuir DD8 4SA
Iain Nelson
T: 01575 540452

This is a long, sloping and terraced garden at over 800 feet in the Braes of Angus, developed to be a garden for all seasons. Half is dominated by bulbs, rhododendrons, azaleas, primulas, meconopsis and clematis. The other half mainly later summer bulbs, herbaceous plants and roses. There is also a rockery/scree and fernery.

Open: Thursdays 10 & 24 May, 7 & 21 June, 5 & 19 July, 9 & 23 August, 6 & 20 September, 2pm - 5pm, admission £3.00, children free. Car parking beside the church (50 yards away) and by the village hall opposite.

Directions: From Kirriemuir take the B955 (sign-posted to *The Glens*) to Dykehead (about five miles).   From there follow the *Prosen* sign for about five miles. Inchmill is the white fronted cottage beside the phone box.

· *The Archie Foundation*

12 KIRKTON HOUSE
Kirkton of Craig, Montrose DD10 9TB
Campbell Watterson
T: 01674 673604 E: campbellkirktonhouse@btinternet.com

A regency manse set in over two acres of garden. The walled garden includes herbaceous borders, a sunken garden, lime allee, statuary and formal rose garden. The wild garden includes a pond and water lilies. There is also a large flock of Jacobs sheep in the adjoining glebe.

Open: Open by arrangement 1 May - 30 September, admission £4.00, children free.

Directions: One mile south of Montrose, off the A92 at the Balgove turn-off.

· *All proceeds to SGS Beneficiaries*

Angus & Dundee

13

LANGLEY PARK GARDENS
Montrose DD10 9LG
Marianne and Philip Santer
T: 01674 810735 E: philipsanter1@gmail.com
W: www.langleyparkgardens.co.uk

Set overlooking Montrose basin, Langley Park Gardens include 27 acres of policies containing woodland walks w th snowdrops nestling at the base of ancient and younger trees. Large drifts of snowdrops of many varieties can be admired around the wall of the three walled gardens and in the small arboretum. Walk down through the 20 acre wildflower meadow to see the snowdrops along the bank of the wildlife pond, enjoying the views of Montrose basin, Montrose, the hills and sea beyond. You will also be welcome to wander around the walled gardens to see them coming to life after their winter slumbers and see the promise of things to come.

Open: Sunday 25 February, 10am - 4pm for the Snowdrop Festival, admission £5.00, children free.

Directions: Just off the A935 Montrose to Brechin Road, 1.5 miles from Montrose.

· *MS Centre (Therapy Centre)*

14

LAWTON HOUSE
Inverkeilor, by Arbroath DD11 4RU
Katie & Simon Dessain

Woodland garden of beech trees carpeted with snowdrops and crocuses in spring set around a Georgian House. There is also a walled garden planted with fruit trees and vegetables. The property was owned for many years by E izabeth and Patrick Allan Fraser who built Hospitalfield House in Arbroath.

Open: Sunday 4 March, 2pm - 5pm for the Snowdrop Festival, admission £3.00, children free.

Directions: Take B965 between Inverkeilor and Friockheim, turn right at sign for *Angus Chain Saws*. Drive approximately 200 metres, then take first right.

· *The Julia Thomson Memorial Trust*

15

MELGUND CASTLE
Melgund, Aberlemno, Brechin DD9 6TD
Martyn and Penelope Gregory

The restoration of Melgund Castle, built in 1542 for Cardinal Beaton, was completed in 2000. In 2007 a drystone wall was also built. The new garden within is laid out in an interpretation of the medieval style. Raised beds and exedra contain a profusion of unusual culinary and medicinal herbs. Old roses and flowers of the medieval period surround the central herber. A rowan arch leads to an orchard of mostly historic fruit cultivars in a flowery mead. A pretty walk takes you alongside a burn and through indigenous meadows and specimen trees.

Open: Sunday 15 July, 2pm - 5pm, admission £4.00, children free.

Directions: Melgund Castle is situated three miles east of Aberlemno. Take the B9134 between Brechin and Forfar. Roughly half way and north of Aberlemno a small sign will direct you along a narrow road, through the farm, when you will see the castle on the left.   Grid ref: No 5460956630.

· *Aberlemno Parish Church Of Scotland*

Angus & Dundee

16

MONTROSE GARDENS
Montrose DD10 8AL
The Gardeners of Montrose

. . . .

A variety of beautiful gardens in the seaside town of Montrose which this year includes a new garden with a stunning show of begonias. Other gardens include formal, woodland walks, herbaceous border and some 'works in progress', novel design ideas, a nature haven, fruit trees and vegetable plots.

36 The Mall Montrose DD10 8SS (Peter Wood)
Arwin House 17 Renny Crescent, Montrose DD10 9BW (Trish and Andy Winton)
Dorward House 24 Dorward Road, Montrose DD10 8SB (The Trustees of Dorward House)
Library Garden 214 High Street, Montrose DD10 8PH (Brian McCallum)
Straton House Garden 10 Castle Place, Montrose DD10 8AL (Tony and Allison Sutton)

Open: Sunday 5 August, 1pm - 5pm, admission £5.00, children free. Teas at Dorward House. Tickets and maps available on the day from Straton House.

Directions: All gardens are within walking distance of the town centre.

· *Dorward House*

17

PITMUIES GARDENS
Guthrie, By Forfar DD8 2SN
Jeanette and Ruaraidh Ogilvie
E: ogilvie@pitmuies.com
W: www.pitmuies.com

. . . .

Two semi-formal walled gardens adjoin the 18th century house and shelter long borders of herbaceous perennials, superb delphiniums, old fashioned roses and pavings with violas and dianthus. Spacious lawns, river and lochside walks beneath fine trees. There is a wide variety of shrubs with good autumn colour and an interesting picturesque turreted doocot and 'Gothick' wash house. Myriad spring bulbs include carpets of crocus following the massed snowdrops.

Open: 1 April - 31 October, 10am - 5pm, admission £5.00, children free. Dogs on leads please.

Directions: A932. Friockheim 1½ miles.

· *Donation to SGS Beneficiaries*

Are you a gardening guru and a social media wizard? Help run our Facebook pages!

Angus & Dundee

18

THE GARDENS OF BRECHIN
Locations across Brechin DD9 6EU
The Gardeners of Brechin

Come and see this lovely collection of gardens scattered across Brechin.

9, Pearse Street DD9 6JR (Irene and James Mackie): A recently redesigned garden with an interesting and colourful herbaceous border, huge collection of ferns and lovely rural feel.
24 North Latch Road DD9 6LE (Alistair and Mary Gray): Expertly grown competitive vegetables along with a spectacular display of colourful bedding full greenhouses.
30 Drumachlie Park DD9 7BU (Dave and Pam Henderson): Roses and monardas flourish amidst a garden also featuring bedding plants, greenhouse and patio and all inspired by the memory of Dave's mum.
Airlie House 20 Airlie Street, DD9 6JP (Laura Croll): A fantasy garden and summer house themed for summer in an enchanted forest.
Golf View DD9 7QU (Kathleen Stephen): Plants, mostly in containers, provide wonderful colour contrasting with this green and peaceful garden, also featuring a pond and white stemmed birches.
East Kintrockat DD9 6RP (Colin and Moira Sandeman): A large open country garden with island beds, natural pond, kitchen garden and riverside walk.
Lower Duncraig 2, Castle Street, DD9 6JN (Jan Oag): A small town garden recently redesigned with plants selected mainly for their value to wildlife and including a small pond, a few trees and twenty different roses.
Pearse Croft 8-10 Pearse Street DD9 6JR (Dr. Hamish and Gail Greig): A classic Scottish town garden reflecting mature box hedges and shrubs, fruit trees, roses underplanted with herbaceous and bulbs and a wildlife haven for birds and bees.
Brechin Community Garden Montrose Street DD9 7EF: Started in 2015 on an abandoned allotment site, this community scheme shares experience and learning skills involved in gardening for their own use and for local people.

Open: Sunday 22 July, 2pm - 5pm, admission £5.00, children free. Tickets and teas at Brechin Cathedral Hall, Church Lane, DD9 6EU.

Directions: Free parking and car parks are available around the city of Brechin.

· *The Attic SCIO & Save Bellfield Campaign*

19

THE HERBALIST'S GARDEN AT LOGIE
Logie House, Kirriemuir DD8 5PN
Terrill and Gavin Dobson
E: terrill@angusherbalists.co.uk
W: www.angusherbalists.co.uk

This garden, featured on *The Beechgrove Garden* in 2014, is set amid an 18th century walled garden and large Victorian greenhouse within Logie's organic farm. Featuring more than 150 herbs, the physic garden is divided into eight rectangles including medicinal herbs for different body systems. All the herbs are labelled with a brief description of actions to help novices learn more about this ancient art. The garden also features a herbaceous border and productive fruit and vegetable garden.

Open: Saturday/Sunday, 28/29 July, 2pm - 5pm, admission £4.00, children free.

Directions: From the A926 leaving Kirriemuir, fork left at Beechwood Place onto the single track road (or if approaching Kirriemuir take sharp left after *Welcome to Kirriemuir sign*). Take the first left and follow signs to The Walled Garden.

· *The Glens and Kirriemuir Old Parish Church of Scotland: Messy Church & Thrums Tots*

ARGYLL & LOCHABER

Scotland's Gardens Scheme 2018 Guidebook is sponsored by INVESTEC WEALTH & INVESTMENT

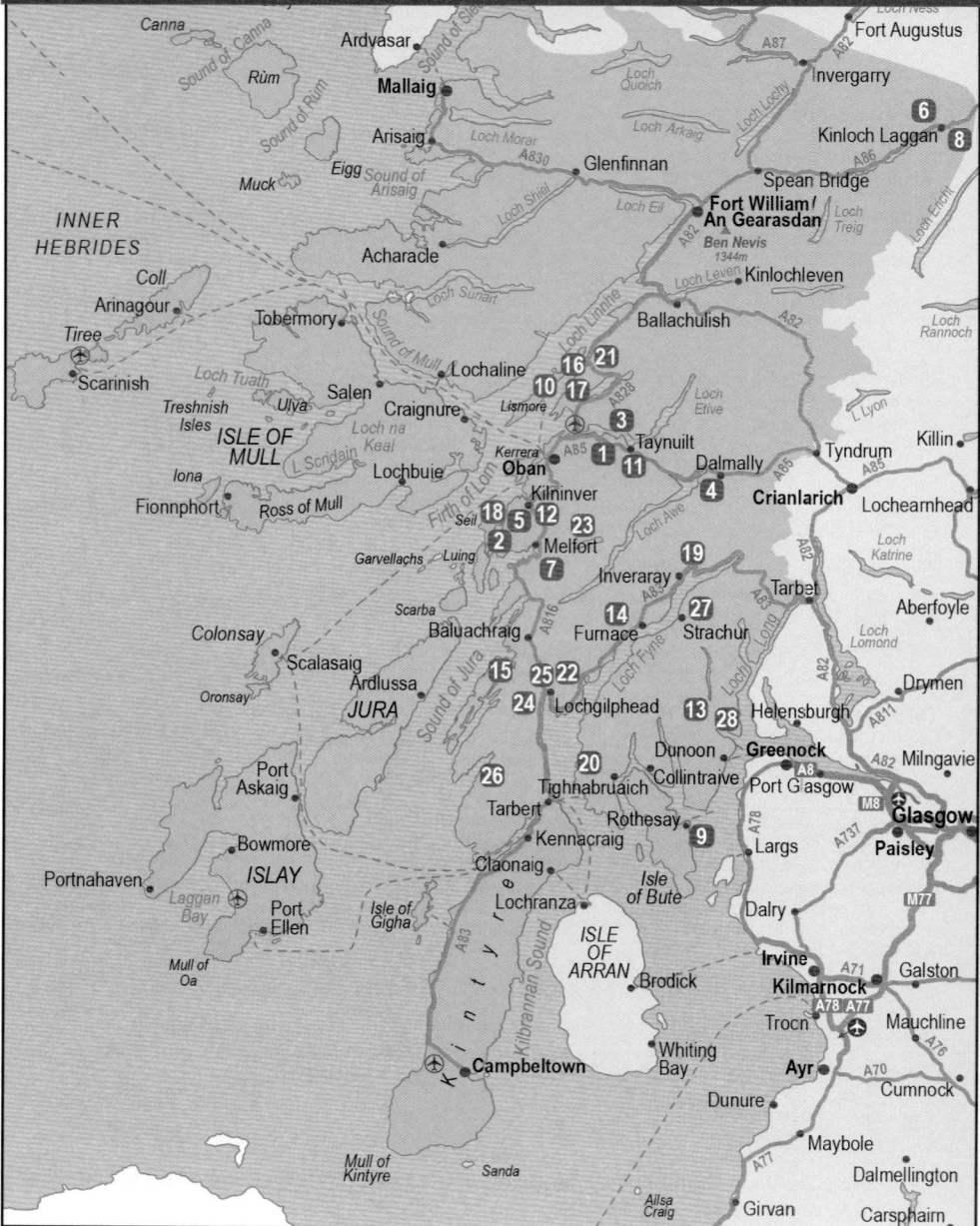

Canna
Rùm
Sound of Canna
Ardvasar
Sound of Sleat
Loch Ness
Fort Augustus
A87
A82
Mallaig
Loch Quoich
A86
Invergarry
Rùm
Sound of Rum
Arisaig
Loch Morar
A830
Loch Arkaig
Loch Lochy
Kinloch Laggan   6
8
Muck
Eigg
Sound of Arisaig
Glenfinnan
Loch Shiel
Loch Eil
Spean Bridge
A82
Fort William /
An Gearasdan
Loch Treig
Loch Ericht
INNER
HEBRIDES
Acharacle
Loch Sunart
Ben Nevis
1344m
Loch Leven
Kinlochleven
Coll
Arinagour
Tiree
Tobermory
Sound of Mull
Lochaline
Ballachulish
A82
Loch Rannoch
Scarinish
Loch Tuath
Treshnish
Isles
Ulva
Salen
Loch na
Keal
Craignure
Lismore
Loch Scridain
16 21
10 17
Loch Linnhe
Loch Etive
L Lyon
Killin
ISLE OF
MULL
Iona
Lochbuie
Kerrera
Oban
A85
3
1
Taynuilt
11
Dalmally
Tyndrum
A85
Fionnphort
Ross of Mull
Firth of Lorn
Seil
18 5 12
2   23
Melfort
7
Kilninver
4
Crianlarich
A85
Lochearnhead
Garvellachs
Luing
19
Loch Awe
A82
Loch Katrine
Scarba
Baluachraig
A816
Furnace
14
Inveraray
27
Strachur
Tarbet
Aberfoyle
Colonsay
Scalasaig
Ardlussa
Oronsay
JURA
Sound of Jura
15 25 22
24
Lochgilphead
13 28
Helensburgh
Loch Fyne
Loch Long
Loch Lomond
A811
Drymen
Milngavie
A82
Port
Askaig
26
Tighnabruaich
Tarbert
20
Collintraive
Dunoon
Greenock
Port Glasgow
A78
A8
M8
Glasgow
Bowmore
ISLAY
Kennacraig
Rothesay
9
Largs
A737
Paisley
Portnahaven
Laggan
Bay
Port
Ellen
Isle of
Gigha
A83
Claonaig
Lochranza
Isle
of Bute
Dalry
M77
Mull of
Oa
Kintyre
Kilbrannan Sound
ISLE
OF
ARRAN
Brodick
Irvine
Kilmarnock
A71
A78 A77
Galston
Trocn
Mauchline
A76
Campbeltown
Whiting
Bay
Ayr
A70
Cumnock
Mull of
Kintyre
Sanda
Dunure
Maybole
A77
Dalmellington
Ailsa
Craig
Girvan
Carsphairn

ARGYLL & LOCHABER

OUR VOLUNTEER ORGANISERS

District Organiser:	Minette Struthers	Ardmaddy Castle, Balvicar, By Oban, PA34 4QY E: argyll@scotlandsgardens.org
Area Organisers:	Yvonne Anderson	Melfort House, Kilmelford, By Oban, PA34 4XD
	Grace Bergius	Craignish House, Ardfern, By Lochgilphead, PA31 8QN
	Mary Lindsay	Dal an Eas, Kilmore, Oban, PA34 4XU
	Patricia McArthur	Bute Cottage, Newton, Strachlachan, PA27 8DB
Treasurer:	Minette Struthers	Ardmaddy Castle, Balvicar, By Oban, PA34 4QY

GARDENS OPEN ON A SPECIFIC DATE

Crarae Garden, Inveraray	Tuesday, 17 April
Crarae Garden, Inveraray	Sunday, 22 April
Benmore Botanic Garden, Benmore, Dunoon	Sunday, 22 April
Arduaine Garden, Oban	Sunday, 29 April
Dalnashean, Port Appin, Appin	Saturday/Sunday, 12/13 May
Inveryne Woodland Garden, Kilfinan, Tighnabruaich	Saturday/Sunday, 12/13 May
Maolachy's Garden, Lochavich, by Taynuilt	Saturday/Sunday, 19/20 May
Strachur House Flower & Woodland Gardens, Strachur	Saturday/Sunday, 19/20 May
Ardverikie with Aberarder, Kinlochlaggan	Sunday, 27 May
The Shore Villages, by Dunoon	Saturday/Sunday, 16/17 June
Ardchattan Priory, North Connel	Sunday, 29 July

GARDENS OPEN REGULARLY

Ardkinglas Woodland Garden, Cairndow	Daily
Ardmaddy Castle, by Oban	1 January - 26 January
Barguillean's "Angus Garden", Taynuilt	Daily
Achnacloich, Connel, Oban	1 January - 31 December (Saturdays only)
Ardtornish, by Lochaline, Morvern	Daily
Ardmaddy Castle, by Oban	27 January - 11 March
Kinlochlaich Gardens, Appin	3 March - 15 October
Ardmaddy Castle, by Oban	12 March - 31 December
Ardchattan Priory, North Connel	29 March - 31 October
Druimneil House, Port Appin	30 March - 31 October
Ar Cala, Ellenabeich, Isle of Seil	1 April - 31 October
Ascog Hall Garden and Fernery, Ascog, Isle of Bute	1 April - 31 October
Inveraray Castle Gardens, Inveraray	1 April - 31 October
Crinan Hotel Garden, Crinan	1 May - 31 August
Oakbank, Ardrishaig	1 May - 31 August
Baile Geamhraidh, Isle of Lismore, Oban, Argyll	1 May - 1 October (Wednesdays only)

Argyll & Lochaber

GARDENS OPEN BY ARRANGEMENT

Kinlochlaich Gardens, Appin	1 Jan- 2 March & 16 Oct - 31 Dec
Ormsary House, Ormsary, Lochgilphead, Argyll	On request
Maolachy's Garden, Lochavich, by Taynuilt	27 January - 11 March
Oakfield, Lochgilpead	1 April - 30 September
Knock Cottage, Lochgair	15 April - 15 June
Barochreal, Kilninver, Oban, Argyll	1 May - 30 September
Baile Geamhraidh, Isle of Lismore, Oban, Argyll	1 May - 1 October
Eas Mhor, Cnoc-a-Challtuinn, Clachan Seil, Oban	1 May - 30 September

KEY TO SYMBOLS

NEW	New garden		Full wheelchair access		Dogs on leads
	Basic teas		Partial wheelchair access	NPC	National plant collection
H	Homemade teas		Plants for sale		Champion trees
C	Cream teas		Children's activities		Designed landscape
	Refreshments		Accessible by public transport		Snowdrop opening

All our gardens open to raise money for charity. Each opening may nominate a charity(s) to receive up to 60% of the takings and these are included with each listing. The net remaining raised supports our core beneficiaries. Information about our core beneficiaries can be found in the front section of the book. More information about our charity scheme and our symbols can be found in the back foldout section of the book under 'Tips for Using Your Guidebook'.

Argyll & Lochaber

1

ACHNACLOICH
Connel, Oban PA37 1PR
Mr T E Nelson
T: 01631 710796 E: charlie_milne@msn.com

Scottish baronial house by John Starforth of Glasgow. Succession of wonderful bulbs, flowering shrubs, rhododendrons, azaleas, magnolias and primulas. Woodland garden with ponds above Loch Etive. Good autumn colours.

Open: 1 January - 31 December (Saturdays only), 10am - 4pm, admission £4.00, children free.

Directions: On the A85 three miles east of Connel. Parking is on the right at the bottom of the drive.

· *Macmillan Cancer Support*

2

AN CALA
Ellenabeich, Isle of Seil PA34 4QY
Mrs Shelia Downie
W: www.gardens-of-argyll.co.uk/view-details.php?id=447

A wonderful example of a 1930s designed garden, An Cala sits snugly in its horseshoe shelter of surrounding cliffs. A spectacular and very pretty garden with streams, waterfall, ponds, many herbaceous plants as well as azaleas, rhododendrons and cherry trees in spring.   Archive material of Mawson's design were found recently.

Open: 1 April - 31 October, 10am - 6pm, admission £4.00, children free.

Directions: Proceed south from Oban on Campbeltown Road for eight miles, turn right at *Easdale* sign, a further eight miles on B844; garden is between the school and village. Bus Oban - Easdale.

· *Donation to SGS Beneficiaries*

3

ARDCHATTAN PRIORY
North Connel PA37 1RQ
Mrs Sarah Troughton
T: 01796 481355 E: sh.troughton@gmail.com
W: www.ardchattan.co.uk

Beautifully situated on the north side of Loch Etive. In front of the house there is a rockery, extensive herbaceous and rose borders, with excellent views over the loch. West of the house there are shrub borders and a wild garden, numerous roses and many different varieties of sorbus providing excellent autumn colour. The Priory, founded in 1230, is now a private house. The ruins of the chapel and graveyard are in the care of *Historic Scotland* and open with the garden.

Open: Sunday 29 July, 12pm - 5pm. Also open 29 March - 31 October, 9:30am - 5:30pm. Admission £4.00, children free. Sunday 29th is a fête.

Directions: Oban ten miles. From north, turn left off A828 at Barcaldine onto B845 for six miles. From East/Oban on A85, cross Connel Bridge and turn first right, proceed east on Bonawe Road.

· *Donation to SGS Beneficiaries*

Argyll & Lochaber

4

ARDKINGLAS WOODLAND GARDEN
Cairndow PA26 8BG
Ardkinglas Estate
T: 01499 600261
W: www.ardkinglas.com

In a peaceful setting overlooking Loch Fyne the garden contains one of the finest collections of rhododendrons and conifers in Britain. This includes the mightiest conifer in Europe, a silver fir, as well as many other champion trees. There is a gazebo with an unique 'Scriptorium' based around a collection of literary quotes. The garden now has the only Gruffalo trail in Scotland, come and find him! It is a *VisitScotland* 3-star garden.
Champion Trees: 'Grand Fir' tallest tree in Britain and others.

Open: Daily, Dawn - Dusk, admission details can be found on the garden's website. See garden website for details on Tree Shop, Plant Centre and Cafe.

Directions: Entrance through Cairndow village off the A83 Loch Lomond/Inveraray road.

· *Donation to SGS Beneficiaries*

5

ARDMADDY CASTLE
by Oban PA34 4QY
Mr and Mrs Charles Struthers
T: 01852 300353 E: minette@ardmaddy.com W: ardmaddy.com/places-visit/

The gardens, in a most spectacular setting, are shielded by mature woodlands, carpeted with bluebells and daffodils and protected from the winds by the elevated castle. The walled garden is full of magnificent rhododendrons, a collection of rare and unusual shrubs and plants, the 'Clock Garden' with its cutting flowers, the new crevice garden, fruit and veg grown with labour saving formality, all within dwarf box hedging. Beyond, a woodland walk, with its 60 foot hydrangea, leads to the water gardens - in early summer a riot of *Candelabra primulas*, irises, rodgersias and other damp loving plants and grasses. Lovely autumn colour. A plantsman's garden for all seasons.

Open: 27 January - 11 March, 9am - Dusk for the Snowdrop Festival. Also open daily, 9am - Dusk. Admission £4.50, children free. Seasonal vegetables, summer fruit and plant stall. Toilet suitable for the disabled. See garden website for other details.

Directions: Take the A816 south of Oban for eight miles. Turn right B844 to Seil Island/Easdale. Four miles on, turn left on to Ardmaddy Road (signed) for a further two miles.

· *Donation to SGS Beneficiaries*

6

ARDTORNISH
by Lochaline, Morvern PA80 5UZ
Mrs John Raven

Wonderful gardens of interesting mature conifers, rhododendrons, deciduous trees, shrubs and herbaceous, set amid magnificent scenery.

Open: Daily, 10am - 6pm, admission £4.00, children free.

Directions: A884 Lochaline three miles.

· *Donation to SGS Beneficiaries*

Argyll & Lochaber

7

ARDUAINE GARDEN
Oban PA34 4XQ
The National Trust for Scotland
T: 01852 200366 E: arduaine@nts.org.uk
W: www.nts.org.uk/arduaine

Outstanding 20 acre coastal garden created over 100 years ago on the south facing slope of a promontory separating Asknish Bay from Loch Melfort. This remarkable hidden paradise, protected by tall shelterbelts and influenced favourably by the North Atlantic Drift, grows a wide variety of plants from all over the globe. Internationally known for its rhododendron species collection, the garden also features magnolias, camellias, azaleas and other wonderful trees and shrubs, many being tender and rarely seen. A broad selection of perennials, bulbs, ferns and water plants ensure year-long interest. Champion Trees: Nine including *Gevuina avellana*.

Open: Sunday 29 April, 9:30am - 4:30pm, admission details can be found on the garden's website. Teas available in adjacent hotel.

Directions: Off the A816 Oban-Lochgilphead, sharing an entrance with the Loch Melfort Hotel.

· *Donation to SGS Beneficiaries*

8

ARDVERIKIE WITH ABERARDER
Kinlochlaggan PH20 1BX
Mrs P Laing & Mrs E T Smyth-Osbourne and The Feilden Family

Aberarder: The garden has been laid out over the last 20 years to create a mixture of spring and autumn plants and trees, including rhododendrons, azaleas and acers . The elevated view down Loch Laggan from the garden is exceptional.
Ardverikie: Lovely setting on Loch Laggan with magnificent trees. Walled garden with large collection of acers, shrubs and herbaceous. Architecturally interesting house (not open) featured in *Monarch of the Glen* and *The Crown*.

Open: Sunday 27 May, 2pm - 5:30pm, admission £5.50, children free.

Directions: On the A86 between Newtonmore and Spean Bridge. Ardverikie's entrance is at the east end of Loch Laggan by the gate lodge over the bridge. For Aberarder go up the drive 200 yards west of the Ardverikie entrance Lodge, adjoining a cottage.

· *Laggan Parish Church & Highland Hospice*

60% of a garden opening's
proceeds can be donated
to the Garden Owner's
nominated charity

Argyll & Lochaber

9

ASCOG HALL GARDEN AND FERNERY
Ascog, Isle of Bute PA20 9EU
Karin Burke
T: 01700 503461 E: info@ascogfernery.com
W: www.ascogfernery.com

....

The outstanding feature of this three acre garden is the Victorian Fernery, a magnificent gilded structure fed by natural spring waters and housing many fern species, including Britain's oldest exotic fern, a 1,000 year old *Todea babara* or King Fern. Rare and unusual species await the visitor wandering the original garden 'rooms' while the stables and coach house ruins feed the imagination with memories of long lost times. The garden is generally well labelled and contains a plant hunter's trail. New for 2018 is a climate change biotape.

Open: 1 April - 31 October, 10am - 5pm, admission £5.00, children free. Restricted mobility parking at the top of the drive (close to the house). Personal assistance available for disabled access to the Fernery.

Directions: Three miles south of Rothesay on A844. Close to the picturesque Ascog Bay. Bus every half hour Rothesay - Kilchattan.

· *Donation to SGS Beneficiaries*

10

BAILE GEAMHRAIDH
Isle of Lismore, Oban, Argyll PA34 5UL
Eva Tombs
T: 01631 760128 E: eva.tombs@gmail.com

....

This unique garden forms part of a biodynamic farm on the Island of Lismore in the Inner Hebrides. Created quite recently from a field, the garden has a strong geometric layout that reflects the ecclesiastical history of the island. It has a vegetable garden, a tree nursery, a physic garden, and an orchard. Wildflowers, birds, bees and butterflies abound. Standing stones, meadows, new woodlands, mountains and the sea encompass the whole. Not without weeds and long grass for the horned cattle that roam the fields.

Open: 1 May - 1 October (Wednesdays only), 2pm - 6pm. Also open by arrangement 1 May - 1 October. Admission £4.00, children free.

Directions: From the Oban to Lismore Ferry (4/5 per day) travel first west then orth for seven miles till you see the 'SGS' yellow sign. Travel up the track over two cattle grids and follow the arrows. From Port Appin to Lismore ferry (foot and cycles) travel 1.5 miles till you see the 'SGS' yellow sign and do the same.

NEW

· *All proceeds to SGS Beneficiaries*

Argyll & Lochaber

11

BARGUILLEAN'S "ANGUS GARDEN"
Taynuilt PA35 1HY
The Josephine Marshall Trust
T: 01866 822333 E: info@barguillean.co.uk
W: www.barguillean.co.uk
....

Nine acre woodland garden around an 11 acre loch set in the Glen Lonan Hills. Spring flowering shrubs and bulbs, extensive collection of rhododendron hybrids, deciduous azaleas, conifers and unusual trees. The garden contains a large collection of North American rhododendron hybrids from famous contemporary plant breeders. Some paths can be steep. Three marked walks from 30 minutes to 1½ hours.

Open: Open Daily, 9am - Dusk, admission £3.50, children free. Coach tours by appointment.

Directions: Three miles south off A85 Glasgow/Oban road at Taynuilt, road marked Glen Lonan, three miles up single track road, turn right at the sign.

· **Donation to SGS Beneficiaries**

"Love your garden?
Why not share it with others
and open in 2019?

12

BAROCHREAL
Kilninver, Oban, Argyll PA34 4UT
Nigel and Antoinette Mitchell
T: 01852 316151 E: toni@themitchells.co.uk
W: www.barochreal.co.uk
....

A young garden evolving since 2006. After much fencing, stone clearing and rewalling, digging and ditching, each year another area has been completed to provide a bank of rhododendrons and azaleas, a rose garden, water feature with rockery, a pond with island, raised vegetable beds and a wild garden with beehives, waterfalls and burns.   Maintained walking tracks in the fields and to viewpoints. The two hard winters of 2010/11 and 2011/12 destroyed many plants in their infancy which are being replaced and added to constantly.

Open: Open by arrangement 1 May - 30 September, admission £3.00, children free.

Directions: On the main A816 Oban to Lochgilphead road just to the south of the village of Kilninver on the left hand side of the road. Please disregard SatNav. Bus Oban - Lochgilpead, stops at Kilninver School, short walk after.

· **Argyll Animal Aid**

Argyll & Lochaber

13

BENMORE BOTANIC GARDEN
Benmore, Dunoon PA23 8QU
A Regional Garden of the Royal Botanic Garden Edinburgh
T: 01369 706261 E: benmore@rbge.org.uk/benmore
W: www.rbge.org.uk

Benmore's magnificent mountainside setting is a joy to behold. Its 120 acres boast a world-famous collection of plants from the Orient and Himalayas to North and South America. An impressive avenue of giant redwoods, one of the finest entrances to any botanic garden in the world. Established in 1863, these majestic giants stand over 50 metres high. Seven miles of trails throughout lead to a restored Victorian Fernery and dramatic viewpoint at 140 metres looking out to surrounding mountains and Holy Loch. Traditional Bhutanese and Chilean pavilions and the magnificent Golden Gates.
National Plant Collection: *Abies*, South American Temperate Conifers, *Picea*.

Open: Sunday 22 April, 10am - 6pm, admission details can be found on the garden's website.

Directions: Seven miles north of Dunoon or 22 miles south from Glen Kinglass below *Rest and Be Thankful* pass. On A815. Bus service is limited.

· *Donation to SGS Beneficiaries*

**Opening your garden is
a fun and rewarding
experience**

14

CRARAE GARDEN
Inveraray PA32 8YA
The National Trust for Scotland
T: 01546 886614 E: kcogan@nts.org.uk
W: www.nts.org.uk/Property/Crarae-Garden/

Crarae is a rugged woodland garden which has spectacular displays of rhododendrons in May and June, a narrow gorge with waterfalls, pools, and varied wildlife from red squirrels and pine martens to otters. Above the garden is the forest garden, a very wild area which was planted in the 1930s as an experiment. This area now has stands of fine tall trees in a unique wild setting but is not open to the public.
National Plant Collection: *Nothofagus*.
Champion Trees: *Abies, acer* and *chamaecyparis*.

Open: Tuesday 17 April, 10am - Dusk. Also open Sunday 22 April, 10am - Dusk. Admission details can be found on the garden's website. Disabled access only to part of the lower garden.

Directions: On A83 ten miles south of Inveraray. Bus Invereray-Lochgilpead

· *Donation to SGS Beneficiaries*

Argyll & Lochaber

Crinan Hotel Garden © Liam Anderstrem

15

CRINAN HOTEL GARDEN
Crinan PA31 8SR
Mr and Mrs N Ryan
T: 01546 830261 E: nryan@crinanhotel.com
W: www.crinanhotel.com

(25)

Small rock garden with azaleas and rhododendrons created in a steep hillside over a century ago with steps leading to a sheltered, secluded garden with sloping lawns, herbaceous beds and spectacular views of the canal and Crinan Loch.

Open: 1 May - 31 August, Dawn - Dusk, admission by donation. Raffle of paintings by Frances MacDonald (Ryan). Tickets available at coffee shop, art gallery and hotel.

Directions: Lochgilphead A83, then A816 to Oban, then A841 Cairnbaan to Crinan. Local service bus three times daily.

· *Feedback Madagascar*

Argyll & Lochaber

16

DALNASHEAN
Port Appin, Appin PA38 4DE
Allister & Kathleen Ferguson
....

Established garden sheltered by a beechwood hill giving views over Loch Linnhe and Lismore. Camellias, rhododendrons and magnolias as well as many unusual shrubs and trees. More recent planting in adjoining field with ponds surrounded by rhododendrons and azaleas and tree and shrub borders.

Open: Saturday/Sunday, 12/13 May, 1pm - 6pm, admission £4.00, children free. Woodcrafts for sale.

Directions: Take the A828 to Appin then the road signposted to *Port Appin* and *Lismore Ferry*. After two miles, turn into the drive opposite the large mirror on roadside.

· Appin Parish Church (Church of Scotland) & Mary's Meals

17

DRUIMNEIL HOUSE
Port Appin PA38 4DQ
Mrs J Glaisher (Gardener: Mr Andrew Ritchie)
T: 01631 730228 E: druimneilhouse@btinternet.com
....

Large garden overlooking Loch Linnhe with many fine varieties of mature trees and rhododendrons and other woodland shrubs. Nearer the house, an impressive bank of deciduous azaleas is underplanted with a block of camassia and a range of other bulbs. A small Victorian walled garden is currently being restored.

Open: 30 March - 31 October, Dawn - Dusk, admission by donation. Teas normally available. Lunch by prior arrangement.

Directions: Turn in for Appin off A828 (Connel/Fort William Road). After two miles, sharp left at Airds Hotel, second house on right.

· Appin Parish Church (Church of Scotland)

18

EAS MHOR
Cnoc-a-Challtuinn, Clachan Seil, Oban PA34 4TR
Mrs Kimbra Lesley Barrett
T: 01852 300 469 E: kimbra1745@gmail.com
....

All the usual joys of a west coast garden plus some delightful surprises! A small contemporary garden on a sloping site - the emphasis being on scent and exotic plant material. Unusual and rare blue Borinda bamboos (only recently discovered in China) and bananas. The garden is at its best in mid to late summer when shrub roses and sweet peas fill the air with scent. The delightful sunny deck overlooks stylish white walled ponds with cascading water blades. Also recent addition of 20 foot citrus house, chinese pergola walk and peony border.

Open: Open by arrangement 1 May - 30 September, admission £4.00, children free. Owner will meet visitors at the bottom of the public road Choc-a-Challtuinn.

Argyll & Lochaber

Directions: Turn off A816 from Oban onto B844 signed Easdale. Over the Bridge onto Seil Island, pass Tigh an Truish pub and turn right after ¼ mile up Cnoc-a-Challtuin road. Public car park on the left at the bottom, please park there and walk up the road. Eas Mhor on right after second speed bump. Please do not block driveway. Bus Oban - Clachan Seil 2-3 per day.

· *MS Centre (Therapy Centre): Oban*

19 INVERARAY CASTLE GARDENS
Inveraray PA32 8XF
The Duke and Duchess of Argyll
T: 01499 302203 E: enquiries@inveraray-castle.com
W: www.inveraray-castle.com
....

Rhododendrons and azaleas abound and flower from April to June. Very fine specimens of *Cedrus deodars, Sequoiadendron wellingtonia, Cryptomeria japonica, Taxus baccata* and others thrive in the damp climate. The 'Flag-Borders' on each side of the main drive with paths in the shape of Scotland's national flag, the St.Andrew's Cross, are outstanding in spring with *Prunus 'Ukon'* and *P. subhirtella* and are underplanted with rhododendrons, Eucryphias, shrubs and herbaceous plants giving interest all year. Bluebell Festival during flowering period in May.

Open: 1 April - 31 October, 10am - 5:45pm, admission £5.00, children free. Wheelchair users please note that there are gravel paths. Guidedogs are welcome. Last admission to garden is 5.00pm.

Directions: Inveraray is 60 miles north of Glasgow on the banks of Loch Fyne on the A83 and 15 miles from Dalmally on the A819. Regular bus service from Glasgow - Lochgilpead.

· *Donation to SGS Beneficiaries*

20 INVERYNE WOODLAND GARDEN
Kilfinan, Tighnabruaich PA21 2ER
Mrs Jane Ferguson
....

In ten acres of a 100 year old amenity wood at Inveryne Farm, on a sloping site, somewhat sheltered from the loch, the garden was begun in 1994. Scrub birches were gradually cleared, bridges installed and amongst rocky outcrops were planted rhododendrons, azaleas, dogwoods, Japanese maples, sorbuses, eucryphias, hydrangeas and more. Gunnera, skunk cabbage, primulas and rodgersias cling to the banks of the burn and ferns provide the backdrop for our growing shrubs. Storms have varied its character and created features, and it is still a work in progress. Spring and autumn colour and an interest in varied vistas and textures of bark and leaf inspire us.

Open: Saturday/Sunday, 12/13 May, 1pm - 5pm, admission £3.50, children free. Parking is opposite the disused tennis court. Wellies are required. Dog owners please note that there are sheep in the fields.

Directions: Approximately six miles north of Tighnabruaich towards Kilfinan on the B8000. After turning right at the crossroads at Millhouse, follow the road past the turning to Ardmarnock, over the little bridge at the bottom. The next track on the left is unpaved and leads to Inveryne.

· *Cowal Elderly Befrienders SCIO*

Argyll & Lochaber

21

KINLOCHLAICH GARDENS
Appin PA38 4BD
Miss F M M Hutchison
T: 07881 525754 E: fiona@kinlochlaich.plus.com
W: www.kinlochlaichgardencentre.co.uk

Walled garden incorporating a large Nursery Garden Centre. Amazing variety of plants growing and for sale. Extensive grounds with woodland walk and spring garden. Many rhododendrons, azaleas, trees, shrubs and herbaceous, including many unusual - embothrium, davidia, stewartia, magnolia, eucryphia and tropaeolum. A quarter of the interior of the walled garden is borders packed with many unusual and interesting plants, espaliered fruit trees, and with an ancient yew in the centre.

Open: 3 March - 15 October, 11am - 4pm. Also open by arrangement. Admission £3.00, children free.

Directions: On the A828 in Appin between Oban, 18 miles to the south, and Fort William, 27 miles to the north.   The entrance is next to the police station. Bus Oban to Fort William.

· *The Appin Village Hall & Feis na h'apainne*

22

KNOCK COTTAGE
Lochgair PA31 8RZ
Mr and Mrs Hew Service
T: 01546 886628 E: corranmorhouse@aol.com

The six acre woodland garden is centred on a small waterfall, an 80 metre lochan and lily pond. From the 1960s there was constant planting with major plantings in 1989 and the 90s. The storms of 2011/12 caused great damage to trees and bushes, thus a replanting phase of azaleas, rhododendrons, camellias and other shrubs. There are over 80 species of rhododendron and hybrids. Among the mature and young trees are cut leaf oak and alder, specimen conifers, eucalyptus, acers, prunus and beech.

Open: Open by arrangement 15 April - 15 June, admission £4.00, children free. Please note there is limited parking. Waterproof footwear is recommended.

Directions: On the A83 from Lochgilphead, Half a mile south of Lochgair Hotel and on the left, and from Inveraray, half a mile after the Lochgair Hotel and on the right between two sharp bends. Bus Inveraray to Lochgilpead

· *MND Scotland*

Argyll & Lochaber

23

MAOLACHY'S GARDEN
Lochavich, by Taynuilt PA35 1HJ
Georgina Dalton
T: 01866 844212

Three acres of woodland garden with a tumbling burn - created in a small glen over 40 years.   At an altitude of 450 feet and two weeks behind the coastal changes we have a shorter growing season. By not struggling to grow tender or late species we can enjoy those that are happy to grow well here and give us all much pleasure. Snowdrops, followed by early rhododendrons, masses of daffodils in many varieties, bluebells, wildflowers and azaleas, primulas and irises.   A productive vegetable patch and tunnel feed the gardener and family.

Open: Open by arrangement 27 January - 11 March for the Snowdrop Festival. Also open Saturday/Sunday, 19/20 May, 1pm - 6pm. Admission £4.00, children free. Main path is gravelled, but some others are narrow, steep and not for the faint hearted. Sensible shoes recommended. The garden steps are being upgraded.

Directions: A816 to Kilmelford. Turn uphill between shop and church, signposted *Lochavich 6*, steep and twisty road with hairpin bend shortly after leaving village, check for passing places. Maolachy Drive is four miles from village. Cross three county cattle grids; after the third. *Ignore the foresty tracks* to left and right. Continue downhill towards Loch Avich, and Maolachy is up on the left, first house after Kilmelford. Ignore SatNav.

· **Hope: Oban**

Knock Cottage

Argyll & Lochaber

24 OAKBANK
Ardrishaig PA30 8EP
Helga Macfarlane
T: 01546 603405 E: helga@macfarlane.one
W: www.gardenatoakbank.blogspot.com
....

This unusual and delightful garden will appeal to adults and children alike with lots for each to explore, including a secret garden. It extends to some three acres of hillside with a series of paths winding among a varied collection of trees, shrubs, bulbs and wild flowers. There are several small ponds, many wonderful wood carvings, an active population of red squirrels and a viewpoint overlooking Loch Fyne to the Isle of Arran.

Open: 1 May - 31 August, 10:30am - 6pm, admission £4.00, children free.

Directions: On the Tarbert (south) side of Ardrishaig - entry to the garden is at the junction of Tarbert Road (A83) and Oakfield Road opposite the more southerly *Scottish Water* lay-by.

· *Diabetes UK*

25 OAKFIELD
Lochgilpead PA31 8NQ
Mrs Jane Renfrew and Mr Graeme Carpenter
T: 07745 115371 E: janerenfrew@live.co.uk
....

Magnificient trees in a picturesque sheltered glen with old specimen rhododendrons, azaleas, and magnolias. Walks through the glen over bridges across the burn. This is an old garden currently being reclaimed. Also a walled garden undergoing restoration. Some rhododendrons have a William Hooker association. The trees were planted 1797-1850 and the rhododendrons and azaleas later.

Open: Open by arrangement 1 April - 30 September, admission £4.00, children free.

Directions: Cross Miller's Bridge on Crinan Canal at Lochgilpead/Tarbert roundabout. Straight up drive 200 metres through pillars at the top. Follow the track to the right. Park at the 'U' shaped Steadings.

· *World Horse Welfare*

26 ORMSARY HOUSE
Ormsary, Lochgilphead, Argyll PA31 8PE
Lady Lithgow
T: 01880 770738 E: mclithgow@ormsary.com
....

Ormsary is on the shore of Loch Caolisport looking across to Islay and Jura. The house policies are resplendent in spring with bluebells and daffodils under fine oak trees. There are woodland gardens with azaleas, rhododendrons and a collection of trees and shrubs. The walled garden, which has evolved over a couple of centuries, is on two levels. The top half is a kitchen garden producing plants, fruit and vegetables for the house; a winter garden and Muscat of Alexandria vinery have been heated by hydroelectric power for a 100 years. A magnificent *Polylepis australis* beckons to the lower 'secret garden' with its lawn, roses, magnolias and long mixed border. It opens onto the banks of Ormsary Water. There are woodland walks accessed through the upper woodland garden.

Argyll & Lochaber

Open: Open by arrangement, admission £5.00, children free.

Directions: Take the A82 road from Lochgilphead towards Campbeltown for four miles, then take B8024 signed to Kilberry and travel ten miles and follow signs to the *Estate office* to collect directions to the garden.

· *All proceeds to SGS Beneficiaries*

27

STRACHUR HOUSE FLOWER & WOODLAND GARDENS
Strachur PA27 8BX
Sir Charles and Lady Maclean

Directly behind Strachur House the flower garden is sheltered by magnificent beeches, limes, ancient yews and Japanese maples. There are herbaceous borders, a burnside rhododendron and azalea walk and a rockery. Old fashioned and species roses, lilies, tulips, spring bulbs and Himalayan poppies make a varied display in this informal haven of beauty and tranquillity. The garden gives onto Strachur Park, laid out by General Campbell in 1782, which offers spectacular walks through natural woodland with two hundred year old trees, rare shrubs and a lochan rich in native wildlife.

Open: Saturday/Sunday, 19/20 May, 1pm - 5pm, admission £4.00, children free.

Directions: Turn off A815 at Strachur House Farm entrance. Park in farm square. Bus Dunoon - Inveraray. From Edinburgh/Glasgow take Ferry from Gourock to Dunoon.

· *British Red Cross: Dunoon*

28

THE SHORE VILLAGES
by Dunoon PA23 8SE
The Gardeners of The Shore Villages
T: 07796 945609 E: mcarthur.patricia@yahoo.co.uk

Seven very different gardens on a seven mile stretch off the A880, overlooking the Holy Loch, the Clyde and Loch Long. Gardening for wildlife, colour combinations and for low maintenance with terracing, sculpture, a wildlife meadow, a cascade of water and a pond.

Open: Saturday/Sunday, 16/17 June, 1pm - 5pm, admission £6.00, children free. Teas are at The Ferry House. Tickets with garden information can be purchased from all the gardens.

Directions: Approaching Dunoon from the north on the A815, take the left hand turning for Kilmun and follow the *SGS* yellow arrows. From Ardentinny follow the A880 right round to Kilmun. All gardens will have yellow balloons at entrance.

· *All proceeds to SGS Beneficiaries*

Make the most of family
friendly walks in bluebell
and snowdrop woods –
spot the signs of spring

AYRSHIRE & ARRAN

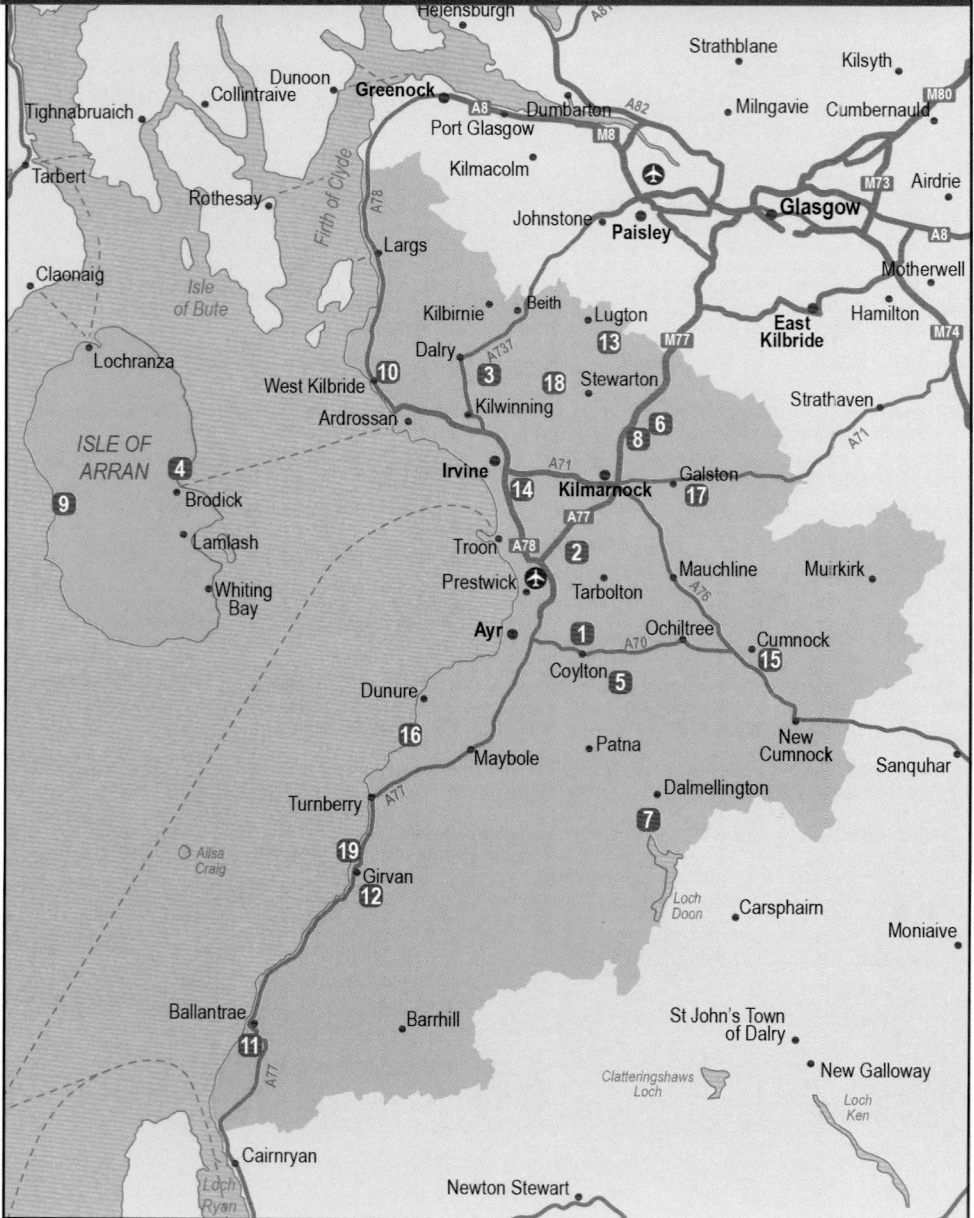

Helensburgh
Strathblane
Kilsyth
Dunoon
Collintraive
Greenock
Port Glasgow
Dumbarton
Milngavie
Cumbernauld
M80
Tighnabruaich
Kilmacolm
Airdrie
M73
Tarbert
Rothesay
Johnstone
Paisley
Glasgow
A8
Largs
Motherwell
Claonaig
Isle of Bute
Kilbirnie
Beith
Lugton
East Kilbride
Hamilton
M74
Lochranza
Dalry
13
Stewarton
Strathaven
West Kilbride
10
Kilwinning
18
6
Ardrossan
8
Galston
ISLE OF ARRAN
4
Irvine
14
Kilmarnock
17
9
Brodick
3
Lamlash
Troon
2
Mauchline
Muirkirk
Whiting Bay
Prestwick
Tarbolton
Ayr
1
Ochiltree
Cumnock
15
Coylton
5
Dunure
16
Patna
New Cumnock
Sanquhar
Maybole
Turnberry
Dalmellington
19
7
Ailsa Craig
Girvan
12
Loch Doon
Carsphairn
Moniaive
Ballantrae
Barrhill
St John's Town of Dalry
11
New Galloway
Clatteringshaws Loch
Loch Ken
Cairnryan
Loch Ryan
Newton Stewart

AYRSHIRE & ARRAN

OUR VOLUNTEER ORGANISERS

District Organisers:	Rose-Ann Cuninghame	45 Towerhill Avenue, Kilmaurs, Kilmarnock, KA3 2TS
	Kim Donald	19 Waterslap, Fenwick, Kilmarnock, KA3 6AJ
	Lavinia Gibbs	Dougarie, Isle of Arran, KA27 8EB
		E: ayrshire@scotlandsgardens.org
Area Organisers:	Anne MacKay	Pierhill, Annbank, Ayr, KA6 5AW
	Kim Main	Afton Cottage, 2 Dunlop Road, Stewarton, KA3 5BE
	Fiona McLean	100 Main Road, Fenwick, KA3 6DY
	Wendy Sandiford	Harrowhill Cottage, Kilmarnock, KA3 6HX
	Jane Tait	The Wildings, Bankwood, Galston, KA4 8LH
Treasurers:	Kim Donald	19 Waterslap, Fenwick, Kilmarnock, KA3 6AJ
	Lizzie Adam	Bayview, Pirnmill, Isle of Arran KA27 8HP

GARDENS OPEN ON A SPECIFIC DATE

Craufurdland Estate, Nr Fenwick, Kilmarnock	Saturday, 17 February
Blair House, Blair Estate, Dalry, Ayrshire	Sunday, 18 February
Brodick Castle & Country Park, Brodick, Isle of Arran	Wednesday, 2 May
Storytelling Event at Culzean, Culzean, Maybole	Monday, 7 May
The Wildings, Bankwood, Galston	Saturday, 19 May
Craigengillan Est Scottish Dark Sky Observatory, Dalmellington	Sunday, 20 May
1 Burnside Cottages, Sundrum, Coylton	Sunday, 3 June
Holmes Farm, Drybridge, by Irvine	Saturday/Sunday, 9/10 June
Barnweil Garden, Craigie, Nr Kilmarnock	Sunday, 17 June
Gardens of West Kilbride and Seamill, West Kilbride	Saturday, 23 June
Blair House, Blair Estate, Dalry, Ayrshire	Sunday, 24 June
Netherthird Community Garden, Craigens Road, Netherthird	Saturday, 30 June
Glendoune House Walled Garden, Coalpots Road, Girvan	Sunday, 1 July
Dougarie, Isle of Arran	Tuesday, 3 July
Clover Park, Langdyke, Waterside, Kilmarnock	Sunday, 15 July
Whitewin House, Golf Course Road, Girvan	Saturday/Sunday, 21/22 July
Whitewin House, Golf Course Road, Girvan	Saturday/Sunday, 28/29 July
Whitewin House, Golf Course Road, Girvan	Saturday/Sunday, 4/5 August
Whitewin House, Golf Course Road, Girvan	Saturday/Sunday, 11/12 August
Netherthird Community Garden, Craigens Road, Netherthird	Saturday, 8 September

GARDENS OPEN BY ARRANGEMENT

Glenapp Castle, Ballartrae, Girvan	17 March - 22 December
1 Burnside Cottages, Sundrum, Coylton	1 April - 30 September
Netherthird Community Garden, Craigens Road, Netherthird	1 April - 31 October
Whitewin House, Golf Course Road, Girvan	1 April - 31 August
Burnside, Littlemill Road, Drongan	1 April - 31 August
Glendoune House Walled Garden, Coalpots Road, Girvan	1 April - 30 September

Ayrshire & Arran

GARDENS OPEN BY ARRANGEMENT (CONTD.)

Clover Park, Langdyke, Waterside, Kilmarnock	1 April - 30 September
Townend of Kirkwood, Stewarton	15 April - 31 October
High Fulwood, Stewarton	1 May - 31 August

KEY TO SYMBOLS

NEW New garden	Full wheelchair access	Dogs on leads
Basic teas	Partial wheelchair access	NPC National plant collection
H Homemade teas	Plants for sale	Champion trees
C Cream teas	Children's activities	Designed landscape
Refreshments	Accessible by public transport	Snowdrop opening

All our gardens open to raise money for charity. Each opening may nominate a charity(s) to receive up to 60% of the takings and these are included with each listing. The net remaining raised supports our core beneficiaries. Information about our core beneficiaries can be found in the front section of the book. More information about our charity scheme and our symbols can be found in the back foldout section of the book under 'Tips for Using Your Guidebook'.

Craigengillan Estate and Scottish Dark Sky Observatory by David Blatchford

Ayrshire & Arran

1

1 BURNSIDE COTTAGES
Sundrum, Coylton KA6 5JX
Carol Freireich
T: 01292 570617 E: carol.freireich@btinternet.com

A sheltered cottage garden of 1.3 acres, based on a rescued orchard of 1930s varieties. In the 1990s other varieties were added, chosen to tolerate the northerly conditions. Even though the soil is heavy and there is poor drainage, the fruit crops amazingly. The organically cultivated native trees and many wild flowers encourage wide varieties of bird and insect life. There is a garden pond, vegetable garden, fruit cage, ornamental beds and a stream running through a small wood. Children are encouraged to enjoy the freedom and exploration this garden offers.

Open: Sunday 3 June, 2pm - 5pm. Also open by arrangement 1 April - 30 September. Admission £4.00, children free.

Directions: A70 three miles from Ayr signed left at Sundrum Castle Caravan Park. Go up the road for ¾ mile and then left down dirt track where there is limited parking or continue to Coylton first left at Barclaugh Drive round to the right, park at Woodhead Road and walk for five minutes to the garden. Look for signposts. Buses 45 or 48 Ayr/Cumnock to foot of Barclaugh Drive and follow signed route.

· *The Pancreatic Cancer Research Fund*

Scotland's Gardens Scheme is supported by hundreds of inspiring volunteers

2

BARNWEIL GARDEN
Craigie, Nr Kilmarnock KA1 5NE
Mr and Mrs Ronald W Alexander
E: ronaldwalexander@btinternet.com

Begun in 1972 this garden has evolved and developed ever since. Pure clay soil and being on the north side of the hill are two of the challenges and wind has also been a problem, but solved by planting beech hedging and shelter belts. The lawn on the south side of the early 19th Century house is enclosed by herbaceous borders, giving way to shrub roses and then the woodland garden where the golden borders (a particular favourite) always seem sunny even on a grey day. A planting of meconopsis and *Primula japonica* 'Postford white' are two of the sights amongst azaleas and species and hybrid rhododendrons. The north side has formal borders framing the view from the house to Craigie Castle and (on a clear day) Ben Lomond, with modern shrub rose borders on each side. Recent work has seen the beginnings of a bog garden.

Open: Sunday 17 June, 2pm - 5pm, admission £5.00, children free.

Directions: Craigie two miles. Right off the B730, two miles south of A77 heading to Tarbolton.

· *Tarbolton Parish Church of Scotland & CLDF: Children's Liver Disease Foundation*

Ayrshire & Arran

3

BLAIR HOUSE, BLAIR ESTATE
Dalry, Ayrshire KA24 4ER
Charles and Sallie Hendry
T: 01294 833100 E: enquiries@blairestate.com
W: www.blairestate.com

. . . .

Blair is a 'Sleeping Beauty' of a garden which is being lovingly restored. There is an atmosphere of a grand 19th century park with masses of changes in mood: sweeping vistas, magnificent trees, shady promenades, and secret groves - everything that is typical of the period. A start on the walled garden has been made with the removal of 600 Christmas trees and we are compiling ideas for future renovation. In February enjoy beautiful displays of snowdrops. Walks on the estate will include access to the private gardens. Please wear stout footwear.

Open: Sunday 18 February, 11am - 4pm for the Snowdrop Festival. Also open Sunday 24 June, 11am - 4pm. Admission £5.00, children free.

Directions: From A737 in Dalry, take road signposted to the station and continue for ½ mile. Access via North Lodge Gates on the right. A one way system will be in place. Public transport to Dalry.

· **Girlguiding Ayrshire North**

4

BRODICK CASTLE & COUNTRY PARK
Brodick, Isle of Arran KA27 8HY
The National Trust for Scotland
T: 01770 302202 E: brodickcastle@nts.org.uk
W: www.nts.org.uk/Visit/Brodick-Castle-and-Country-Park/

. . . .

At any time of year the gardens are well worth a visit, though especially in spring when the internationally acclaimed rhododendron collection bursts into full bloom. There are exotic plants and shrubs, a walled garden and a woodland garden to be enjoyed by garden enthusiasts, families and children. Venture out into the country park and discover wildflower meadows where Highland cows graze, woodland trails and tumbling waterfalls. There is something for everyone.
National Plant Collection: *Rhododendron* (subsect *Grandia*, subsect *Falconera*, and subsect *Maddenia*)
Champion Trees: Several

Open: Wednesday 2 May, tours at 12pm and 2pm, admission details can be found on the garden's website. Booking not essential.   Dogs on leads welcome outside the walled garden.

Directions: Brodick two miles. Buses from Brodick Pier to Castle. Regular sailings from Ardrossan and Claonaig (Argyll). Info from Caledonian MacBrayne, Gourock, 01475 650100.

· **Donation to SGS Beneficiaries**

Our Volunteers run
the District accounts
and social media,
want to help?

Ayrshire & Arran

5

BURNSIDE
Littlemill Road, Drongan KA6 7EN
Sue Simpson and George Watt
T: 01292 592445

This young six and a half acre garden was started in 2006. There is a wide range of plants from trees to alpines. Features include a 200 yard woodland border along the burn, herbaceous beds, screes, an ericaceous garden, three alpine houses, a large collection of alpine troughs and a pond. The informal arboretum is underplanted with groups of daffodils, camassia, fritillaries and crocus.

Open: Open by arrangement 1 April - 31 August, admission £4.00, children free.

Directions: From A77 Ayr bypass take A70 Cumnock for 5¼ miles, at Coalhall, turn onto B730 Drongan (south) for 2½ miles. Burnside entrance immediately adjacent before black/white parapeted bridge. Ordnance survey grid ref: NS455162.

· *Alzheimer Scotland*

Alpine troughs and pots at Burnside

6

CLOVER PARK
Langdyke, Waterside, Kilmarnock KA3 6JA
Alistair Paterson and Iain MacClure
T: 01560 700555 E: clover.park@outlook.com

Clover Park began life nine years ago as a flat field. It has been developed by the owners into an array of mixed ornamental and atmospheric features - with a woodland walk, fernery, rockery, gunnera bog, azalea walk, extensive herbaceous borders and a secluded pond walkway. A paddock is home to a small herd of friendly pygmy goats. There are quiet seating areas throughout the garden for contemplation and relaxation. The owners have in a short time created a garden of great interest.

Open: Sunday 15 July, 2pm - 5:30pm. Also open by arrangement 1 April - 30 September. Admission £4.00, children free.

Directions: From Glasgow on the M77 take J6 on to A77. After about 1.5 miles take left for Galston A719. Drive through hamlet of Waterside, a little further on there is a dip in the road over the Hareshaw Water, look for the sign for *Langdyke & Clover Park* on the left hand side (farm road). From Ayr/Kilmarnock take J7 off the M77 heading north on to A77. At the Fenwick/ Stewarton roundabout follow signs to Galston. After one mile turn right onto the A719 Galston as above.

· *CLIC Sargent*

Ayrshire & Arran

7

CRAIGENGILLAN ESTATE AND SCOTTISH DARK SKY OBSERVATORY
Dalmellington KA6 7PZ
Mark Gibson and Fi McLelland
T: 01292 551118 E: fi@craigengillan.com
W: www.scottishdarkskyobservatory.co.uk

Peacefully set in a rugged 'Highland' landscape recognised by Historic Scotland's Inventory of Gardens and Designed Landscapes. Beautiful gardens, recently uncovered 'rock and water garden' by James Pulham & Sons. Extensive displays of native bluebells - great swathes of vibrant blue under the fresh greens of newly forming leaf canopies. At night there are some of the darkest skies that most people will ever see with stars, planets, comets and constellations all visible.

Open: Sunday 20 May, 2pm - 5pm, admission £4.00, children free. Immersive Planetarium and Stellarium Presentation available at the Dark Sky Observatory at 2pm, 3pm and 4pm. See the Observatory website for prices and to book (advanced booking recommended).

Directions: A713 from Ayr, at the round red 30mph sign on entering Dalmellington turn right (signed Craigengillan Stables) - drive for approx 2¼ m to Craigengillan House. From Carsphairn, stay on the main road through Dalmellington then take first turning on left after the Jet petrol station.

· *The Scottish Dark Sky Observatory*

Share your gardening knowledge for us online

8

CRAUFURDLAND ESTATE
Nr Fenwick, Kilmarnock KA3 6BS
Mr and Mrs Simon Craufurd
T: 01560 600760
W: www.craufurdland.co.uk

Coming through the gates, drive along to the Fishery - the road continues to the Castle. You will see that the woods around the Castle have wonderful examples of many different types of snowdrops. You can stroll through the woodland at leisure, on paths we have created - viewing the best Craufurdland snowdrops along the way.

Open: Saturday 17 February, 12pm - 3pm for the Snowdrop Festival, admission £4.00, children free. Tickets available by the Fishery. Sturdy footwear required. Soup, tea and coffee can be purchased at the Castle.

Directions: For SatNav follow Marchbank House KA3 6BX. Once in Fenwick Village at the bottom of Main Road, turn into Waterslap, follow the road out of the village for approximately one mile, Marchbank is on the left, a little further on there is a sharp bend, the gates to Craufurdland Estate are straight ahead. Parking at the Fishery/Wee Cafe car park.

· *Friends of Craufurdland SCIO*

9

DOUGARIE
Isle of Arran KA27 8EB
Mr and Mrs S C Gibbs
E: office@dougarie.com

Most interesting terraced garden in castellated folly built in 1905 to celebrate the marriage of the 12th Duke of Hamilton's only child to the Duke of Montrose. Good selection of tender and rare shrubs and herbaceous border. Small woodland area with trees including azara, abutilon, eucryphia, hoheria and nothofagus.

Ayrshire & Arran

Open: Tuesday 3 July, 2pm - 5pm, admission £3.50, children free. The opening date is subject to change. Check the SGS website before making arrangements to travel.

Directions: Blackwaterfoot five miles. Regular ferry sailing from Ardrossan and Claonaig (Argyll). Information from Caledonian MacBrayne, Gourock, T: 01475 650100

· *Pirnmill Village Association*

10 GARDENS OF WEST KILBRIDE AND SEAMILL
West Kilbride KA23 9EN
The Gardeners of West Kilbride and Seamill
E: rhonalinda@btinternet.com

A variety of gardens, well favoured by the usually mild coastal climate, will open on the Saturday only when visitors will also be able to enjoy the excellent shopping facilities of the "Craft Town".

Open: Saturday 23 June, 1pm - 5pm, admission £5.00, children free. Tickets, maps and refreshments at the Village Hall, 1 Arthur Street.

Directions: Heading from Dalry take B781 for seven miles. Alternatively take the A78 south for eight miles from Largs or the A78 north for seven miles from Kilwinning. Signposted to Village Hall for tickets and maps marked with gardens opening, disabled access shown as applicable. Accessible by train.

· *North Ayrshire Cancer Care*

11 GLENAPP CASTLE
Ballantrae, Girvan KA26 0NZ
Mr Paul Szkiler
T: 01465 831212 E: gm@glenappcastle.com
W: www.glenappcastle.com

The 36 acre grounds at Glenapp Castle are totally secluded and private. There are many rare and unusual plants and shrubs to be found, including magnificent specimen rhododendrons. Paths wander round the azalea pond, and through established woodland, leading to the wonderful walled garden with its 150 foot Victorian glasshouse. Fresh herbs and fruit from the garden are used every day in the castle kitchen. Much of the gardens were designed by Gertrude Jekyll (1843-1932) who was a world famous garden architect applying the principles of the Arts and Crafts Movement and who worked in collaboration with Edwin Lutyens.

Open: Open by arrangement 17 March - 22 December, admission £5.00, children free.

Directions: When approaching from the North take the A77 South. Pass through the village of Ballantrae, crossing the River Stinchar as you leave. Take the first turning on the right, 100 yards beyond the river (not sign posted). From the South take the A77 North and turn left 100 yards before the bridge over the River Stinchar at Ballantrae. The gates of the castle are located one mile along this road.

· *Donation to SGS Beneficiaries*

Ayrshire & Arran

12

GLENDOUNE HOUSE WALLED GARDEN
Coalpots Road, Girvan KA26 0HN
Mr and Mrs WJ Briggs
T: 07870 919505 E: kilhenzie@aol.com

The owners of Glendoune House have set about the enormous task of restoring this well known walled garden to its former glory. The garden had lain neglected for many years, but they have inherited good records of the property and are working towards putting it back to its original condition, including repairing the glasshouses. There are walkways and paths, lined with old fruit trees, old roses and many herbaceous shrubs and perennials. The garden is bordered by magnificent specimens of old trees and glorious rhododendrons. The southerly part of the walled garden is home to a large vegetable garden. A work in progress.

Open: Sunday 1 July, 2pm - 5pm. Also open by arrangement 1 April - 30 September. Admission £4.00, children free.

Directions: Heading south to Girvan on the A77, at the roundabout before going in to Irvine take the B734 (Old Dailly), after a short distance take the road on the right, Coalpots Road, which is the Girvan by-pass to the East of the town. Glendoune House is on the left heading towards Stranraer - approximately half a mile beyond the railway bridge.

H   NEW

· Haemophilia Scotland

13

HIGH FULWOOD
Stewarton KA3 5JZ
Mr and Mrs Crawford
T: 01560 484705

One acre of mature garden, particularly fine in late spring with rhododendrons, azaleas, trillium, hellebores and other spring flowering plants and bulbs. There is also an acre of developing garden with herbaceous borders, vegetable garden and orchard at its best during July and August and there are two acres of native broadleaf woodland being created. No neat edges but lots to see at any time.

Open: Open by arrangement 1 May - 31 August, admission £4.00, children free.

Directions: From Stewarton Cross take the B760 Old Glasgow Road for one mile - turn onto the road marked to Dunlop (from Glasgow this turning is half a mile past Kingsford). Continue for two miles and turn right at T junction. High Fulwood is a short distance on the right hand side.

· Hessilhead Wildlife Rescue

14

HOLMES FARM
Drybridge, by Irvine KA11 5BS
Mr Brian A Young
T: 01294 311210 E: hfplants@live.co.uk
W: www.holmesfarmplants.com

A plantsman's garden created by a confirmed plantaholic. Meandering paths guide the eye through predominantly herbaceous plantings, with small trees and shrubs. The garden opening will hopefully be timed for the peak bloom of some of the 400 iris in the garden. Some areas of the garden are currently undergoing a partial replant. The plant nursery Holmes Farm Plants is located at the garden where a wide selection of plants from the garden can be purchased along with a gift too.

Ayrshire & Arran

Open: Saturday/Sunday, 9/10 June, 1pm - 5pm, admission £5.00, children free.

Directions: Holmes is the only farm between Drybridge and Dreghorn on B730.

· *Plant Heritage*

Holmes Farm by Rob Davis

NETHERTHIRD COMMUNITY GARDEN

Craigens Road, Netherthird, Cumnock KA18 3AR
Netherthird Community Development Group
E: jamielor@aol.com
W: Facebook (Netherthird Community Development Group)

Netherthird Community Garden is an oasis of calm in the centre of the Ayrshire countryside. We have a lovely cottage garden, flower beds, vegetable beds, and wooden gazebos funded by The Prince Charles Foundation.   There is also a beach, play area, vintage cafe, a new nature trail, fairy door hunt and lots more. Volunteers run the garden which is used by a wide range of community groups and all the children and nursery children from the adjacent Netherthird Primary during the week.

Open: Saturday 30 June, 12pm - 4pm. Also open Saturday 8 September, 12pm - 4pm. And open by arrangement 1 April - 31 October. Admission £3.00, children free.

Directions: Driving south on the A76 Cumnock by-pass look for the roundabout signed B7083, take this exit which heads to Cumnock, after few hundred yards take right turn into Craigens Road, Netherthird Primary School is on the right. Parking available here, Community Garden nearby. Disabled parking at garden.

· *Netherthird Community Development Group*

Ayrshire & Arran

16 ## STORYTELLING AT CULZEAN
Culzean, Maybole KA19 8LE
NTS Culzean and Scotland's Gardens Scheme
W: www.nts.org.uk/Visit/Culzean-Castle-and-Country-Park

Once upon a time...

Culzean Castle perches on top of the spectacular cliffs of the Ayrshire coast, looking out to sea on one side and over its historic gardens and grounds on the other, acting simultaneously as a viewing platform and as a splendid backdrop for the extensive gardens. Hear how Culzean's unique situation and climate allow many usually tender plants to flourish outdoors such as the exotic pineapple guava *Acca sellowiana*, 2 metres high Canary Island echiums, or the Loquat tree *Eriobotrya japonica*. Hear about the walled garden, created in a double plan blunt diamond shape to maximise sunlight but also to create working and pleasure gardens in one space. And how the land where the walled garden now sits was once the property of a former slave called Scipio, who was brought to Culzean as a child, but earned his freedom and the right to this high value plot of land. Join Scotland's Gardens Scheme and The Scottish International Storytelling Festival in "Growing Stories". A fun packed way to explore some of Scotland's gardens. See gardens with new eyes once you hear stories, from local storytellers, about their creation, history and interaction with the environment. For more information see Scotland's Gardens Scheme website.

Open: Monday 7 May, 1pm - 4pm, admission details can be found on the garden's website. Admission to the storytelling event is £5.00, in addition to general admission.

Directions: On the A719 twelve miles south of Ayr, four miles west of Maybole. Bus 60 Stagecoach, Ayr/Girvan via Maidens to the entrance. One mile walk downhill from the stop to the Castle/Visitor Centre.

· *Culzean's Walled Gardens*

17 ## THE WILDINGS
Bankwood, Galston KA4 8LH
Mr and Mrs Jim Tait

The Wildings is opening as a Spring Garden this year. The garden was created 18 years ago and is now well established, providing year round interest. A cottage style front garden leads to a more formal area with a terrace lined with an abundance of climbing plants in pots, stone walls, lawn, imaginatively planted beds, a pond well stocked with water plants, raised vegetable beds and potting shed. A pathway winds up through a mature garden planted with a variety of rhododendrons, azaleas, various shrubs and mature trees. A bluebell wood lies further up the garden planted with mature rhododendrons. This garden is a haven for wildlife.

Open: Saturday 19 May, 11am - 4pm, admission £4.00, children free.

Directions: Take Sorn Road from Galston and follow for approxImately 1½ miles. Just before reaching Sorn Hill, turn left where signposted *Gibbs Animal Feeds*. Turn left again immediately and The Wildings is the first house on the left.

· *Compassion UK Christian Child Development*

Our Volunteers organise open days and promote gardens, could this be you?

Ayrshire & Arran

18 TOWNEND OF KIRKWOOD
Stewarton KA3 3EN
Mrs Katrina Clow
T: 01560 483926 / 07914 316119 E: katrina.clow@btinternet.com

Townend of Kirkwood is a new garden - started on three acres of wet field in 2013. There is an excellent range of interesting shrubs and young trees. To the rear of the house there is a small sheltered garden with lawn and herbaceous beds full of plants, and a path that leads to a small young orchard with productive trees. On the left of the driveway leading to the house there is a wildlife pond.

Open: Open by arrangement 15 April - 31 October, admission £6.00, children free. Open only for groups of 6-25.   Reasonable parking and access for mini-bus.

Directions: Provided when applying.

· *The Younger (Benmore) Trust*

19 WHITEWIN HOUSE
Golf Course Road, Girvan KA26 9HW
Linda Finnie and Graeme Finnie
T: 01465 712358 E: lafinnie@hotmail.com

Whitewin House and gardens have an interesting history. It was the first house to be built on Golf Course Road by the Tate & Lyle sugar refining family in the late 1800's. It has a prime location with stunning views over the Firth of Clyde and to Ailsa Craig and the Kintyre Peninsula. There are four separate gardens: the Ailsa Craig Garden at the front; The Gable Garden; the Central Rear Garden and the Rear Golf Course Garden. The layout is formal with lawns, borders, shrubs, rockeries and statuary - complementing the Victorian architecture of Whitewin.

Open: Saturday/Sunday, 21/22 and 28/29 July and Saturday/Sunday 4/5 and 11/12 August, 1pm - 5pm. And open by arrangement 1 April - 31 August. Admission £3.50, children free. Teas & coffee served in conservatories.

Directions: Approaching Girvan from the North on the A77 the turning to Golf Course Road is on the right hand side of the road before the town centre (follow signs for the *Golf Course*). From the South on the A77 come through Girvan, turn left at the lights, then first left and follow signs for the *Golf Course*, Entrance to the property will be signed.

· *All proceeds to SGS Beneficiaries*

Scotland's Gardens
Scheme is supported
by hundreds of
inspiring volunteers

BERWICKSHIRE

Scotland's Gardens Scheme 2018 Guidebook is sponsored by INVESTEC WEALTH & INVESTMENT

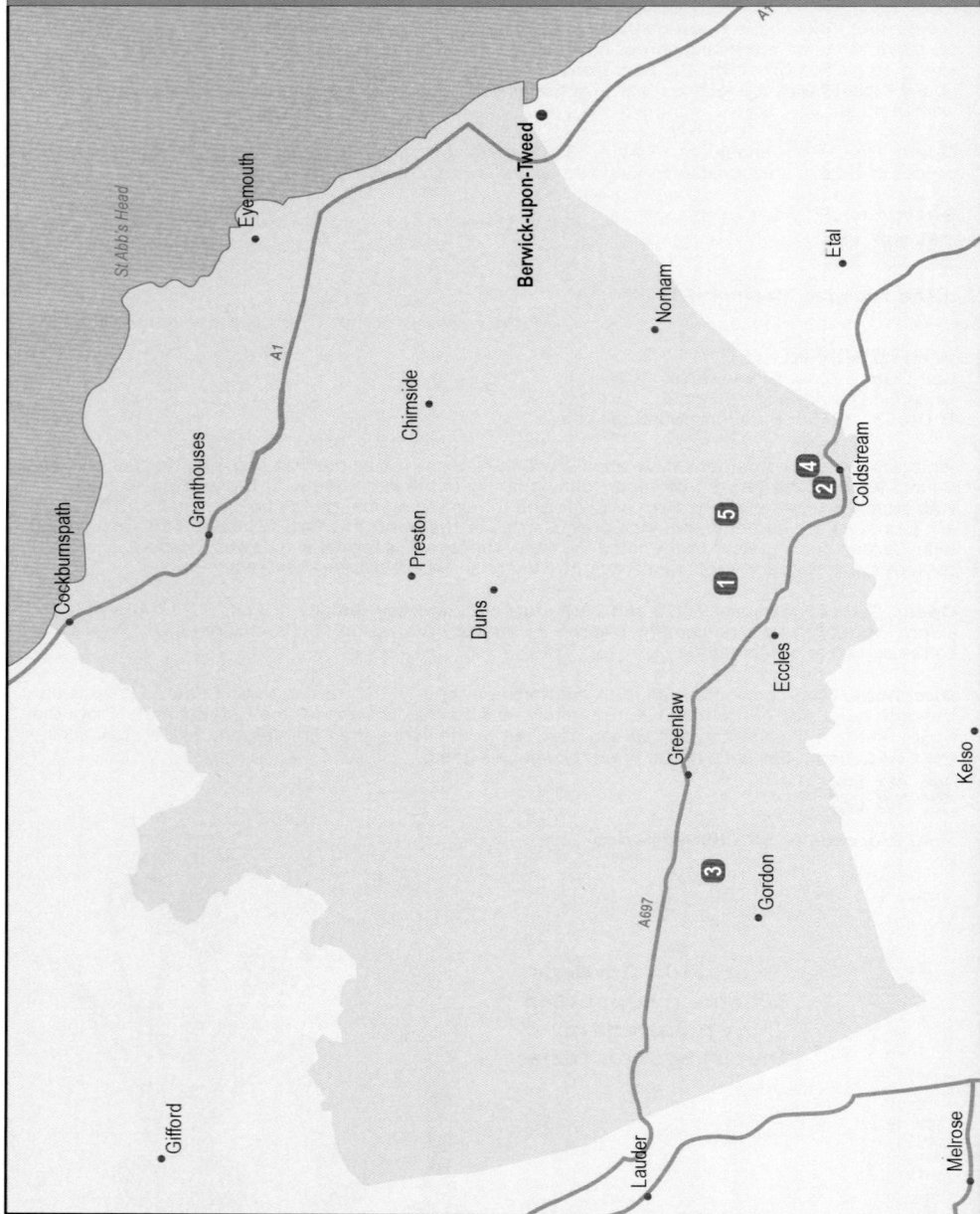

St Abb's Head

Eyemouth

Berwick-upon-Tweed

Etal

Norham

A1

Chirnside

Granthouses

Coldstream

4

Preston

2

5

Cockburnspath

1

Duns

Eccles

Greenlaw

Kelso

A697

3

Gordon

Gifford

Lauder

Melrose

BERWICKSHIRE

OUR VOLUNTEER ORGANISERS

District Organiser:	Christine McLennan	Marlfield, Coldstream, TD12 4JT
		E: berwickshire@scotlandsgardens.org
Treasurer:	Forbes McLennan	Marlfield, Coldstream, TD12 4JT

GARDENS OPEN ON A SPECIFIC DATE

East Gordon Smiddy, Gordon	Sunday, 24 June
Lennel Bank, Coldstream	Sunday, 1 July
Coldstream Open Gardens, Coldstream Community Centre	Sunday, 8 July
Marlfield and Ruthven Gardens, Coldstream	Sunday, 22 July

GARDENS OPEN REGULARLY

Bughtrig, Near Leitholm, Coldstream	1 June - 31 August

GARDENS OPEN BY ARRANGEMENT

Lennel Bank, Coldstream	On request

KEY TO SYMBOLS

NEW New garden	Full wheelchair access	Dogs on leads
Basic teas	Partial wheelchair access	NPC National plant collection
H Homemade teas	Plants for sale	Champion trees
C Cream teas	Children's activities	Designed landscape
Refreshments	Accessible by public transport	Snowdrop opening

All our gardens open to raise money for charity. Each opening may nominate a charity(s) to receive up to 60% of the takings and these are included with each listing. The net remaining raised supports our core beneficiaries. Information about our core beneficiaries can be found in the front section of the book. More information about our charity scheme and our symbols can be found in the back foldout section of the book under 'Tips for Using Your Guidebook'.

Berwickshire

1

BUGHTRIG
Near Leitholm, Coldstream TD12 4JP
Mr and Mrs William Ramsay
T: 01890 840777 E: ramsay@bughtrig.co.uk

A traditional hedged Scottish family garden with an interesting combination of sculpture, herbaceous plants, shrubs, annuals and fruit. It is surrounded by fine specimen trees which provide remarkable shelter.

Open: 1 June - 31 August, 2pm - 5pm, admission £5.00, children free.

Directions: Quarter of a mile east of Leitholm on the B6461.

· *Donation to SGS Beneficiaries*

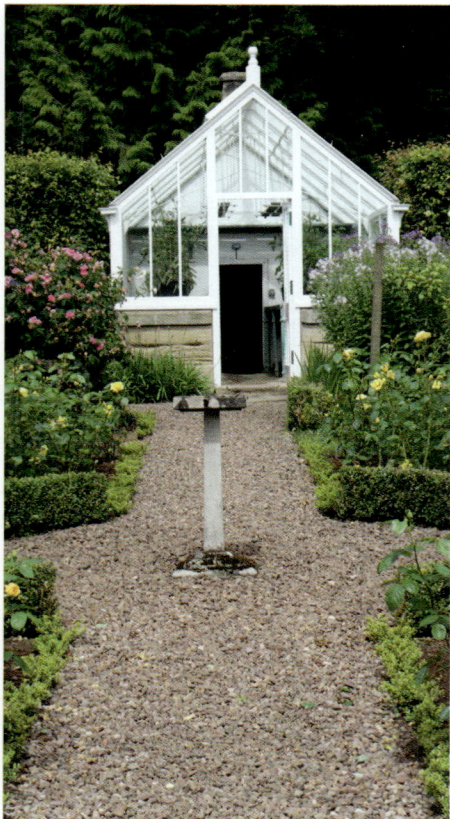

Herbaceous borders and greenhouse at Bughtrig by Kenneth Patterson

Berwickshire

2

COLDSTREAM OPEN GARDENS
Coldstream Community Centre, High Street, Coldstream TD12 4AP
The Gardeners of Coldstream
T: 01890 840700

Historic Coldstream, Scotland's 'First True Border Town' is home of Coldstream's Guards, the country's second oldest infantry regiment. Cross the bridge over the river Tweed which forms a natural boundary between England and Scotland, pausing to admire the wonderful views along the river to the Cheviots and beyond. Coldstream, as the Borders Floral Gateway Awards best large village winner 2017, will have a great variety of gardens open for the garden enthusiast to explore. Wander around and chat to an exponent of permaculture, a giant vegetable grower and numerous other garden owners who will be delighted to share their gardening triumphs and interests with you.

Open: Sunday 8 July, 1pm - 5pm, admission £5.00, children free. Tickets, teas, plant sales and facilities at the Community Centre.

Directions: Coldstream is on the A697 equidistant between Kelso and Berwick-on-Tweed. The Community Centre (an old church building) is in the west end of town. There is ample parking on the street and in nearby car parks.

· *Coldstream Gateway Association*

3

EAST GORDON SMIDDY
Gordon TD3 6JY
Martyn and Judith Welch

A garden newly created from farmland in 2008 with wonderful panoramic views towards the Cheviot Hills. Herbaceous borders, shrubbery, extensive vegetable garden and fruit trees. There is a pond, woodland and a wildflower meadow. The whole garden is divided by mature hornbeam hedging, grass pathways and interesting corners to sit and contemplate.

Open: Sunday 24 June, 11am - 5pm, admission £5.00, children free.

Directions: On the A6105 between Gordon and Greenlaw at East Gordon. On top of the hill at the farm entrance.

· *Sustrans Ltd*

Berwickshire

4

LENNEL BANK
Coldstream TD12 4EX
Mrs Honor Brown
T: 01890 882297

....

Lennel Bank is a terraced garden overlooking the River Tweed, consisting of wide borders packed with shrubs and perennial planting, some unusual. The water garden, built in 2008, is surrounded by a rockery and utilises the slope ending in a pond. There is a small kitchen garden with raised beds in unusual shapes. Different growing conditions throughout the garden from dry, wet, shady and sunny lend themselves to a variety of plants, which hopefully enhance interest in the garden.

Open: Sunday 1 July, 10:30am - 5pm. Also open by arrangement. Admission £5.00, children free.

Directions: On A6112 Coldstream to Duns road, one mile from Coldstream.

· *British Heart Foundation*

Lennel Bank by Kenneth Patterson

Berwickshire

5

MARLFIELD AND RUTHVEN GARDENS
Coldstream TD12 4JT
Christine & Forbes McLennan and Karen & Keith Fountain
T: 01890 840700

Set in the rolling Berwickshire countryside, Marlfield and Ruthven are two large family gardens, previously part of working farms. The gardens are approximately one mile apart which is either a nice walk or simple drive.

Marlfield TD12 4JT: Two and a half acre garden with extensive lawns, specimen trees, shrubberies, flower beds, a half acre woodland wind break, half acre paddock with a large allotment type raised vegetable garden, fruit cage and small orchard. The present owners have worked extensively over the past five years to create the allotment and fruit beds from a vacant field. The main garden is still a work in progress, restoring or creating order from what was a very neglected garden. The rockery and fish pond are almost complete. Marlfield is a lovely tranquil garden where one can honestly hear nothing but birds singing and our bees buzzing.
Ruthven House TD12 4JU: Lovely views toward the Cheviots and is accessed via a sweeping driveway. There are three acres divided into various interconnected areas, including a traditional knot garden, gravel gardens, an orchard set in meadow planting, a newly establish rose garden and informal herbaceous borders which lead to the garden's main feature, two ponds connected by a winding stream. The owners have over the last few years expanded the garden extensively from the original small beds around the house - adding different areas as inspiration struck. The most recent additions are a substantial kitchen garden and (perhaps optimistically) a small lavender field.

Open: Sunday 22 July, 1pm - 5pm, admission £5.00, children free.

Directions: From Coldstream, turn up at the side of the Mercedes dealer and follow the road for approximately four miles. From the A697, take the B6461 towards Berwick. Two miles past Leitholm, take the first right at Swinton Mill crossroads and follow this road for one mile. From Swinton, take the B6461 towards Kelso. After two miles, go left at the Swinton Mill crossroad and follow the road for one mile. Both gardens will be well signposted.

· *Macmillan Cancer Support: Borders*

Scotland's Gardens Scheme
started in 1931 and
HRH King George V opened
the gardens at Balmoral

CAITHNESS & SUTHERLAND

Scotland's Gardens Scheme 2018 Guidebook is sponsored by INVESTEC WEALTH & INVESTMENT

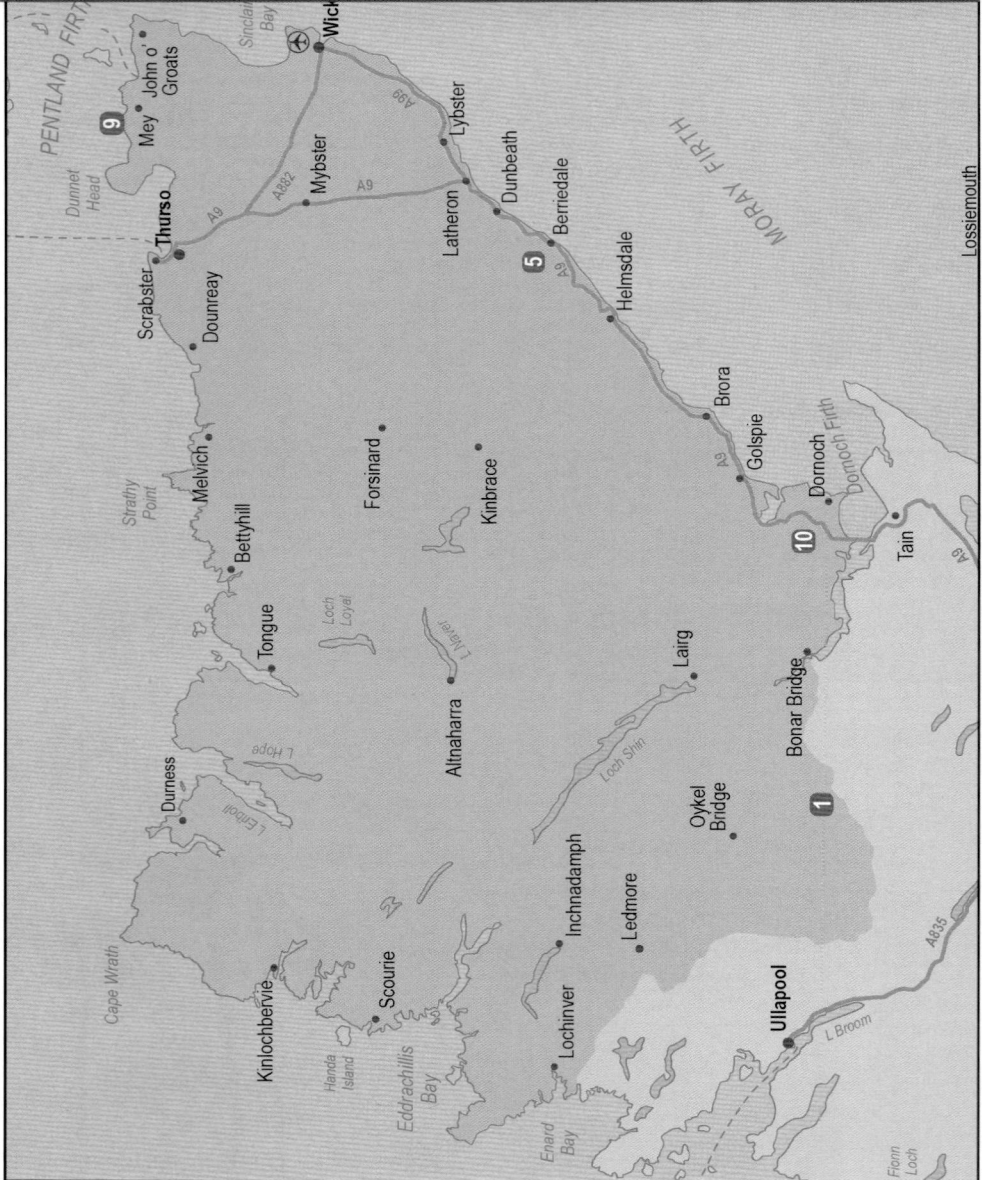

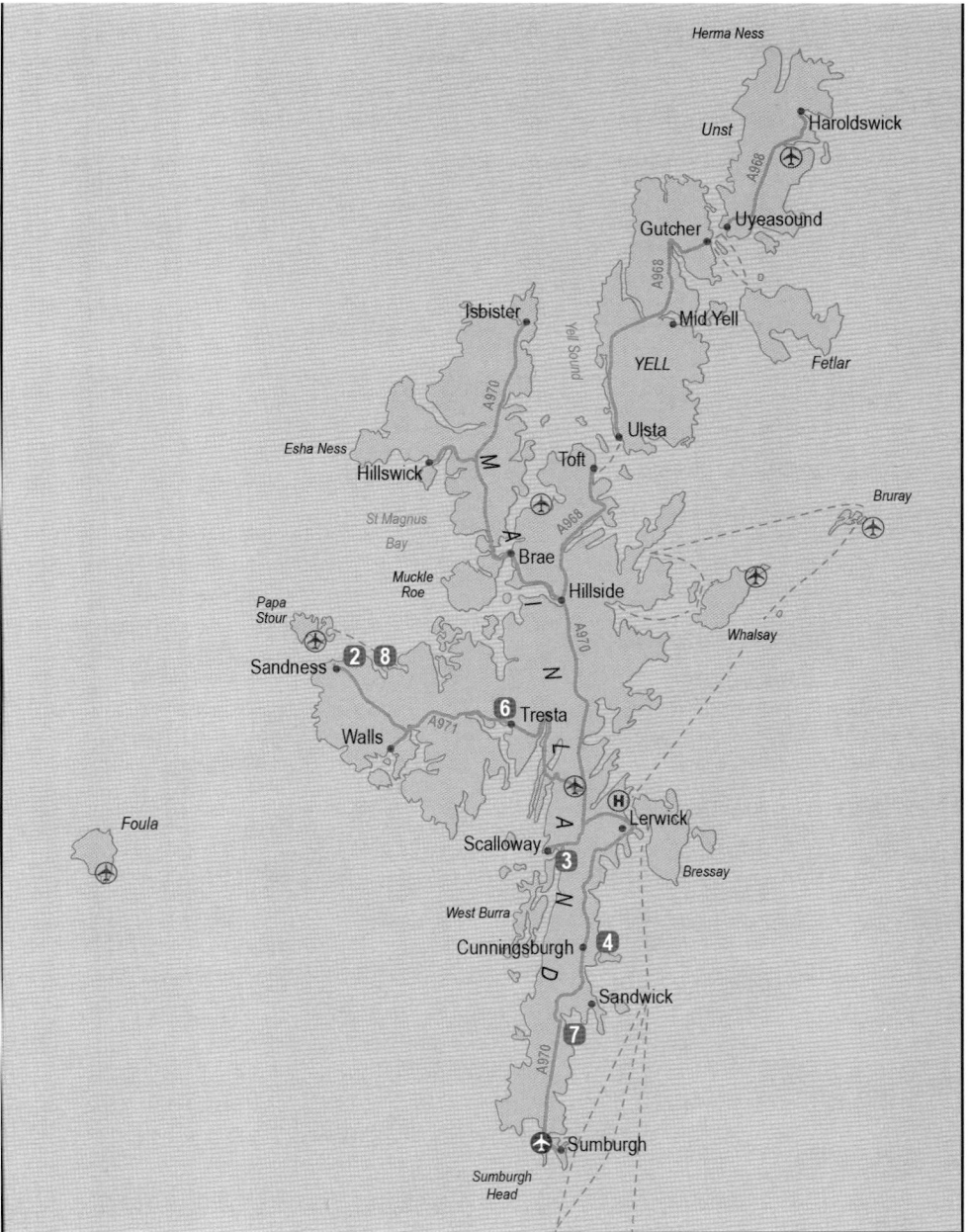

SHETLAND

Herma Ness

Unst

Haroldswick

A968

Gutcher

Uyeasound

A968

Isbister

Mid Yell

YELL

Yell Sound

A970

Fetlar

Ulsta

Esha Ness

Toft

Hillswick

Bruray

A968

St Magnus Bay

Brae

M A I N L A N D

Whalsay

Muckle Roe

Hillside

A970

Papa Stour

2 8

Sandness

6 Tresta

Walls

A971

Foula

H

Lerwick

Scalloway

3

Bressay

West Burra

Cunningsburgh   4

Sandwick

7

A970

Sumburgh

Sumburgh Head

CAITHNESS, SUTHERLAND, ORKNEY & SHETLAND

OUR VOLUNTEER ORGANISERS

District Email		caithness@scotlandsgardens.org
Area Organisers:	Caroline Critchlow	The Quoy of Houton, Orphir, Orkney, KW17 2RD
	Mary Leask	VisitScotland, Market Cross, Lerwick, Shetland, ZE1 0LU
	Steve Mathieson	VisitScotland, Market Cross, Lerwick, Shetland, ZE1 0LU
	Sara Shaw	Amat, Ardgay, Sutherland, IV24 3BS
Treasurer:	Nicola Vestey	The Old School House, Bunloit, Drumnacrochit, IV63 6XG

GARDENS OPEN ON A SPECIFIC DATE

Amat, Ardgay	Saturday/Sunday, 9/10 June
The Gardens of Dornoch, Dornoch	Saturday, 21 July
Langwell, Berriedale	Monday, 6 August

GARDENS OPEN REGULARLY

Norby, Burnside, Sandness, SHETLAND	Daily
Lea Gardens, Tresta, SHETLAND	1 March - 31 October (not Thursdays)
Nonavaar, Levenwick, SHETLAND	15 April - 2 September (Fridays & Sundays)
The Castle & Gardens of Mey, Mey	15 May - 30 September

GARDENS OPEN BY ARRANGEMENT

Cruisdale, Sandness, SHETLAND	On request
Nonavaar, Levenwick, SHETLAND	15 April - 2 September
Highlands, East Voe, Scalloway, SHETLAND	1 May - 30 September
Keldaberg, Cunningsburgh, SHETLAND	1 June - 30 September

KEY TO SYMBOLS

NEW New garden	Full wheelchair access	Dogs on leads
Basic teas	Partial wheelchair access	NPC National plant collection
H Homemade teas	Plants for sale	Champion trees
C Cream teas	Children's activities	Designed landscape
Refreshments	Accessible by public transport	Snowdrop opening

All our gardens open to raise money for charity. Each opening may nominate a charity(s) to receive up to 60% of the takings and these are included with each listing. The net remaining raised supports our core beneficiaries. Information about our core beneficiaries can be found in the front section of the book. More information about our charity scheme and our symbols can be found in the back foldout section of the book under 'Tips for Using Your Guidebook'.

Caithness, Sutherland, Orkney & Shetland

1

AMAT
Ardgay IV24 3BS
Jonny and Sara Shaw
E: sara.amat@aol.co.uk

Riverside garden surrounded by the old Caledonian Amat Forest. Herbaceous borders and rockery set in a large lawn looking onto a salmon pool. Old and new rhododendrons with woodland and river walk, plus large specimen trees in policies.

Open: Saturday/Sunday, 9/10 June, 2pm - 5pm, admission £5.00, children free.

Directions: Take the road from Ardgay to Croick, nine miles. Turn left at the red phone box and the garden is 500 yards on the left.

· *Trellis*

Meconopsis at Amat by Colin Gregory

2

CRUISDALE
Sandness, SHETLAND ZE2 9PL
Alfred Kern
T: 01595 870739

The garden is in a natural state with many willows, several ponds and a variety of colourful hardy plants that grow well in the Shetland climate. It is a work in progress, started about 16 years ago and growing bigger over the years with more work planned.

Open: Open by arrangement, admission £3.00, children free.

Directions: From Lerwick head north on the A970, then at Tingwall take the A971 to Sandness, on the west side of Shetland. Opposite the school, on the right hand side with a wind generator in the field.

· *Royal Voluntary Service*

Caithness, Sutherland, Orkney & Shetland

3

HIGHLANDS
East Voe, Scalloway, SHETLAND ZE1 0UR
Sarah Kay
T: 01595 880526 E: info@easterhoull.co.uk
W: www.selfcatering-shetland.co.uk/the-garden/

The garden is in two parts. The upper garden is mostly a rockery, with a large selection of plants, shallow pond, seating area and newly built 'polycrub' and greenhouse with fruit and vegetables. The lower garden is on a steep slope with a spectacular sea view over the village of Scalloway. There is a path to lead visitors around. The garden features a large collection of plants, vegetable patch, deep pond and pergola. It was awarded a *Shetland Environmental Award* in 2014 for its strong theme of recycling.

Open: Open by arrangement 1 May - 30 September, admission £3.50, children free. Visitors are welcome to wander around, if no-one is in. There is also an arts and crafts studio.

Directions: Follow the A970 main road towards the village of Scalloway. Near the top of the hill heading towards Scalloway take a sharp turn to the left, signposted *Easterhoull Chalets*. Follow the road to chalets (painted blue with red roofs) and you will see the yellow *SGS* sign for the garden. Bus 4 from Lerwick/Scalloway.

· *Glasgow Children's Hospital Charity: Yorkhill*

Money raised supports over 200 different charities annually

4

KELDABERG
Cunningsburgh, SHETLAND ZE2 9HG
Mrs L Johnston
T: 01950 477331 E: linda.keldaberg@btinternet.com

A 'secret garden' divided into four areas. A beach garden of grasses, flowers and driftwood. The main area is a sloping perennial border leading down to a greenhouse, vegetable plot, up to a decked area with containers and exotic plants including agaves, pineapple lilies, cannas and gunneras. The new part has trees, raised vegetable beds, a rockery, retaining walls and an arbour in which to rest. There is a pond with goldfish and aquatic plants. Now, with the addition of a polycrub to grow vegetables, fruit trees and grapevine.

Open: Open by arrangement 1 June - 30 September, admission £3.50, children free. Homemade teas on request.

Directions: On the A970 south of Lerwick is Cunningsburgh, take the Gord junction on the left after passing the village hall. Continue along the road to the second house past the *Kenwood* sign.

· *Chest Heart & Stroke Scotland*

Caithness, Sutherland, Orkney & Shetland

5

LANGWELL
Berriedale KW7 6HD
Welbeck Estates
T: 01593 751278/751237 E: caithness@welbeck.co.uk

A beautiful and spectacular old walled garden with outstanding borders situated in the secluded Langwell Strath. Charming wooded access drive with a chance to see deer.

Open: Monday 6 August, 1pm - 5pm, admission £4.00, children free.

Directions: Turn off the A9 at Berriedale Braes, up the private (tarred) drive signposted *Private - Langwell House*.   It is around 1¼ miles from the A9.

· *RNLI*

6

LEA GARDENS
Tresta, SHETLAND ZE2 9LT
Rosa Steppanova
T: 01595 810454

Lea Gardens, started in the early 1980s, now cover almost two acres. The plant collection, the largest north of Inverewe Gardens, consists of 1,500 different species and cultivars from all over the world, including phyto-geographic elements of collections of plants from New Zealand, South Africa and South America. Planted to provide all year round interest it has been divided into a variety of habitats: woodland and shade, borders, wetland, raised beds, and acid and lime lovers. A winner of the 2011 *Shetland Environmental Award*.

Open: 1 March - 31 October (not Thursdays), 2pm - 5pm, admission £4.00, children free.

Directions: From Lerwick take the A970 north, turn left at Tingwall onto the A971 past Weisdale along Weisdale Voe and up Weisdale hill. Coming down, Lea Gardens is on your right surrounded by trees.

· *All proceeds to SGS Beneficiaries*

7

NONAVAAR
Levenwick, SHETLAND ZE2 9HX
James B Thomason
T: 01950 422447

This is a delightful country garden, sloping within drystone walls, and overlooking magnificent coastal views. It contains ponds, terraces, trees, bushes, varied perennials, annuals, vegetable garden and greenhouse.

Open: 15 April - 2 September (Fridays & Sundays), 11am - 6pm. Also open by arrangement 15 April - 2 September. Admission £3.00, children free.

Directions: Head south from Lerwick. Turn left at *Levenwick* sign soon after Bigton turnoff. Follow the road to third house on the left after Midway stores. Park where there is a *Garden Open* sign. Bus 6 from Lerwick - Sumburgh.

· *Cancer Research UK*

Caithness, Sutherland, Orkney & Shetland

8

THE CASTLE & GARDENS OF MEY
Mey KW14 8XH
The Queen Elizabeth Castle of Mey Trust
T: 01847 851473 E: enquiries@castleofmey.org.uk
W: www.castleofmey.org.uk

Her Majesty Queen Elizabeth The Queen Mother bought what was then Barrogill Castle in 1952 before renovating and restoring the z-plan castle and creating the beautiful gardens you see today, renaming it The Castle and Gardens of Mey. This romantic and unique garden is a reminder that, however daunting the weather, it is often possible with a little vision and energy to create and maintain a garden in the most unlikely of locations. The castle now includes an animal centre, gift shop and tearoom serving delicious locally sourced food and drinks, often using produce from the castle's very own gardens.

Open: 15 May - 30 September, 10am - 5pm, admission details can be found on the garden's website. Castle opening times can also be found on the garden's website.

Directions: On the A836 between Thurso and John O'Groats.

· *Donation to SGS Beneficiaries*

The Castle and Gardens of Mey by Colin Gregory

Caithness, Sutherland, Orkney & Shetland

9

THE GARDENS OF DORNOCH
Dornoch IV25 3NH
The Gardeners of Dornoch

Four gardens that are located very close to Dornoch, all opening for the first time.
42 Astle IV25 3NH (Fay Wilkinson): Organic wildlife garden at the edge of boggy moorland. Mixed planting of trees, shrubs, herbaceous perennials, fruit and vegetables, many on raised beds for improved drainage. There is a natural pond.
Auchlea IV25 3HY (John & Fiona Garvie): The creation from its natural state as a wetland of rushes and whins began in 1998 with the drainage and sowing of a lawn on introduced topsoil. The planting of trees, mostly around its periphery was also begun. Extensive, herbaceous borders with a wide variety of colour and species has gradually developed. Sheltered vegetable garden and recently re-planted bog garden. The continued use of garden and household compost has progressively improved stony ground around the boundary where a mixed hedge has made good progress. The resulting overall feel is that of a maturing cottage garden.
Skelbo House IV25 3QG (Alison Bartlett): Extensive woodland garden with spectacular views over Loch Fleet. Mixed herbaceous borders, rose garden and shrubberies around the house and set in lawns sloping down to a small lochan and river walkway. Mature trees throughout. Large kitchen garden.
The Old Smithy IV25 3RW (Donald and Mary Kennedy): This quite wild garden overlooks the Dornoch Firth, with a wide view over a field. It has a rockery, herbaceous border, raised beds, grass areas with trees.

Open: Saturday 21 July, 10am - 5pm, admission £5.00, children free. Includes entry to all four gardens. Maps/tickets available at all gardens, cream teas at Auchlea.

Directions: 42 Astle: From A9 south, pass turn off to Dornoch, take first left after *Tall Pines Restaurant*, signposted *Astle*. After 1½ miles take left fork, cross river and no. 42 is second house on left. From A9 north, turn right 100m before *Tall Pines Restaurant*, then as above. **Auchlea**: Situated on the B9168. This B road is on the right driving up the A9. Take B road and Auchlea is 1st house on right. **Skelbo House**: From the south of the A9 take the small turning opposite the Trentham Hotel (just past Dornoch turn offs). At the side of Loch Fleet turn left, at ruined castle take the 2nd farm road which is fairly rough, and follow round to your right. From north take the Loch Fleet road signposted to *Embo* from the A9.
The Old Smithy: On the Cuthill road, between A9 and Dornoch. Off the A9 at sign for *Cuthill*, turn right, over the bridge, and The Old Smithy, is the 2nd house on left. The sign for *Cuthill*, is ¼ mile, after crossing the Dornoch Bridge.

C **NEW**

· *Mary's Meals, Marie Curie, Bumblebee Conservation Trust & Mission Africa*

DUMFRIESSHIRE

Scotland's Gardens Scheme 2018 Guidebook is sponsored by INVESTEC WEALTH & INVESTMENT

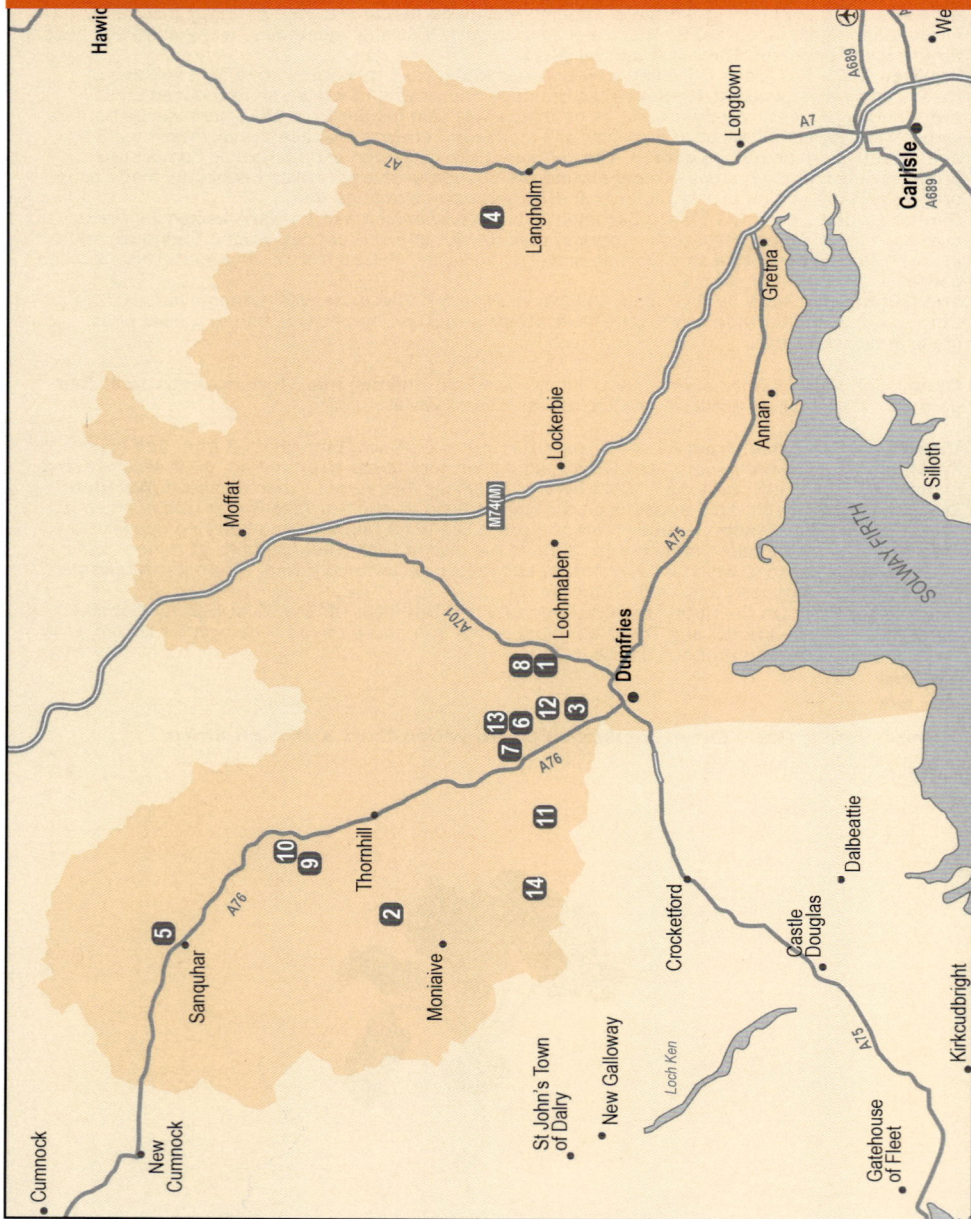

DUMFRIESSHIRE

OUR VOLUNTEER ORGANISERS

District Organiser:	Sarah Landale	Dalswinton House, Dalswinton, Dumfries, DG2 0XZ E: dumfriesshire @scotlandsgardens.org
Area Organisers:	Fiona Bell-Irving Guy Galbraith Liz Mitchell	Bankside, Kettleholm, Lockerbie, DG11 1BY Stanemuir Parkgate, Dumfries, DG1 3NE Drumpark, Irongray, DG2 9TX
Treasurer:	Harold Jack	The Clachan, Newtonairds, Dumfries, DG2 0JL

GARDENS OPEN ON A SPECIFIC DATE

Craig, Langholm	Sunday, 18 February
Crawick Multiverse, Crawick, Sanquhar	Sunday, 6 May
Portrack, The Garden of Cosmic Speculation, Holywood	Sunday, 6 May
Dalswinton House, Dalswinton	Sunday, 13 May
Cowhill Tower, Holywood	Sunday, 27 May
Capenoch, Penpont, Thornhill	Sunday, 3 June
Glenae, Amisfield	Sunday, 10 June
Kirkcaldy House, Kirkcaldy, Burnsands, Thornhill	Friday, 22 June
Newtonairds Lodge, Newtonairds	Sunday, 24 June
Kirkcaldy House, Kirkcaldy, Burnsands, Thornhill	Friday, 29 June
Kirkcaldy House, Kirkcaldy, Burnsands, Thornhill	Friday, 6 July
Whiteside, Dunscore	Sunday, 8 July
Amisfield Tower, Amisfield	Sunday, 15 July
Dalswinton Mill, Dalswinton, Dumfries	Sunday, 5 August
Storytelling Event at Dalswinton, Dalswinton	Sunday, 21 October

GARDENS OPEN BY ARRANGEMENT

Holehouse, Near Penpont, Thornhill	1 May - 30 June
Dalswinton Mill, Dalswinton, Dumfries	6 August - 31 August

Gardens are perfect for younger visitors to explore and open their minds

Dumfriesshire

KEY TO SYMBOLS

NEW	New garden	♿	Full wheelchair access	🐕	Dogs on leads
☕	Basic teas	♿	Partial wheelchair access	NPC	National plant collection
H	Homemade teas	🌷	Plants for sale	🌳	Champion trees
C	Cream teas	👥	Children's activities	🌿	Designed landscape
🍹	Refreshments	🚌	Accessible by public transport	🌱	Snowdrop opening

All our gardens open to raise money for charity. Each opening may nominate a charity(s) to receive up to 60% of the takings and these are included with each listing. The net remaining raised supports our core beneficiaries. Information about our core beneficiaries can be found in the front section of the book. More information about our charity scheme and our symbols can be found in the back foldout section of the book under 'Tips for Using Your Guidebook'.

Drifts of bluebells at Dalswinton House © Val Corbett

Dumfriesshire

1 ### AMISFIELD TOWER
Amisfield DG1 3PA
Mrs Jane Johnstone
E: amisfield@hotmail.com

Large walled garden and greenhouses run by Coverglen Support Services for Adults with Learning Difficulties. Extensive policies around the house and border tower offer a good and interesting walk.

Open: Sunday 15 July, 1pm - 5pm, admission £4.00, children free.

Directions: Take A701 from Dumfries towards Moffat. In Amisfield Village, after five miles, turn left at the crossroads towards Auldgirth and Duncow. Go straight over the next crossroads.   Keep left and house is one mile further on on the right.

· *Cloverglen Support Services*

2 ### CAPENOCH
Penpont, Thornhill DG3 4LZ
Mr and Mrs Robert Gladstone
E: maggie.gladstone@gmail.com

There are rare trees throughout the grounds and the main garden is the remnant of that laid out in Victorian times. There is a pretty little raised knot garden called the Italian Garden and a lovely old Victorian conservatory. Parking is available at the house but you may prefer to park in Penpont Village and walk up the drive to Capenoch as there are lovely bluebells and wild flowers in the oak woods on either side of the drive.

Open: Sunday 3 June, 2pm - 5pm, admission £4.00, children free.

Directions: Take the A702 west from Thornhill, drive through Penpont and the entrance to the house is at the lodge on the left hand side, just at the speed restriction sign.

· *The Jo Walters Trust*

3 ### COWHILL TOWER
Holywood DG2 0RL
Mr and Mrs P Weatherall
T: 01387 720304 E: cmw@cowhill.co.uk

This is an interesting walled garden. There are topiary animals, birds and figures and a beautiful woodland walk. Splendid views can be seen from the lawn right down the Nith Valley. There are also a variety of statues from the Far East.

Open: Sunday 27 May, 2pm - 5pm, admission £5.00, children free.

Directions: Holywood is one and a half miles off A76, five miles north of Dumfries.

· *Maggie's Centres*

Dumfriesshire

4 CRAIG

Langholm DG13 0NZ
Mr and Mrs Neil Ewart
T: 013873 70230 E: nmlewart@googlemail.com

Craig snowdrops have evolved over the last 30 or so years. Round the house and policies, a large variety have been planted with a varied flowering season stretching from the start of January until April and peaking mid-February. Large drifts of *Leucojum vernum* (Winter Snowflake) have started to naturalise here and along the riverbank a variety of snowdrops swept down by the river have naturalised in the adjacent woodland, known as the Snowdrop Walk.

Open: Sunday 18 February, 12pm - 4pm for the Snowdrop Festival, admission £4.00, children free.

Directions: Craig is three miles from Langholm on the B709 towards Eskdalemuir. The Village Hall serving teas is at Bentpath, one mile further towards Eskdalemuir.

· *Kirkandrews Kirk Trust*

Many of our gardens run children's activities for younger visitors

5 CRAWICK MULTIVERSE

Crawick, Sanquhar DG4 6ET
Charles Jencks
T: 01659 50242 E: info@crawickmultiverse.co.uk
W: www.crawickmultiverse.co.uk

Crawick Multiverse is a major land art restoration project on the Duke of Buccleuch's Queensberry Estate in Dumfriesshire. Created by landscape architect Charles Jencks, the former open cast coal mine has been transformed into a stunning representation of theories of the universe, linking the themes of space, astronomy and cosmology, using the ecology of the site, and the materials found within, to inspire its design.

Open: Sunday 6 May, 10am - 4pm, admission £5.00, children £2.00. Concessions £4.00. Note that Portrack, The Garden of Cosmic Speculation, also designed by Charles Jencks, will be open on the same day.

Directions: From Sanquhar, head to Kirkconnel, turn left on the B740 Crawfordjohn, as you travel on the B740 after 250 metres you will pass under a viaduct (rail bridge) take the 2nd exit on the left approximately 100 metres past the viaduct. See website for more details.

· *Maggie's Centres*

Dumfriesshire

6

DALSWINTON HOUSE

Dalswinton DG2 0XZ
Mr and Mrs Peter Landale
T: 01387 740220 E: sarahlandale@gmail.com

Late 18th century house sits on top of a hill surrounded by herbaceous beds and well established shrubs, including rhododendrons and azaleas overlooking the loch. Attractive walks through woods and around the loch. It was here that the first steamboat in Britain made its maiden voyage in 1788 and there is a life-size model beside the water to commemorate this. Over the past years, there has been much clearing and development work around the loch, which has opened up the views considerably.

Open: Sunday 13 May, 2pm - 5pm, admission £5.00, children free.

Directions: Take A76 north from Dumfries to Thornhill. After seven miles, turn right to Dalswinton. Drive through Dalswinton Village, past the orange church on the right and follow estate wall on the right. Entrance is by either the single lodge or double lodge entrance set in the wall.

· *Kirkmahoe Parish Church of Scotland*

© Crawick Multiverse

Dumfriesshire

7 **DALSWINTON MILL**
Dalswinton, Dumfries DG2 0XY
Colin and Pamela Crosbie
T: 01387 740070 E: colin.crosbie@talktalk.net
....

A newly created plantsman's garden set around an 18th century watermill with the Pennyland Burn running through it. The garden contains a wide range of perennials, trees and shrubs which favour the local climate. Throughout the garden a wide range of statuary can be found.

Open: Sunday 5 August, 2pm - 6pm. Also open by arrangement 6 August - 31 August. Admission £4.00, children free.

Directions: Garden lies in Dalswinton, halfway between A76 and A701 on the Auldgirth to Kirkton Road. From Auldgirth take the first left after the Dalswinton Village Hall. The Mill is on the corner before the bridge.

· IFDAS

8 **GLENAE**
Amisfield DG1 3NZ
Mrs Totty Morley
T: 01387 710236 E: tottsmorley@btinternet.com
....

A beautiful, well established, walled garden, well stocked with interesting plants, four small lawns surrounded by colourful herbaceous borders, a woodland garden and a restored Victorian glasshouse.

Open: Sunday 10 June, 2pm - 5pm, admission £5.00, children free.

Directions: One and a half miles north of Amisfield on A701. Turn left to Duncow and Auldgirth and one mile on right.

· Stewartry Care, Dumfries

9 **HOLEHOUSE**
Near Penpont, Thornhill DG3 4AP
Lord and Lady Norrie
T: 01848 600303
....

Holehouse is a newly established garden which has been beautifully and carefully landscaped and developed in, around, and through a farm steading over the past 12 years. Its secluded location high on a hillside offers some wonderful views over the Dumfriesshire hills and nearby Drumlanrig Estate. It is a garden of great variety including a labyrinth, pond, some lovely roses, shrubs and early trees and a working vegetable garden laid out beside the Orchard. A great number of trees have been planted and these are really starting to take shape.

Open: Open by arrangement 1 May - 30 June, admission £5.00, children free.

Directions: From Penpont Village crossroads, take Sanquhar Rd, passing triangle on left after 2.1 miles. Carry on 1.2 miles and take next left in front of the white farmhouse. Turn right at next T-Junction with three white cottages. Continue past farm on the left.   Holehouse is next on right.

· Buccleuch And Queensberry Caledonia Pipe Band

Dumfriesshire

10

KIRKCALDY HOUSE
Kirkcaldy, Burnsands, Thornhill DG3 4AL
Professor and Mrs Robert McClelland

The garden is set on a hillside with spectacular views over the Nith Valley and Lowther Hills. Although the foundations of the garden were in place, it has been extended over the past 12 years by the owners. It is a compact garden with a variety of trees, shrubs, herbaceous plants, roses, a pond, decorative dykes and sculptures.

Open: Fridays 22 & 29 June and 6 July, 2pm - 5pm, admission £5.00, children free.

Directions: Take the A76 through Thornhill and Carronbridge and past the turning to Drumlanrig Castle. At the next turning left just before the *Picnic Area* (about four miles) turn left and then immediately left after crossing the Glenairlie Bridge. Kirkcaldy is the second house at the top of the hill.

`NEW`

· *All proceeds to SGS Beneficiaries*

11

NEWTONAIRDS LODGE
Newtonairds DG2 0JL
Mr and Mrs J Coutts
W: www.newtonairds-hostasandgarden.co.uk

An interesting 1.2 acre plantsman's garden punctuated with topiary, trees and shrubs, surrounding a 19th century listed baronial lodge. The National Collection is integrated with a further 150 other hosta varieties on a natural terraced wooded bank.
National Plant Collection: *Hosta plantaginea* cvs. and hybrids.

Open: Sunday 24 June, 2pm - 5pm, admission £5.00, children free.

Directions: From Dumfries take A76 north. At Holywood take B729 (Dunscore). After one mile turn left (Morrinton). After three miles red sandstone lodge is on right, behind black iron railings.

· *Peter Pan Moat Brae Trust*

Scotland's Gardens
Scheme welcomes all
varieties of gardens

Dumfriesshire

12

PORTRACK, THE GARDEN OF COSMIC SPECULATION
Holywood DG2 0RW
John Jencks
W: www.thegardenofcosmicspeculation.com

Forty major areas, gardens, bridges, landforms, sculpture, terraces, fences and architectural works. Covering thirty acres, The Garden of Cosmic Speculation uses nature to celebrate nature, both intellectually and through the senses, including the sense of humour. A water cascade of steps recounts the story of the universe; a terrace shows the distortion of space and time caused by a black hole; a 'Quark Walk' takes the visitor on a journey to the smallest building blocks of matter and a series of landforms and lakes recall fractal geometry.

Open: Sunday 6 May, 11am - 5pm, admission £10.00, children free. Admission is via prepaid ticket only. Many more people than anticipated came to the 2017 opening and we have therefore had to introduce a ticket limit against the capacity of the car parking fields (1,500 spaces) to keep everyone safe and the traffic moving through the small lanes around the private estate. The tickets will be available from 1st February at Eventbrite (browse for 'Portrack' in the search box).   Please note that the garden is not open to the public at any other time. The Upper Nithsdale Pipe Band will perform (weather permitting). Crawick Multiverse, also designed by Charles Jencks, will be open on the same day.

Directions: Holywood is one and a half miles off A76, five miles north of Dumfries.

· *Maggie's Centres*

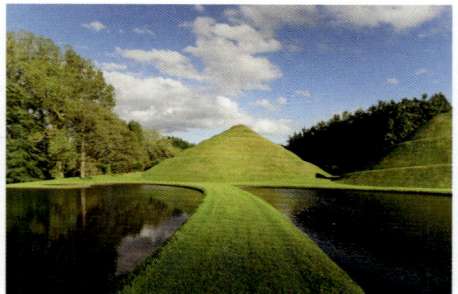

All photographs © Ming Thein, 2015

Dumfriesshire

13

STORYTELLING AT DALSWINTON
Dalswinton DG2 0XZ
Mr and Mrs Peter Landale
T: 01387 740220 E: sarahlandale@gmail.com

Once upon a time...

Keen to listen to stories about the maiden voyage of Britain's first steamboat? Huddle around the boat itself to hear tales the brave Red Comyn, who lived at Dalswinton and was killed by Robert the Bruce in 1306. Or step back in time and hear tales about Romans who encamped upon the hills nearby. Soak in the garden's history and stand in awe at the large man made loch with island folly. Join Scotland's Gardens Scheme and The Scottish International Storytelling Festival in "Growing Stories". A fun packed way to explore some of Scotland's gardens. See gardens with new eyes once you hear stories, from local storytellers, about their creation, history and interaction with the environment. For more information see Scotland's Gardens Scheme website.

Open: Sunday 21 October, 2pm - 5pm, admission £5.00, children free.

Directions: Take A76 north from Dumfries to Thornhill. After seven miles, turn right to Dalswinton. Drive through Dalswinton Village, past the orange church on the right and follow estate wall on the right. Entrance is by either the single lodge or double lodge entrance set in the wall.

· *Pituitary Foundation*

Gardening teaches children patience and appreciation for the natural world

14

WHITESIDE
Dunscore DG2 0UU
John and Hilary Craig
T: 01387 820501 E: hjcraig19@gmail.com

The Garden, which extends to several acres is 200 metres above sea level on a north facing slope with views across to Queensberry and the Lowther Hills. There are some mature trees around the house but the rest of the garden is relatively new, having been created from a bare hillside since 2000. There are shrubs, young trees, a rowan avenue, a walled vegetable garden, orchard and courtyard garden. Several burns run through the property and there is a pond and two duck enclosures.

Open: Sunday 8 July, 12pm - 5pm, admission £5.00, children free.

Directions: From Dunscore, take the Corsock road. Continue two miles on, turn right opposite the postbox. Continue on for 1¾ miles, over the humpback bridge and past the white farmhouse on the left. Whiteside is signed on the left.

· *Music in Dumfries*

DUNBARTONSHIRE

Scotland's Gardens Scheme 2018 Guidebook is sponsored by INVESTEC WEALTH & INVESTMENT

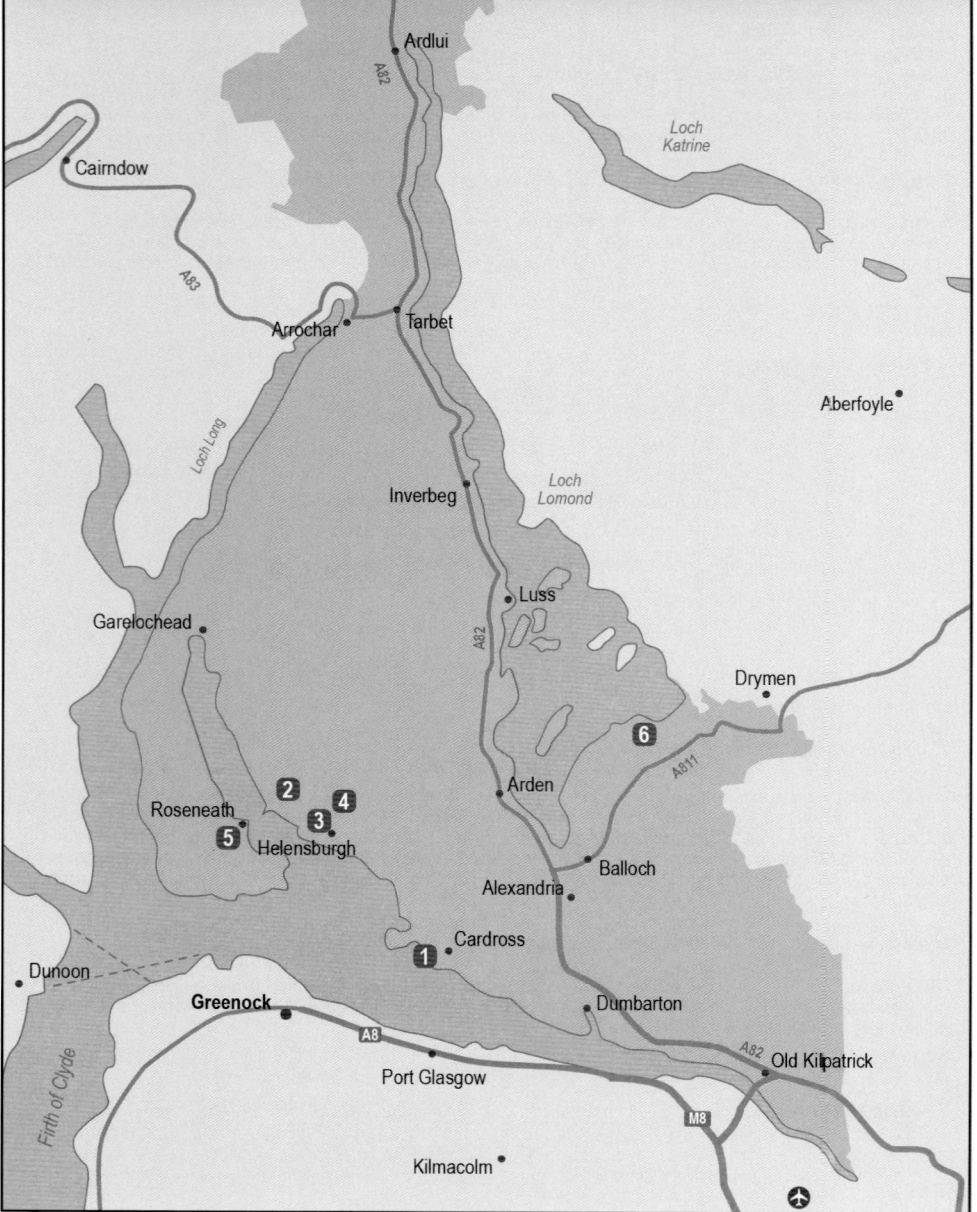

DUNBARTONSHIRE

OUR VOLUNTEER ORGANISERS

District Organiser:	Tricia Stewart	High Glenan, 24a Queen St, Helensburgh, G84 9LG E: dunbartonshire@scotlandsgardens.org
Area Organisers:	Joyce Goel Graham Greenwell	33 West Argyle Street, Helensburgh, G84 8XR Avalon, Shore Road, Mambeg Garelochhead, G84 0EN
Treasurer:	Kathleen Murray	7 The Birches, Shandon, Helensburgh, G84 8HN

GARDENS OPEN ON A SPECIFIC DATE

Kilarden, Rosneath	Sunday, 15 April
High Glenan with Westburn, Helensburgh	Sunday, 13 May
Ross Priory, Gartocharn	Sunday, 20 May
Geilston Garden, Main Road, Cardross	Sunday, 10 June
Hill House Plant Sale, Helensburgh	Sunday, 2 September

GARDENS OPEN REGULARLY

Glenarn, Glenarn Roac, Rhu, Helensburgh	21 March - 21 September

KEY TO SYMBOLS

NEW	New garden		Full wheelchair access		Dogs on leads
	Basic teas		Partial wheelchair access	NPC	National plant collection
H	Homemade teas		Plants for sale		Champion trees
C	Cream teas		Children's activities		Designed landscape
	Refreshments		Accessible by public transport		Snowdrop opening

All our gardens open to raise money for charity. Each opening may nominate a charity(s) to receive up to 60% of the takings and these are included with each listing. The net remaining raised supports our core beneficiaries. Information about our core beneficiaries can be found in the front section of the book. More information about our charity scheme and our symbols can be found in the back foldout section of the book under 'Tips for Using Your Guidebook'.

Dunbartonshire

1

GEILSTON GARDEN
Main Road, Cardross G82 5HD
The National Trust for Scotland
T: 01389 849187 E: geilstongarden@nts.org.uk
W: www.nts.org.uk/Property/Geilston-Garden/

Geilston Garden has many attractive features including the walled garden with the herbaceous border providing summer colour, tranquil woodland walks and a large working kitchen garden. This is the ideal season for viewing the Siberian iris in flower along the Geilston Burn and the Japanese azaleas.

Open: Sunday 10 June, 1pm - 5pm, admission details can be found on the garden's website. During the summer months, July to September, there is a range of fresh fruit and vegetables for sale from the large kitchen garden.

Directions: On the A814, one mile from Cardross towards Helensburgh.

· *All proceeds to SGS Beneficiaries*

Geilston Garden © National Trust for Scotland

Dunbartonshire

2

GLENARN
Glenarn Road, Rhu, Helensburgh G84 8LL
Michael and Sue Thornley
T: 01436 820493 E: masthome@btinternet.com
W: www.gardens-of-argyll.co.uk

Glenarn survives as a complete example of a ten acre garden which spans from 1850 to the present day. There are winding paths through miniature glens under a canopy of oaks and limes, sunlit open spaces, a vegetable garden with beehives, and a rock garden full of surprise and season-long colour, with views over the Gareloch. The famous collections of rare and tender rhododendrons and magnolias give way in midsummer to roses rambling through the trees and climbing hydrangeas, followed by the starry white flowers of hoherias and eucryphias to the end of the season.

Open: 21 March - 21 September, Dawn - Dusk, admission £5.00, children free.

Directions: On the A814, two miles north of Helensburgh, up Pier Road. Cars to be left at the gate unless passengers are infirm.

· *Donation to SGS Beneficiaries*

Tree Magnolias at Glenarn

Dunbartonshire

3

HIGH GLENAN WITH WESTBURN
Helensburgh G84 9LG
Tom & Tricia Stewart and Professor & Mrs Baker
....

Two delightful Helensburgh Gardens.
High Glenan Helensburgh G84 9LG (Tom and Tricia Stewart): A secluded garden with burn and waterside plants, gravel garden, herb and herbaceous borders, kitchen garden with selection of fruit and vegetables.   Extensive programme of hard landscaping has been undertaken over the last eight years.
Westburn 50 Campbell Street G84 9NH (Professor & Mrs Baker)
A woodland garden of just over two acres. The Glenan Burn runs through a woodland of oak and beech trees with bluebells in the springtime. Some of the paths are steep, but there are bridges over the burn and handrails in places. There is also an air raid shelter, and the remains of a kiln where James Ballantyne Hannay manufactured artificial diamonds in the 1800s. A lawn is surrounded by rhododendrons and azaleas, and there is a vegetable garden. Over the years the garden has been enjoyed by children, with lots of room to play and fish in the burn.

Open: Sunday 13 May, 2pm - 5pm, admission £4.00, children free.

Directions: High Glenan: The garden is situated in West Helensburgh, approximately ½ mile along Queen Street from its junction with Sinclair Street on the right hand side. **Westburn**: Proceed along West Montrose Street from Sinclair Street and take the fourth turn on the right, the entrance of Wesburn is 100 yards up Campbell Street on the right hand side.

· *Prostate Cancer UK & St Michael & All Angels Church: Helensburgh*

**Are you snap happy?
Send us your garden
photographs**

4

HILL HOUSE PLANT SALE
Helensburgh G84 9AJ
The National Trust for Scotland and SGS
T: 01436 673900 E: gsmith@nts.org.uk
....

The plant sale is held in the garden of Hill House which has fine views over the Clyde estuary and is considered Charles Rennie Mackintosh's domestic masterpiece. The sale includes a wide selection of nursery grown perennials and locally grown trees, shrubs, herbaceous, alpine and house plants.

Open: Sunday 2 September, 11:30am - 4pm, admission by donation. This is a provisional date as the garden is under reconstruction, please check the *SGS* website for updates.

Directions: Follow signs to The Hill House.

· *All proceeds to SGS Beneficiaries*

Dunbartonshire

5

KILARDEN
Rosneath G84 0PU
Carol Rowe

Sheltered hilly ten acre woodland part of a 20 acre property with a notable collection of species and hybrid rhododendrons gathered over a period of 50 years by the late Neil and Joyce Rutherford as seen on the *Beechgrove Garden*. The collection has been augmented in the last 18 years by the current owner. Elsewhere during this time hurricane and severe storm damaged broad leaved trees and mature specimens of conifers have been cleared as have commercial conifers and *Rhododendron ponticum*. Fruit trees and bushes have been established, of which apples and blueberries are particularly successful, despite a far from favourable north facing shady site.

Open: Sunday 15 April, 2pm - 5pm, admission £3.00, children free. Organ music will be played in St Modan's church and Shandon Ukelele Band will play in the garden.

Directions: A ¼ of a mile from Rosneath off the B833.

· *Friends of St. Modan's, Rosneath*

6

ROSS PRIORY
Gartocharn G83 8NL
University of Strathclyde

Mansion house with glorious views over Loch Lomond with adjoining garden. Wonderful rhododendrons and azaleas are the principal plants in the garden, with a varied selection of trees and shrubs throughout. Spectacular spring bulbs, border plantings of herbaceous perennials, shrubs and trees. Extensive walled garden with glasshouses, pergola and ornamental plantings. Play area and putting green beside house.

Open: Sunday 20 May, 2pm - 5pm, admission £5.00, children free. Please note that the house is not open to view. Dogs on leads welcome except in the walled garden. Homemade teas and plant stall in the walled garden.

Directions: Gartocharn 1½ miles off the A811. The Balloch to Gartocharn bus leaves Balloch at 13:52.

· *Friends Of Loch Lomond & The Trossachs & Children's Hospice Association Scotland*

Ross Priory

EAST LOTHIAN

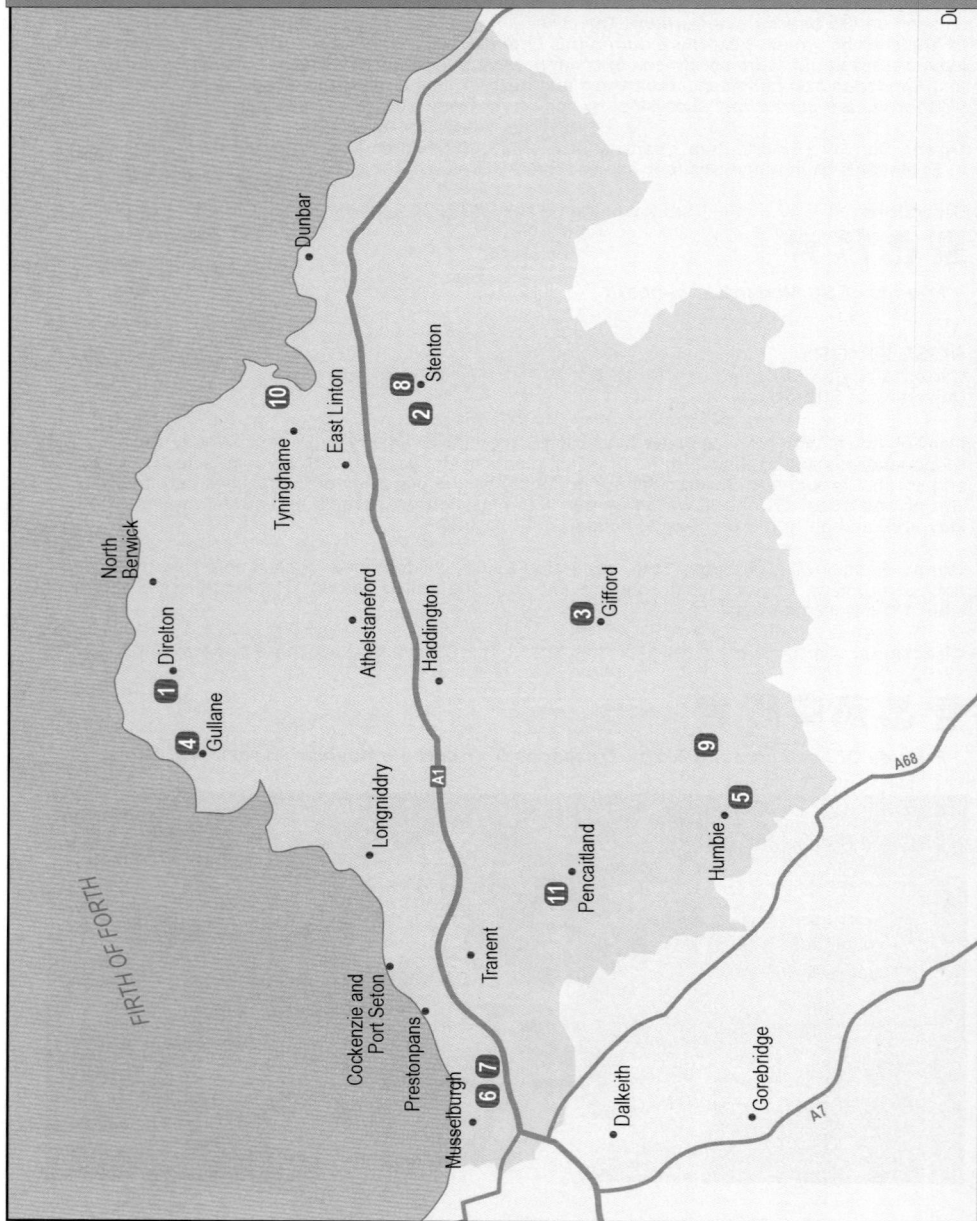

EAST LOTHIAN

OUR VOLUNTEER ORGANISERS

District Organiser:	Joan Johnson	The Round House, Woodbush, Dunbar, EH42 1HB E: eastlothian@scotlandsgardens.org
Area Organisers:	Becca Duncan	St Michael's Lodge, Inveresk, EH21 7UA
	Frank Kirwan	Humbie Dean, Humbie, EH36 5PW
	Beryl McNaughton	Macplants Berrybank Nursery, EH34 5BA
	Ian Orr	6 Grannus Mews, Inveresk, EH21 7TT
	Judy Riley	The Old Kitchen, Tyninghame House, EH42 1XW
Treasurer:	Colin Wilson	5 Tenterfield Drive, Haddington, EH41 3JF

GARDENS OPEN ON A SPECIFIC DATE

Shepherd House, Inveresk, Musselburgh	Saturday/Sunday, 24/25 February
Winton Castle, Pencaitland	Sunday, 15 April
Eastfield and Redcliff Gardens, Whittingehame	Sunday, 29 April
Shepherd House, Inveresk, Musselburgh	Saturday/Sunday, 5/6 May
Tyninghame House and The Walled Garden, Dunbar	Sunday, 13 May
Stenton Village, East Lothian	Sunday, 3 June
Dirleton Village, North Berwick	Saturday/Sunday, 9/10 June
Inveresk Village, Musselburgh	Sunday, 17 June
Tyninghame House and The Walled Garden, Dunbar	Sunday, 24 June
Gifford Village and Broadwoodside, Gifford	Sunday, 8 July
Greywalls, Gullane	Saturday, 4 August

GARDENS OPEN REGULARLY

Shepherd House, Inveresk, Musselburgh	13 Feb - 6 March (Tuesdays & Thursdays)
Shepherd House, Inveresk, Musselburgh	17 April - 12 July (Tuesdays & Thursdays)

GARDENS OPEN BY ARRANGEMENT

Stobshiel House , Humbie	1 March - 1 December
Humbie Dean, Humbie	1 April - 31 July
Tyninghame House and The Walled Garden, Dunbar	1 May - 31 August
Inveresk Village, Musselburgh	1 July - 31 August

East Lothian

KEY TO SYMBOLS

NEW — New garden	Full wheelchair access	Dogs on leads
Basic teas	Partial wheelchair access	NPC — National plant collection
H — Homemade teas	Plants for sale	Champion trees
C — Cream teas	Children's activities	Designed landscape
Refreshments	Accessible by public transport	Snowdrop opening

All our gardens open to raise money for charity. Each opening may nominate a charity(s) to receive up to 60% of the takings and these are included with each listing. The net remaining raised supports our core beneficiaries. Information about our core beneficiaries can be found in the front section of the book. More information about our charity scheme and our symbols can be found in the back foldout section of the book under 'Tips for Using Your Guidebook'.

Shell house, designed by Lachlan Stewart, at Shepherd House

East Lothian

1 DIRLETON VILLAGE
North Berwick EH39 5EH
The Gardeners of Dirleton and Historic Scotland
....

Dirleton is a beautiful conservation village with a large green, historic church and castle. Gardens of various sizes and types are open throughout the village, including that of Dirleton Castle.

Open: Saturday/Sunday, 9/10 June, 2pm - 6pm, admission £6.00, children free.

Directions: Dirleton Village is two miles west of North Berwick off the A198.

· *RNLI*

2 EASTFIELD AND REDCLIFF GARDENS
Whittingehame EH41 4QA
Mr & Mrs J Harper and Mr & Mrs D Shaw-Stewart
T: 01368 850210
....

These complementary gardens, very different in style and planting, are set against the backdrop of Deuchrie Dod and Pressmannan Wood.
Eastfield Whittingehame, Haddington EH41 4QA (Mr & Mrs D Shaw-Stewart): Eastfield has recently been created from a farm steading building. All young planting, new hedges and large courtyard garden.
Redcliff Whittinghame, Haddington EH41 4QA (Joe and Jenny Harper): Redcliff was built as the factor's house to Whittingehame Estate, home of Prime Minister A J Balfour. The established garden is terraced and runs down to the Whittingehame water.

Open: Sunday 29 April, 1pm - 6pm, admission £5.00 per garden, children free. The gardens are connected by a path - there is limited parking at Redcliff and priority will be for visitors with limited mobility.

Directions: A199 to East Linton bypass and turn right, follow road to Whittinghame for 2.4 miles. From Haddington, A199 to East Linton bypass and turn right, follow road to Whittinghame for 2.4 miles. Redcliff is the red sandstone house at the top of the hill at Whittinghame.

NEW

· *Leuchie*

Redcliff Garden

Creating an inspiring, rewarding and enjoyable experience for volunteers and visitors alike

East Lothian

3

GIFFORD VILLAGE AND BROADWOODSIDE
Gifford EH41 4QY
The Gardeners of Gifford and Mr & Mrs Dalrymple

. . . .

Gifford Village: The gardens vary in size and type, from the compact and informal, to the large and formal with a wide range of plants, shrubs and trees. Gifford was laid out early in the 18th century and has retained much of its original charm. The village includes a beautiful church built in 1708, the Lime Avenue of Yester House, the Goblin Ha' and Tweeddale Hotels and a wide range of gardens all within walking distance of each other.
Broadwoodside: The garden at Broadwoodside is planted in and around a farm steading, rescued from dereliction. While people often talk of starting a new garden with a blank canvas, Broadwoodside was more like painting by numbers - planting the garden has been like an exercise in 'colouring-in' with the layout determined by the footprint of existing buildings and the old walls surrounding them. But, unlike a picture in a frame, a garden is always a work in progress.

Open: Sunday 8 July, 1pm - 5pm, admission £6.00, children free.

Directions: Gifford sits between the A1 and A68 roads about five miles south of Haddington. The village is well signposted from Haddington, Pencaitland and Duns.

· *Gifford Horticultural Society & Local Charities*

4

GREYWALLS
Gullane EH31 2EG
Mr and Mrs Giles Weaver
W: www.greywalls.co.uk

. . . .

Six acre formal garden, attributed to Gertrude Jekyll, surrounding Greywalls Hotel, with stunning views over East Lothian and the Forth.   Late season colour as featured in the *Beechgrove Garden* in September 2015. Highlights of the garden are the walls: straight walls and curved walls which create rooms and vistas, and radiating paths which link entrances and exits. Everywhere there are places to sit, in sun and in shade.

Open: Saturday 4 August, 2pm - 5pm, admission £5.00, children free.

Directions: Signposted on the A198 southeast of Gullane. From Edinburgh take A1 south, then A198 to Gullane last turning on left side. From south take A1 north to Haddington, Gullane is signposted. Further information is on our website.

· *Leuchie*

5

HUMBIE DEAN
Humbie EH36 5PW
Frank Kirwan
T: 07768 996382 E: frank.kirwan@which.net
W: www.humbiedean.com

. . . .

A two acre ornamental and woodland garden at 600 feet which has been under renovation and major extension since 2008. The aim is to provide interest throughout a long season. A limited palette of plants with hosta, primula, meconopsis and spring bulbs, herbaceous and shrubaceous planting, bluebell meadow, mature and recent azalea and rhododendron planting. A short woodland walk has been created.

Open: Open by arrangement 1 April - 31 July, admission £5.00, children free. Short notice, weather-dependent openings throughout the season, please check the SGS website for more details. Access to the woodland walk is via multiple steps.

East Lothian

Directions: Enter Humbie from the A68, pass the school and village hall on the left then immediately turn right just before the Humbie Hub. Take second left and Humbie Dean is on the left between two small bridges.

· *Mamie Martin Fund*

6 INVERESK VILLAGE
Musselburgh EH21
The Gardeners of Inveresk
E: ianorrgardens@gmail.com
....

A collection of walled and domestic gardens, including Shepherd House and also allotments, in an historic village. Each has its own individual character displaying a wide variety of interesting and unusual trees, shrubs and plants. Three new gardens, including a Japanese Garden added this year.

Open: Sunday 17 June, 2pm - 5pm. Also open by arrangement 1 July - 31 August. Admission £7.00, children free (Sunday 17 June) and £10.00, children free (1 July - 31 August). On the 17th June there will be lawn croquet. By arrangement visits for 'The Garden and Historic Tour' will involve visits to at least two gardens and a historic tour, including 'The Gunpowder Plot of Inveresk' and 'The Strange Case of the Knocking Coffin'. Contact Ian Orr for details: ianorrgardens@gmail.com.

Directions: South side of Musselburgh, Inveresk Village Road - A6124.

· *Edinburgh Young Carers Project*

7 SHEPHERD HOUSE
Inveresk, Musselburgh EH21 7TH
Sir Charles and Lady Fraser
T: 0131 665 2570 E: annfraser@talktalk.net
W: www.shepherdhousegarden.co.uk
....

Shepherd House and its one acre garden form a walled triangle in the middle of the 18th century village of Inveresk. The main garden is to the rear of the house where the formality of the front garden is continued with a herb parterre and two symmetrical potagers. A formal rill runs the length of the garden, beneath a series of rose and clematis arches and connects the two ponds. There is a growing collection of specialist snowdrops which are mainly grown in beds and borders, some of which will be displayed in our 'Snowdrop Theatre'. An addition to the garden in 2014 was a Shell House, designed by Lachlan Stewart. The garden has been featured in many magazines and in 2015 appeared in Alan Titchmarsh's *Britain's Best Back Gardens*.

Open: Saturday/Sunday, 24/25 February, 11am - 4pm for the Snowdrop Festival. Also open Saturday/Sunday, 5/6 May, 11am - 4pm. And open 13 February - 6 March and 17 April - 12 July (Tuesdays & Thursdays), 2pm - 4pm. Admission £5.00, children free. Artists cards by Ann Fraser will be on sale at all openings.

Directions: The garden is near Musselburgh. From the A1 take the A6094 exit signed *Wallyford* and *Dalkeith* and follow signs to *Inveresk*.

· *Edinburgh Young Carers Project*

East Lothian

8 **STENTON VILLAGE**
East Lothian EH42 1TE
The Gardeners of Stenton Village
....

Stenton (Stane Toon) with its ancient cottages of purple hued sandstone and pantiled roofs has been awarded *Outstanding Conservation* status. There is a thriving Horticultural Society and the gardens, large and small, are of extraordinary variety and interest. Stenton is also renowned for its generous teas on Open Days.

Open: Sunday 3 June, 2pm - 5:30pm, admission £5.00, children free.

Directions: Follow signs from A199/A1.

· *To be confirmed*

9 **STOBSHIEL HOUSE**
Humbie EH36 5PD
Mr Maxwell and Lady Sarah Ward
T: 01875 833646 E: stobshiel@gmail.com
....

A large garden to see for all seasons. Walled garden adjacent to the house, box-edged borders filled with bulbs, roses and lavender beds. There is also a rustic summerhouse, glasshouse, formal lily pond and castellated yew hedge. The shrubbery has rhododendrons, azaleas and bulbs. Growing in the water and woodland garden are meconopsis and primulas. Enjoy the beautiful woodland walks.

Open: Open by arrangement 1 March - 1 December, admission £5.00, children free.

Directions: On the B6368 Haddington/Humbie road; sign to *Stobshiel* one mile.

· *Circle Supporting Families in Scotland*

10 **TYNINGHAME HOUSE AND THE WALLED GARDEN**
Dunbar EH42 1XW
Tyninghame Gardens Ltd and Mrs C.Gwyn
E: tyninghamegardens@btinternet.com
....

Once upon a time...

Splendid 17th century sandstone Scottish baronial house, remodelled in 1829 by William Burn. The gardens include herbaceous border, formal rose garden, Lady Haddington's Secret Garden with old fashioned roses and an extensive "wilderness" spring garden with rhododendrons, azaleas, flowering trees and bulbs. Grounds include a one mile beech avenue to the sea. The Romanesque ruin of St Baldred's Church commands views across the Tyne Estuary and Lammermuir Hills. Tyninghame has been awarded 'Outstanding' for every category in the Inventory of Gardens and Designed Landscapes of Scotland.

Storytelling at Tyninghame
13 May: Folklore and facts come to life at Tyninghame, with echoes of the lost village, or the Romanseque ruin of St Baldred's Church overlooking the Tyne Estuary and Lammermuir Hills. The site has been inhabited since the 11th century, and the gardens grown with the secrets of time past. Take in Lady Haddington's 'Secret Garden', the 'apple walk' and sculptured hedges. Join Scotland's Gardens Scheme and The Scottish International Storytelling Festival in "Growing Stories". A fun packed way to explore some of Scotland's Gardens. See gardens with new eyes once you hear stories, from local Storytellers, about their creation, history and interaction with the environment. For more information please see Scotland's Gardens Scheme website.
Champion Trees: Two British and seven Scottish.

East Lothian

Open: Sunday 13 May, 1pm - 5pm. Also open Sunday 24 June, 1pm - 5pm. And open by arrangement 1 May - 31 August. Admission £5.00, children free (Sunday 13 May & Sunday 24 June) and by donation (1 May - 31 August).

Directions: Gates on the A198 at Tyninghame Village. Bus 120.

· *Lynton Day Centre (Sunday 13 May) & Leuchie (Sunday 24 June)*

Tyninghame House from the south lawn

WINTON CASTLE

11

Pencaitland EH34 5AT
Sir Francis Ogilvy Winton Trust
T: 01875 340222
W: www.wintoncastle.co.uk

....

The gardens continue to develop and improve. In addition to the natural areas around Sir David's Loch and the Dell, extensive mixed borders are taking shape for the terraces and walled garden. In spring a glorious covering of daffodils makes way for cherry and apple blossoms. Enjoy an informative tour of this historic house and walk off delicious lunches and home baking around the estate. A visit to Winton Castle is a wonderful family day out.

Open: Sunday 15 April, 12pm - 4:30pm, admission £5.00, children free. Their open day is essentially a family event with bouncy castle, archery, falconry displays, Luca's ice cream sold from a vintage Bentley, tours of the house, games on the lawn, treasure hunts, face painting etc.

Directions: Entrance off the B6355 Trent/Pencaitland Road.

· *Marie Curie*

EDINBURGH, MIDLOTHIAN & WEST LOTHIAN

Scotland's Gardens Scheme 2018 Guidebook is sponsored by INVESTEC WEALTH & INVESTMENT

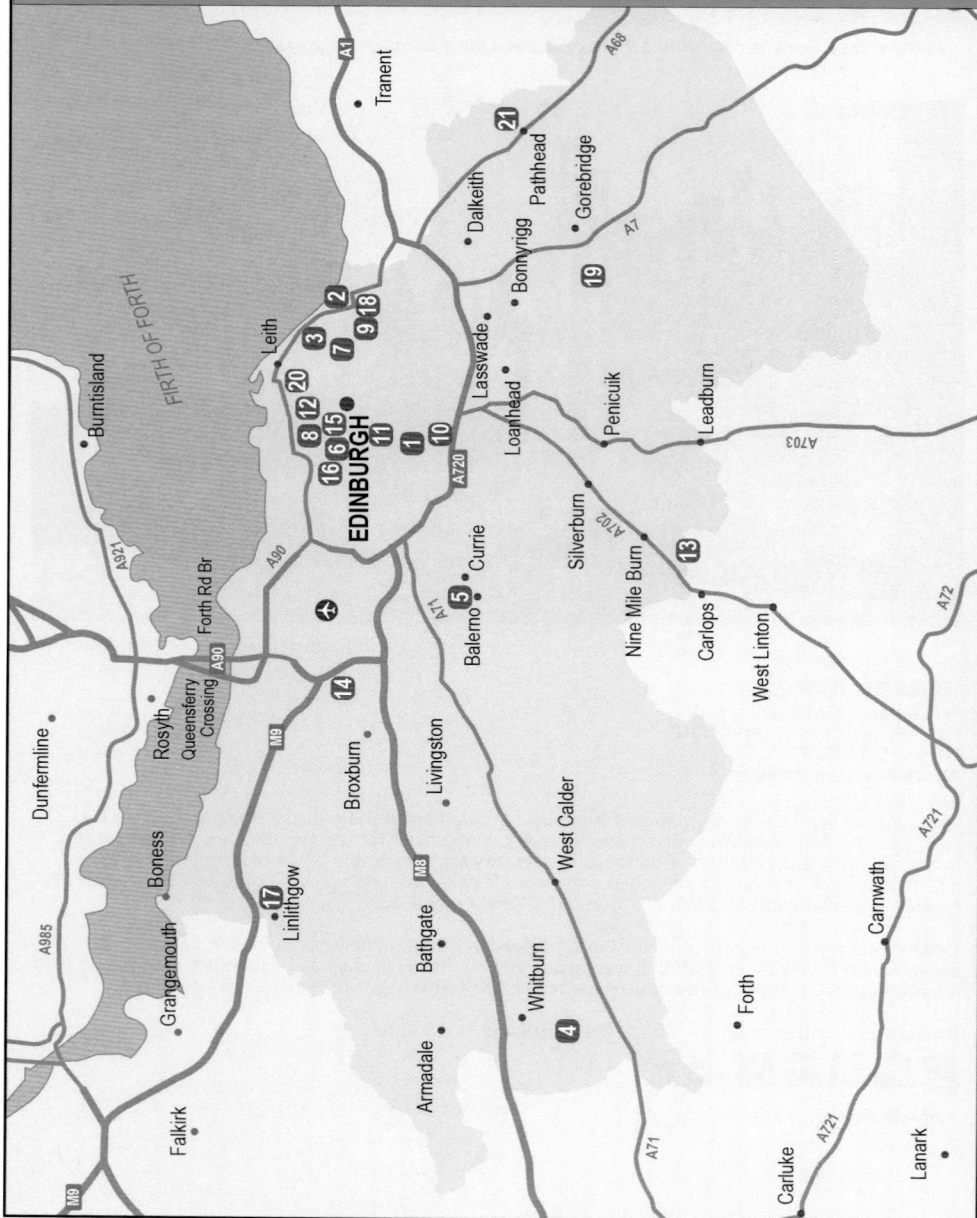

EDINBURGH, MIDLOTHIAN & WEST LOTHIAN

OUR VOLUNTEER ORGANISERS

District Organiser:	Victoria Reid Thomas	Riccarton Mains Farmhouse, Currie, EH14 4AR E: edinburgh@scotlandsgardens.org
Area Organisers:	Chris Gregson Jerry Gregson Caroline Pearson	101 Greenbank Crescent, Edinburgh, EH10 5TA 101 Greenbank Crescent, Edinburgh, EH10 5TA 42 Pentland Avenue, Edinburgh, EH13 0HY
Treasurer:	Michael Pearson	42 Pentland Avenue, Edinburgh, EH13 0HY

GARDENS OPEN ON A SPECIFIC DATE

Dr Neil's Garden, Duddingston Village	Saturday/Sunday, 5/6 May
Redcroft, 23 Murrayfield Road, Edinburgh	Sunday, 6 May
Storytelling at Dr Neil's Garden, Duddingston Village	Monday, 7 May
Moray Place and Bank Gardens, Edinburgh	Sunday, 13 May
101 Greenbank Crescent, Edinburgh	Sunday, 20 May
Balerno Lodge, 36 Johnsburn Road, Balerno	Saturday, 26 May
The Glasshouses at the Royal Botanic Garden Edinburgh	Sunday, 10 June
Temple Village Gardens, Temple	Sunday, 10 June
Dean Gardens, Edinburgh	Sunday, 17 June
Open Gardens of the Lower New Town, 24 Fettes Row	Saturday, 23 June
Merchiston Cottage, 16 Colinton Road, Edinburgh	Sunday, 24 June
14 East Brighton Crescent, Portobello, Edinburgh	Sunday, 24 June
Rivaldsgreen House, 48 Friars Brae, Linlithgow.	Saturday, 21 July
Hunter's Tryst, 95 Oxgangs Road, Edinburgh	Sunday, 22 July
45 Northfield Crescent, Longridge, Bathgate	Saturday/Sunday, 28/29 July
39 Nantwich Drive, Edinburgh	Saturday, 4 August
Craigentinny and Telferton Allotments, Telferton Road, Edinburgh	Sunday, 5 August
101 Greenbank Crescent, Edinburgh	Sunday, 12 August
Whitburgh House Walled Garden, Pathhead, Midlothian	Sunday/Monday/Tuesday, 19/20/21 August
Belgrave Crescent Gardens, Edinburgh	Sunday, 2 September

GARDENS OPEN REGULARLY

Newliston, Kirkliston	2 May - 3 June

GARDENS OPEN BY ARRANGEMENT

Hunter's Tryst, 95 Oxgangs Road, Edinburgh	On request
101 Greenbank Crescent, Edinburgh	15 April - 26 August
Newhall, Carlops	1 July - 31 August

Edinburgh, Midlothian & West Lothian

KEY TO SYMBOLS

NEW New garden	♿ Full wheelchair access	🐕 Dogs on leads
Basic teas	Partial wheelchair access	**NPC** National plant collection
H Homemade teas	Plants for sale	Champion trees
C Cream teas	Children's activities	Designed landscape
Refreshments	Accessible by public transport	Snowdrop opening

All our gardens open to raise money for charity. Each opening may nominate a charity(s) to receive up to 60% of the takings and these are included with each listing. The net remaining raised supports our core beneficiaries. Information about our core beneficiaries can be found in the front section of the book. More information about our charity scheme and our symbols can be found in the back foldout section of the book under 'Tips for Using Your Guidebook'.

Redcroft © Shelia Sim

Edinburgh, Midlothian & West Lothian

101 GREENBANK CRESCENT

1

Edinburgh EH10 5TA
Mr and Mrs Jerry and Christine Gregson
T: 0131 447 6492 E: jerry_gregson@yahoo.co.uk

The front of the house is on a busy town bus route, but the back of the house is in the country, with views to the Pentland Hills and over the adjoining Braidburn Valley Park. The garden shows what can be done on a steeply sloped site. Paths and steps join a variety of distinct areas and terraces, each with a different character. The aim is to have colour, contrast and interest all year round.

Open: Sunday 20 May, 2pm - 5pm. Also open Sunday 12 August, 2pm - 5pm. And open by arrangement 15 April - 26 August. Admission £4.00, children free.

Directions: From city centre take the A702 through Morningside. Continue uphill and turn right at Greenbank Church on to Greenbank Crescent. On 5 and 16 bus routes, the stop is for Greenbank Row.

· **Shelter Scotland**

101 Greenbank Crescent

14 EAST BRIGHTON CRESCENT

2

Portobello, Edinburgh EH15 1LR
Mr and Mrs Jim and Sue Hurford

Roughly two thirds of an acre suburban garden, developed over 35 years. People have said the following about it: "A little bit of countryside in the town"; "Booming with green"; "A bosky bower" and "There is such a wide range of plant material and every little corner holds a new gem".

Open: Sunday 24 June, 2pm - 5pm, admission £4.00, children free. There will be a plant stall and an apple pressing demonstration. A list of local eateries will be available on the day.

Directions: Buses 21, 42 and 49 to Brighton Place, and 15, 26, 40 and 45 to Portobello High Street. Brighton Place intersects Portobello High Street just east of the bus stops.

· **Save Bellfield**

Edinburgh, Midlothian & West Lothian

3

39 NANTWICH DRIVE
Edinburgh EH7 6RA
Michael and Susan Burns

Large wildlife friendly garden, run on organic principles. Includes mini orchard, pond, mixed borders, greenhouse and a secret garden. There are mini woodland walks and an allotment for vegetables, plus a compost area, worm bin and rotary bin.

Open: Saturday 4 August, 2pm - 5pm, admission £4.00, children free.

Directions: Bus 19 to Craigentinny Road or bus 26 to Kekewich Drive.

· *The Henry Doubleday Research Association : Garden Organic*

4

45 NORTHFIELD CRESCENT
Longridge, Bathgate EH47 8AL
Mr Jamie Robertson
T: 07885 701642 E: jamierobertson04@hotmail.co.uk

A delightful garden with a wide variety of shrubs, herbaceous, bedding and dozens of dahlia plants. Large pond with a small waterfall and a colourful decked area with an attractive selection of bedding plants. There is a vegetable patch with raised beds. A 12 by 8 foot feature greenhouse shows award winning pot plants. The garden is the current holder of the *Oatridge College* award and has won several gold medals. The owner has won the *West Lothian Gardener of the Year* prize four times and is chairman of the Livingston and District Horticultural Society.

Open: Saturday/Sunday, 28/29 July, 2pm - 5pm, admission £3.00, children free

Directions: From A71 turn right after Breith at traffic lights, go about a mile and turn right into the Crescent. From Whitburn, take A706 Longridge Road to Longridge and last left into the Crescent.

· *Worldwide Cancer Research*

45 Northfield Crescent

Edinburgh, Midlothian & West Lothian

BALERNO LODGE
36 Johnsburn Road, Balerno EH14 7DX
Gilly Corstorphine

Balerno Lodge is a two acre mature garden consisting of rhododendrons, azaleas, shrubbery and a small pretty stream leading into a pond. Within the walled garden there is a large central herbaceous border and a newly created insect friendly bed.

Open: Saturday 26 May, 2pm - 5pm, admission £4.00, children free. Plant stall run by Macplants Nursery. Soft ball tennis, mini football and other exciting children's activities.

Directions: A70 to Balerno, leave school on the left, over a small roundabout up Johnsburn Road and it is the second opening on the right. Bus 44A.

· *Harmeny Education Trust Limited*

BELGRAVE CRESCENT GARDENS
Edinburgh EH4 3AJ
The Residents of Belgrave Crescent

City centre private garden of seven acres beside the historic Dean Bridge. Shrubs, trees, herbaceous and mixed borders provide a haven of peace close to the city, with wild areas and magnificent views of the Dean Bridge, over the Water of Leith.

Open: Sunday 2 September, 2pm - 5pm, admission £4.00, children free.

Directions: The garden is a five minute walk from the West End. Enter from the East Gate in Belgrave Crescent. Buses 36, 41, 47, 19.

· *Fresh Start*

CRAIGENTINNY AND TELFERTON ALLOTMENTS
Telferton Road, off Portobello Road, Edinburgh EH7 6XG
The Gardeners of Craigentinny and Telferton
W: www.ctallotments.com

Established in 1923, this independent allotment site is a tranquil and charming space. Hidden away in a built up area, the local community benefit from growing their own vegetables and fruit. Come and enjoy tea, homebaking and chat with our friendly plot holders.

Open: Sunday 5 August, 2pm - 5pm, admission £3.00, children free.

Directions: Park on Telferton Road.   Lothian Regional Transport buses 15, 26, 45.

· *Craigentinny Telferton Allotments*

Edinburgh, Midlothian & West Lothian

8 | DEAN GARDENS

Edinburgh EH4 1QE
Dean Gardens Management Committee
W: www.deangardens.org

....

Nine acres of semi-woodland garden with spring bulbs on the steep banks of the Water of Leith in central Edinburgh. Founded in the 1860s by local residents, the Dean Gardens contain part of the great structure of the Dean Bridge, a Thomas Telford masterpiece of 1835. Lawns, paths, trees, and shrubs with lovely views to the weir in the Dean Village and to the St Bernard's Well. There is also a children's play area.

Open: Sunday 17 June, 2pm - 5pm, admission £3.00, children free. There will be live music, along with teas and cakes.

Directions: Entrance at Ann Street or Eton Terrace.

· All proceeds to SGS Beneficiaries

Dr Neil's Garden

9 | DR NEIL'S GARDEN

Duddingston Village EH15 3PX
Dr Neil's Garden Trust
E: info@drneilsgarden.co.uk
W: www.drneilsgarden.co.uk

....

Wonderful secluded, landscaped garden on the lower slopes of Arthur's Seat including conifers, heathers, alpines, a physic garden, herbaceous borders and ponds. Also Thompson's Tower with the Museum of Curling and beautiful views across Duddingston Loch.

Open: Saturday/Sunday, 5/6 May, 2pm - 5pm, admission £3.00, children free.

Directions: Park at kirk car park on Duddingston Road West and then follow signposts through the manse garden.

· Dr. Neils Garden Trust

Edinburgh, Midlothian & West Lothian

10

HUNTER'S TRYST
95 Oxgangs Road, Edinburgh EH10 7BA
Jean Knox
T: 0131 477 2919 E: jean.knox@blueyonder.co.uk

Well stocked and beautifully designed mature, medium sized town garden comprising herbaceous and shrub beds, lawn, fruit and some vegetables, water features, seating areas and trees. This is a wildlife friendly garden that has been transformed from a wilderness 30 years ago and continues to evolve. The project for 2017 was the construction and planting of two raised beds in the front garden, so there's a lot more to see this year. This hidden treasure of a garden was featured on the *Beechgrove Garden* in June 2015 and on *The Instant Gardener* in June 2016.

Open: Sunday 22 July, 2pm - 5pm. Also open by arrangement. Admission £4.00, children free.

Directions: From Fairmilehead crossroads head down Oxgangs Road to Hunter's Tryst roundabout, last house on the left. Take buses 4, 5, 18 or 27. The bus stop is at Hunter's Tryst and the garden is opposite.

· *Lothian Cat Rescue*

11

MERCHISTON COTTAGE
16 Colinton Road, Edinburgh EH10 5EL
Esther Mendelssohn

Romantic walled garden within a mile of the city centre providing a haven for wildlife based on a tapestry of habitats including numerous water features. It has been gardened on organic principles for nearly 30 years with productive fruit trees, apples, pears, plums, quince, medlar and black mulberry. Soft fruit including gooseberries, raspberries, blueberries and red, white and blackcurrants all benefit from the pollinating bees kept in hives in the garden which also give us the added bonus of honey. A recently completed new addition of a roof garden devoted to growing fruit and vegetables has greatly enhanced the garden and provided new planting opportunities.

Open: Sunday 24 June, 2pm - 5pm, admission £4.00, children free. Talks on bee keeping will take place during the afternoon and when possible the bees can be seen at close quarters in an observation hive.

Directions: Near Holy Corner, opposite Watson's College School. Take Lothian buses 11 or 16.

· *ALYN Hospital, Jerusalem*

12

MORAY PLACE AND BANK GARDENS
Edinburgh EH3 6BX
The Residents of Moray Place and Bank Gardens

Well worth a visit to these two exquisite gardens.
Bank Gardens Nearly six acres of secluded wild gardens with lawns, trees and shrubs with banks of bulbs down to the Water of Leith. Stunning vistas across the Firth of Forth.
Moray Place Private garden of 3½ acres in Georgian New Town. Shrubs, trees and beds offering atmosphere of tranquillity in the city centre.

Open: Sunday 13 May, 2pm - 5pm, admission £4.00, children free.

Directions: **Bank Gardens** Enter by the gate at the top of Doune Terrace.
Moray Place Enter by the north gate in Moray Place.

· *Euan Macdonald Centre for Motor Neurone Disease Research*

Edinburgh, Midlothian & West Lothian

13

NEWHALL
Carlops EH26 9LY
John and Tricia Kennedy
T: 01968 660206 E: tricia.kennedy@newhalls.co.uk

Traditional 18th century walled garden with huge herbaceous border, shrubberies, fruit and vegetables. Stunning glen running along the North Esk river in the process of restoration (stout shoes recommended). Large pond with evolving planting. Young arboretum and ccllection of *Rosa pimpinellifolia*. As in *Good Gardens Guide 2010, Scottish Field, Gardens Monthly* and *Scotland on Sunday*.

Open: Open by arrangement 1 July - 31 August, admission £5.00, children free. Homemade teas available by prior arrangement. Light lunches available for groups by prior arrangement.

Directions: On the A702 Edinburgh/Biggar, ½ mile after Ninemileburn and a mile before Carlops. Follow signs.

· *All proceeds to SGS Beneficiaries*

Newhall from the air

14

NEWLISTON
Kirkliston EH29 9EB
Mr and Mrs R C Maclachlan
T: 0131 333 3231 E: mac@newliston.fsnet.co.uk

18th century designed landscape with good rhododendrons and azaleas. The house, designed by Robert Adam, is open.

Open: 2 May - 3 June, 2pm - 6pm, admission £4.00, children free.

Directions: Four miles from the Forth Road Bridge, entrance off B800.

· *Children's Hospice Association Scotland*

Edinburgh, Midlothian & West Lothian

15 OPEN GARDENS OF THE LOWER NEW TOWN
24 Fettes Row EH3 6RH
The Gardeners of the Lower New Town

A group of New Town amateur gardeners have combined to show their approach to greening the city with a densely planted courtyard garden in a former back green, a tranquil shade garden in a back lane, a small but perfectly formed patio garden in a modern apartment block and a glorious street planting in a charming mews. All the gardens have year round interest with a mix of seasonal planting and structural evergreens and the gardeners will be on hand to talk about their own selections.

Open: Saturday 23 June, 2pm - 5pm, admission £5.00, children free.

Directions: Tickets/maps from 24 Fettes Row which is the last Georgian block at the end of Fettes Row West, left off Dundas Street from Princes Street. Map will direct you to the other open gardens. Buses 23 or 27.

· *Medicines sans Frontieres (UK)*

16 REDCROFT
23 Murrayfield Road, Edinburgh EH12 6EP
James and Anna Buxton
T: 0131 337 1747 E: annabuxtonb@aol.com

A walled garden surrounding an Arts and Crafts villa which provides an unexpected haven off a busy road. Planted and maintained with shape and texture in mind. Acid soil and relative shelter allow a wide range of plants to be grown. In early May there should be a fine display of colour from rhododendrons and other flowering shrubs, trees in flower and plenty of tulips and other bulbs, both in pots and in the garden

Open: Sunday 6 May, 2pm - 5pm, admission £4.00, children free. Large plant sale.

Directions: Murrayfield Road runs north from Corstorphine Road to Ravelston Dykes. There is easy parking available which is free. Buses 12, 26, 31, get off at Murrayfield Stadium and 38 which goes down Murrayfield Road.

· *The Church of the Good Shepherd, Murrayfield: Edinburgh*

17 RIVALDSGREEN HOUSE
48 Friars Brae, Linlithgow. EH49 6BG
Dr Ian Wallace
T: 01506 845700 E: Ianwjw1940@gmail.com

Mature two acre garden with lovely mixed herbaceous, rose and tree planting.

Open: Saturday 21 July, 12pm - 5pm, admission £5.00, children free.

Directions: For final directions if necessary call the number listed above. There is car parking available.

· *St Peters Episcopal Church*

Edinburgh, Midlothian & West Lothian

18 STORYTELLING AT DR NEIL'S GARDEN
Duddingston Village   EH15 3PX
Dr Neil's Garden Trust
E: info@drneilsgarden.co.uk
W: www.drneilsgarden.co.uk

Once upon a time...

Step back in time in an oasis of calm at Dr Neil's garden with the soothing sounds of the nearby Duddingston Loch. Hear tales of the bronze age hoard discovered beneath the waters in the 1800s. The garden, tenderly created by the doctors from scratch, was often used by their patients. Get up close and personal with the soft, rubbery needles of the *Abries concolor* tree and hear the story of the three sequoias.

Join Scotland's Gardens Scheme and The Scottish International Storytelling Festival in "Growing Stories". A fun packed way to explore some of Scotland's Gardens. See gardens with new eyes once you hear stories, from local Storytellers, about their creation, history and interaction with the environment. For more information see Scotland's Gardens Scheme website.

Open: Monday 7 May, 2pm - 5pm, admission £5.00, children free.

Directions: Park at kirk car park on Duddingston Road West and then follow signposts through the Manse Garden.

♿ NEW

· **Dr. Neils Garden Trust**

19 TEMPLE VILLAGE GARDENS
Temple EH23 4SQ
Temple Village Gardeners
T: 01875 830253 E: delapsandy@gmail.com

Temple Village is situated on the east bank of the River South Esk, to the south west of Gorebridge and is one of Midlothian's most attractive and historic conservation villages. Between the 12th and 14th centuries Temple was the headquarters of the Knights Templar, more recently the village has been home to Sir William Gillies the famous Scottish painter.   A number of village gardens will be open, from the charming riverside garden of The Mill House, to the delightful front and rear gardens of some of the village houses on the Main Street. Planted in a variety of different styles, they display contrasting designs and plant combinations, reflecting the villager's many distinctive horticultural interests.

Open: Sunday 10 June, 2pm - 5pm, admission £5.00, children free.

Directions: On the B6372, 3 miles off the A7 from Gorebridge.

· **Temple Village Halls Association**

Gardens are perfect for younger visitors to explore and open their minds

Edinburgh, Midlothian & West Lothian

20

THE GLASSHOUSES AT THE ROYAL BOTANIC GARDEN EDINBURGH
20A Inverleith Row, Edinburgh EH3 5LR
Royal Botanic Garden Edinburgh
T: 0131 248 2909
W: www.rbge.org.uk

The Glasshouses with ten climatic zones are a delight all year round. The Orchids and Cycads House brings together primitive cycads which dominated the land flora some 65 million years ago, and a diverse range of orchids, the most sophisticated plants in the world. In summer, giant water lilies, *Victoria amazonica*, are the star attraction in the Tropical Aquatic House. Plants with vibrant flowers and fascinating foliage thrive in the Rainforest Riches House and the complex ecosystems of life in the world's deserts are explored in the Arid Lands House. A large collection of gingers, *Zingiberaceae*, one of the largest collections of vireya rhododendrons in the world and a case housing carnivorous plants are among other attractions.

Open: Sunday 10 June, 10am - 5pm, admission details can be found on the garden's website.

Directions: Located off the A902, one mile north of the city centre. Entrances at Inverleith Row and Arboretum Place. Lothian Buses 8, 23 and 27 stop close to the East Gate entrance on Inverleith Row. The Majestic Tour Bus stops at Arboretum Place.

· **Donation to SGS Beneficiaries**

21

WHITBURGH HOUSE WALLED GARDEN
Pathhead, Midlothian EH37 5SR
Mrs Elizabeth Salvesen

This contemporary, stylish one acre walled garden, 700 feet above sea level, is a lively forward looking and unexpected gem. The solidity and graphic quality of clipped foliage act as a foil for the many perennials, grasses, annuals, fruit and vegetables. A spiral path leads through an acre of white birches. There is also a variety of ponds and fine sculptures spread around 14 acres of policies. Whitburgh garden has featured recently in *Gardens Illustrated* and other publications.

Open: Sunday/Monday/Tuesday, 19/20/21 August, 2pm - 5pm, admission £6.00, children free.

Directions: From the north - ½ mile south of Pathhead on the A68 turn left and follow the SGS signs. From the south - one mile north of Blackshiels on the A68 turn right at the sign to *Fala Dam* and follow SGS signs. Whitburgh House is a short two miles from either turn off and southeast of Pathhead.

· **Horatio's Garden: Scotland**

Gardening teaches children
patience and appreciation
for the natural world

FIFE

Scotland's Gardens Scheme 2018 Guidebook is sponsored by INVESTEC WEALTH & INVESTMENT

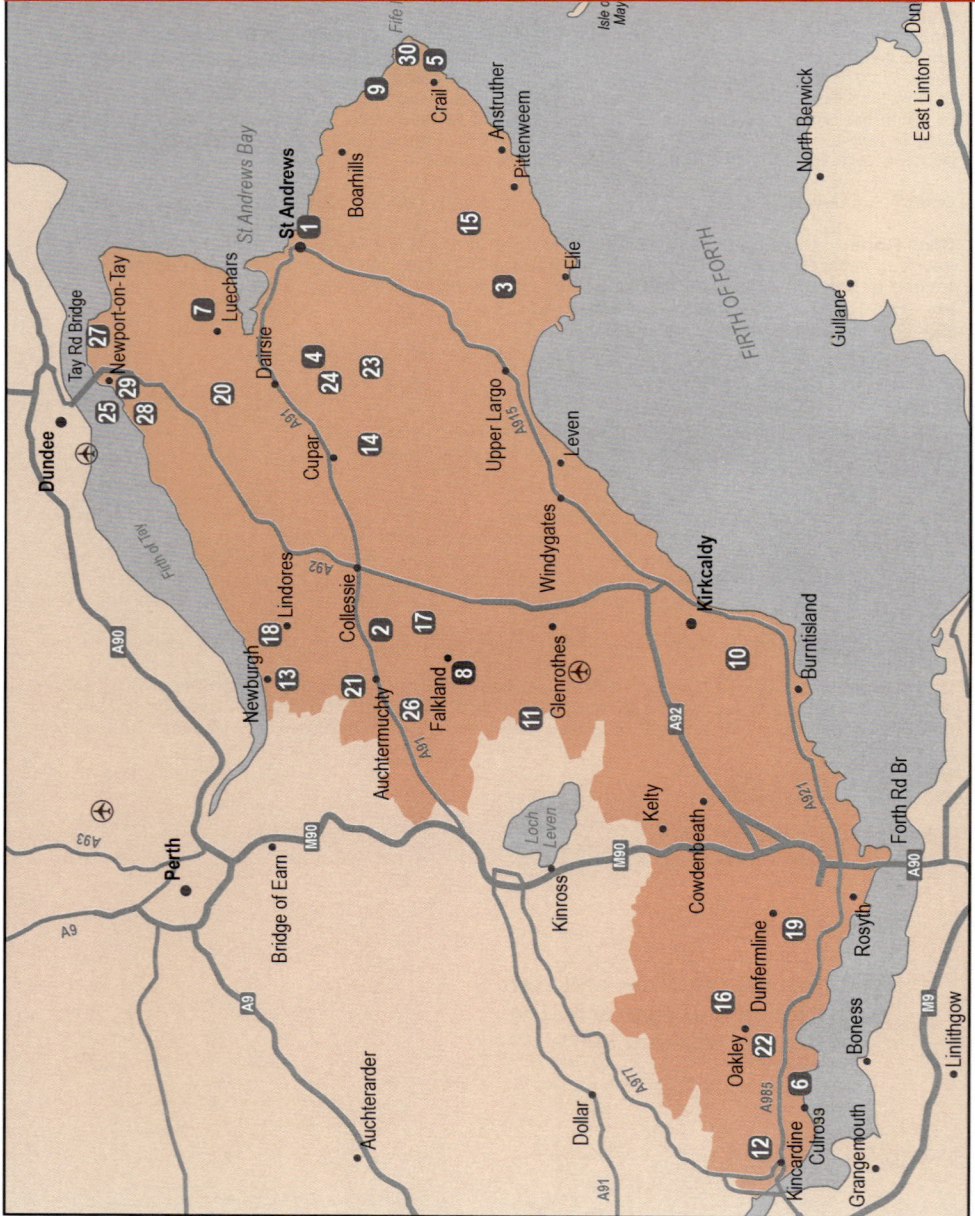

FIFE

OUR VOLUNTEER ORGANISERS

District Organisers:	Catherine Erskine	Cambo House, Kingsbarns, KY16 8QD
	Louise Roger	Chesterhill, Boarhills, St Andrews, KY16 8PP
		E: fife@scotlandsgardens.org
Area Organisers:	Alison Aiton	Craigview Cottage, Blebo Craigs, Cupar, KY15 5UQ
	Jeni Auchinleck	2 Castle Street, Crail, KY10 3SQ
	Oenone Baillie	
	Pauline Borthwick	96 Hepburn Gardens, St Andrews, KY16 9LP
	Evelyn Crombie	Keeper's Wood, Over Rankeilour, Cupar, KY15 4NQ
	Caroline Macpherson	Edenside, Strathmiglo, KY14 7PX
	Lorna McHardy	Gardeners Cottage, Shore Road, Crombie Point Crombie, Dunfermline, KY12 8LQ
	Lindsay Murray	Craigfoodie, Dairsie, Cupar, KY15 4RU
	April Simpson	The Cottage, Boarhills, St Andrews, KY16 8PP
	Fay Smith	37 Ninian Fields, Pittenweem, Anstruther, KY10 2QU
	Julia Young	South Flisk, Blebo Craigs, Cupar, KY15 5UQ
Treasurer:	David Buchanan-Cook	Helensbank, 56 Toll Road, Kincardine, FK10 4QZ

GARDENS OPEN ON A SPECIFIC DATE

Lindores House, By Newburgh	Sunday, 18 February
Fife Spring Trail, Various locations across Fife	Tuesday - Thursday, 10/11/12 April
Fife Spring Trail, Various locations across Fife	Sunday, 15 April
Fife Spring Trail, Various locations across Fife	Tuesday - Thursday, 17/18/19 April
Fife Spring Trail, Various locations across Fife	Tuesday - Thursday, 24/25/26 April
Balcarres, Colinsburgh	Sunday, 29 April
Fife Spring Trail, Various locations across Fife	Tuesday, 1 May
Fife Spring Trail, Various locations across Fife	Thursday/Friday, 3/4 May
Fife Spring Trail, Various locations across Fife	Thursday, 10 May
Willowhill, Tayfield and St Fort Woodland, Newport-on-Tay	Sunday, 13 May
Fife Spring Trail, Various locations across Fife	Wednesday, 16 May
Earlshall Castle, Leuchars	Sunday, 20 May
Kirklands, Saline	Sunday, 20 May
Fife Spring Trail, Various locations across Fife	Wednesday, 23 May
Lindores House, By Newburgh	Sunday, 27 May
46 South Street, St Andrews	Sunday, 27 May
Earlshall Castle, Leuchars	Sunday, 3 June
Newton Mains and Newton Barns, Auchtermuchty	Saturday/Sunday, 9/10 June
Old Inzievar House, Oakley, Dunfermline	Saturday/Sunday, 9/10 June
Hidden Gardens of Newburgh, Newburgh, Fife	Sunday, 17 June
Culross Palace Garden, Culross	Sunday, 24 June
Strathmiglo Village Gardens, Fife	Sunday, 24 June
Backhouse at Rossie Estate, By Collessie	Sunday, 1 July
Lathrisk Gardens, Lathrisk	Sunday, 8 July
Crail: Small Gardens in the Burgh, Crail	Saturday/Sunday, 14/15 July

Fife

GARDENS OPEN ON A SPECIFIC DATE (CONTD.)

Falkland Palace and Garden, Falkland, Cupar	Sunday, 15 July
Tayport Gardens, Tayport	Sunday, 22 July
The Tower, 1 Northview Terrace, Wormit	Saturday, 11 August
Kellie Castle with Balcaskie, Pittenweem	Saturday/Sunday, 18/19 August
Blebo Craigs Village Gardens, Cupar	Saturday/Sunday, 25/26 August
Hill of Tarvit Plant Sale and Autumn Fair, Hill of Tarvit, Cupar	Sunday, 30 September

GARDENS OPEN REGULARLY

Glassmount House, By Kirkcaldy	1 April - 30 September (not Sundays)
Wormistoune House, Crail	1 June - 30 September (Tuesdays only)
Lucklaw House, Logie, Cupar	6 June - 25 July (Wednesdays only)

GARDENS OPEN BY ARRANGEMENT

Rosewells, Pitscottie	1 April - 30 September
Kirklands, Saline	1 April - 30 September
The Tower, 1 Northview Terrace, Wormit	1 April - 30 September
Logie House, Crossford, Dunfermline	1 May - 30 Sept. (not Weds, Sats & Suns)
South Flisk, Blebo Craigs, Cupar	1 May - 15 June
St Fort Woodland Garden, St Fort Farm, Newport-on-Tay	1 May - 30 November
Greenhead Farmhouse, Greenhead of Arnot, Leslie	1 June - 31 July
Helensbank, Kincardine	1 June - 31 July
Old Inzievar House, Oakley, Dunfermline	1 June - 30 June

KEY TO SYMBOLS

NEW	New garden	♿	Full wheelchair access	🐕	Dogs on leads
	Basic teas	♿	Partial wheelchair access	NPC	National plant collection
H	Homemade teas	🌷	Plants for sale	🌳	Champion trees
C	Cream teas	👥	Children's activities		Designed landscape
	Refreshments	🚌	Accessible by public transport		Snowdrop opening

All our gardens open to raise money for charity. Each opening may nominate a charity(s) to receive up to 60% of the takings and these are included with each listing. The net remaining raised supports our core beneficiaries. Information about our core beneficiaries can be found in the front section of the book. More information about our charity scheme and our symbols can be found in the back foldout section of the book under 'Tips for Using Your Guidebook'.

Fife

1

46 SOUTH STREET
St Andrews KY16 9JT
Mrs June Baxter
T: 01334 474 995

Renowned town garden in medieval long rig, with orchard, clematis, spring bulbs and many spring flowering shrubs. An historic and unique feature in St Andrews, but also a wonderfully planted space where different styles of planting complement the range of plants used. Historic doocot.

Open: Sunday 27 May, 2pm - 5pm, admission £5.00, children free.

Directions: Entry for the garden is off South Street.

· *Save the Children UK*

2

BACKHOUSE AT ROSSIE ESTATE
By Collessie KY15 7UZ
Caroline Thomson and Andrew Thomson
E: caroline.thomson@rofsie-estate.com
W: www.rofsie-estate.com

A wonderful series of arches covered in scented roses is just one of the centre piece attractions here. Herbaceous borders with wispy grasses, colourful perennials, lillium and allium planting surrounding a grass labyrinth add to this spectacular walled garden lovingly restored over ten years. Culinary and medicinal herbs, vegetable and cut flowers fill the potager, with old espaliered fruit trees trained on the walls. Interesting scree and rock garden, peat bed plantings and woodland walk leading to a ruined tomb.
National Plant Collection: *Narcissus* (Backhouse cvs.).

Open: Sunday 1 July, 2pm - 5pm, admission £5.00, children free.

Directions: Between Auchtermuchty and Collessie on A91. One mile east of Auchtermuchty turn right for Charlottetown, turn first right into Rossie Estate onto an untarred drive.

· *Fife Voluntary Action*

3

BALCARRES
Colinsburgh KY9 1HN
The Earl and Countess of Crawford and Balcarres
T: 01333 340205 (Estate Office)

The garden at Balcarres is always very exciting in the Spring with interesting plants and a profusion of colour. There will be a multitude of daffodils, snowdrops, primroses, polyanthus and smilacina together with many other spring plants. The Woodland Walk will also be bursting with life with much variety and colour including hostas, trillium and a multitude of bulbs.

Open: Sunday 29 April, 2pm - 5pm, admission £6.00, children free.

Directions: Half a mile north of Colinsburgh off A942. Bus to Colinsburgh.

· *Colinsburgh Galloway Library*

Fife

4 BLEBO CRAIGS VILLAGE GARDENS
Cupar KY15 5UF
The Gardeners of Blebo Craigs
E: findlaysatblebo@btinternet.com
....

The lovely village of Blebo Craigs welcomes you to visit a selection of our special and varied gardens with its wonderful hedgerows, cottages and superb views. We are opening later than usual to give visitors a new seasonal experience. Meet the gardeners, collect a few gardening tips and be surprised by the produce we grow.

Open: Saturday/Sunday, 25/26 August, 1pm - 5pm, admission £5.00, children free. Parking is available near the Village Hall. Disabled toilet in the Village Hall. The Village Hall will be serving teas from 2pm - 4pm.

Directions: From St Andrews take the B939 and after four miles, turn right onto village road. From Cupar take the B940 to Pitscottie then turn left onto B939 signposted St Andrews. After two miles, turn left at sign into Blebo Craigs.

· **Blebo Craigs Village Hall 2000 Trust**

5 CRAIL: SMALL GARDENS IN THE BURGH
Crail KY10 3SQ
The Gardeners of Crail
T: 01333 450538
....

Three new gardens this year! A number of small gardens in varied styles: cottage, historic, plantsman's and bedding. The stunning coastal location of the gardens presents some challenges for planting but also allows a great range of more tender species to flourish.

Open: Sat/Sun, 14/15 July, 1pm - 5pm, admission £5.00, children free. Tickets and maps available from Mrs Jeni Auchinleck, 2 Castle Street and Ian & Margaret Moonie, 52 Marketgate South.

Directions: Approach Crail from either St Andrews or Anstruther by A917. Park in the Marketgate.

· **Crail Preservation Society**

6 CULROSS PALACE GARDEN
Culross KY12 8JH
The National Trust for Scotland
T: 01383 880359 E: larnot@nts.org.uk
W: www.nts.org.uk/Property/Royal-Burgh-of-Culross
....

Relive the domestic life of the 16th and 17th centuries amid the old buildings and cobbled streets of this Royal Burgh on the River Forth. Explore the recreated 17th century garden behind the Culross Palace laid out to show the range of plants that were grown for culinary, medicinal and ornamental use. Don't miss the Scot's Dumpy chickens!

Open: Sunday 24 June, 12pm - 5pm, admission details can be found on the garden's website. Meet the Head Gardener with tours starting at 12:30 pm and 3:30 pm for £6.00. Fruit and vegetable stalls with produce grown at Culross Palace.

Fife

Directions: Off A985, three miles east of Kincardine Bridge, six miles west of Dunfermline. Buses Stagecoach, Stirling to Dunfermline or First, Edinburgh to Dunfermline. Falkirk station 12 miles, Dunfermline station six miles.

· *Donation to SGS Beneficiaries*

7

EARLSHALL CASTLE
Leuchars KY16 0DP
Paul & Josine Veenhuijzen
T: 01334 839205
....

Celebrat ng over 50 years of opening for charity with Scotland's Gardens Scheme. Extensive and interesting garden designed by Sir Robert Lorimer. Fascinating topiary lawn, for which Earlshall is renowned, rose terrace, croquet lawn with herbaceous borders, shrub border, box garden, orchard, kitchen and herb garden. Spectacular spring bulbs.

Open: Sunday 20 May, 2pm - 5pm. Also open Sunday 3 June, 2pm - 5pm. Admission £5.00, children free.

Directions: On Earlshall Road, three quarters of a mile east of Leuchars Village (off A919). Bus/train to Leuchars.

· *Royal Scots Dragoon Guards Regimental Trust (Sunday 20 May) & Leuchars St Athernase Parish Church (Sunday 3 June)*

Donate your plants to a plant stall to raise money for charity

8

FALKLAND PALACE AND GARDEN
Falkland, Cupar KY15 7BU
The National Trust for Scotland
T: 01337 857397 E: wpurvis@nts.org.uk
W: www.nts.org.uk/Property/Falkland-Palace-and-Garden
....

Set in a medieval village, the Royal Palace of Falkland is a superb example of Renaissance architecture, surrounded by a beautiful garden. Come and enjoy this fantastic Herb Day, which will provice an opportunity to learn more about herbs, including how these versatile plants have been usec through the ages. From creating perfumes and flavouring foods, to treating ailments. Activities for all the family, from cookery to growing tips!
Champion Trees: *Acer platanoides* 'Crimson King'.

Open: Sunday 15 July, 12pm - 4:30pm, admission details can be found on the garden's website.

Directions: A912, ten miles from M90, junction 8, eleven miles north of Kirkcaldy.
Bus - Stacecoach Fife stops in the High Street (about 100 metres from the garden).

· *Donation to SGS Beneficiaries*

Fife

9 FIFE SPRING TRAIL
Various locations across Fife KY
The Fife Gardeners
E: fife@scotlandsgardens.org

Running duringthe Spring this year in April and May, the Fife Gardeners are offering an opportunity to visit 12 privately owned gardens across Central and East Fife. This offers a very flexible way to keep up your weekly dose of beautiful gardens, and excellent value for money. Fife can look quite bleak in March, with brown arable fields and fringed by a cold North Sea, but by April, the countryside is starting to burst into verdant colours, and our gardens are also starting to bloom. A wide variety of gardens is on offer, from bluebell and daffodil woodlands, through natural style plantings of rhododendrons and other spring flowering shrubs, to more formal garden settings in some of Fife's most notable gardens, large and small.

Cambo Plant Fair Kingsbarns KY16 8QD (Trustees of Cambo Heritage Trust)
Craigfoodie Dairsie KY15 4RU (Mr and Mrs James Murray)
Crail Gardens
2 Castle Street Crail KY10 3SQ (Mrs Jeni Auchinleck)
17 Marketgate Crail KY10 3TL (Jim and Kathleen Main)
Kenlygreen House Boarhills, St Andrews KY16 8PT (Mr & Mrs John Kilgour)
Myres Castle Auchtermuchty KY14 7EW (Henry and Amanda Barge)
South Flisk Blebo Craigs, Cupar KY15 5UQ (Mr and Mrs George Young)
Straiton Farmhouse Straiton Farm, Balmullo KY16 0BN (Mrs Barbara Pickard)
The Murrel Aberdour KY3 0RN (Mr and Mrs Alistair Bowen)
The Tower 1 Northview Terrace, Wormit DD6 8PP (Peter and Angela Davey)
Wemyss Castle Gardens Coaltown of Wemyss KY1 4TE (Mr and Mrs Michael Wemyss and Wemyss Estates Trustees)
Wormistoune House Crail KY10 3XH (Baron and Lady Wormiston)

Open: The Fife Spring Trail is open at various dates over April and May.   Admission £25.00, children free, pre-sales tickets available from Eventbrite (browse 'SGS Fife Spring Trail') or at the gardens on the day.   See Pages 36-37 for more information.

Directions: Directions to each garden will be provided with the tickets.

· *Rhet Fife Countryside Initiative Limited & RDA: Fife*

Kenlygreen House, Fife Spring Trail

Fife

10

GLASSMOUNT HOUSE
By Kirkcaldy KY2 5UT
Peter, James and Irene Thomson
T: 01592 890214 E: mcmoonter@yahoo.co.uk

Densely planted walled garden with surrounding woodland. An A-listed sun dial, Mackenzie & Moncur greenhouse and historical doocot are complemented by a number of newer built structures. Daffodils are followed by a mass of candelabra and cowslip primula, meconopsis and *Cardiocrinum giganteum*. Hedges and topiary form backdrops for an abundance of bulbs, clematis, rambling roses and perennials, creating interest through the summer into September.

Open: 1 April - 30 September (not Sundays), 2pm - 5pm, admission £5.00, children free.

Directions: From Kirkcaldy - head west on the B9157. Turn left immediately after the railway bridge on the edge of town. Follow the single track road for 1½ miles and cross the crossroads. Glassmount House is the first turning on your right.

· *Parkinsons UK*

11

GREENHEAD FARMHOUSE
Greenhead of Arnot, Leslie KY6 3JQ
Mr and Mrs Malcolm Strang Steel
T: 01592 840459
W: www.fife-bed-breakfast-glenrothes.co.uk

The south facing garden combines a sense of formality in its symmetrical layout, with an informal look of mixed herbaceous and shrub borders and a large display of alliums throughout. The garden is constantly evolving with new themes and combinations of plants, all unified by a fantastic use of colour. There is also a well stocked polytunnel which is used to augment the highly productive fruit and vegetable garden.

Open: Open by arrangement 1 June - 31 July, admission £5.00, children free.

Directions: A911 between Auchmuir Bridge and Scotlandwell.

· *Milnathort Guide Group*

A stalwart supporter of the
Queen's Nursing Institute
Scotland

Fife

12

HELENSBANK
Kincardine FK10 4QZ
David Buchanan-Cook and Adrian Miles
T: 07739 312912 E: Helensbank@aol.com

An 18th century walled garden, with main feature a Cedar of Lebanon, reputedly planted in 1750 by the sea captain who built the house. It provides challenges for planting in terms of shade and needle fall. Distinctive garden 'rooms' in part of the garden comprise a perennial blue and white cottage garden, a formal rose garden and an 'Italian' garden with citrus trees in pots. A 'hot' courtyard contains exotics such as bananas, acacias, Iochromas, melianthus and brugmansia. A shaded walk along the bottom of the garden leads to a Japanese pagoda. A large conservatory/greenhouse houses various climbing plants including varieties of passiflora.

Open: Open by arrangement 1 June - 31 July, admission £4.00, children free.

Directions: On request. Bus to Kincardine.

· *Marie Curie*

A quiet spot in the walled garden at Helensbank

13

HIDDEN GARDENS OF NEWBURGH
Newburgh, Fife KY14 6AJ
The Gardeners of Newburgh
T: 07763 340362

Hidden behind the 18th century facades of Newburgh High Street is a jumble of wonderful old gardens, many with spectacular views of the Tay estuary. Includes a plantsman's garden; a birdwatcher's garden; an original Newburgh orchard garden, plus a community orchard; a phoenix-risen-from-the-ashes garden in its second year of backbreaking refurbishment; some allotment gardens with prize-winning vegetables; fruit, vegetables, herbaceous borders.

Open: Sunday 17 June, 12pm - 5pm, admission £5.00, children free.

Directions: There is a car park at each end of the village, with tickets and teas available nearby and signposted.

· *Newburgh Cub Scouts*

Fife

14

HILL OF TARVIT PLANT SALE AND AUTUMN FAIR

Hill of Tarvit, Cupar KY15 5PB
The National Trust for Scotland/Scotland's Gardens Fife
E: fife@scotlandsgardens.org

This long established plant sale is a fantastic opportunity to purchase bare root and potted plants from an enormous selection on offer. We also welcome donations of plants prior to the sale. Please deliver to Hill of Tarvit on the Friday or Saturday. Hill of Tarvit is one of Scotland's finest Edwardian mansion houses. Surrounding the mansion house are spectacular gardens designed by Robert Lorimer, woods, open heath and parkland to explore.

Open: Sunday 30 September, 10:30am - 3pm, admission £2.00, children free. Children's activities - make a willow crown.

Directions: Two miles south of Cupar off A916.

· *All proceeds to SGS Beneficiaries*

Hill of Tarvit Plant Sale and Autumn Fair

15

KELLIE CASTLE WITH BALCASKIE

Pittenweem KY10 2RF
The National Trust for Scotland and the Anstruther Family
T: 01333 720271 (Kellie Castle)

Balcaskie (The Anstruther Family): These superb formal gardens are undergoing a period of imaginative restoration. New parterre borders on the themes of air, earth, fire and water will be ablaze with crocosmia, kniphofia, hedychium and other unusual perennials. These are set off with a variety of dwarf hedging, as alternatives to box is trialled. The garden frames stunning views out to sea.
Kellie Castle (National Trust for Scotland): This superb garden, around 400 years old, was sympathetically restored by the Lorimer family in the late 19th century. The Arts and Crafts style garden has a selection of old-fashioned roses and herbaceous plants, cultivated organically, and hosts an amazing 30 varieties of rhubarb and 75 different types of apple.

Open: Saturday/Sunday, 18/19 August, 12pm - 5pm, admission £8.00, children free.

Directions: Access to Balcaskie and Kellie Castle via Kellie Castle only, a free minibus will transport visitors between the gardens.   B9171, three miles NNW of Pittenweem. There is bus from local villages available by pre-booking.

· *Donation to SGS Beneficiaries*

Fife

16

KIRKLANDS

Saline KY12 9TS
Peter & Gill Hart
T: 01383 852737 E: gill@i-comment360.com
W: www.kirklandshouseandgarden.co.uk

25

Kirklands, built in 1832 on the site of an older house, has been the Hart family home for nearly 40 years. Over the years we have created an ever expanding garden with a woodland garden, herbaceous borders, bog garden, a terraced wall garden on a slope with raised vegetable and flower beds, 18 espalier fruit trees, rhododendrons and a display of red and yellow tulips. In the woodland garden there is a carpet of snowdrops followed by bluebells, meconopsis, trilliums, fritillaries, erythroniums, candelabra primulas and wonderful shrubs and trees all picked for their form and colour. In the bog garden by the side of Saline burn we have giant *Gunnera manicata* and *Darmera peltata*.   A treehouse for the grandchildren was recently built, as seen on the *Beechgrove Garden*.

Open: Sunday 20 May, 2pm - 5pm. Also open by arrangement 1 April - 30 September. Admission £5.00, children free.

Directions: Junction 4, M90, then B914. Parking in the centre of the village, then a short walk to the garden. Limited disabled parking at Kirklands.

· *Saline Environmental Group*

17

LATHRISK GARDENS

Lathrisk KY15 7HX
Fiona Skinner, Elspeth Skinner and Tober & Vera Reilly
T: 01337 857419

Three delightful gardens around Lathrisk House. In 2009, one acre of former field was added to the tiny garden of Wester Lathrisk. There Elspeth Skinner has planted trees and mixed borders so as to enhance the view of East Lomond Hill. Also Burnside, which features contemporary stone sculptures, enhancing a mixed garden containing woodland area and pond.

Open: Sunday 8 July, 2pm - 4pm, admission £5.00, children free.

Directions: Off the A914, north of Freuchie, or off B936 on Lathrisk Road at Newton of Falkland.

NEW

· *Alzheimer's Research UK*

Scotland's Gardens
Scheme welcomes all
varieties of gardens

Fife

18 **LINDORES HOUSE**
By Newburgh KY14 6JD
Mr and Mrs R Turcan
T: 01337 840369
....

Lindores House, overlooking the Loch. Woodland walk beside the loch and stunning views from the garden. Herbaceous borders, rhododendrons and species tress including *Nothofagus* and *Davidia involucrata*, the handkerchief tree.

Open: Sunday 18 February, 11:30am - 3pm for the Snowdrop Festival. Also open Sunday 27 May, 2pm - 5pm. Admission £4.00, children free (Sunday 18 February) and £5.00, children free (Sunday 27 May). Snowdrop opening with soup (11:30-3). Plant sale with *Leucojum vernum*, snowdrops, tr llium and candelabra primulae and other plants from the garden in season.

Directions: Off A913 two miles east of Newburgh. Bus from Cupar.

· Bumblebee Conservation Trust (Sunday 18 February) & Abdie & Dunbog Parish Church of Scotland (Sunday 27 May)

19 **LOGIE HOUSE**
Crossford, Dunfermline KY12 8QN
Mr and Mrs Jonathan Hunt
T: 07867 804020
....

Central to the design of this walled garden is a path through a double mixed border. Long rows of vegetables and fruit also contribute to colour and design when seen from the house and terrace. A long border of repeat flowering roses and rose and annual beds contribute to an extended season of colour and interest. There is a magnificent and very productive Mackenzie & Moncur greenhouse in excellent condition with fully working vents and original benches and central heating system. The garden is surrounded by a belt of mixed woodland with walks.

Open: Open by arrangement 1 May - 30 September (not Wednesdays, Saturdays & Sundays), admission £5.00, children free. Dogs welcome outwith the walled garden.

Directions: M90 exit 1 for Rosyth and Kincardine Bridge (A985). After about two miles turn right to Crossford. At traffic lights, turn right and the drive is on the right at the end of the village main street.

· Scottish Veterans Residences

20 **LUCKLAW HOUSE**
Logie, Cupar KY15 4SJ
Kate and Robert Campbell
E: katie.elliott@btopenworld.com
....

Large country garden set on a challenging north facing slope that drops steeply down to a burn, backed by woodland. The planting around the house is grassy and naturalistic, leading to mixed borders planted for scent, and a woodland garden.

Open: 6 June – 25 July (Wednesdays only), 2pm - 5pm, admission £5.00, children free.

Directions: From A92, take turning signposted *Logie* for two miles up the hill. From A914, follow signpost to *Logie at Thai Teak*, turning right at top of hill. Please park on the verge outside the garden wall.

· Medicines sans Frontieres (UK)

Fife

NEWTON MAINS AND NEWTON BARNS
21

Auchtermuchty KY14 7HR
Ruth and Tony Lear and John and Jess Anderson
T: 01337 827345

Newton Mains Confronted with the challenge of an exposed south facing site, visited frequently by deer and hares in search of a tasty snack, sheltered areas have been created and planted with a variety of trees, shrubs and perennials. Curving dry stone walls outline beds, pathways and seating areas that merge into the naturalised field. Wonderful views across the Eden Valley to the Lomond Hills.

Newton Barns The borders at Newton Barns are planted with choice shrubs, trees and rhododendrons. Central to the garden is a huge rockery and stream. Sweeping lawns and generous borders slope towards Pitmedden Wood and there are breathtaking views across the top of the garden towards the Lomond Hills.

Open: Saturday/Sunday, 9/10 June, 11am - 4pm, admission £6.00, children free.

Directions: On A91 from Cupar turn right in Auchtermuchty on to B936. Follow SGS signs.

· *Diabetes UK*

Newton Mains

Fife

22

OLD INZIEVAR HOUSE
Oakley, Dunfermline KY12 8HA
Mr and Mrs Tim Hall
T: 07711 368574 E: elizabethhall06@btinternet.com
....

A recently restored walled garden with lime walk, herbaceous borders, knot garden, rose gardens, fruit trees and a small amount of vegetables. Lovely views over the lower south facing wall.

Open: Saturday/Sunday, 9/10 June, 11am - 5:30pm. Also open by arrangement 1 June - 30 June. Admission £5.00, children free.

Directions: A985 heading west for Kincardine Bridge turn right at sign to Oakley 2 miles after Cairneyhill roundabout. After ½ mile take a right turn to Linvid Pet Hotel. Bus to Oakley. Follow SGS signs.

· *Church of the Holy Name, Oakley*

Opening your
garden is a fun and
rewarding experience

23

ROSEWELLS
Pitscottie KY15 5LE
Birgitta and Gordon MacDonald
E: birgittamac@hotmail.co.uk
....

Rosewells, designed by the garden owners, has developed over the last 20 years with an underlying theme that each part of the garden should work in relation to the rest to create one overall effect. The design centres on texture and foliage to provide a lively effect with structure and shape all year. The winter 'bones' are provided with trees and shrubs with features such as contorted stems and peeling or coloured bark. In spring and summer, texture and coloured foliage of shrubs and perennials add to the overall design. Birgitta sees flowers as an added bonus with scent and colour being important and combinations of yellow, blue and white colour schemes are preferred. The garden has many varieties of cornus, magnolias, trilliums, meconopsis, agapanthus, rhododendrons, primulas, auriculas, fritillaries, erythroniums, peonies and acers which are favourites.

Open: Open by arrangement 1 April - 30 September, admission £4.00, children free. Children are welcome.

Directions: B940 between Pitscottie and Peat Inn, one mile from Pitscottie. Rosewells is the ochre coloured house.

· *Save the Children UK*

Fife

24

SOUTH FLISK
Blebo Craigs, Cupar KY15 5UQ
Mr and Mrs George Young
T: 01334 850859 E: julia@standrewspottery.co.uk
W: www.standrewspottery.co.uk

A flooded former quarry forms the centrepiece of the enchanting three acre garden at South Flisk. There are spectacular views of north Fife and beyond. Boulders, cliffs and the many big, mature trees form a backdrop for all manner of spring bulbs, rhododendrons, magnolias, azaleas, and carpets of colourful primulas while the woodland area sports meconopsis, trilliums, podophyllums and some beautiful hellebores. At the front of the house (a former smiddy) is a charming, mature walled garden with traditional cottage garden planting.

Open: Open by arrangement 1 May - 15 June, admission £5.00, children free.

Directions: Six miles west of St Andrews off the B939 between Strathkinness and Pitscottie. There is a small stone bus shelter opposite the road into the village and a small sign saying Blebo Craigs. Or check out the map on our website. Bus to Blebo Craigs.

· *Wateraid*

25

ST FORT WOODLAND GARDEN
St Fort Farm, Newport-on-Tay DD6 8RE
Mr and Mrs Andrew Mylius
T: 07974 083110
W: www.stfort.co.uk

Inspired by a visit to Ruskin's house and woodland garden at Brantwood. Azaleas and specimen rhododendrons are the principal plants as the acid soil within the wood makes them ideal, along with ability to withstand roe deer browsing. The rhododendrons include a wide selection of both specimen and hybrids. Azaleas are mainly *Azalea pontica* chosen for scent and autumn colour. Around 30 acres, Northwood is home to red squirrels, and offers spectacular views northwards over the River Tay. Also of interest are eucryphia, cercidiphyllum, tulip tree, various red acers, rowans, liquidambar, metasequoia and magnolias. Spectacular late autumn foliage.

Open: Open by arrangement 1 May - 30 November, admission £4.00, children free.

Directions: 1¾ miles south of the Tay Road Bridge off the A92, between the Forgan and Five Roads roundabouts. St Fort is approached with a woodland walk of about 400 metres from the car park and garden entrance.

· *Brooke Action for Working Horses & Donkeys*

26

STRATHMIGLO VILLAGE GARDENS
Fife KY14 7PX
The Gardeners of Strathmiglo
T: 01337 860213

Strathmiglo lies under the beautiful West Lomond Hill and the river Eden runs through the village. A selection of lovely gardens will be on display covering many styles: open aspect, mature trees, walled and courtyard, cottage gardens, vegetable, topiary and herbaceous borders.

Fife

Open: Sunday 24 June, 1pm - 5pm, admission £5.00, children free. Parking, tickets and maps, and homemade teas available at the Village Hall. Parking overflow spaces nearby.

Directions: Off the A91 to St Andrews and two miles west of Auchtermuchty, enter village from either the east or the west end and follow signs to the parking areas.

· *Alzheimer Scotland*

Tayport Gardens

27

TAYPORT GARDENS
Tayport DD6 9HX
The Gardeners of Tayport
E: admin@tayportgarden.org

Several gardens in this historic harbour town will be open in the afternoon. Explore a lovely selection of town gardens in a variety of styles, many of them featuring old fruit trees. Wonderful views across the Tay. Tayport was awarded Gold in the *2017 Beautiful Fife* competition, with Tayport Community Garden (one of the gardens to visit) given the *Judge's Prize* and also short listed for the *RSPB's Nature of Scotland Awards*. The Community Garden is run by PLANT - Tayport's Community Trust's garden group.

Open: Sunday 22 July, 1pm - 5pm, admission £5.00, children free. Tickets and maps are available at all the gardens which will be clearly signposted. Refreshments available at the Harbour Cafe.

Directions: South of the Tay Road Bridge, take the B946 to Tayport.

· *Tayport Community Trust*

Fife

28

THE TOWER
1 Northview Terrace, Wormit DD6 8PP
Peter and Angela Davey
T: 01382 541635 M: 07768 406946 E: adavey541@btinternet.com

Situated four miles south of Dundee, this one acre Edwardian landscaped garden has panoramic views over the River Tay. Set on a hill, a series of paths meander around ponds and a small stream, rockeries featuring hellebores and low level planting, a curved lawn and larger borders. Original woodland paths lead to a granite grotto with waterfall pool. At the rear of the house the vegetable garden features raised beds made from granite sets. We have recently removed rhododendrons to create more space for seating and flower beds.

Open: Saturday 11 August, 12pm - 5pm. Also open by arrangement 1 April - 30 September. Admission £4.00, children free. Homemade teas on request for arranged visits.

Directions: From B946 park on Naughton Road outside Spar shop and walk up path on left following signs.

· *Stop and Talk (Fife)*

Encouraging, promoting and supporting garden openings since 1931

29

WILLOWHILL, TAYFIELD AND ST FORT WOODLAND GARDEN
Newport-on-Tay DD6 8RA
Eric Wright and Sally Lorimore, Mr and Mrs William Berry, and Mr & Mrs Andrew Mylius
T: 01382 542890 E: e.g.wright@dundee.ac.uk

Willowhill DD6 8RA: An evolving three acre garden. The house is surrounded by a series of mixed borders designed with different vibrant colour combinations for effect all season. Spectacular tulips planted through the wide borders are a highlight in the spring.
Tayfield House DD6 8RA: A wide variety of shrubs and fine trees, many to mark celebrations of the family who have lived here for over 200 years. Large tree rhododendrons and wonderful views over the Tay.
St Fort Woodland Garden DD6 8RE: A beautiful selection of rhododendrons and azaleas planted over 30 acres amongst specimen trees including eucryphia, acers, liquidambar, metasequoia and magnolias. A rich home for wildlife.

Open: Sunday 13 May, 1pm - 5pm, admission £5.00, children free. Plant sale at Willowhill. St Fort is approached by a woodland walk of 400 metres from the car park and garden entrance.

Directions: Willowhill and Tayfield: 1½ miles south of Tay Road Bridge, take the B995 to Newport off the Forgan roundabout. St Fort: 1¾ miles south of the Tay Road Bridge off the A92, between the Forgan and Five Roads roundabouts.

· *Forgan Arts Centre SCIO*

Fife

The Tower

30 **WORMISTOUNE HOUSE**
Crail KY10 3XH
Baron and Lady Wormiston
T: Katherine Taylor, Head Gardener 07905 938449 E: ktaylor.home@googlemail.com

....

The 17th century tower house and gardens have been painstakingly restored over the last 20 years. The walled garden is a series of 'rooms', including a wildlife meadow bursting with fritillaries, cowslips and primroses, productive potager, magical Griselinia garden, wildlife ponds and rill, and recently planted mid and late season perennial borders. The garden's backbone is the splendid midsummer herbaceous border peaking in early July. Outside the walled garden, enjoy woodland walks around the newly re-landscaped lochan.

Open: 1 June - 30 September (Tuesdays only), 2pm - 4pm, admission £5.00, children free.

Directions: One mile north of Crail on the A917 Crail to St Andrews road. Crail/St Andrews bus.

· *Maggies Centre: Fife*

GLASGOW & DISTRICT

Scotland's Gardens Scheme 2018 Guidebook is sponsored by INVESTEC WEALTH & INVESTMENT

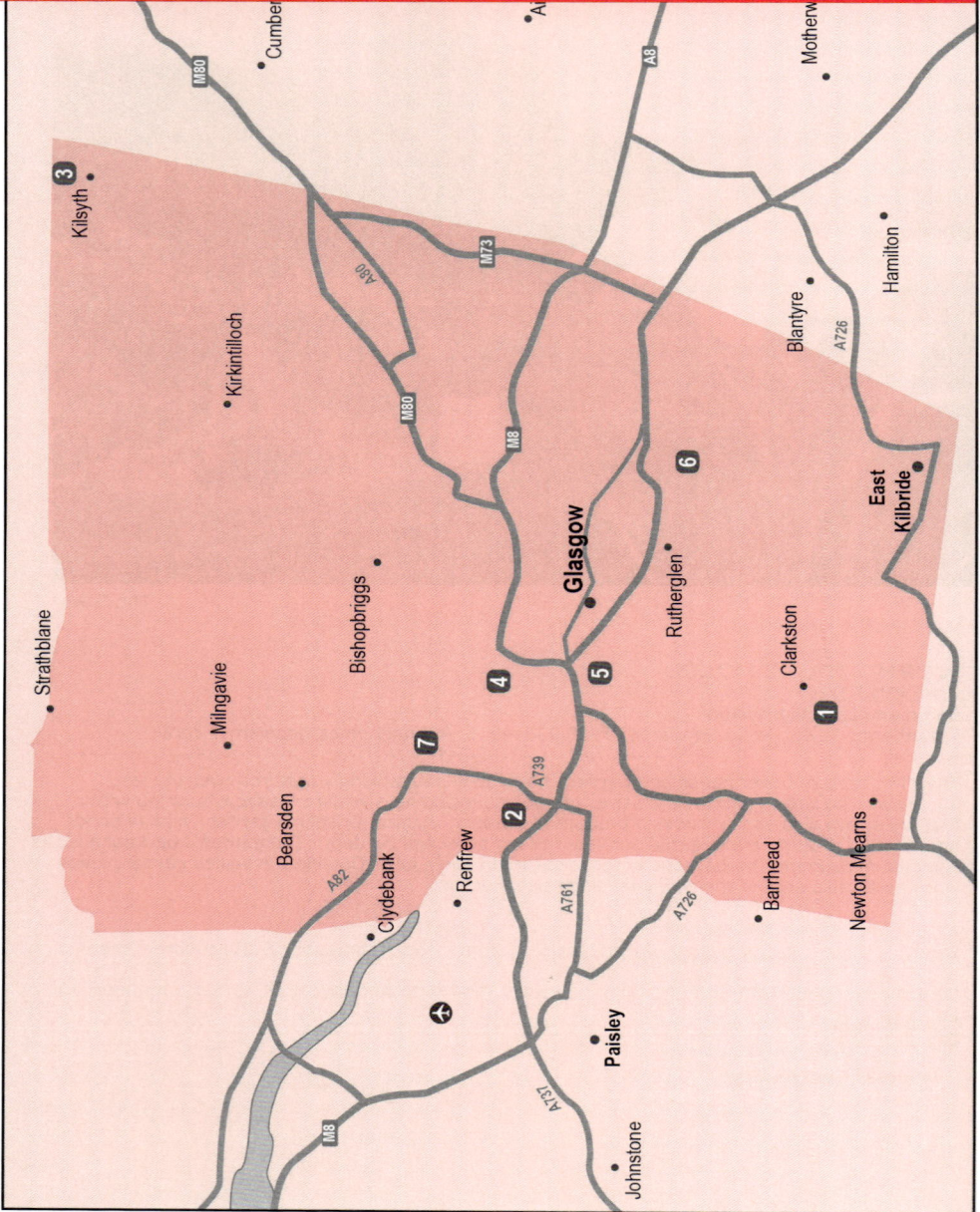

GLASGOW & DISTRICT

OUR VOLUNTEER ORGANISERS

District Organiser	Heidi Stone	0/1 109 Hyndland Road, Glasgow, G12 9JD E: glasgow@scotlandsgardens.org
Area Organisers:	Caroline Anderson	64 Partickhill Road, Glasgow, G11 5NB
	Mandy Hamilton	Springfield, Colintravie, Argyll & Bute, PA22 3AH
	Mary Marshall	14 Hughenden Gardens, Glasgow, G12 9XW
	Audrey Mason	Hillend House, Drakemyre, Dalry, KA24 5JR
	Anne Murray	44 Gordon Road, Netherlee, Glasgow, G44 3TW
Treasurer:	Jim Murray	44 Gordon Road, Netherlee, Glasgow, G44 3TW

GARDENS OPEN ON A SPECIFIC DATE

Kilsyth Gardens, Allanfauld Road, Kilsyth	Sunday, 20 May
Whittingehame Drive Gardens, Glasgow	Sunday, 3 June
Greenbank Garden, Flenders Road, Clarkston	Saturday/Sunday, 9/10 June
Kirklee Circus, 14 Kirklee Circus	Saturday, 9 June
Strathbungo Garden, March Street	Sunday, 1 July
Horatio's Gardens, Queen Elizabeth Hospital	Saturday, 1 September
The Good Life Gardens, 12 & 14 Chatelherault Avenue	Sunday, 2 September

GARDENS OPEN BY ARRANGEMENT

Kilsyth Gardens, Allanfauld Road, Kilsyth	1 April - 30 September

KEY TO SYMBOLS

NEW	New garden		Full wheelchair access		Dogs on leads
	Basic teas		Partial wheelchair access	NPC	National plant collection
H	Homemade teas		Plants for sale		Champion trees
C	Cream teas		Children's activities		Designed landscape
	Refreshments		Accessible by public transport		Snowdrop opening

All our gardens open to raise money for charity. Each opening may nominate a charity(s) to receive up to 60% of the takings and these are included with each listing. The net remaining raised supports our core beneficiaries. Information about our core beneficiaries can be found in the front section of the book. More information about our charity scheme and our symbols can be found in the back foldout section of the book under 'Tips for Using Your Guidebook'.

Glasgow & District

1

GREENBANK GARDEN
Flenders Road, Clarkston G76 8RB
The National Trust for Scotland
T: 0141 616 5126 E: greenbankgarden@nts.org.uk
W: www.nts.org.uk/property/greenbank-garden
....

An unique walled garden with plants and designs of particular interest to suburban gardeners.
There is also a fountain and a woodland walk.
National Plant Collection: *Bergenia* cvs. & spp.

Open: Saturday/Sunday, 9/10 June, 11am - 4:30pm, admission details can be found on the
garden's website.   Annual schools' wheelbarrow competition and treasure hunt. Come along
and vote for your favourite wheelbarrow, decorated by local school children. There will also
be a children's treasure hunt round the garden with prizes. Dogs on leads are welcome in
the woodland, only assistance dogs are allowed in the garden. There is no disabled access to
Greenbank House but there is full access to the garden. There is a tearoom on site for light lunches
and refreshments.

Directions: Flenders Road, off Mearns Road, Clarkston. Off M77 and A727, follow signs for East
Kilbride to Clarkston Toll. Bus 4a, Glasgow to Newton Mearns. Rail - Clarkston station 1¼ miles.
w Buses - 4 and 4a, Glasgow to Newton Mearns. Rail - Clarkston Station 1¼ miles.

· *Donation to SGS Beneficiaries*

2

HORATIO'S GARDENS
Queen Elizabeth Hospital G51 4TF
Horatio's Gardens
E: sallie@horatiosgarden.org.uk
W: Horatiosgarden.org.uk
....

Opened in 2016, award winning Horatio's Garden at the Scottish National Spinal Unit, was
designed by acclaimed garden designer and RHS judge, James Alexander-Sinclair. Visit to see how
this high profile national charity creates cleverly designed, contemporary, accessible gardens in the
heart of the NHS.

Open: Saturday 1 September, 2pm - 5pm, admission £6.00, children free. Guests will be guided
around on tours by the knowledgeable Head Gardener and volunteer team.

Directions: From the east or west of the city: On the M8 motorway to Junction 25, follow signs
for the Clyde Tunnel (A739) for ¾ mile, then follow signs for the Queen Elizabeth Hospital. Turn
left into Govan Road and the hospital is on the left. From north of the River Clyde: Go through the
Clyde tunnel (A739) and follow signs for the hospital.

· *Horatio's Garden*

**Many of our gardens
run children's activities
for younger visitors**

Glasgow & District

3

KILSYTH GARDENS
Allanfauld Road, Kilsyth G65 9DE
Mr & Mrs A Patrick and Mr & Mrs George Murdoch
T: 07743 110908 E: alan.patrick3@googlemail.com

Aeolia A third of an acre woodland garden developed since 1960 and designed to have something in flower every month of the year. The garden contains a large variety of mature specimen trees and shrubs, maples, primulas, hardy geraniums and herbaceous plants. Spring bulbs provide early colour and lilies and dahlias provide late season interest. There are a couple of small ponds for wildlife, two greenhouses and a fruit production area. The owners are members of the *Scottish Rhododendron Society* and have a collection of over 100 specimens, some grown from seed. Areas of the garden are often under development to provide something new to see and provide material for the extensive plant sale, which is all homegrown.
Blackmill Across the road from Aeolia, Blackmill is a garden of two parts in that the Garrel Burn runs through the property. On one side is an acre of mature specimen trees, rhododendrons and shrubs on the site of an old waterpowered sickle mill. There is an ornamental pond and a rock pool built into the remains of the mill building. On the other side a further two acres of woodland glen with paths along the Garrel Burn with views to many cascading waterfalls, one with a seven metre drop. New is a large area of wildflowers alongside the burn, a micro hydro scheme is on view along with many different types of dry stone walls.

Open: Sunday 20 May, 2pm - 5pm. Also open by arrangement 1 April - 30 September. Admission £6.50, children free. Includes entry to both gardens and homemade teas. Well stocked plant stall with a good variety of home grown plants. There is a minimum of six visitors for the By Arrangement openings.

Directions: A803 to Kilsyth, through main roundabout. Turn left into Parkburn Road up to the crossroads. Short walk up Allanfauld Road. Buses - X86 Glasgow-Falkirk, 24 Stirling-Kilsyth, 89 Glasgow-Kilsyth. The 89 service has a stop at the bottom of Allanfauld Road, a couple of minutes walk from the gardens. If extra parking is required the nearby Church of God car park can be used, with a shuttle up the hill to the gardens in place.

· *Strathcarron Hospice*

Primulas at Aeolia, Kilsyth Gardens

Glasgow & District

4

KIRKLEE CIRCUS
14 Kirklee Circus G12 0TW
The Gardeners of Kirklee Circus
T: 07765 769097

Kirklee Circus Garden is a delightful oasis of calm enclosed by a discreet enclave of Victorian houses west of the Botanic Gardens. Over the years a dense circle of 32 lime trees has been reduced to five and replaced in stages with a large variety of interesting plants, many defying the shady location. This process will be continued into the future which will encourage a return visit. Since 2013 a new flower bed and path has been established. To the rear of the villas and terraced houses are the residents' walled gardens, 12 of which will be on show. These display an amazing variety reflecting the aspirations and character of generations of owners as well as present residents.

Open: Saturday 9 June, 1:30pm - 5pm, admission £6.00, children free. Various stalls, entertainment, music and children's activities.

Directions: Enter from Kirklee Road, second on the right from the Great Western Road/ Kirklee Road junction and traffic lights. Parking on Kirklee Road. There are frequent bus services along Great Western Road. Nearest subway station is Hillhead Station on Byres Road. Kirklee Circus is a 10 minute walk from the station, either along Great Western Road or through the Botanic Gardens to the Kirklee Gate.

· Friends Of Glasgow Botanic Gardens, RCS Endowment Trust & Beatson West of Scotland Cancer Centre

5

STRATHBUNGO GARDEN
March Street G41 2PX
Frank Burns

wAn unexpected and interesting terrace, cottage style walled garden in the city, showing what can be turned into a lovely colourful space for all the occupants of the terrace to enjoy. Inventive container planting is a key feature of this distinct urban retreat.

Open: Sunday 1 July, 2pm - 5pm, admission £4.00, children free.

Directions: From the south take the M74 to junction 1A Polmadie. Turn left onto Polmadie Road, then turn right at the next traffic lights onto Calder Street. Proceed to Nithsdale Drive, then turn left into March Street, where ample parking can be found.   From the M8, join the M74 and turn right into Polmadie Road at Junction 1A.

· ALVO Rural South Lanarkshire

6

THE GOOD LIFE GARDENS
12 & 14 Chatelherault Avenue G72 8BJ
Paul & Sheona Brightey and Andy & Amanda Bateman
T: 07894 265469

Two gardens of around a third of an acre each.
12 Chatelherault Avenue The front garden of no. 12 is split into a gravel garden and a small white woodland garden. Go through the gate and you will find a garden the aim of which is to grow as many different edibles as possible, herbs, fruit arches, vegetable beds and edible hedging. There are herbaceous perennials and a cut flower bed, a wildlife pond, a pizza oven and around the corner a food smoker.

Glasgow & District

14 Chatelherault Avenue An established garden that has been revived since the owners arrived three years ago. As the overgrowth was removed more and more beautiful surprises emerged. The garden is now a lovely calm sanctuary, artistically planted with a wide range of herbaceous perennials surrounded by beautiful trees.

Open: Sunday 2 September, 2pm - 5pm, admission £6.00, children free. As well as homemade teas there will be fresh pizza from the pizza oven, plants and fresh flowers for sale and live music to celebrate the maiden opening of these two gardens.

Directions: M74 Glasgow to Cambuslang at junction two, exit onto Cambuslang Road/A724 towards Rutherglen. At the roundabout, take the first exit and stay on Cambuslang Road/A724. Continue to follow A724. Turn right onto Buchanan Drive, then right onto Richmond Drive. Richmond Drive turns left and becomes Chatelherault Avenue.

· *NAS: Glasgow*

WHITTINGEHAME DRIVE GARDENS
Glasgow G12 0XS
The Gardeners of Whittingehame Drive

The gardens are well established and have good displays of mature shrubs and varied planting.
5a and 5 Whittingehame Drive (Jock & Margaret Fleming and Jane and Pete Craig): The soil is well suited to camellias, magnolias, poppies, heathers and there is extensive herbaceous planting. With a waterfall and small pond surrounded by water loving plants it is an oasis within the West End.
12 Whittingehame Drive (Mike and Gill Craig): The smallest of the Whittingehame gardens, originally laid out in the early 1900's after the house was built. The front garden contains a very colourful variety of spring flowering shrubs. The small private back garden was re-modelled in 2011 when two patios and raised beds were created. A selection of flowering shrubs, herbaceous plants and pots create a colourful palette from early spring to late autumn.
20 Whittingehame Drive G12 0XS (Bob and Connie Simpson): A delightful and intriguing small town garden with lots of surprises. Colourful shrubs and flowers include enkianthus, eucrivia, philadelphus, rhododendrons and corsican broom. Shrub and climbing roses include rosa mundi and the apothecary's rose. A herb garden, raised beds, a chamomile seat and an impressive, flourishing fig tree. A breakfast patio with hostas, hanging baskets, window boxes and a green wall with ivy, clematis, honeysuckle and flowering annuals. Look for the novel way to grow a fig tree.
22 Whittingehame Drive (Robert and Helen Jamieson): The garden was laid out in the 1960s by a *Beechgrove Garden* presenter. A strong structure of garden rooms, some overlapping, prevails. The soil is well worked clay, ericaceous plants abound, poppies and meconopsis feature with about 40 clematis often used in companion planting. Much use is made of pots displaying Asiatic and oriental lilies, alliums, begonias and garlic. A cedar greenhouse contains cacti succulents and is used for growing vegetables, tomatoes and chilies. See how many of the 40 clematis you can find and identify.

Open: Sunday 3 June, 2pm - 5pm, admission £6.50, children free. There will be a well stocked plant stall at 22 Whittingehame Drive. Homemade cakes and teas will be served at 5 Whittingehame Drive.

Directions: Take the M8 junction exit 17; From A82 (Great Western Road), past Gartnavel Hospital and the next left is Whittingehame Drive.

· *Vine Trust & Franciscan Missionaries of the Divine Motherhood*

INVERNESS, ROSS, CROMARTY & SKYE

Scotland's Gardens Scheme 2018 Guidebook is sponsored by INVESTEC WEALTH & INVESTMENT

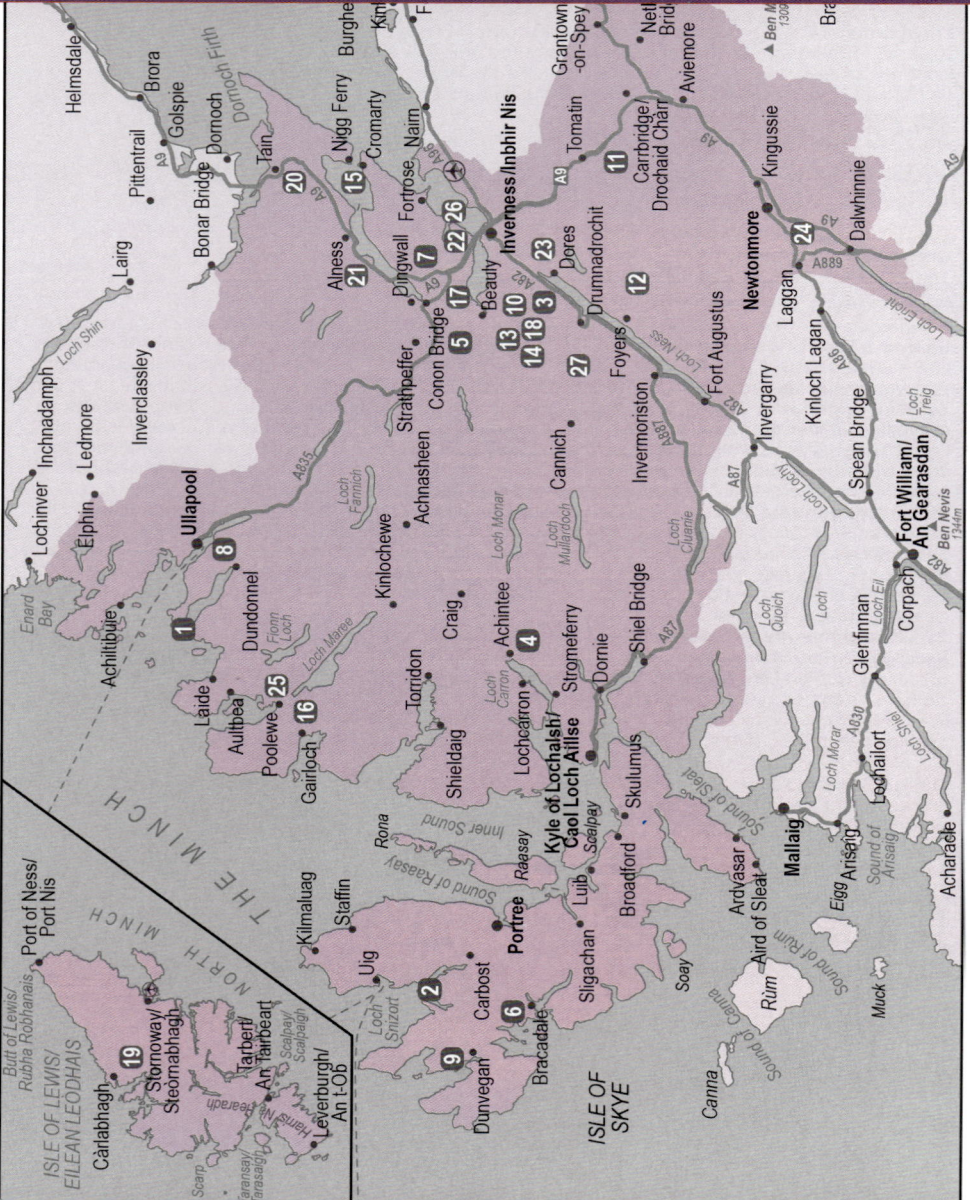

INVERNESS, ROSS, CROMARTY & SKYE

OUR VOLUNTEER ORGANISERS

District Organiser:	Lucy Lister-Kaye	House of Aigas, Aigas, Beauly, IV4 7AD E: inverness@scotlandsgardens.org
Area Organiser:	Emma MacKenzie	Glenkyllachy, Tomatin, IV13 7YA
Treasurer:	Sheila Kerr	Lilac Cottage, Struy, By Beauly, IV4 7JU

GARDENS OPEN ON A SPECIFIC DATE

Dundonnell House, Little Loch Broom, Wester Ross	Thursday, 12 April
Storytelling at Inverewe Garden, Poolewe, Achnasheen	Saturday, 12 May
Inverewe Garden and Estate, Poolewe, Achnasheen	Wednesday, 16 May
Old Allangrange, Munlochy	Saturday, 26 May
Hugh Miller's Birthplace Cottage & Museum, Church St, Cromarty	Sunday, 27 May
Novar, Evanton	Sunday, 27 May
Dundonnell House, Little Loch Broom, Wester Ross	Thursday, 31 May
Gorthleck House Garden, Stratherrick	Friday/Saturday, 1/2 June
Inverewe Garden and Estate, Poolewe, Achnasheen	Monday, 4 June
Field House, Belladrum, Beauly	Sunday, 10 June
Glenkyllachy, Tomatin	Sunday, 17 June
House of Aigas and Field Centre, By Beauly	Sunday, 24 June
Torcroft, Balnain, Glenurquhart	Saturday/Sunday, 7/8 July
Malin, Glenaldie, Tain	Saturday/Sunday, 14/15 July
2 Durnamuck, Little Loch Broom, Wester Ross	Sunday, 22 July
Kiltarlity Gardens, Kiltarity	Sunday, 22 July
5 Knott, Clachamish, Portree, Isle of Skye	Sunday, 29 July
House of Aigas and Field Centre, By Beauly	Sunday, 29 July
Dundonnell House, Little Loch Broom, Wester Ross	Thursday, 16 August
Old Allangrange, Munlochy	Saturday, 18 August
2 Durnamuck, Little Loch Broom, Wester Ross	Sunday, 19 August
Kilcoy Castle, Redcastle, by Muir of Ord	Sunday, 19 August
2 Durnamuck, Little Loch Broom, Wester Ross	Sunday, 9 September
Glenkyllachy, Tomatin	Sunday, 7 October

Inverness, Ross, Cromarty & Skye

GARDENS OPEN REGULARLY

Highland Liliums, 10 Loaneckheim, Kiltarlity	Daily
Oldtown of Leys Garden, Inverness	Daily
Abriachan Garden Nursery, Loch Ness Side	1 February - 30 November
Dunvegan Castle and Gardens, Isle of Skye	1 April - 15 October
Attadale, Strathcarron	1 April - 28 October
Leathad Ard, Upper Carloway, Isle of Lewis	1 May - 30 September (not Sundays)
Balmeanach House, Balmeanach, near Struan, Isle of Skye	1 May - 6 October (Tuesdays & Fridays)
The Lookout, Kilmuir, North Kessock	1 May - 31 August (Sundays only)
5 Knott, Clachamish, Portree, Isle of Skye	28 June - 14 September (Thurs & Fridays)
Torcroft, Balnain, Glenurquhart	1 July - 31 August (Mondays & Tuesdays)

GARDENS OPEN BY ARRANGEMENT

Novar, Evanton	On request
Aultgowrie Mill, Aultgowrie, Urray, Muir of Ord	1 February - 1 September
2 Durnamuck, Little Loch Broom, Wester Ross	1 April - 30 September
5 Knott, Clachamish, Portree, Isle of Skye	1 April - 31 October
Dundonnell House, Little Loch Broom, Wester Ross	1 April - 31 October (not Saturdays & Sundays)
Leathad Ard, Upper Carloway, Isle of Lewis	1 April - 30 April
House of Aigas and Field Centre, By Beauly	1 April - 31 October
The Lookout, Kilmuir, North Kessock	1 May - 31 August
Glenkyllachy, Tomatin	1 May - 30 October
Shanvall, Glentruim, Newtonmore	1 June - 30 August
Brackla Wood, Culbokie, Dingwall	1 July - 31 July

KEY TO SYMBOLS

NEW	New garden		Full wheelchair access		Dogs on leads
	Basic teas		Partial wheelchair access	NPC	National plant collection
H	Homemade teas		Plants for sale		Champion trees
C	Cream teas		Children's activities		Designed landscape
	Refreshments		Accessible by public transport		Snowdrop opening

All our gardens open to raise money for charity. Each opening may nominate a charity(s) to receive up to 60% of the takings and these are included with each listing. The net remaining raised supports our core beneficiaries. Information about our core beneficiaries can be found in the front section of the book. More information about our charity scheme and our symbols can be found in the back foldout section of the book under 'Tips for Using Your Guidebook'.

Inverness, Ross, Cromarty & Skye

2 DURNAMUCK

Little Loch Broom, Wester Ross IV23 2QZ
Will Soos and Susan Pomeroy
T: 01854 633761 E: sueandwill@icloud.com

Our garden is situated on the edge of Little Loch Broom and is south east facing. It is a coastal plantsman's garden with a rich mix of herbaceous borders, trees and shrubs, vegetables, drystone wall planting, South African plants, Mediterranean plants, wild meadow and stunning views. Many of the plants have been collected from all over the world and growing them in Durnamuck has provided the obvious challenges but with an overall pleasing outcome. We were lucky enough to be featured on *Gardener's World* in 2016 and *Garden Magazine* and *Country Life* in 2017.

Open: Sunday 22 July, 12pm - 5pm. Also open Sunday 19 August, 12pm - 5pm. And open Sunday 9 September, 12pm - 5pm. And open by arrangement 1 April - 30 September. Admission £4.00, children free. Homemade teas on 19 August and 9 September only.

Directions: On the A832, between Dundonnell and Ullapool. Take the turning along the single track road signed *Badcaul*, continue to the yellow salt bin, turn right, go to the bottom of the hill and it's the house with the red roof. There is parking down by the house if needed.

· *Target Ovarian Cancer (Sunday 22 July & 1 April - 30 September), Research project: Unique Understanding Chromosome Disorders (Sunday 19 August & 1 April - 30 September) & Dementia Research UK (Sunday 9 September & 1 April - 30 September)*

5 KNOTT

Clachamish, Portree, Isle of Skye IV51 9NZ
Brian and Joyce Heggie
T: 01470 582213 E: jbheggie@hotmail.co.uk

An informal, organic garden on a gently sloping ½ acre site. Perimeter hedging has enabled a sheltered, tranquil oasis to be created. Winding paths meander through densely planted borders filled with a diverse range of perennials, annuals and shrubs. The house overlooks a sheltered bay with regular sightings of otters, sea eagles and harbour porpoises. There is a separate vegetable and herb area with raised beds. Garden seating in several locations. The garden is situated in an easily reached, particularly quiet and scenic area of Skye.

Open: Sunday 29 July, 2pm - 5pm. Also open 28 June - 14 September (Thursdays & Fridays), 2pm - 5pm. And open by arrangement 1 April - 31 October. Admission £3.00, children free. Groups welcome by prior arrangement.

Directions: From Portree, take the A87 to Uig/Dunvegan. After approximately three miles, take the A850 towards Dunvegan. Six miles on, past the Treaslane sign, look for the red phonebox on the right. Turn right on the bend at the signpost for Knott.

· *Crossroads Care Skye & Lochalsh*

Scotland's Gardens Scheme welcomes all varieties of gardens

Inverness, Ross, Cromarty & Skye

3

ABRIACHAN GARDEN NURSERY
Loch Ness Side IV3 8LA
Mr and Mrs Davidson
T: 01463 861232 E: info@lochnessgarden.com
W: www.lochnessgarden.com

This is an outstanding garden with over four acres of exciting plantings with winding paths through native woodlands. Seasonal highlights include snowdrops, hellebores, primulas, meccnopsis, hardy geraniums and colour themed summer beds. Views over Loch Ness.

Open: 1 February - 30 November, 9am - 7pm, admission £3.00, children free.

Directions: On the A82 Inverness/Drumnadrochit road, approximately eight miles south of Inverness.

· *Highland Hospice*

4

ATTADALE
Strathcarron IV54 8YX
Mr and Mrs Ewen Macpherson
T: 01520 722603 E: info@attadalegardens.com
W: www.attadalegardens.com

The Gulf Stream, surrounding hills and rocky cliffs, create a microclimate for 20 acres of outstanding water gardens, old rhododendrons, unusual trees and a fern collection in a geodesic dome. There is also a sunken fern garden developed on the site of an early 19th century drain, a waterfall into a pool with dwarf rhododendrons, sunken garden, peace garden and kitchen garden. Other features include a conservatory, Japanese garden, sculpture collection and giant sundial.

Open: 1 April - 28 October (Monday - Saturday), 10am - 5:30pm, (Sundays), 2pm - 5pm. Admission £8.00, children £1.00. OAP's £6.00. Wheelchair users plus one carer free. Disabled car parking by the main house. Self service teas.

Directions: On the A890 between Strathcarron and South Strome.

· *Strathcarron Project & Strathcarron Project Ltd Development Fund*

5

AULTGOWRIE MILL
Aultgowrie, Urray, Muir of Ord IV6 7XA
Mr and Mrs John Clegg
T: 01997 433699 E: john@johnclegg.com

Aultgowrie Mill is an 18th century converted water mill set in gardens, river and woodlands of 13 acres. Features include a wooded island, a half acre wildflower meadow and a wildlife pond, all with outstanding views of the surrounding hills. The maturing gardens have terraces, lawns, two mixed orchards and raised vegetable beds with glasshouse and a third of a mile river walk. The *Beechgrove Garden* featured this garden in July 2014.

Open: Open by arrangement 1 February - 1 September, admission £4.50, children free. Teas are available by arrangement.

Directions: From the south, turn left at Muir of Ord Distillery, Aultgowrie Mill is 3.2 miles. From the north and west, after Marybank Primary School, Aultgowrie Mill is 1.7 miles up the hill.

· *RNLI*

Inverness, Ross, Cromarty & Skye

BALMEANACH HOUSE

Balmeanach, near Struan, Isle of Skye IV56 8FH
Mrs Arlene Macphie
T: 01470 572320 E: info@skye-holiday.com
W: www.skye-holiday.com

During the late 1980s, a third of an acre of croft land was fenced in to create a garden. Now there is a glorious herbaceous border, bedding plants area and a small azalea/rhododendron walk. In addition, there is a woodland dell with fairies, three ponds and a small shrubbery. Lots of seating areas are provided and visitors are welcome to rest, or even picnic, remembering, please to take all litter away.

Open: 1 May - 6 October (Tuesdays & Fridays), 10:30am - 3pm, admission £3.00, children free.

Directions: A87 to Sligachan, turn left, Balmeanach is five miles north of Struan and five miles south of Dunvegan.

· *Scottish SPCA*

Herbeceous border at Balmeanach House

BRACKLA WOOD

Culbokie, Dingwall IV7 8GY
Susan and Ian Dudgeon
T: 01349 877765 E: susmadud@gmail.com

Mature one acre plot consisting of woodland, wildlife features, ponds, mixed borders, a kitchen garden, rockery and mini-orchard. Spring bulbs and hellebores, rhododendrons, wisteria and roses followed by crocosmia, clematis and deciduous trees provide continuous colour and interest throughout the seasons. There is always the chance to see red squirrels.

Open: Open by arrangement 1 July - 31 July, admission £3.00, children free.

Directions: From the north, take the A9 turn to Culbokie. At the end of the village, turn right to Munlochy. A mile up the road, turn right into *No Through Road* to Upper Braefindon.
From the south, take the A9 to Munlochy. At the end of the village, turn right and then sharp left up road signposted *Culbokie and Killen*. After about 4½ miles turn left onto road signposted *Upper Braefindon*. Brackla Wood is the first house on the left.

· *Macmillan Cancer Support: Black Isle*

Inverness, Ross, Cromarty & Skye

8 **DUNDONNELL HOUSE**
Little Loch Broom, Wester Ross IV23 2QW
Dundonnell Estates
T: 07789 390028

Camellias, magnolias and bulbs in spring, rhododendrons and laburnum walk in this ancient walled garden. Exciting planting in new borders gives all year colour centred around one of the oldest yew trees in Scotland.   A new water sculpture, midsummer roses, restored Edwardian glasshouse, riverside walk, arboretum - all in the valley below the peaks of An Teallach. Champion Trees: Yew and Holly.

Open: Thursdays 12 April, 31 May and 16 August, 2pm - 5pm. And open by arrangement 1 Apri - 31 October (not Saturdays & Sundays). Admission £3.50, children free. Homemade teas are only available on 31 May

Directions: Turn off the A835 at Braemore on to the A832. After 11 miles take the Badralloch turn for ½ mile.

· *Save the Elephant & David Nott Foundation*

**We've raised over
£1 million for charity
in the last five years**

9 **DUNVEGAN CASTLE AND GARDENS**
Isle of Skye IV55 8WF
Hugh Macleod of Macleod
T: 01470 521206 E: info@dunvegancastle.com
W: www.dunvegancastle.com

Five acres of formal gardens dating from the 18th century. In contrast to the barren moorland of Skye, the gardens are an oasis featuring an eclectic mix of plants, woodland glades, shimmering pools fed by waterfalls and streams flowing down to the sea. After the water garden with its ornate bridges and islands replete with a rich and colourful plant variety, wander through the elegant surroundings of the formal round garden. The walled garden is worth a visit to see its colourful herbaceous borders and recently added Victorian style glasshouse. In what was formerly the castle's vegetable garden, there is a garden museum and a diverse range of plants and flowers which complement the features including a waterlily pond, a neoclassical urn and a larch pergola. Replanting and landscaping has taken place over the last 30 years to restore and develop the gardens.

Open: 1 April - 15 October, 10am - 5:30pm, admission £12.00, children £7.00. OAP's £9.00

Directions: One mile from Dunvegan Village, 23 miles west of Portree. Follow the signs for Dunvegan Castle.

· *Donation to SGS Beneficiaries*

Inverness, Ross, Cromarty & Skye

10 **FIELD HOUSE**
Belladrum, Beauly IV4 7BA
Mr and Mrs D Paterson
W: www.dougthegarden.co.uk

An informal country garden in a one acre site with mixed borders, ponds and some unusual plants - a plantsman's garden. Featured in *The Beechgrove Garden*.

Open: Sunday 10 June, 2pm - 4:30pm, admission £4.00, children free.

Directions: Four miles from Beauly on the A833 Beauly to Drumnadrochit road, then follow signs to Belladrum.

· *Highland Disability Sport Lochaber: Swim Team*

11 **GLENKYLLACHY**
Tomatin IV13 7YA
Mr and Mrs Philip Mackenzie
E: emmaglenkyllachy@gmail.com

In a magnificent Highland glen, at 1,150ft Glenkyllachy offers a glorious garden of shrubs, herbaceous plants, rhododendrons, trees and spectacular views down the Findhorn River. There are some rare specimens and an embryonic arboretum.   Rhododendrons and bulbs flower in May/June, herbaceous plants bloom through July/August. Experience the wildflower meadow in summer and glorious autumn colours from September. Original sculptures and a Highgrove-inspired wall provide year-round interest. New bronze sculpture and waterfall feature for 2018.

Open: Sundays 17 June and 7 October, 2pm - 5pm. And open by arrangement 1 May - 30 October. Admission £5.00, children free. Includes tea.

Directions: Turn off the A9 at Tomatin and take the Coignafearn/Garbole single track road down the north side of the River Findhorn, there is a cattle grid and gate on the right 500 metres AFTER the humpback bridge and the sign to Farr.

· *Marie Curie*

12 **GORTHLECK HOUSE GARDEN**
Stratherrick IV2 6UJ
Steve & Katie Smith
T: 07710 325903 E: visit@gorthleckgarden.co.uk

An unusual 20 acre woodland garden built in an unlikely place, on and around an exposed rocky ridge. The layout of the garden works with the natural features of the landscape rather than against them, with numerous paths, hedges and shelter belts creating clearly defined spaces that enable a large collection of plants and trees to thrive. It has extensive collections of rhododendrons and bamboos. The ridge offers long views of the surrounding countryside in the 'borrowed landscape' tradition of Japanese gardens. The garden didn't exist a dozen years ago and is very much a work in progress.

Open: Friday/Saturday, 1/2 June, 10am - 9pm, admission £5.00, children free.

Directions: From the A9, join the B862. Go through the village of Errogie where there is a sharp left-hand bend on the road. Approximately one mile after this bend there is a small church on the left. The Gorthleck drive is directly opposite the church and the house can be seen on the hill to the left as you follow the drive (follow it to the left of the new house). Park outside the house on the gravel.

· *Maggies Centre: Highlands*

Inverness, Ross, Cromarty & Skye

13 ### HIGHLAND LILIUMS
10 Loaneckheim, Kiltarlity IV4 7JQ
Neil and Frances Macritchie
T: 01463 741365 E: neil.macritchie@btconnect.com
W: www.highlandliliums.co.uk

A working retail nursery with spectacular views over the Beauly valley and Strathfarrar hills. A wide selection of home grown plants available including alpines, ferns, grasses, herbaceous, herbs, liliums, primulas and shrubs. This garden is also open on a daily basis, see their individual entry for details.

Open: Daily 9am - 5pm. Also open as part of the Kiltarlity Gardens on Sunday 22 July.

Directions: Signposted from Kiltarlity village, which is just off the Beauly to Drumnadrochit road (A833), approximately 12 miles from Inverness.

· *Donation to SGS Beneficiaries*

14 ### HOUSE OF AIGAS AND FIELD CENTRE
By Beauly IV4 7AD
Sir John and Lady Lister-Kaye
T: 01463 782443 E: sheila@aigas.co.uk
W: www.aigas.co.uk

The House of Aigas has a small arboretum of named Victorian specimen trees and modern additions. The garden consists of extensive rockeries, herbaceous borders, ponds and shrubs. Aigas Field Centre rangers lead regular guided walks on nature trails through woodland, moorland and around a loch.
Champion Trees: Douglas fir, Atlas cedar and *Sequoiadendron giganteum*.

Open: Sunday 24 June, 2pm - 5pm. Also open Sunday 29 July, 2pm - 5pm. And open by arrangement 1 April - 31 October (lunches/teas available by request). Admission £4.00, children free. Homemade teas served in the house.

Directions: Four and a half miles from Beauly on the A831 Cannich/Glen Affric road.

· *Highland Hospice: Aird Branch*

15 ### HUGH MILLER'S BIRTHPLACE COTTAGE & MUSEUM
Church Street, Cromarty IV11 8XA
The National Trust for Scotland
T: 01381 600245 E: millersmuseum@nts.org.uk
W: www.nts.org.uk/Visit/Hugh-Millers-Birthplace

Domestic gardens, including the garden of wonders, created in 2008, with its theme of natural history, features fossils, exotic ferns, ornamental letter-cutting and a mystery stone. The sculptural centrepiece of this award-winning small but beautiful area is a scrap metal ammorite created by Helen Denerley. While at the birthplace, see the cobbled courtyard and the garden room - space for reflection and a walk around the garden named after Hugh's wife, Lydia. The crescent-shaped, sandstone path of fragrant climbing roses, herbs and wild plant areas which reflect Miller's own love of nature and curiosity in the natural landscape.

Open: Sunday 27 May, 1pm - 5pm, admission details can be found on the garden's website.

Inverness, Ross, Cromarty & Skye

Directions: By road via Kessock Bridge and A832 to Cromarty. Twenty-two miles north east of Inverness.

🚌

· **Donation to SGS Beneficiaries**

16 INVEREWE GARDEN AND ESTATE
Poolewe, Achnasheen IV22 2LG
The National Trust for Scotland
T: 01445 712952 E: inverewe@nts.org.uk
W: www.nts.org.uk/Property/Inverewe-Garden-and-Estate

Magnificent 54 acre Highland garden, surrounded by mountains, moorland and sea loch. Created by Osgood Mackenzie in the late 19th century, it now includes a wealth of exotic plants from Australian tree ferns to Chinese rhododendrons to South African bulbs. Plantings include a grove of Wollemi pines and other fossil trees.
National Plant Collection: *Olearia, Rhododendron* (subsect. *Barbata*, subsect. *Glischra*, subsect. *Maculifera*).
Champion Trees: Over 20.

Open: Wednesday 16 May, 10am - 5:30pm. Also open Monday 4 June, 10am - 5:30pm. Admission details can be found on the garden's website. 16 May - The Head Gardener's walk will focus on woodland gardening.
4 June - The First Gardener's walk will take in the National Collection plantings.
Meet at the Visitor Centre at 2pm for all walks, please book in advance to avoid disappointment. We have an electric buggy and two wheelchairs that are available to use free of charge. A shop and self-service restaurant are available.

Directions: Signposted on A832 by Poolewe, six miles northeast of Gairloch.

🅗 🍴 ♿ 🌳 NPC

· **Donation to SGS Beneficiaries**

17 KILCOY CASTLE
Redcastle, by Muir of Ord IV6 7RX
Kilcoy Castle Estate
T: 01463 871138

At the front of the castle are steps and grass terraces surrounded by shrubs and trees and the walled garden leads off to the east. The area farthest from the castle was restyled three years ago and s based on the poem *Solitude* by Thomas Merton. The shape is rhomboid with a central point taken from which the design radiates. Pleached hornbeam, under planted with willow. Hawthorn, holly and yew hedges are still to grow to fruition. Work on the first half will start in autumn 2017.

Open: Sunday 19 August, 2pm - 5pm, admission £6.00, children free. Admission price includes teas.

Directions: Take the Muir of Ord road, A832 off Tore roundabout go past Fettes Sawmill on the left. Kilcoy Kindergarten is on the right which is an old church. Turn right at the church heading towards Kilcoy, go along the single road for about ¼ mile and the gates to the castle are on the left.

🅗 ♿ 🐕 NEW

· **ENF; EN Foundation: Elsie Normington Foundation, The Haven Project**

Inverness, Ross, Cromarty & Skye

18 **KILTARLITY GARDENS**
Kiltarity IV4 7JQ
The Gardeners of Kiltarity
....

Aird View 30a Camault Muir, Kiltarlity IV4 7JH (Sheila Ross): A fairly new garden developed over the past two years. Mixed borders and beds, water features and arbour.
Foinaven Loaneckheim, Kiltarlity, Beauly IV4 7JQ (Sue Mullins): The garden at 'Foinaven' is approximately ½ acre in size, and is blessed with several mature Scots Pine trees. The garden is a 'plantaholics' garden with many different varieties of shrubs, trees and herbaceous plants. There is a natural pond and the garden has untamed areas for wildlife and pollinators. Honeybees live here and are well catered for by the selection of plants with flowers for pollen and nectar, and the birds are fed well by the resultant berries.
Highland Liliums 10 Loaneckheim, Kiltarlity IV4 7JQ (Neil and Frances Macritchie): A working retail nursery with spectacular views over the Beauly valley and Strathfarrar hills. A wide selection of home grown plants available including alpines, ferns, grasses, herbaceous, herbs, liliums, primulas and shrubs. This garden is also open on a daily basis, see their individual entry for details.

Open: Sunday 22 July, 12pm - 5pm, admission £3.00, children free. Admission tickets can be purchased at any of the three gardens. Teas and discounted plants at Highland Liliums.

Directions: All Gardens will be signposted from Kiltarlity Village

· *Highland Hospice*

19 **LEATHAD ARD**
Upper Carloway, Isle of Lewis HS2 9AQ
Rowena and Stuart Oakley
T: 01851 643204 E: stuart.oakley1a@gmail.com
W: www.whereveriam.org/leathadard
....

A one acre sloping garden with stunning views over East Loch Roag. It has evolved along with the shelter hedges that divide the garden into a number of areas giving a new view at every corner. With shelter and raised beds, the different conditions created permit a wide variety of plants to be grown.   Beds include herbaceous borders, cutting borders, bog gardens, grass garden, exposed beds, patio, a new pond and vegetable and fruit patches, some of which are grown to show.

Open: 1 May - 30 September (not Sundays), 10am - 6pm. Also open by arrangement 1 April - 30 April. Admission £4.00, children free.

Directions: A858 Shawbost - Carloway. First right after Carloway football pitch. First house on right. The Westside circular bus ex Stornoway to road end and ask for the Carloway football pitch.

· *British Red Cross*

20 **MALIN**
Glenaldie, Tain IV19 1ND
Ivan Brockway
T: 07538 379208 E: ikbrock@btinternet.com
....

The garden has a wide range of trees, shrubs and other plants including alpines, perennials, and a large collection of over 130 roses. In a damp area hostas and primulas grow with many ferns. A pergola has a vine and other climbers including wisteria and jasmine. Rhododendrons and azaleas have been planted in the woodland and main garden. There is a large pond with 60 ducks and geese, and a stream with Rogersia, Gunnera and Meconopsis. The garden also has a polytunnel, greenhouses and an alpine house. The two acre garden was lovingly developed by Ivan and his

Inverness, Ross, Cromarty & Skye

late wife Mary, mostly from a bare farm field, beginning in 1994. Since Mary's death in 2015 Ivan has continued to develop the garden with the help of good friends.

Open: Saturday/Sunday, 14/15 July, 11am - 5pm, admission £3.00, children free. Homemade teas £3.00

Directions: From the south near Tain, on the A9, turn left signposted Glenaldie and Rosemount. Just over ½ a mile along this road at the end of the woodland, the garden entrance is on the left.

· *Highland Hospice*

21 NOVAR

Evanton IV16 9XL
Mr and Mrs Ronald Munro Ferguson
T: 01349 831062 E: enquiries@novarestate.co.uk

Water gardens have been renovated and replanted since the last garden opening. There is a new terrace garden. Five acre walled garden, rhododendrons and azaleas. Newly planted apple orchard.

Open: Sunday 27 May, 2:30pm - 5pm. Also open by arrangement to groups of a minimum of eight people. Admission £6.00, children free.

Directions: Off the B817 between Evanton and junction with A836. Turn west onto the drive to Novar.

· *Diabetes UK: Endowment Fund, Raigmore Hospital*

22 OLD ALLANGRANGE

Munlochy IV8 8NZ
J J Gladwin
T: 01463 811304 E: jayjaygladwin@gmail.com

A 17th century lime washed house is the backdrop to a formal(ish) garden with many fine old trees including an ancient stand of yews. We use sculpted hedges to play with perspective. There is an ice house, vegetable garden, a mound, orchard and two large polytunnels where we grow vegetables biodynamically. We are establishing a nursery where plants attractive to invertebrates are grown. We plant particularly for wildlife so wildflowers and beneficial weeds are encouraged. New beds planted in 2017 along with significant additional planting in the orchard. Champion Trees: Yew.

Open: Saturday 26 May, 10:30am - 5pm. Also open Saturday 18 August, 10:30am - 5pm. Admission £7.50, children free.

Directions: From Inverness head four miles north on the A9, and follow the directions for Black Isle Brewery. Park in the brewery car park and you will be given directions in the shop.

· *Black Isle Bee Gardens*

**Are you snap happy?
Send us your garden
photographs**

Inverness, Ross, Cromarty & Skye

23 ## OLDTOWN OF LEYS GARDEN
Inverness IV2 6AE
David and Anne Sutherland
T: 01463 238238 E: ams@oldtownofleys.com
....

Large garden established in 2003 on the outskirts of Inverness and overlooking the town. Herbaceous beds with lovely rhododendron and azalea displays in spring.   There are specimen trees, three ponds surrounded by waterside planting and a small woodland area. A new rockery area was created in 2015 and is still developing.

Open: Daily, Dawn - Dusk, admission by donation.

Directions: Turn off Southern distributor road (B8082) at Leys roundabout towards Inverarnie (B861). At the T-junction turn right. After 50 metres turn right into Oldtown of Leys.

· *Local Charities*

24 ## SHANVALL
Glentruim, Newtonmore PH20 1BE
George and Beth Alder
T: 01540 673213 E: beth.alder@yahoo.co.uk
....

The garden is two thirds of an acre at 900 ft. above sea level, surrounding a 19th century cottage. On the south side of the River Spey, it has lovely views of the Creag Dubh and Creag Meagaidh mountains. There are ruined buildings of an old township within the garden. To the south is a garden of roses and perennials. Within a stone wall, there are fruit cages, a small orchard and organic vegetable beds which have been cultivated for about 200 years. The garden on the north slopes has trees, shrubs, herbaceous border, wildflowers, a pond and is rich with wildlife, including woodpeckers and red squirrels.

Open: Open by arrangement 1 June - 30 August, admission £5.00, children free. Includes tea.

Directions: Shanvall is on the minor road running along the south side of the Spey, linking the A9 south of Newtonmore at Glentruim and the A889 at Catlodge. The garden gate is on the right about 1½ miles from the A9. Further details on request.

· *Laggan Parish Church*

25 ## STORYTELLING AT INVEREWE GARDEN
Poolewe, Achnasheen IV22 2LG
The National Trust of Scotland
T: 01445 712952 E: inverewe@nts.org.uk
W: www.nts.org.uk/Property/Inverewe-Garden-and-Estate

Once upon a time...

....

Inverewe Garden is a magical place nestling on the shores of Loch Ewe in the rugged North West Highlands- it's an oasis of plants, trees, animals and birds – giving inspiration to many gardeners, artists, poets, musicians and bards over the decades. Traditionally storytellers have been inspired by this amazing place. Inverewe is about building dreams and making them happen. Come and hear many of the stories written over the years, stand at the foot of giants and find out what is the very special spirit of Inverewe.   For more information see Scotland's Gardens Scheme website.
National Plant Collection: *Olearia, Rhododendron* (subsect. *Barbata*, subsect. *Glischra*, subsect. *Maculifera*).
Champion Trees: Over 20.

Inverness, Ross, Cromarty & Skye

Open: Saturday 12 May, 2pm - 5pm, admission £5.00, children free.

Directions: Signposted on A832 by Poolewe, six miles northeast of Gairloch.

· *The National Trust for Scotland: Inverewe*

26 THE LOOKOUT
Kilmuir, North Kessock IV1 3ZG
David and Penny Veitch
T: 01463 731489 E: david@veitch.biz

A ¾ acre elevated coastal garden with incredible views over the Moray Firth which is only for the sure-footed. This award winning garden featured on the *Beechgrove Garden* is created out of a rock base with shallow pockets of ground, planted to its advantage to encourage all aspects of wildlife. There is a small sheltered courtyard, raised bed vegetable area, pretty cottage garden, scree and rock garden, rose arbour, rhododendrons, flowering shrubs, bamboos, trees and lily pond with waterside plants.

Open: 1 May - 31 August (Sundays only), 12pm - 4pm. Also open by arrangement 1 May - 31 August. Admission £3.00, children free.

Directions: From Inverness, take North Kessock left turn from A9, and third left at roundabout to go on underpass then sharp left onto Kilmuir Road. From Tore, take slip road for North Kessock and immediately right for Kilmuir. Follow signs for Kilmuir (three miles) until you reach the shore. The Lookout is near the far end of the village with a large palm tree on the grass in front.

· *Alzheimer Scotland*

27 TORCROFT
Balnain, Glenurquhart IV63 6TJ
Barbara Craig

This garden is about ¾ of an acre on a hillside overlooking Loch Meiklie in Glen Urquhart. It is a wild garden, with its own character and style. There are weeds, cardamine for the orange tip butterflies, a nettle patch, but most of all there are plants in profusion from acer, anemone and astrantia to *Veronicastrum, Verbascum, Weigela* and water lilies. It has a natural stream coming into the garden, meandering into various small ponds. In the spring there are masses of bog primula of all types and colours. There is a fern bed, a rockery, herbs, wooded area. New for 2018 a stumpery, beds and another pond.

Open: Saturday/Sunday, 7/8 July, 2pm - 5pm. Also open 1 July - 31 August (Mondays & Tuesdays), 2pm - 5pm. Admission £3.00, children free. Garden open includes tea on 7/8 July £6.00.

Directions: From Inverness turn right at Drumnadrochit and go towards Cannich.   After four miles, sign *Balnain*, there is a very sharp right-hand bend with a high retaining wall on the right. At the end of the wall take the turning to right signposted *Torcroft Lodges*.

· *Munlochy Animal Aid & Send a Cow*

KINCARDINE & DEESIDE

Scotland's Gardens Scheme 2018 Guidebook is sponsored by INVESTEC WEALTH & INVESTMENT

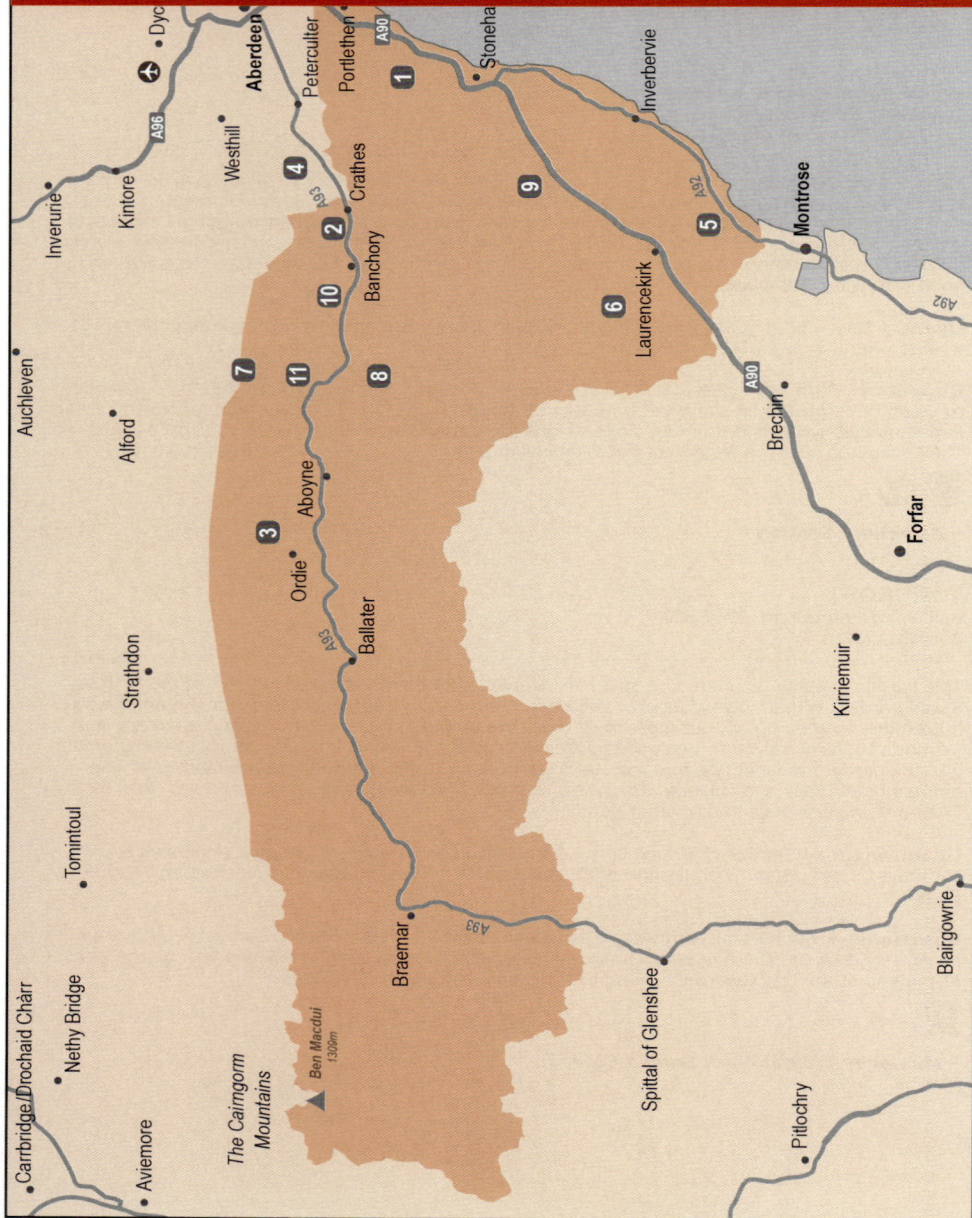

KINCARDINE & DEESIDE

OUR VOLUNTEER ORGANISERS

District Organisers:	Tina Hammond	Sunnybank, 7 Watson Street, Banchory, AB31 5UB
	Julie Nicol	Cedarwood Lodge, Rhu-Na-Haven Rd, Aboyne, AB34 5JB
		E: kincardine@scotlandsgardens.org
Area Organisers:	Wendy Buchan	Inneshewen, Dess, Aboyne, AB31 5BH
	Gavin Farquhar	Ecclesgreig Castle, St Cyrus, DD10 0DP
	Hillary Greensill	Broomhill, Tarland, Aboyne, AB34 4UJ
	Helen Jackson	
	Catherine Nichols	Westerton Steading, Dess, Aboyne, AB34 5AY
	David Younie	Bealltainn, Ballogie, Aboyne, AB34 5DL
	Patsy Younie	Bealltainn, Ballogie, Aboyne, AB34 5DL
Treasurer:	Tony Coleman	Templeton House, Arbroath, DD11 4QP

GARDENS OPEN ON A SPECIFIC DATE

Ecclesgreig Castle, St Cyrus	Sunday, 4 March
Inchmarlo House Garden, Inchmarlo, Banchory	Sunday, 20 May
Kincardine Castle, Kincardine O'Neil	Sunday, 10 June
Ecclesgreig Castle, St Cyrus	Sunday, 17 June
Finzean House, Finzean, Banchory	Sunday, 17 June
Clayfolds, Bridge of Muchalls, Stonehaven	Sunday, 24 June
Drum Castle Garden, Drumoak, by Banchory	Wednesday, 4 July
Drum Castle Garden, Drumoak, by Banchory	Wednesday, 11 July
Douneside House, Tarland	Sunday, 15 July
Drum Castle Garden, Drumoak, by Banchory	Wednesday, 18 July
Findrack, Torphins	Sunday, 22 July
Drum Castle Garden, Drumoak, by Banchory	Wednesday, 25 July
Crathes Castle Garden, Banchory	Saturday, 28 July
Glenbervie House, Drumlithie, Stonehaven	Sunday, 5 August
Fasque House, Fettercairn, Laurencekirk	Sunday, 12 August

Encouraging, promoting and supporting garden openings since 1931

Kincardine & Deeside

KEY TO SYMBOLS

NEW New garden	Full wheelchair access	Dogs on leads
Basic teas	Partial wheelchair access	**NPC** National plant collection
H Homemade teas	Plants for sale	Champion trees
C Cream teas	Children's activities	Designed landscape
Refreshments	Accessible by public transport	Snowdrop opening

All our gardens open to raise money for charity. Each opening may nominate a charity(s) to receive up to 60% of the takings and these are included with each listing. The net remaining raised supports our core beneficiaries. Information about our core beneficiaries can be found in the front section of the book. More information about our charity scheme and our symbols can be found in the back foldout section of the book under 'Tips for Using Your Guidebook'.

Douneside House

Kincardine & Deeside

1 CLAYFOLDS
Bridge of Muchalls, Stonehaven AB39 3RU
Andrea Sinclair

An informal country garden extending to half an acre, with a further six acres of wildflowers, native trees and a pond.   The main garden is laid out with lawn and mixed borders which are filled with shrubs and a wide range of hardy perennials and includes a 'hot' border with various flaxes and a variety of hot coloured plants. Small cottage style garden to the front of the house. Follow the tracks through the recently developed six acre 'wilderness garden' and see what native fauna and flora you can spot.

Open: Sunday 24 June, 12:30pm - 3:30pm, admission £4.00, children free. Children must be accompanied. Children's activity 'A Hunt on the Wildside'.

Directions: SatNav - AB39 3RU but travel inland a further one and a half miles to Clayfolds. Travelling in either direction on the A90, three miles north of Stonehaven, take the road signposted *Netherley 3*, continue travelling inland for approximately one and a half miles and you will then be directed where to park.

· *Scottish SPCA*

Mr Lowry at Clayfolds

2 CRATHES CASTLE GARDEN
Banchory AB31 5QJ
The National Trust for Scotland
T: 01330 844525 E: crathes@nts.org.uk
W: www.nts.org.uk/Visit/Crathes-Castle/

Crathes Castle is a magical turreted castle set within glorious gardens. Wander through the walled garden and admire yew hedges, planted as early as 1702, and spot a rich variety of wildlife along the six trails, including roe deer, red squirrels, woodpeckers, buzzards and herons.
National Plant Collection: *Dianthus Malmaison*.
Champion Trees: Four champions including *Zelkova* x *verschaffeltii*.

Open: Saturday 28 July, Bug Walks at 11am, 1pm and 3pm, children £5.00 (accompanying adult free).   Help us discover Crathes Castle Garden's bugs and beasties. Find out more about our helpful pollinators and meet the mini monsters lurking in the shrubbery. Minibeast walks, opening the moth trap set up from the night before and minibeast crafts. Booking is essential, for details visit the Crathes Garden website.

Directions: On the A93, 15 miles west of Aberdeen and three miles east of Banchory.

· *All proceeds to SGS Beneficiaries*

Kincardine & Deeside

3

DOUNESIDE HOUSE
Tarland AB34 4UD
The MacRobert Trust
W: www.dounesidehouse.co.uk

Douneside is the former home of Lady MacRobert who developed these magnificent gardens in the early to mid 1900s. Ornamental borders and water gardens surround a spectacular infinity lawn overlooking the Deeside hills. A large walled garden supplies vegetables and cut flowers and also houses a large ornamental greenhouse. A new arboretum displays over 130 trees amongst mown grass paths and walking trails behind Douneside which offer breathtaking views across the Howe of Cromar and beyond.

Open: Sunday 15 July, 2pm - 5pm, admission £5.00, children free (concessions £3.00). There will be a local pipe band and raffle.

Directions: B9119 towards Aberdeen. Tarland one mile.

· *Perennial*

4

DRUM CASTLE GARDEN
Drumoak, by Banchory AB31 5EY
The National Trust for Scotland
T: 01330 700334 E: drumcastle@nts.org.uk
W: www.nts.org.uk/Visit/Drum-Castle

The Trust has established a collection of old-fashioned roses which is at its peak for blossom and colour during July. Other garden areas include a pond and bog garden, wildlife meadow, wildlife garden, a cutting garden and new viewing platform and stumpery.

Open: Guided Walks, Wednesdays 4, 11, 18 & 25 July (2pm), admission £5.00, children free. Join the Head Gardener for a walk through the historic rose garden each Wednesday at 2:00pm throughout July. Booking essential via the garden website.

Directions: On the A93, three miles west of Peterculter. Ten miles west of Aberdeen and eight miles east of Banchory.

· *All proceeds to SGS Beneficiaries*

5

ECCLESGREIG CASTLE
St Cyrus DD10 0DP
Mr Gavin Farquhar
T: 01224 214301 E: enquiries@ecclesgreig.com
W: www.ecclesgreig.com

Ecclesgreig Castle, Victorian Gothic on a sixteenth century core, is internationally famous as an inspiration for Bram Stoker's Dracula. The snowdrop walk (150+ varieties of snowdrop) starts at the castle, meanders around the estate, along woodland paths and the pond, ending at the garden. In the Italian balustraded gardens there is a 140 feet long herbaceous border, classical statues and stunning shaped topiary with views across St Cyrus to the sea. Started from a derelict site, development continues. Also to be found in the grounds is the well of St Cyrus.

Open: Sunday 4 March, 1pm - 4pm for the Snowdrop Festival. Also open Sunday 17 June, 1pm - 5pm. Admission £4.00, children free. Children's activities on 17 June.

Kincardine & Deeside

Directions: *Ecclesgreig* will be signposted from the A92 Coast Road and from the A937 Montrose/Laurencekirk Road.

· *AHF (Sunday 4 March), The Architectural Heritage Society of Scotland (Sunday 17 June) & Girl Guiding Montrose (Sunday 4 March & Sunday 17 June)*

6

FASQUE HOUSE
Fettercairn, Laurencekirk AB30 1DN
Mr and Mrs Douglas Dick-Reid
W: www.fasquehouse.co.uk

....

Fasque Castle the former family home of William Gladstone, four times Prime Minister under Queen Victoria, is set deep within its own forested parkland at the end of a drive through a private deer park. The current owners have restored the house to its former glory and the gardens are becoming more stunning each year. Landscaping of the West Garden took place in 2013 with a sunken terrace garden containing a formal pond and a mixture of formal and herbaceous plants. There are some magnificent trees and beautiful long walks in the surrounding woodlands.

Open: Sunday 12 August, 2pm - 5pm, admission £5.00, children free. Wheelchair users may find t difficult as there are gravel paths.

Directions: Off the B974 Cairn O'Mount road 1¼ miles north of Fettercairn.

· *Fettercairn Community Allotments & Home Start Stonehaven*

7

FINDRACK
Torphins AB31 4LJ
Mr Hal Salvesen

....

Findrack is a large mixed garden on a working estate with snapshot views to Clachna Ben. Woodland gardens, ponds, burn bed, sunken garden, vegetable garden, orchard and woodland walks, plus croquet and many other lawns which may take some time to fully explore! The walled garden has herbaceous borders with varying themes which are currently going through rejuvenation works. This garden has something for everyone, with a children's trail and family friendly features throughout the gardens waiting to be enjoyed.

Open: Sunday 22 July, 2pm - 5pm, admission £5.00, children free.

Directions: Leave Torphins on the A980 to Lumphanan after ½ a mile turn off, signposted Tornaveen. There is a stone gateway one mile up on the left.

· *The Bread Maker*

Scotland's Gardens Scheme
started in 1931 and
HRH King George V opened
the Balmoral Gardens

Kincardine & Deeside

8

FINZEAN HOUSE
Finzean, Banchory AB31 6NZ
Mr and Mrs Donald Farquharson

Finzean House was the family home of Joseph Farquharson, the Victorian landscape painter, and the garden was the backdrop for several of his paintings. The garden has lovely views over the historic holly hedge to the front of Clachnaben. There is a spring woodland garden, extensive lawns with herbaceous and shrub borders and a working cut flower garden for late summer alongside a recently restored pond area.

Open: Sunday 17 June, 2pm - 5pm, admission £5.00, children free. OAP's £4.00

Directions: On the B976, South Deeside Road, between Banchory and Aboyne.

· Forget Me Not Care & Counselling

9

GLENBERVIE HOUSE
Drumlithie, Stonehaven AB39 3YA
Mr and Mrs A Macphie

The nucleus of the beautiful present day house dates from the 15th century with additions in the 18th and 19th centuries. A traditional Scottish walled garden on a slope with roses, herbaceous and annual borders along with fruit and vegetables. One wall is taken up with a Victorian style greenhouse with many species of pot plants and climbers including peach and figs. A woodland garden by a burn is punctuated with many varieties of plants, primula to name but one.

Open: Sunday 5 August, 2pm - 5pm, admission £5.00, children free. Please note some steep pathways and tree roots can make walking difficult in places. Gravel paths are not accessible for electric wheelchairs. Please no dogs. Garden visits available by arrangement, apply in writing.

Directions: Drumlithie one mile. Garden 1½ miles off the A90.

· RNLI

10

INCHMARLO HOUSE GARDEN
Inchmarlo, Banchory AB31 4AL
Skene Enterprises (Aberdeen) Ltd
T: 01330 826242 E: info@inchmarlo-retirement.co.uk
W: www.inchmarlo-retirement.co.uk

Beautiful five acre woodland garden filled with azaleas and rhododendrons beneath ancient Scots pines, Douglas firs and silver firs (some over 42 metres tall). Also beeches, rare and unusual trees including pindrow firs, Pere David's maple, Erman's birch and a mountain snowdrop tree. The Oriental Garden features a Kare Sansui, a dry slate stream designed by Peter Roger, a *RHS Chelsea* gold medal winner. The Rainbow Garden, within the keyhole-shaped purple *Prunus cerasifera* hedge, has been designed by Billy Carruthers, an eight times gold medal winner at the *RHS Scottish Garden Show*.

Open: Sunday 20 May, 1:30pm - 4:30pm, admission £5.00, children free.

Directions: From Aberdeen via North Deeside Road on the A93, one mile west of Banchory turn right at the main gate to the Inchmarlo Estate.

· Alzheimer Scotland & Forget Me Not Care & Counselling

Kincardine & Deeside

KINCARDINE CASTLE

11

Kincardine O'Neil AB34 5AE
Mr and Mrs Andrew Bradford

A superb series of gardens around a Victorian Castle with great views across Deeside. Walled garden with a world-class laburnum walk, a mixture of herbaceous and shrub borders, vegetables and fruit trees. Extensive lawns, wildflower meadows and a thought provoking Planetary Garden. A woodland garden with 120 varieties of rhododendrons and azaleas, many of recent planting, set amongst mature trees. Sculpture by Lyman Whittaker of Utah.   A great day out.

Open: Sunday 10 June, 1:30am - 5pm, admission £5.00, children free.

Directions: Kincardine O'Neil on the A93. Gates and lodge are opposite the village school.

· Christ Church: Kincardine O'Neil & Children 1st

Laburnam Walk at Kincardine Castle

KIRKCUDBRIGHTSHIRE

Scotland's Gardens Scheme 2018 Guidebook is sponsored by INVESTEC WEALTH & INVESTMENT

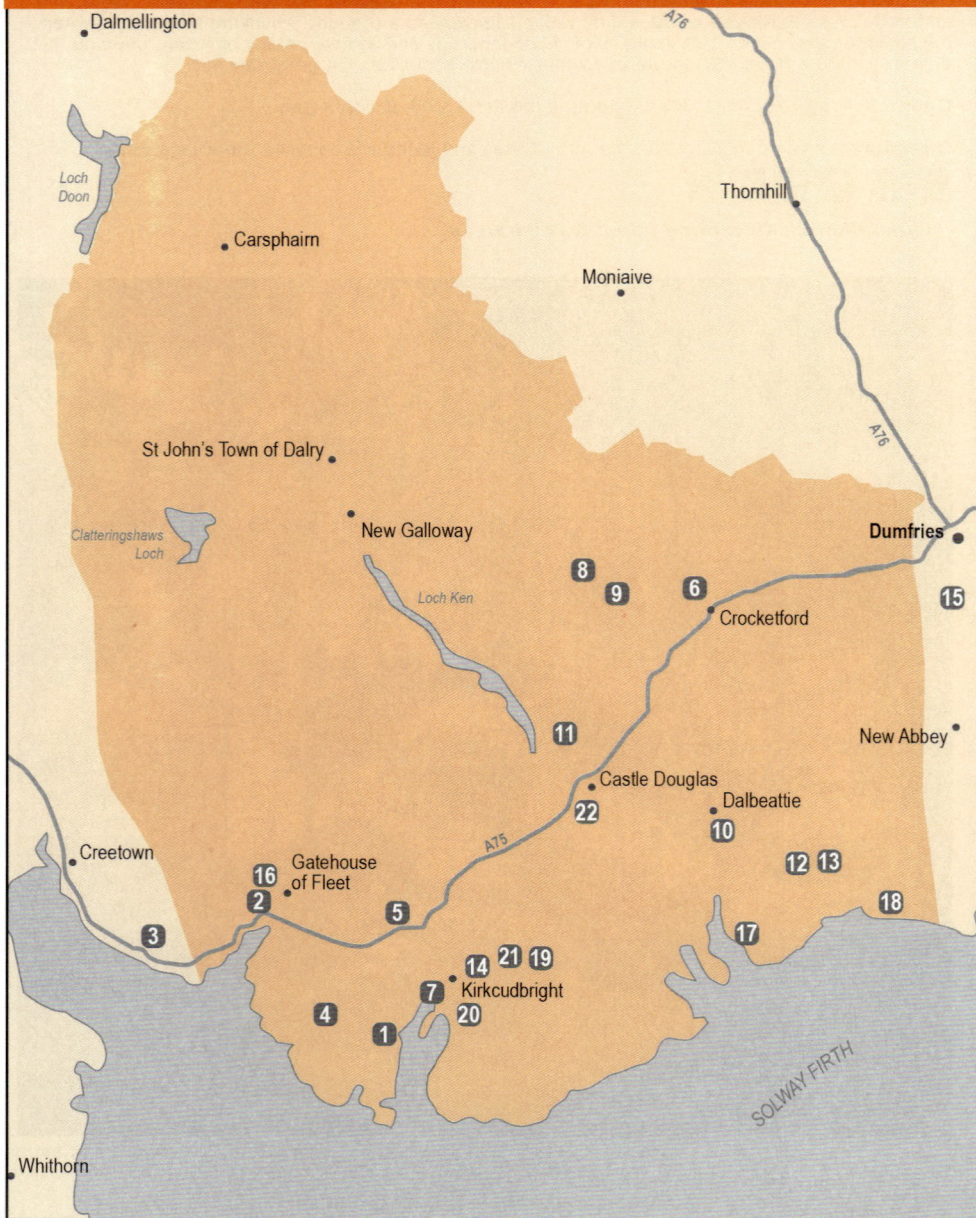

Dalmellington

A76

Loch
Doon

Thornhill

Carsphairn

Moniaive

St John's Town of Dalry

Clatteringshaws
Loch

New Galloway

Dumfries

8

9

6

Loch Ken

Crocketford

15

11

New Abbey

Castle Douglas

22

Dalbeattie

10

Creetown

12 13

16

Gatehouse
of Fleet

2

18

3

5

17

14 21 19

7

Kirkcudbright

4

20

1

A75

SOLWAY FIRTH

Whithorn

KIRKCUDBRIGHTSHIRE

OUR VOLUNTEER ORGANISERS

District Organisers:	Theodora Stanning	Seabank, Merse Rd, Rockcliffe, Dalbeattie, DG5 4QH
	Julian Stanning	Seabank, Merse Rd, Rockcliffe, Dalbeattie, DG5 4QH
		E: kirkcudbrightshire@scotlandsgardens.org
Area Organisers:	Hedley Foster	Deer Park, Fleet Forest, Gatehouse of Fleet, DG7 2DN
	Lesley Pepper	Anwoth Old Schoolhouse, Gatehouse of Fleet, DG7 2EF
	Vivien Scott	14 Castle Street, Kirkcudbright, DG6 4JA
	Audrey Slee	Holmview, New Galloway, Castle Douglas, DG7 3RN
	George Thomas	Savat, Meikle Richorn, Dalbeattie, DG5 4QT
Treasurer:	Duncan Lofts	Balcary Tower, Auchencairn, Castle Douglas, DG7 1QZ

GARDENS OPEN ON A SPECIFIC DATE

Danevale Park, Crossmichael	Sunday, 18 February
3 Millhall, Shore Road, Kirkcudbright	Sunday, 15 April
Threave Garden, Castle Douglas	Sunday, 6 May
Corsock House, Corsock, Castle Douglas	Sunday, 27 May
Barmagachan House, Borgue, Kirkcudbright	Sunday, 3 June
Broughton House Garden, 12 High Street, Kirkcudbright	Thursday, 7 June
Linden Lea, Islesteps, Dumfries	Sunday, 10 June
Glenlivet, Kirkcudbright	Sunday, 17 June
The Limes, Kirkcudbright	Sunday, 17 June
Drumstinchall Cottage, Drumstinchall, Dalbeattie	Sunday, 24 June
Drumstinchall House, Drumstinchall, Dalbeattie	Sunday, 24 June
Broughton House Garden, 12 High Street, Kirkcudbright	Thursday, 28 June
Southwick House, Southwick	Sunday, 1 July
Seabank, The Merse, Rockcliffe	Sunday, 8 July
Crofts, Kirkpatrick Durham, Castle Douglas	Sunday, 22 July
Threave Garden, Castle Douglas	Sunday, 5 August
Dalbeattie Community Allotments Association, Port Rd	Sunday, 12 August
3 Millhall, Shore Road, Kirkcudbright	Sunday, 2 September

GARDENS OPEN BY ARRANGEMENT

Stockarton, Kirkcudbright	On request
The Limes, Kirkcudbright	On request
Brooklands, Crocketford	15 January - 11 March
Barwhinnock House, Twynholm, Kirkcudbright	14 February - 28 February
Anwoth Old Schoolhouse, Anwoth, Gatehouse of Fleet	15 February - 15 November
Barholm Castle, Gatehouse of Fleet	15 February - 15 October
Brooklands, Crocketford	12 March - 30 November
Luckie Harg's, Anwoth, Gatehouse of Fleet, Castle Douglas	1 April - 31 July
Corsock House, Corsock, Castle Douglas	1 April - 30 June
The Waterhouse Gardens at Stockarton, Kirkcudbright	1 May - 30 September
Seabank, The Merse, Rockcliffe	1 June - 31 August

Kirkcudbrightshire

KEY TO SYMBOLS

NEW New garden	Full wheelchair access	Dogs on leads
Basic teas	Partial wheelchair access	NPC National plant collection
H Homemade teas	Plants for sale	Champion trees
C Cream teas	Children's activities	Designed landscape
Refreshments	Accessible by public transport	Snowdrop opening

All our gardens open to raise money for charity. Each opening may nominate a charity(s) to receive up to 60% of the takings and these are included with each listing. The net remaining raised supports our core beneficiaries. Information about our core beneficiaries can be found in the front section of the book. More information about our charity scheme and our symbols can be found in the back foldout section of the book under 'Tips for Using Your Guidebook'.

Dusty light at The Limes

Kirkcudbrightshire

1 3 MILLHALL
Shore Road, Kirkcudbright DG6 4TQ
Mr Alan Shamash

Impressive five acre garden with a large collection of mature shrubs, including over 200 rhododendron species, many camellias, perennials, over 300 hydrangeas and many rare Southern Hemisphere plants. The garden is on a steep hillside running along the rocky shore of the Dee Estuary in Kirkcudbright Bay, close to the beach at the Dhoon and three miles from Kirkcudbright.

Open: Sunday 15 April, 2pm - 5pm. Also open Sunday 2 September, 2pm - 5pm. Admission £5.00, children free.

Directions: On the B727 between Kirkcudbright and Borgue on the west shore of the Dee Estuary. Parking at Dhoon beach public car park, about three miles south of Kirkcudbright. There is a five to ten minute walk to the house.

H

· *Kirkcudbright Hospital League Of Friends & Alzheimer's Research UK*

2 ANWOTH OLD SCHOOLHOUSE
Anwoth, Gatehouse of Fleet DG7 2EF
Mr & Mrs Pepper
T: 01557 814444 E: lesley.pepper@btinternet.com

Two acres of delightful cottage style gardens behind the old schoolhouse and cottage in a picturesque setting opposite Anwoth Old Church (in ruins) and graveyard. Winding paths alongside a burn, informally planted with unusual woodland perennials and shrubs. Wildlife pond, fish pond, rock garden, vegetable garden, wildflower area and viewpoint.

Open: Open by arrangement 15 February - 15 November, admission £3.00, children free.

Directions: Driving west on the A75, take the Anwoth turnoff about half a mile after Gatehouse of Fleet. Anwoth Church is about half a mile along the road and Anwoth Old Schoolhouse is a little further along, opposite Anwoth Old Church (in ruins).

· *Dogs for Good*

3 BARHOLM CASTLE
Gatehouse of Fleet DG7 2EZ
Dr John and Dr Janet Brennan
E: barholmcastle@gmail.com

Barholm Castle, a sixteenth century tower, was restored from a ruin in 2006 and the owners moved in permanently in 2011. Since the restoration, the three acre gardens surrounding the tower have been mostly developed from scratch. There is a small walled garden, a wooded ravine, a greenhouse, shrub borders, ponds, rockeries and herbaceous beds. Good snowdrop display in February. Lots of colour March - October. The views over Wigtown Bay are magnificent.

Open: Open by arrangement 15 February - 15 October, admission £4.00, children free.

Directions: Off the A75 at the Cairn Holy turn off, fork right three times up a steep narrow road for ½ mile.

· *Home-Start Wigtownshire*

Kirkcudbrightshire

4

BARMAGACHAN HOUSE
Borgue, Kirkcudbright DG6 4SW
Andy and Carolyn McNab
T: 01557 870225

This new garden surrounds an eighteenth century house on a rocky knoll overlooking Wigtown Bay. It is profusely planted with a large variety of alpines, perennials and shrubs, including rhododendrons. Two themes are plants from SW China and Australia e.g. meconopsis, Asian primulas, eucryphia, and hebe. Many plants have been chosen for their wildlife value. The grounds also include an orchard, wall trained fruit, soft fruit area, potager and meadow. The woodland is rich in bird life. There is a thirteenth century motte.

Open: Sunday 3 June, 2pm - 5pm, admission £4.00, children free.

Directions: From Borgue follow the coast (Carrick) road up hill past the church and down. Take the first and only right turn and follow the lane winding past farms for about half a mile. Barmagachan House is on the left by a wood.

· *Scottish Wildlife Trust Ltd & The National Trust for Scotland: Threave Ospreys*

5

BARWHINNOCK HOUSE
Twynholm, Kirkcudbright DG6 4PF
Mrs Serena Haszard
T: 01557 860212/07814 142247 E: serenahaszard@icloud.com

A beautiful regency house with a spectacular show of snowdrops in the spring. Also a collection of more than 30 unusual snowdrops. Lovely dell walk by the burn to the oval walled garden which is planted with fruit trees, herbaceous and rose borders, and vegetable plots. Woodland walks abound with yet more splashes of snowdrops.

Open: Open by arrangement 14 February - 28 February for the Snowdrop Festival, admission £4.00, children free.

Directions: On A75, from Dumfries go past two turnings to Twynholm, road then goes into three lanes, drive is on the right 300 yards into the three lane section. From Stranraer go past turning to Twynholm, road goes into three lanes. Drive is on the left 100 yards after layby.

· *Twynholm Action Group SCIO*

6

BROOKLANDS
Crocketford DG2 8QH
Mr and Mrs Robert Herries
T: Head Gardener John Geddes 01556 690685

Large old walled garden, richly planted with a wide variety of perennials, including many unusual species, soft fruit and vegetables. Mature woodland garden full of rhododendrons and carpeted with snowdrops in February and daffodils in spring.

Open: Open by arrangement 15 January - 11 March for the Snowdrop Festival. Also open by arrangement 12 March - 30 November. Admission £4.00, children free.

Directions: Turn off the A712 Crocketford to New Galloway Road one mile outside Crocketford at the Gothic gatehouse (on the right travelling north).

· *All proceeds to SGS Beneficiaries*

Kirkcudbrightshire

7

BROUGHTON HOUSE GARDEN
12 High Street, Kirkcudbright DG6 4JX
The National Trust for Scotland
T: 01557 330437 E: broughtonhouse@nts.org.uk
W: www.nts.org.uk/property/broughton-house-and-garden

Broughton House Garden is a fascinating townhouse garden that belonged to E. A. Hornel - artist, collector and one of the 'Glasgow boys'. Full of colour, with mostly herbaceous plants, old apple trees, greenhouse with old pelargonium varieties, and fruit and vegetable garden.

Open: Thursday 7 June, 6pm - 9pm. Also open Thursday 28 June, 10am - 12pm. Admission £5.00, children free.   7 June 'Broughton House at sunset': an evening of live music and refreshments (included in the entry price). It is an opportunity to meet the Head Gardener and see the garden in a different light. 28 June 'Broughton House Garden Early Bird': appreciate the garden in morning light, at a peaceful and calmer time of day. Tea or coffee (included in the entry price) will be available in the beautiful surroundings of Broughton House and the Head Gardener will be available to provide gardening advice.

Directions: Off A711/A755 on Kirkcudbright High Street. Stagecoach buses 500/X75 and 501 from Dumfries and Castle Douglas. By bike, NCN 7.

· *The National Trust for Scotland: for Broughton House*

8

CORSOCK HOUSE
Corsock, Castle Douglas DG7 3DJ
The Ingall Family
T: 01644 440250

Corsock House garden includes an amazing variety of designed landscape, from a strictly formal walled garden, through richly planted woodlands full of different vistas, artfully designed water features and surprises to manicured lawns showing off the Bryce baronial mansion. This is an Arcadian garden with pools and temples, described by Ken Cox as 'the most photogenic woodland garden in Scotland'.

Open: Sunday 27 May, 2pm - 5pm. Also open by arrangement 1 April - 30 June. Admission £5.00, children free.

Directions: Off A75 Dumfries 14 miles, Castle Douglas ten miles, Corsock village ½ mile on A712.

· *Corsock & Kirkpatrick Durham Church Of Scotland*

9

CROFTS
Kirkpatrick Durham, Castle Douglas DG7 3HX
Mrs Andrew Dalton
T: 01556 650235 E: jenniedalton@mac.com

Victorian country house garden with mature trees, a walled garden with fruit and vegetables and glasshouses, hydrangea garden and a pretty water garden. Delightful woodland walk, colourfully planted with bog plants, with a stream running through.

Open: Sunday 22 July, 2pm - 5pm, admission £4.00, children free.

Directions: A75 to Crocketford, then three miles on A712 to Corsock and New Galloway.

· *Corsock & Kirkpatrick Durham Church Of Scotland*

Kirkcudbrightshire

Sculpture in the walled garden at Crofts

10 DALBEATTIE COMMUNITY ALLOTMENTS ASSOCIATION
Port Road, Dalbeattie DG54AZ
Dalbeattie Community Allotments Association

Dalbeattie Community Allotments Association was formed in 2008 and the site was officially opened in August 2010. A local land owner has leased the land for 25 years at £1 per year, initially providing for 47 plots. The initial results were so successful that the area is now increased to provide for 81 productive plots where local residents can grow their own fruit, vegetables and flowers. Come and enjoy a stroll around the site, chat to members or relax in one of the community areas. Information will be available and photos of the development of the site will be on display.

Open: Sunday 12 August, 2pm - 5pm, admission £3.00, children free.

Directions: The allotment site can be found on the Dalbeattie bypass (A710) next to Craignair Health Centre.

· *Dalbeattie Community Initiative*

11 DANEVALE PARK
Crossmichael DG7 2LP
Mrs M R C Gillespie
T: 01556 670223 E: danevale@tiscali.co.uk

First opening for snowdrops in 1951, these mature grounds have a wonderful display of snowdrops as well as aconites and many other wildflowers. Walks through the woods and alongside the River Dee make this a memorable day.

Open: Sunday 18 February, 1pm - 4pm for the Snowdrop Festival, admission £3.00, children free.

Directions: On the A713 two miles from Castle Douglas and one mile short of Crossmichael.

· *Earl Haig Fund Poppy Scotland*

Kirkcudbrightshire

12

DRUMSTINCHALL COTTAGE
Drumstinchall, Dalbeattie DG5 4PD
Ginny and Abel Quintanilla
T: 01387 780571

A small informal quintessentially cottage style garden surrounded by farmland and hills, and with views to Criffel and Drumstinchall Loch. The main area has been reclaimed from agricultural land over the last seven years and continues to evolve, with the emphasis on growing a wide range of vegetables, herbs and fruit organically. Unusual varieties are combined with as many colourful wildlife friendly flowers as possible. There is a wildlife pond area and a few rescue chickens pottering about.

Open: Sunday 24 June, 2pm - 5pm, admission £5.00, children free. Open with Drumstinchall House, admission is for both gardens.

Directions: From the A711 just east of Dalbeattie, take the B793 towards Southwick/ Caulkerbush. After 4.2 miles take a right turn signposted Drumstinchall and follow this road for 0.8 miles to Drumstinchall Cottage.

· Soul Soup & Brooke Action for Working Horses & Donkeys

13

DRUMSTINCHALL HOUSE
Drumstinchall, Dalbeattie DG5 4PD
Melanie and Mark Parry & Celia Hanbury
T: 01387 780278

An extensive and established garden, surrounded by mature trees, with fine views to the sea two miles away. There are colourful herbaceous and mixed borders, and a rose garden in front of the house. A variety of paths wind their way through more borders, a rock garden, rhododendrons and azaleas, and past the ruin of the original house to a woodland walk around the edge of the garden. There is a vegetable garden, including a polytunnel, on your way to Drumstinchall Cottage.

Open: Sunday 24 June, 2pm - 5pm, admission £5.00, children free. Open with Drumstinchall Cottage, admission is for both gardens.

Directions: From the A711 just east of Dalbeattie, take the B793 towards Southwick/ Caulkerbush. After 4. 2 miles take a right turn signposted Drumstinchall and follow this road for 0. 8 miles to Drumstinchall House.

· Soul Soup & Brooke Action for Working Horses & Donkeys

Make the most of family friendly walks in bluebell and snowdrop woods – spot the signs of spring

Kirkcudbrightshire

14

GLENLIVET
Kirkcudbright   DG6 4UR
Mr & Mrs Blackadder

This new town garden of half an acre on the edge of Kirkcudbright has been developed by the owners from scratch over the past ten years. It has a remarkably mature appearance already and is packed with colour and a huge variety of thriving plants, shrubs and trees, all carefully tended. There are two small ponds connected by a rill, with fountains at each end, herbaceous beds, gravel beds and a variety of statuary and garden structures. The garden is in a lovely position overlooking the River Dee.

Open: Sunday 17 June, 1pm - 5pm, admission £5.00, children free. Open with The Limes, admission is for entry to both gardens.

Directions: Coming in to Kirkcudbright via the A711 and Tongland Bridge, on the outskirts of the town pass the Arden House Hotel on the left. Glenlivet is about half a mile further on the right. It is exactly half a mile from the town centre crossroads on the Tongland Road. Parking is on the main road.

· *Friends Of Kirkcudbright Swimming Pool*

15

LINDEN LEA
Islesteps, Dumfries DG28ES
Jeanette Cairns

Formal front garden with fish stocked pond, leading past a small cottage garden and down to a pebble garden with a quiet seating area. From there a kitchen garden leads through to a small apple orchard. A summer house at the top of the orchard looks out over informal shrubs to a herbaceous garden that surrounds a sunken patio. At the top is a woodland garden from which runs a stream through the informal area.

Open: Sunday 10 June, 1pm - 4pm, admission £4.00, children free.

Directions: Islesteps is on the A701 to New Abbey, about one and a half miles outside Dumfries. Linden Lea is the last house along a lane that leaves the A701 to the right, immediately over the hump bridge at the entrance to the village.

· *Alzheimer's Research UK: Dumfries Support Group*

16

LUCKIE HARG'S
Anwoth, Gatehouse of Fleet, Castle Douglas DG7 2EF
Drs Carole and Ian Bainbridge
T: 01557 814141 E: luckiehargs@btinternet.com

A new and developing garden on the outskirts of Gatehouse. A rock and spring herbaceous garden with a wide range of alpines, Himalayan and New Zealand plants, rock garden, crevices, troughs, large alpine house and bulb frame. Under the extension new beds and woodland area are being developed. Small productive vegetable and fruit garden, plus a bluebell bank in May.

Open: Open by arrangement 1 April - 31 July, admission £4.00, children free.

Kirkcudbrightshire

Directions: From Gatehouse High Street, turn north onto Station Road, immediately west at the Fleet Bridge (by Ship Inn). After almost one mile turn left (signed to *Anwoth Old Church*). Luckie Harg's is first on right after 400 yards. Nearest bus stop on Gatehouse High Street, walk about 15 minutes to Luckie Harg's.

· *Scottish Rock Garden Club*

17

SEABANK
The Merse, Rockcliffe DG5 4QH
Julian and Theodora Stanning
T: 01556 630244
....

The one and a half acre garden extends to the high water mark with fine views across the Urr Estuary, Rough Island and beyond. Mixed shrub and herbaceous borders surround the house and there is a new walled garden for fruit and vegetables. A plantswoman's garden with a range of interesting and unusual plants.

Open: Sunday 8 July, 2pm - 5pm. Also open by arrangement 1 June - 31 August. Admission £4.00, children free.

Directions: Park in the public car park at Rockcliffe. Walk down the road about 50 metres towards the sea and turn left along The Merse, a private road. Seabank is the sixth house on the left.

· *Marie Curie*

Views across the Urr Estruary at Seabank

18

SOUTHWICK HOUSE
Southwick DG2 8AH
Mr and Mrs R H L Thomas
....

The extensive gardens at Southwick House comprise three main areas. The first is a traditional formal walled garden with potager and large glasshouse producing a range of fruit, vegetables and cutting flowers. Adjacent to this is a hedged formal garden with herbaceous, shrub and rose beds centred around a lily pond, with roses predominating as an interesting feature. Outwith the formal gardens there is a large water garden with two connected ponds with trees, shrubs and lawns running alongside the Southwick Burn.

Open: Sunday 1 July, 2pm - 5pm, admission £5.00, children free.

Directions: On A710 near Caulkerbush. Dalbeattie seven miles, Dumfries seventeen miles.

· *Loch Arthur*

Kirkcudbrightshire

19 **STOCKARTON**
Kirkcudbright DG6 4XS
Lt. Col. and Mrs Richard Cliff
T: 01557 330430

This interesting garden was started in 1995 and contains a collection of unusual shrubs and small trees which are growing well. Our aim has been to create different informal gardens around a Galloway farm house, leading down to a lochan. Above the lochan there is a sweet cottage, used for holiday retreats. It has its own interesting garden. In 1996 a three acre aboretum was planted as a shelter belt and it now contains some rare oak trees.

Open: Open by arrangement, admission £4.00, children free.

Directions: On B727 Kirkcudbright to Gelston Road.   Kirkcudbright three miles, Castle Douglas seven miles.

· *Great Ormond Street Hospital Children's Charity*

Walled garden and glasshouse at Southwick House

20 **THE LIMES**
Kirkcudbright DG6 4XD
Mr and Mrs McHale
E: david.mchale@btinternet.com

This one and a quarter acre plantsman's garden has a variety of different plant habitats: woodland, dry sunny gravel beds, rock garden, crevice garden and mixed perennial and shrub borders. There is also a large productive vegetable garden. The McHales like to grow most of their plants from seed obtained through various international seed exchanges. You can expect to see a large number of unusual and exciting plants. In June the meconopsis should be at their best.

Open: Sunday 17 June, 1pm - 5pm, with Glenlivet. Also open by arrangement. Admission £5.00, children free (Sunday 17 June, admission is entry to both gardens) and £3.50, children free (1 January - 31 December).

Kirkcudbrightshire

Directions: In Kirkcudbright go straight along St Mary Street towards Dundrennan. The Limes is on the right, about half a mile from the town centre crossroads, on the edge of the town.

· **Friends Of Kirkcudbright Swimming Pool**

21

THE WATERHOUSE GARDENS AT STOCKARTON
Kirkcudbright DG6 4XS
Martin Gould & Sharon O'Rourke
T: 01557 331266 E: waterhousekbt@aol.com
W: www.waterhousekbt.co.uk

One acre of densely planted terraced cottage style gardens attached to a Galloway cottage. Three ponds surround the oak framed eco-polehouse 'The Waterhouse'. Climbing roses, clematis and honeysuckles are a big feature as well as a pond-side walk. Over 50 photos on their website. Featured on *Beechgrove Garden* 2007.

Open: Open by arrangement 1 May - 30 September, admission £4.00, children free.

Directions: On the B727 Kirkcudbright to Gelston - Dalbeattie road. Kirkcudbright three miles, Castle Douglas seven miles.

· **Loch Arthur**

22

THREAVE GARDEN
Castle Douglas DG7 1RX
The National Trust for Scotland
T: 01556 502 575 E: rapolley@nts.org.uk
W: /www.nts.org.uk/Property/Threave-Garden-and-Estate

Threave Garden, "The Training Centre for future Professional Gardeners", is home to the School of Heritage Gardening. A place of education and plantsmanship, the garden has been sculptured by generations of students since 1960, resulting in a series of 'rooms' within the garden, each showcasing year round interest; from beautiful spring daffodils, striking autumnal colour and a multitude of summer herbaceous displays. Threave also boasts a fully productive working walled garden that yields a large bounty of home-grown produce each year for sale to the public and use in the on site terrace cafe.
Champion Trees: *Acer platanoides* 'Princeton Gold'.

Open: Sunday 6 May, 10am - 5pm. Also open Sunday 5 August, 10am - 5pm. Admission £5.00, children free. Dogs are welcome on the wider Threave estate, but only assistance dogs in the garden please.

Directions: Off A75, one mile west of Castle Douglas.

· **The National Trust for Scotland: School of Heritage Gardening**

Scotland's Gardens
Scheme welcomes all
varieties of gardens

LANARKSHIRE

Scotland's Gardens Scheme 2018 Guidebook is sponsored by INVESTEC WEALTH & INVESTMENT

LANARKSHIRE

OUR VOLUNTEER ORGANISERS

District Organiser:	Vanessa Rogers	1 Snowberry Field, Thankerton, ML12 6RJ
		E: lanarkshire@scotlandsgardens.org
Area Organisers:	Nicky Eliott Lockhart	Stable House, Cleghorn Farm, Lanark, ML11 7RW
	Janis Sinclair	2 Meadowflatts Cottage, Meadowflatts Rd, ML12 6NF
Treasurer:	Shelia Munro-Tullock	Castlegait House, Strathaven, Lanarkshire, ML10 6FF

GARDENS OPEN ON A SPECIFIC DATE

Cleghorn, Stable House, Cleghorn Farm, Lanark	Sunday, 4 March
5 Fergus Gardens, Hamilton, South Lanarkshire	Sunday, 13 May
20 Smithycroft, Hamilton	Sunday, 10 June
Dippoolbank Cottage, Carnwath	Sunday, 17 June
Symington House, By Biggar	Sunday, 8 July
D ppoolbank Cottage, Carnwath	Sunday, 22 July
Wellbutts, Elsrickle, by Biggar	Sunday, 29 July
Viewpark Allotments and Gardens, Bairds Avenue, Viewpark	Sunday, 5 August
Old Farm Cottage, The Ladywell, Nemphlar, Lanark	Saturday/Sunday, 11/12 August
Culter Allers, Coulter, Biggar	Sunday, 19 August

GARDENS OPEN BY ARRANGEMENT

Carmichael Mill, Hyndford Bridge, Lanark	On request
The Walled Garden, Shieldhill, Quothquan, Biggar	1 April - 30 September
St Patrick's House, Lanark	1 May - 17 June

Helping more than 200 charities annually, big and small

Lanarkshire

KEY TO SYMBOLS

NEW	New garden	♿	Full wheelchair access	🐕	Dogs on leads
	Basic teas	♿	Partial wheelchair access	NPC	National plant collection
H	Homemade teas	🌷	Plants for sale	🌳	Champion trees
C	Cream teas	👫	Children's activities		Designed landscape
	Refreshments	🚌	Accessible by public transport		Snowdrop opening

All our gardens open to raise money for charity. Each opening may nominate a charity(s) to receive up to 60% of the takings and these are included with each listing. The net remaining raised supports our core beneficiaries. Information about our core beneficiaries can be found in the front section of the book. More information about our charity scheme and our symbols can be found in the back foldout section of the book under 'Tips for Using Your Guidebook'.

Blue Skies at The Walled Garden, Sheildhill

Lanarkshire

1 20 SMITHYCROFT

Hamilton ML3 7UL
Mr and Mrs R I Fionda
E: idafionda@hotmail.com

A plantswoman's award-winning garden which has developed into a mature oasis. Phormiums and clematis abound and there is a large range of unusual plants which only flourish in sheltered parts of Scotland.

Open: Sunday 10 June, 12:30pm - 5pm, admission £4.00, children free.

Directions: Off the M74 at Junction 6. One mile on the A72. Garden is well signed. On Hamilton to Larkhall bus route.

· *Mary's Meals*

20 Smithycroft

2 5 FERGUS GARDENS

Hamilton, South Lanarkshire ML3 7DF
Ann and Alistair Hackson
E: event@5fg.co.uk

This modest suburban garden, altered over several years and still developing, reflects the owners' various interests. The garden is set up to have interest throughout the year. The lively colours of the bulbs and plants of early spring lead into vibrant rhododendrons, azaleas, *Magnolia stellata*, and acers. Shrubs, herbaceous planting and roses fill the summer months, before the berry and leaf change to Autumn colours. The framework of hedging and evergreens gives open vistas and hidden views, and interesting contrasts of plant form and colour combinations. The garden contains a productive greenhouse and raised vegetable and fruit beds, and artist's studio, several relaxed seating areas and a wildlife pond.

Open: Sunday 13 May, 1pm - 4:30pm, admission £4.00, children free.

Directions: From Junction 6 (Hamilton) off M74, follow through two traffic lights signed for A72 towards Larkhall. Garden signed right from first small roundabout into Barncluith Road then left into Fergus Gardens. Considerate parking please along left hand side of road.

· *Alzheimer Scotland*

Lanarkshire

3 CARMICHAEL MILL
Hyndford Bridge, Lanark ML11 8SJ
Chris, Ken and Gemma Fawell
T: 01555 665880 E: ken.fawell@btinternet.com

Gardens developed over the last 30 years surrounding the last workable water mill in Clydesdale. Water wheel will be rotating, river levels permitting. A large collection of over 200 different ornamental trees with shrubs and herbaceous and a large vegetable and fruit garden. The mill lade (stream) flows through the centre, providing diverse habitats including *Candelabra primula* in late May. Large collection of tulips and narcissus in early spring followed by glorious display of flowering cherry and crab apples. Wildlife protection and enhancement is a priority. Also visible are archaeological remains of the medieval grain milling, flax processing and a foundry. (The bell in Carmichael village was made here). A vote of thanks following a visit from the Hardy Plant Society: "You have a fantastic garden Ken, but the best part about it is the small water feature on the side" He meant the River Clyde!

Open: Open by arrangement, admission £5.00, children free.

Directions: Just off the A73 Lanark to Biggar road ½ mile east of the Hyndford Bridge.

· *Donation to SGS Beneficiaries*

4 CLEGHORN
Stable House, Cleghorn Farm, Lanark ML11 7RN
Mr and Mrs R Eliot Lockhart
T: 01555 663792 E: elliotlockhart.nicky@gmail.com
W: www.cleghornestategardens.com

Eighteenth century garden which is gradually being renovated. Attractive walks through mature trees and shrubs. Recent replanting of a valley below a 12th century dam. Abundant snowdrops and visitors are welcome to return when the daffodils are in flower.

Open: Sunday 4 March, 2pm - 4pm for the Snowdrop Festival, admission by donation.

Directions: Cleghorn Farm is situated two miles north of Lanark on the A706.

· *Marie Curie*

5 CULTER ALLERS
Coulter, Biggar ML12 6PZ
The McCosh Family

The grounds of Culter Allers centre around its traditional one and a half acre walled garden, within which lies a productive vegetable and fruit garden with espalier fruit trees and berry bushes lining the walls. There are cut flower beds, an apple tree lined walk, a 'secret' herb garden, a wishing well and wide herbaceous borders revolving around an ornamental cherry and lawn. The policies of the house include winding woodland walks, fairy doors, a giant (small one) and an avenue of 125 year old lime trees leading to the village kirk.

Open: Sunday 19 August, 2pm - 5pm, admission £4.00, children free.

Directions: In the village of Coulter, three miles south of Biggar on A702.

· *Coulter Public Library Trust*

Lanarkshire

6

DIPPOOLBANK COTTAGE
Carnwath ML11 8LP
Mr Allan Brash

Artist's intriguing cottage garden. Vegetables are grown in small beds. There are herbs, fruit, flowers and a pond in woodland area with tree house and summer house. The fernery was completed in 2007. This is an organic garden which was mainly constructed with recycled materials.

Open: Sunday 17 June, 2pm - 6pm. Also open Sunday 22 July, 2pm - 6pm. Admission £4.00, children free.

Directions: Off B7016 between Forth and Carnwath near the village of Braehead on the Auchengray road. Approximately eight miles from Lanark. Well signposted.

· *The Little Haven (Forth)*

7

OLD FARM COTTAGE
The Ladywell, Nemphlar, Lanark ML11 9GX
Ian and Anne Sinclair
T: 01555 663345

This property was previously a working farm but is now owned by a beekeeper and a gardener. Opening to show later summer flowering shrubs and herbaceous plants, the garden includes mixed borders, a wild flower area, a pond, an apiary and small orchard. The garden is about an acre and has a large grassed area and putting green. A child friendly garden there are lots of nooks and crannies of discovery and play.

Open: Saturday/Sunday, 11/12 August, 12pm - 4pm, admission £4.00, children free. Guide Dogs Scotland will be in attendance. There will be a demonstation hive with a beekeeper to answer your questions. Honey and hive products available. Ideal for walkers being close to the Nemphlar spur of the Clyde Walkway. Shelter available if wet. Teepees for the children.

Directions: Leave A73 at Cartland Bridge (Lanark to Carluke Road) or A72 (Clyde Valley Road) at Crossford. Both routes well signposted.

· *Guide Dogs*

8

ST PATRICK'S HOUSE
Lanark ML11 9EG
Mr and Mrs Peter Sanders
T: 01555 663800 E: peterjeansanders@gmail.com

A May or June visit to St Patrick's House garden will be rewarded with a stunning display of rhododendrons, azaleas, heathers and shrubs. Created over a 50 year period, the grounds of this five acre garden slope down to the River Clyde. Natural springs have been harnessed to create water features, a large contemporary pond with an arbour begs you to sit a while. Paths wind between beds of varied plantings and perennials, rockeries, and woodland plants which all add to the magic of this unexpected gem.

Open: Open by arrangement 1 May - 17 June, admission £4.00, children free. Steep slopes in places, sturdy shoes recommended if wet.

Directions: A73 into Lanark, after Police Station turn right into Friars Lane. At bottom of hill turn right onto St. Patrick Road. Garden 0.25 mile on the left.

· *Lanark Community Development Trust*

Lanarkshire

9

SYMINGTON HOUSE
By Biggar ML12 6LW
Mr and Mrs James Dawnay

A traditional walled garden and greenhouses saved from dereliction 20 years ago. Now with beautiful herbaceous borders set off by a backdrop of yew hedges. The greenhouses have collections of fuchsias, geraniums and tender fruit. There are woodland and river walks to enjoy too.

Open: Sunday 8 July, 2pm - 5:30pm, admission £4.00, children free.

Directions: Entrance east of Symington Village on A72 between Biggar and Symington. Bus 191 or 91 Biggar to Lanark.

· *Cancer Research UK*

10

THE WALLED GARDEN, SHIELDHILL
Quothquan, Biggar ML12 6NA
Mr and Mrs Gordon
T: 01899 221961 E: nicolagord@gmail.com

This 200 year old walled garden was completely redesigned and planted in 2014/15 with contemporary features within a classic design. The garden incorporates a modern rill and banks of colour with perennial flowers in a variety of borders. The resident bees enjoy the large area of traditional meadow flowers and the rose garden, planted with lavenders, salvias and stock. Outside the wall you will find mature woodland including a giant sequoia and a wildlife pond. If you are interested in fruit and vegetables, take a look at the raised beds and the peach tree and vine in the greenhouse.

Open: Open by arrangement 1 April - 30 September, admission £5.00, children free.

Directions: Turn off the B7016 between Biggar and Carnwath towards Quothquan. After about a mile, look for signs and turn right at the lodge.

· *Médecins Sans Frontières*

11

VIEWPARK ALLOTMENTS AND GARDENS
Bairds Avenue, Viewpark G71 6JH
Viewpark Allotments and Gardens
T: 07967 153798
W: www.viewparkgardenallotments.co.uk

Viewpark is a thriving community of contemporary allotments. These allotments not only provide the opportunity to garden and grow but also provide enjoyment, education and therapy for local groups, families and individuals. Each plot has its own character. Crops grown range from potatoes to peaches, godetia to grapes. Inspiration can be found everywhere, from planting combinations, irrigation methods, use of small spaces, unusual crops etc. Environmental awareness is high on the agenda with a stunning wildflower meadow, hedgehog houses, bug hotels, group orchard and the use of recyclable materials. There is also the opportunity to visit the little known Viewpark Gardens. Adjacent to the allotments these interestingly themed gardens include Japanese, organic, wildlife garden and a wisteria walk. The highlight of the visit being the tropical greenhouses with their wide range of tender plants, koi carp pond and cactus house.

Lanarkshire

Open: Sunday 5 August, 1pm - 4:30pm, admission £4.00, children free. There will be children's activities throughout the afternoon. Adults and childrens alike will enjoy the beekeeping, reptile and moth exhibitions.

Directions: On the A721, New Edinburgh Road between Bellshill and Viewpark.

· *Alzheimer Scotland*

Packed herbaceous borders at Wellbutts

12

WELLBUTTS
Elsrickle, by Biggar ML12 6QZ
Mr and Mrs N Slater

At 960 feet the garden was started in 2000 from a two acre bare site around a renovated croft cottage. In an exposed and elevated position, the hedge and shrub planting gives some protection for the many new and now established varied herbaceous beds, whilst retaining the open views. There are two large natural ponds with ducks, a rill fed 'boggery', greenhouses, fish pond and covered areas for our fine collection of summer begonia baskets.

Open: Sunday 29 July, 1pm - 5pm, admission £4.00, children free.

Directions: Parking on the main road (A721) then walk to the garden (approximately 200 yards).

· *The Sick Kids Friends Foundation: Edinburgh Children's Hospital*

MORAY & NAIRN

Scotland's Gardens Scheme 2018 Guidebook is sponsored by INVESTEC WEALTH & INVESTMENT

MORAY & NAIRN

OUR VOLUNTEER ORGANISERS

District Organiser:	James Byatt	Lochview Cottage, Pitgaveny, Elgin, IV30 5PQ
		E: moraynairn@scotlandsgardens.org
Area Organisers:	Lorraine Dingwall	10 Pilmuir Road West, Forres, Morayshire, IV36 2HL
	David Hetherington	Haugh Garden, College of Roseisle, Moray, IV30 5YE
	Gwynne Hetherington	Haugh Garden, College of Roseisle, Moray, IV30 5YE
	Rebecca Russell	12 Duff Avenue, Elgin, Moray, IV30 1QS
	Annie Stewart	33 Albert Street, Nairn, IV12 4HF
Treasurer:	Michael Barnett	Drumdelnies, Nairn, IV12 5NT

GARDENS OPEN ON A SPECIFIC DATE

Brodie Castle, Brodie, Forres	Saturday/Sunday, 21/22 April
Balnabual Cottage, Dalcross	Wednesdays, 9, 16 & 23 May
10 Stuart Avenue, Ardersier, Inverness	Sunday, 10 June
10 Pilmuir Road West , Forres	Sunday, 8 July
Gordon Castle Walled Garden, Fochabers, Moray	Saturday, 14 July
Glenrinnes Lodge, Dufftown, Keith, Banffshire	Sunday, 29 July
Gordonstoun, Duffus, near Elgin	Sunday, 2 September

GARDENS OPEN REGULARLY

Logie House, Dunphail, Forres	Daily
Gordon Castle Walled Garden, Fochabers, Moray	Daily
Burgie, Between Forres and Elgin	1 April - 31 October

GARDENS OPEN BY ARRANGEMENT

10 Pilmuir Road West , Forres	27 January - 11 March
Haugh Garden, College of Roseisle	1 April - 31 August
Balnabual Cottage, Dalcross	1 May - 30 June
10 Pilmuir Road West , Forres	1 June - 15 August

Moray & Nairn

KEY TO SYMBOLS

NEW	New garden	♿	Full wheelchair access	🐕	Dogs on leads
🍵	Basic teas	♿	Partial wheelchair access	NPC	National plant collection
H	Homemade teas	🌷	Plants for sale	🌳	Champion trees
C	Cream teas	👥	Children's activities	🌿	Designed landscape
🍴	Refreshments	🚌	Accessible by public transport	🌱	Snowdrop opening

All our gardens open to raise money for charity. Each opening may nominate a charity(s) to receive up to 60% of the takings and these are included with each listing. The net remaining raised supports our core beneficiaries. Information about our core beneficiaries can be found in the front section of the book. More information about our charity scheme and our symbols can be found in the back foldout section of the book under 'Tips for Using Your Guidebook'.

Glenrinnes Lodge

Moray & Nairn

10 PILMUIR ROAD WEST

Forres IV36 2HL
Mrs Lorraine Dingwall
T: 01309 674634 E: fixandig@aol.com

Plantsman's small town garden with over 300 cultivars of hostas, an extensive collection of hardy geraniums together with many other unusual plants. Managed entirely without the use of artificial fertilizers or chemicals, the owner encourages hedgehogs, toads and wild birds to control slugs. In early spring there are approximately 150 named snowdrops to be seen, some of which are very rare.

Open: Open by arrangement 27 January - 11 March for the Snowdrop Festival. Also open Sunday 8 July, 1pm - 5pm. And open by arrangement 1 June - 15 August. Admission £3.00, children free. Well stocked plant sales with some rare varieties available, specialising in hostas and geraniums and with snowdrops in season.

Directions: From Tesco roundabout at Forres continue along Nairn Road. Take the first left onto Ramflat Road, then go right at the bottom and first left onto Pilmuir Road West.

· *Macmillan Cancer Support*

10 Pilmuir Road West

10 STUART AVENUE

Ardersier, Inverness IV2 7SA
Mr and Mrs Kevin Reid

A cottage style garden with vibrant rich and dense plantings of perennials and shrubs that bring colour and scent across the seasons,and makes the most of the limited space. Winner of the *Inverness Courier Garden of the Year* (medium category) in 2015, featured in the *Beechgrove Garden* in 2016 and overall winner of the *Inverness Courier Garden of the Year* in 2017.

Open: Sunday 10 June, 10:30am - 4:30pm, admission £3.00, children free.

Directions: From Inverness or Nairn take the A96, then the B9039 to Ardesier. After the 30mph sign turn right to Nairn, then first left into Reaybank Road and left again. Limited parking in Stuart Avenue, more in adjoining streets.

· *JAPES*

Moray & Nairn

3 ### BALNABUAL COTTAGE
Dalcross IV2 7JJ
Mr and Mrs Hamish Mackintosh
T: 01667 493449 E: sue-hamishmackintosh@hotmail.co.uk

One acre mixed garden, as seen on the *Beechgrove Garden* in 2017.   Rhododendrons, azaleas, large rockeries and alpine beds, pond, stream and water features. Greenhouses with large collections of pelargoniums and streptocarpus.   Alpine house, fruit and vegetables. Polytunnel and bog garden new in 2017.   Scree garden and crevice garden under construction.

Open: Wednesdays 9, 16 & 23 May, 12pm - 7pm. Also open by arrangement 1 May - 30 June. Admission £5.00, children free. Admission include tea/coffee and biscuits available in the conservatory. Paintings for sale.

Directions: Eight miles from Inverness, ten miles from Nairn. From the A96 turn off at Tornagrain and go up the hill for one mile.

· *Mary's Meals, Highland Rock Garden Club, Nairn and District Gardening Club & National Vegetable Society: North of Scotland branch*

4 ### BRODIE CASTLE
Brodie, Forres IV36 2TE
The National Trust for Scotland
T: 01309 641371
W: www.nts.org.uk/Property/Brodie-Castle/

The grounds of Brodie Castle are carpeted with daffodils in the spring and include a National Collection of over 110 different cultivars bred at the property by a former laird. Work has been done to continue to improve this collection. Good displays of other spring bulbs and shrubs including dog's tooth violet and rhododendrons.   On these special SGS open days garden staff will be leading guided tours of the garden and talking about the history of the daffodil collection at Brodie.   See the NTS website nearer the date for the tour times.
National Plant Collection: *Narcissus* (Brodie cvs.).

Open: Saturday/Sunday, 21/22 April, 10:30am - 4pm, admission details can be found on the garden's website. Garden tours £5.00.   Pots of daffodils, including very limited stock of Brodie cultivar will be available for purchase.

Directions: Off A96 4½ miles west of Forres and 24 miles east of Inverness.

· *Donation to SGS Beneficiaries*

Over 500 gardens open with us annually. Would you like to join us?

Moray & Nairn

The loch at Burgie

BURGIE

Between Forres and Elgin IV36 2QU
Hamish Lochore
T: 01343 850 231 E: hamish@burgie.org

A rare opportunity to see a sizeable woodland garden / arboretum in its infancy. It has a good collection of rhododendrons, sorbus, alder, birch and tilia but also includes many unusual trees from around the world. The arboretum is zoned into geographic areas and species type. It includes a Japanese garden, bog garden, bog wood, loch and quarry garden. First created in 2005 and is ongoing. Most plants are grown from hand collected seed and propagated in the Georgian greenhouse.

Open: 1 April - 31 October, 8am - 5pm, admission £3.00, children free. Please use honesty box. Disabled persons should get in touch by email so the gate can be opened for buggies.

Directions: A96 between Forres and Elgin. Four miles east of Forres. Six miles west of Elgin. Road end sign *Burgie Mains*. in wrought iron sign with horses and cattle on the top. South off the main road and one mile to the Woodland Garden car park.

· *Sandpiper Trust & World Horse Welfare*

Moray & Nairn

6 GLENRINNES LODGE

Dufftown, Keith, Banffshire AB55 4BS
Mrs Kathleen Locke
T: 01340 820384
W: www.glenrinnes.com

The garden and policies surrounding Glenrinnes Lodge are typical of a Victorian Lodge. There is a semi-formal garden which lends itself to quiet reflection with stunning views up Glenrinnes.   A walled kitchen garden with a large heated greenhouse both of which supply plants, cut flowers and fruit and vegetables. Here you will also find a newly developed herbaceous border displaying vibrant colours through the use of perennial and half hardy plantings. There are delightful walks in the meadow around the pond and into the woodland, watch out for red squirrels! Some major works have been undertaken recently and much of the garden is still a 'work in progress'.   In keeping with the rest of the estate, Glenrinnes Lodge is gardened following organic principles.

Open: Sunday 29 July, 2pm - 5pm, admission £4.00, children free.

Directions: In the centre of Dufftown at the Clock Tower take the B9009 road to Tomintoul for about one mile. After passing Dufftown Golf Club on your right there is a lane to the left which leads to two stone pillars to Glenrinnes Lodge.

· *Alzheimer's Research UK*

Greenhouse at Glenrinnes Lodge

7 GORDON CASTLE WALLED GARDEN

Fochabers, Moray IV32 7PQ
Angus and Zara Gordon Lennox
T: 01343 612317 E: info@gordoncastlescotland.com
W: www.gordoncastlescotland.com

Gordon Castle has one of the largest and oldest walled gardens in Britain. Eight acres in size, it is being lovingly restored to its former glory with a new design by award winning Anne Maynard which includes vegetables, fruit, herbs and cut flower beds alongside the amazing 259 espaliered trees on the 15 foot high walls. This wonderful kitchen garden has a 'Plant.Pick.Plate' ethos for its onsite cafe and there is a children's natural play area and shop.

Open: Saturday 14 July, 10am - 4pm, admission £5.00, children free. Also open 1 June - 31 October, admission £5.00 and the rest of the year admission £2.00. Children are free but there is a £3.00 charge for the children's play area which will be waived on the 14th July open day.

Directions: The main entrance is situated at the western end of the village of Fochabers on the A96, approximately nine miles east of Elgin and 12 miles west of Keith.

· *Fochabers Trust (Saturday 14 July) & Donation to SGS Beneficiaries (other dates)*

Moray & Nairn

8

GORDONSTOUN
Duffus, near Elgin IV30 5RF
Gordonstoun School
T: 01343 837837 E: richardss@gordonstoun.org.uk
W: www.gordonstoun.org.uk

The gardens consist of good formal herbaceous borders around lawns, a terrace and an orchard. The school grounds include Gordonstoun House, a Georgian house of 1775/6 incorporating an earlier 17th century house built for the First Marquis of Huntly, and the school chapel, both of which will be open to visitors. There is also a unique circle of former farm buildings known as the Round Square, and a scenic lake.

Open: Sunday 2 September, 2pm - 4pm, admission £5.00, children free.

Directions: Entrance off B9012, four miles from Elgin at Duffus Village.

· All proceeds to SGS Beneficiaries

9

HAUGH GARDEN
College of Roseisle IV30 5YE
Gwynne and David Hetherington
T: 01343 835790

We are now in the sixth year of developing our two acre garden with walks through mature woodland and young woodland which are planted with shade loving plants, rhododendrons, hydrangeas and spring flowering bulbs. Large lawns bordered by extensive herbaceous borders. Ongoing work to develop the garden around the ruins of an 18th century farmhouse continues. There is a wildlife pond with adjacent bog garden. A small orchard and an organic soft fruit and vegetable garden together with a greenhouse and large polytunnel.

Open: Open by arrangement 1 April - 31 August, admission £4.00, children free.

Directions: From Elgin take the A96 west, then the B9013 Burghead Road to the crossroads at the centre of College of Roseisle. The garden is on the right, enter from the Duffus Road. Village Hall car parking is to the left off Kinloss Road.

· Children's Hospice Association Scotland & Alzheimer Scotland

10

LOGIE HOUSE
Dunphail, Forres IV36 2QN
Alasdair and Panny Laing
E: panny@logie.co.uk
W: www.logie.co.uk

Originally a formal garden with a large area of vegetable production, Logie House garden has been developed since 1991 with emphasis on trees, shrubs and hardy perennials, giving all year round interest. The meandering burn and dry stone walls support the creation of a wide variety of planting habitats from dry sunny banks to damp shady areas. Many of the unusual plants are propagated for sale in the Garden Shop at Logie Steading.   Also features forest and river walks.

Open: 1 January - 31 December, 10am - 5pm, admission £2.00, children free.

Directions: Six miles south of Forres off A940. Follow signs to Logie Steading.

· Donation to SGS Beneficiaries

PEEBLESSHIRE & TWEEDDALE

Scotland's Gardens Scheme 2018 Guidebook is sponsored by INVESTEC WEALTH & INVESTMENT

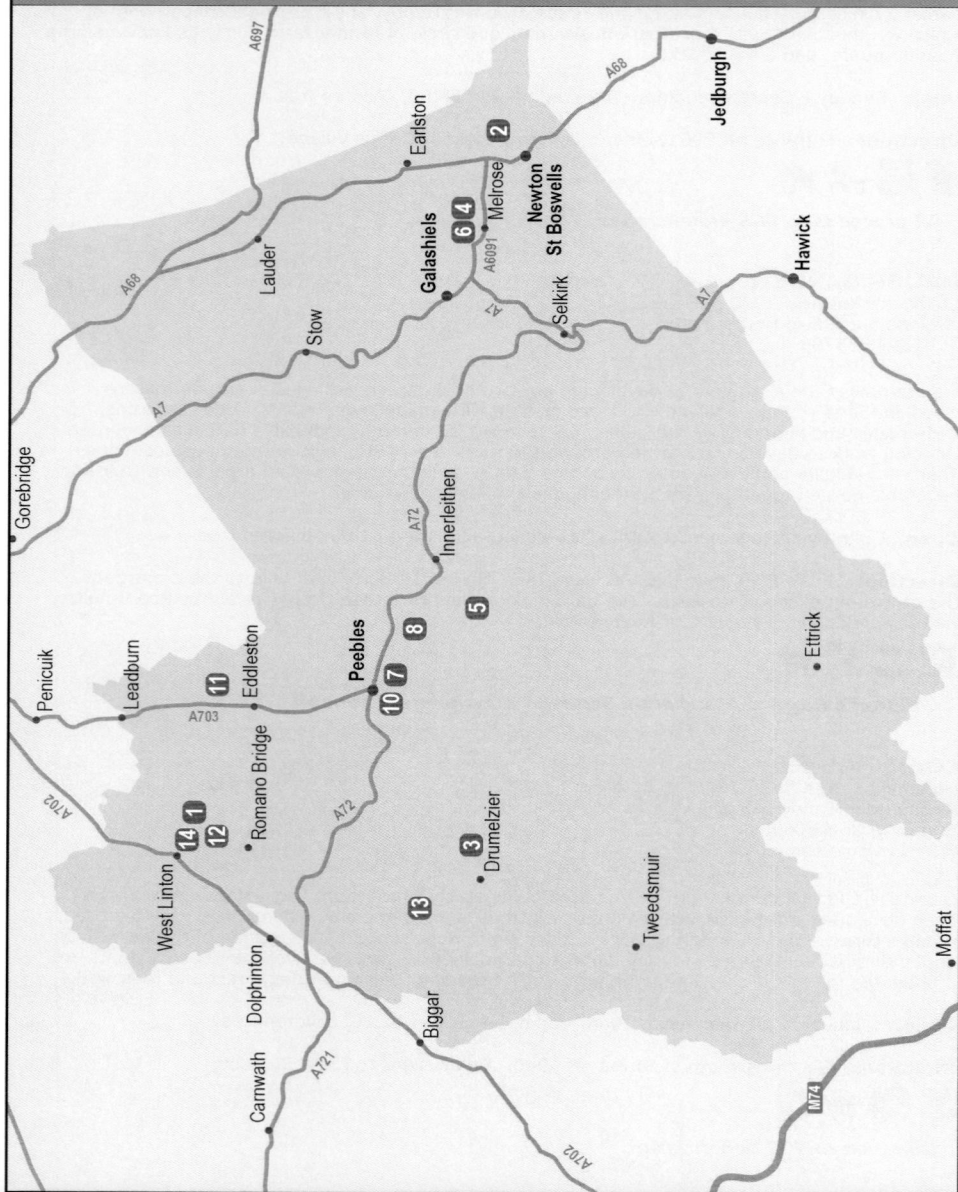

PEEBLESSHIRE & TWEEDDALE

OUR VOLUNTEER ORGANISERS

District Organiser:	Lesley McDavid	Braedon, Medwyn Road, Bridge of Earn, EH46 7HA E: peeblesshire@scotlandsgardens.org
Area Organisers:	Jennifer Barr	Allerly, Gattonside, Melrose, TD6 9LT
	Graham Buchanan-Dunlop	The Potting Shed, Broughton Place, ML12 6HJ
	Jenny Litherland	Laidlawstiel House, Clovenfords, Galashiels, TD1 1TJ
Treasurer:	John Bracken	Gowan Lea, Croft Road, West Linton, EH46 7DZ

GARDENS OPEN ON A SPECIFIC DATE

Kailzie Gardens, Peebles	Sunday, 25 February
Bemersyde, Melrose	Sunday, 22 April
Laidlawstiel House, Clovenfords, Galashiels	Wednesday, 23 May
Haystoun, Peebles	Sunday, 27 May
SGS Plant Sale at Halmyre Mains, West Linton	Sunday, 10 June
Laidlawstiel House, Clovenfords, Galashiels	Wednesday, 13 June
Glen House, Glen Estate, Innerleithen	Sunday, 1 July
West Linton Village Gardens, West Linton	Sunday, 8 July
Harmony and Priorwood Gardens, St Mary's Road, Melrose	Saturday/Sunday, 21/22 July
Gattonside Village Gardens, Gattonside	Sunday, 22 July
Peebles Gardens, Peebles	Sunday, 5 August
8 Halmyre Mains, West Linton	Sunday, 26 August
Dawyck Botanic Garden, Stobo	Sunday, 7 October

GARDENS OPEN REGULARLY

The Potting Shed, Broughton Place, Broughton, Biggar	12 June - 17 July (Tuesdays only)
Portmore, Eddleston	4 July - 29 August (Wednesdays only)

GARDENS OPEN BY ARRANGEMENT

Portmore, Eddleston	1 June - 31 August

Peeblesshire & Tweeddale

KEY TO SYMBOLS

NEW	New garden	♿	Full wheelchair access	🐕	Dogs on leads
☕	Basic teas	♿	Partial wheelchair access	**NPC**	National plant collection
H	Homemade teas	🌷	Plants for sale	🌳	Champion trees
C	Cream teas	👥	Children's activities		Designed landscape
🍸	Refreshments	🚌	Accessible by public transport		Snowdrop opening

All our gardens open to raise money for charity. Each opening may nominate a charity(s) to receive up to 60% of the takings and these are included with each listing. The net remaining raised supports our core beneficiaries. Information about our core beneficiaries can be found in the front section of the book. More information about our charity scheme and our symbols can be found in the back foldout section of the book under 'Tips for Using Your Guidebook'.

A red admiral butterfly rests on a Michaelmas daisy at Glen House

Peeblesshire & Tweeddale

1

8 HALMYRE MAINS
West Linton EH46 7BX
Joyce and Mike Madden
T: 07774 609 547 E: agentromanno@gmail.com

An half an acre organic garden with deep herbaceous borders surrounding the main lawn. Raised plots, a new greenhouse, keder house and polytunnel producing fruit and vegetables. A pergola leads to a sizeable composting area and then down to the pond with restyled viewing areas and sun house.

Open: Sunday 26 August, 2pm - 5pm, admission £4.00, children free. Teas will be provided in the nearby Lamancha Hub.

Directions: Five miles South of Leadburn Junction on the A701 (Moffat).

· *Lamancha Hub*

2

BEMERSYDE
Melrose TD6 9DP
The Earl and Countess of Haig

Sixteenth century peel tower reconstructed in the seventeenth century with added mansion house. Glorious show of daffodils around the house. Woodland garden and walks along the River Tweed, good footwear required.

Open: Sunday 22 April, 2pm - 5pm, admission £4.00, children free.

Directions: From A68 follow signs to Scott's View and then follow the yellow *Scotland's Gardens Scheme* signs to Bemersyde.

· *Earl Haig Fund Poppy Scotland*

3

DAWYCK BOTANIC GARDEN
Stobo EH45 9JU
A Regional Garden of the Royal Botanic Garden Edinburgh
T: 01721 760 254
W: www.rbge.org.uk/dawyck

Stunning collection of rare trees and shrubs. With over 300 years of tree planting, Dawyck is a world-famous arboretum with mature specimens of Chinese conifers, Japanese maples, Brewer's spruce, the unique Dawyck beech and sequoiadendrons from North America which are over 45 metres tall. Bold herbaceous plantings run along the burn. Range of trails and walks. Fabulous autumn colours.
National Plant Collection: *Larix* spp. and *Tsuga* spp.
Champion Trees: Numerous.

Open: Sunday 7 October, 10am - 5pm, admission details can be found on the garden's website.

Directions: Eight miles southwest of Peebles on B712.

· *Donation to SGS Beneficiaries*

Peeblesshire & Tweeddale

4

GATTONSIDE VILLAGE GARDENS
Gattonside TD69NP
The Gardeners of Gattonside
T: 07500 869 041 E: jenbarr@gmx.com
....

Various interesting and colourful village gardens. Some open for the first time.

Open: Sunday 22 July, 2pm - 6pm, admission £5.00, children free. Tickets and maps from Village Hall on Main Street. Teas and plant sale in the Village Hall.

Directions: Two miles from Leaderfoot Bridge on A68. North side of the River Tweed on B6360.

· MND Scotland: Doddie Weir'5 Discretionary Trust

5

GLEN HOUSE
Glen Estate, Innerleithen EH44 6PX
The Tennant Family
T: 01896 830210 E: info@glenhouse.com
W: www.glenhouse.com
....

Surrounding the outstanding Scots Baronial mansion designed by David Bryce in the mid-19th century, Glen House gardens are laid out on a series of shallow terraces overhanging the glen itself, which offers one of the loveliest designed landscapes in the Borders. The garden expands from the formal courtyard through a yew colonnade, and contains a fine range of trees, long herbaceous border and pool garden with pergola, all arranged within the curve of slopes sheltering the house.

Open: Sunday 1 July, 11am - 4pm, admission £5.00, children free. To celebrate 2018 as the Year of Young People, Glen is running a poetry competition on its open day. Write a poem on one of these three topics: 1. Dream Gardens, 2. Twigs or 3. What does Nature mean to you? Two categories: under 10 and 11-16 and three prizes for each: 1st prize £10, 2nd prize £7 and 3rd prize £3. Visitors are welcome to bring a picnic on the day.

Directions: Follow B709 out of Innerleithen for approximately two and a half miles. Right turn at signpost for Glen Estate.

· The Conservation Foundation

6

HARMONY AND PRIORWOOD GARDENS
St Mary's Road, Melrose TD6 9LJ
The National Trust for Scotland
T: 01896 822493 E: aleitch@nts.org.uk
W: www.nts.org.uk/property/harmony-garden
....

Harmony Garden : Wander through this tranquil garden, wonderful herbaceous borders, lawns, fruit and vegetable plots, and enjoy fine views of the Abbey and Eildon Hills.
Priorwood Garden : Overlooked by the Abbey ruins, this unique garden produces plants for a superb variety of dried flower arrangements made and sold here. The orchard also contains many historic apple varieties. Come along for a tour of Priorwood Garden with our knowledgeable staff to learn about the wide variety of dried flowers grown including annuals, herbs and perennials. See the unique flower drying room and discover the traditional skills of this colourful and aromatic ancient art.

Open: Saturday 21 July, 10am - 5pm. Also open Sunday 22 July, 1pm - 5pm. Admission by donation. Seasonal fruits and vegetable for sale on trolley at the entrance of Harmony.

Peeblesshire & Tweeddale

Directions: Off A6091, in Melrose, opposite the Abbey. Bus First from Edinburgh and Peebles.

· *Donation to SGS Beneficiaries*

7 HAYSTOUN
Peebles EH45 9JG
Mrs David Coltman

This sixteenth century house (not open) has a charming walled garden with an ancient yew tree, herbaceous beds and vegetable garden. There is a wonderful burnside walk created since 1980, with azaleas, rhododendrons and primulas leading to a small ornamental loch (cleared in 1990) with stunning views up Glensax Valley.

Open: Sunday 27 May, 1:30pm - 5pm, admission £5.00, children free.

Directions: Cross the River Tweed in Peebles to the south bank and follow *Scotland's Gardens Scheme* sign for approximately one mile.

· *MND Scotland: Doddie Weir'5 Discretionary Trust*

8 KAILZIE GARDENS
Peebles EH45 9HT
Lady Buchan-Hepburn
T: 01721 720007 E: angela.buchanhepburn@btinternet.com
W: www.kailziegardens.com

Semi-formal walled garden with shrubs and herbaceous borders, rose garden and excellent display of plants in large Victorian greenhouses. Woodland and burnside walks among spring bulbs, snowdrops, bluebells, rhododendrons and azaleas. The garden is set among fine old trees including a larch planted in 1725. Watch Osprey with live CCTV recordings of Ospreys nesting in the recently extended nature centre. Kailzie has been featured on *Landward* and *Beechgrove Garden*. Champion Trees: Larch planted 1725.

Open: Sunday 25 February, 10am - 4pm for the Snowdrop Festival, admission £4.00, children free. For details on garden and cafe opening see garden website. There is a children's play area.

Directions: Two and a half miles east of Peebles on B7062.

· *Erskine Hospital*

Release your creativity –
we need writers

Peeblesshire & Tweeddale

9

LAIDLAWSTIEL HOUSE
Clovenfords, Galashiels TD1 1TJ
Mr and Mrs P Litherland

Walled garden containing herbaceous border, fruit, and vegetables in raised beds. There are colourful rhododendrons and azaleas as well as splendid views down to the River Tweed.

Open: Wednesday 23 May, 1pm - 5pm. Also open Wednesday 13 June, 1pm - 5pm. Admission £4.00, children free.
Directions: A72 between Clovenfords and Walkerburn, turn up the hill signposted for *Thornielee*. The house is on the right at the top of the hill.

· *CLIC Sargent*

10

PEEBLES GARDENS
Peebles EH45 9DX
The Gardeners of Peebles
T: 01899 830574 E: buchanandunlop@btinternet.com

A group of four gardens will be opening in the beautiful Borders town of Peebles. The gardens are all different, varying in their size and the varieties of plants grown. You will find well established herbaceous borders, mature shrubs and trees, roses and climbers, and plantings in shade and moist ground. The gardeners are all enthusiastic amateurs who are passionate about their gardens and would love to share them with you.

Open: Sunday 5 August, 2pm - 5pm, admission £5.00, children free. A bus can take visitors between gardens. The bus will start from the Neidpath Road car park and include the car parks at Edinburgh Road and Kingsmeadows Road in its itinerary.

Directions: From Peebles yellow *Scotland's Gardens Scheme* signs direct you to the gardens at Frankscroft, south of the river, Innerleithen Road, near Peebles Hydro, and Connor Ridge.

· *Sandpiper Trust & MIND*

11

PORTMORE
Eddleston EH45 8QU
Mr and Mrs David Reid
T: 07825 294388
W: www.portmoregardens.co.uk

Lovingly created by the current owners over the past 20 years, the gardens surrounding the David Bryce designed mansion house contain mature trees and offer fine views of the surrounding countryside. Large walled garden with box-edged herbaceous borders is planted in stunning colour harmonies, potager, rose garden, pleached lime walk and ornamental fruit cages. The Victorian glasshouses contain fruit trees, roses, geraniums, pelargoniums and a wide variety of tender plants. There is also an Italianate Grotto and water garden with shrubs and meconopsis. The woodland walks are lined with rhododendrons, azaleas and shrub roses. Starred in *Good Gardens Guide* and featured in Kenneth Cox's book *Scotland for Gardeners* and *Beechgrove Gardens*.

Open: 4 July - 29 August (Wednesdays only), 1pm - 5pm. Also open by arrangement 1 June - 31 August. Admission £6.00, children free. Self service refreshments on Wednesdays openings. Homemade cream teas for groups over 15 people by prior arrangement.

Peeblesshire & Tweeddale

Directions: Off A703 one mile north of Eddleston. Bus 62.

· *The Lavender Touch*

12

SGS PLANT SALE AT HALMYRE MAINS
West Linton EH46 7BX
Joyce and Mike Madden

An early season plant sale gives an opportunity to preview the garden ahead of the main opening, when there will be a further sale. There will be a well stocked supply of plants with many having grown in the garden.

Open: Sunday 10 June, 10am - 12pm, admission £2.00, children free.

Directions: Five miles South of Leadburn Junction on the A701 (Moffat).

NEW

· *Lamancha Hub*

13

THE POTTING SHED
Broughton Place, Broughton, Biggar ML12 6HJ
Jane and Graham Buchanan-Dunlop
T: 01899 830574 E: buchanandunlop@btinternet.com

A one acre garden, begun from scratch in 2008, on an exposed hillside at 900 feet. It contains herbaceous plants, climbers, shrubs and trees, all selected for wind resistance and ability to cope with the poor, stony soil. There are (usually) fine views to the Southern Uplands.

Open: 12 June - 17 July (Tuesdays only), 11am - 5pm, admission £4.00, children free.

Directions: Signposted from the main A701 Edinburgh - Moffat Road, immediately north of Broughton Village.

· *Macmillan Cancer Support: Borders General Hospital*

14

WEST LINTON VILLAGE GARDENS
West Linton EH46 7EL
West Linton Village Gardeners
T: 01968 660669 E: j.bracken101@gmail.com

Once again a selection of gardens in the village will be opening. The gardens all vary in their size, design, planting styles and individual features with wide herbaceous borders, specimen trees, greenhouses full of pelargoniums and show begonias, an impressive hosta collection and an organic vegetable and fruit garden with a 'no dig' policy. Like most gardeners they are more than happy to talk about their gardens and offer advice come rain or shine.

Open: Sunday 8 July, 2pm - 5pm, admission £5.00, children free.

Directions: Take the A701 or A702 and follow road signs to West Linton. The hall where we take the admission fee, teas and plant sale is in the centre of the village and will be signposted.

· *Ben Walton Trust & Borders General Hospital, Margaret Kerr Unit*

PERTH & KINROSS

Scotland's Gardens Scheme 2018 Guidebook is sponsored by INVESTEC WEALTH & INVESTMENT

Dundee
Kirriemuir
Coupar Angus
Newport-o
St And
Cupar
Leven
Kirkcaldy
Newburgh
Glenrothes
Falkland
Blairgowrie
Auchtermuchty
Loch Leven
Kelty
Perth
Kinross
Cowdenbeath
Pitlochry
Dunkeld
Auchterarder
Dollar
Alva
Alloa
Blair Atholl
Crieff
Braco
Dunblane
Aberfeldy
Kenmore
Comrie
Callander
Thornhill
Stirling
Killin
Lochearnhead
Aberfoyle
Spean Bridge
Kinlochleven
Tyndrum
Crianlarich
Tarbet

Loch Treig
Loch Ericht
Loch Rannoch
Loch Lyon
Loch Tay
Loch Earn
Loch Katrine
Loch Long

Map markers: 1 2 3 4 5 6 7 8 9 10 11 12 13 14 15 16 17 18 19 20 21 22 23 24 25 26 27 28 29 30 31 32 33 34

PERTH & KINROSS

OUR VOLUNTEER ORGANISERS

District Organiser:	Margaret Gimblett	Fehmarn, Clayton Road, Bridge of Earn, PH2 9AH E: perthkinross@scotlandsgardens.org
Area Organisers:	Henrietta Harland	Easter Carmichael Cottage, Forgandenny Road, Bridge of Earn, PH2 9EZ
	Elizabeth Mitchell	Woodlee, 28 St Mary's Drive, Perth, PH2 7BY
	Lizzie Montgomery	Burleigh House, Milnathort, Kinross, KY13 9SR
	Judy Nichol	Rossie House, Forgandenny, PH2 9EH
	Judy Norwell	Dura Den, 20 Pitcullen Terrace, Perth, PH2 7EQ
	Bumble Ogilvy Wedderburn	Garden Cottage, Lude, Blair Atholl, PH18 5TR
	Richenda Pearson	Spinneyburn, Rumbling Bridge, KY13 0PY
	Clarinda Snowball	The Limes, Dollerie, Crieff, PH7 4JH
	Heather Wood	Mill of Forneth, Forneth, Blairgowrie, PH10 6SP
Treasurer:	Michael Tinson	Parkhead House, Burghmuir Road, Perth, PH1 1JF

GARDENS OPEN ON A SPECIFIC DATE

Branklyn Garden, 116 Dundee Road, Perth	Sunday, 11 February
Kilgraston School, Bridge of Earn	Sunday, 25 February
The Steading at Clunie, Newmill of Kinloch, Clunie, Blairgowrie	Sunday, 29 April
Abernethy Open Gardens, Abernethy	Saturday, 5 May
Fingask Castle, Rait	Sunday, 6 May
Branklyn Garden, 116 Dundee Road, Perth	Sunday, 13 May
Machany House, Auchterarder	Sunday, 13 May
SGS Plant Sale at Pitcurran House, Abernethy	Sunday, 20 May
Bonhard House, Perth	Sunday, 27 May
Explorers Garden, Pitlochry	Sunday, 3 June
Mill of Forneth, Forneth, Blairgowrie	Sunday, 3 June
Muckhart Village, Dollar	Sunday, 10 June
Blair Castle Gardens, Blair Atholl	Saturday, 23 June
The Bield at Blackruthven, Blackruthven House, Tibbermore	Saturday, 30 June
Wester Cloquhat , Bridge of Cally	Sunday, 1 July
Errol Park, Errol	Wednesdays, 11, 18 & 25 July
Drummond Castle Gardens, Crieff	Sunday, 5 August
Storytelling at Fingask, Rait	Thursday, 11 October

GARDENS OPEN REGULARLY

Braco Castle, Braco	28 January - 31 October
Eastbank Cottage, Perth Road, Abernethy	1 February - 30 June
Bolfracks, Aberfeldy	1 April - 31 October
Glendoick, by Perth	1 April - 31 May
Ardvorlich, Lochearnhead	1 May - 3 June
Bradystone House, Murthly	31 May - 26 July (Thursdays only)

Perth & Kinross

GARDENS OPEN BY ARRANGEMENT

Glenericht House Arboretum, Blairgowrie	On request
Glenlyon House, Fortingall	On request
Rossie House, Forgandenny	On request
Fingask Castle, Rait	29 January - 8 March (Mondays & Thursdays)
Briglands House, Rumbling Bridge	1 April - 10 June
Hollytree Lodge, Muckhart, Dollar	1 April - 31 October
Pitcurran House, Abernethy	1 April - 30 September
The Garden at Craigowan, Ballinluig	15 April - 31 July
7 Drum Gate, Abernethy, Perthshire	1 May - 30 June
Carig Dhubh, Bonskeid	1 May - 30 September
Dowhill, Cleish	1 May - 31 May (Wednesdays only)
Parkhead House, Parkhead Gardens, Burghmuir Road, Perth	1 May - 30 September
5 Sutherland Crescent, 5 Sutherland Crescent	14 May - 31 July

KEY TO SYMBOLS

NEW	New garden	Full wheelchair access		Dogs on leads
	Basic teas	Partial wheelchair access	NPC	National plant collection
H	Homemade teas	Plants for sale		Champion trees
C	Cream teas	Children's activities		Designed landscape
	Refreshments	Accessible by public transport		Snowdrop opening

All our gardens open to raise money for charity. Each opening may nominate a charity(s) to receive up to 60% of the takings and these are included with each listing. The net remaining raised supports our core beneficiaries. Information about our core beneficiaries can be found in the front section of the book. More information about our charity scheme and our symbols can be found in the back foldout section of the book under 'Tips for Using Your Guidebook'.

Perth & Kinross

5 SUTHERLAND CRESCENT

5 Sutherland Crescent PH2 9GA
Gill Boardman
T: 07833 576094 E: gillboard@btinternet.com

This garden was designed and planted in late 2011-2012. Originally a very boring modern estate house garden with grass and decking! Mainly perennials and grasses were planted at the side and front. There is a more traditional back garden with shrubs for structure and some perennials. Silver birch trees, rowan trees, laurel hedges, beech hedge and golden privet on the boundaries.

Open: Open by arrangement 14 May - 31 July, admission £3.00, children free.

Directions: Seven miles south of Perth. Leave the M90 at Junction 9 and follow signs for *Abernethy, Newburgh* and *Cupar* on the A912 for approximately five miles.   Garden owner will give detailed directions on request.

· *Marie Curie & The Uphill Trust*

**Scotland's Gardens Scheme
started in 1931 and
HRH King George V opened
Balmoral Gardens**

7 DRUM GATE

Abernethy, Perthshire PH2 9SA
Helen Morrison
E: helen72.hm@gmail.com

What started out in 2004 as just under an acre of bare earth has now turned into an attractive garden split into extensive herbaceous borders, large lawn areas and a young woodland with metasequoias, tulip tree, rhododendrons and wonderful views across the Tay Valley and upwards to the Ochils. The garden continues to develop and mature with earlier planting of topiary and hedging now being able to be sculptured, fruit trees and shrubs bearing produce. Visitors can meander through the garden, pausing in the children's Hideaway Cottage to listen and observe the many species of birds attracted to the garden. Work is ongoing but this is a rare example of what can be achieved from a blank canvas given vision, determination and plenty of time and patience.

Open: Open by arrangement 1 May - 30 June, admission by donation. This garden will also be open as part of the Abernethy Open Gardens on Saturday 5th May.

Directions: Seven miles south of Perth. Leave the M90 at Junction 9 and follow signs for *Abernethy, Newburgh* and *Cupar* on the A912 for approximately five miles.   Garden owner will give detailed directions on request.

· *Search And Rescue Dog Association Scotland*

Perth & Kinross

3

ABERNETHY OPEN GARDENS
Abernethy PH2
The Gardeners of Abernethy

The gardens range from individual plots of a few metres square in a sheltered housing scheme to much bigger gardens with ponds, ornamental trees and orchards.
5 Sutherland Crescent PH2 9GA (Gill Boardman): Once a garden of decking, transformed in 2012 to grasses, perennials and structural shrubs. Silver birch trees, rowan trees, laurel and beech hedges, and golden privet on the boundaries.
7 Drum Gate PH2 9SA (Helen Morrison): An attractive garden with a young woodland with matasequoias, tulip tree, fruit trees, and a children's Hideaway Cottage for bird watching.
An na Beatha 27-29 Main Street, PH2 9JH (Heather and Reid Martin): Situated in the conservation area of Abernethy. There is a small orchard of mainly ancient Scottish apple trees, vegetables beds, and a polytunnel.
Eastbank Cottage Perth Road, PH2 9LR (Mike Thompson): Traditional Scottish cottage, a third of an acre garden, walled and bounded by a small burn to the east and with erythroniums, azaleas, rhododendrons wood anemones, trillium and a fine display of clematis.
James Roy Court PH2 9HZ : A sheltered housing development in the old primary school in the village. The residents, working with thin soils and awkward spaces, have created fantastic individual gardens.
Nurse Peattie's Garden PH2 (Keir Allan): An awkward small triangular shady plot, lovingly cared for by village residents for the community. Nurse Peattie was a much loved District Nurse and the garden was made in her memory.
Struan House Station Road, PH2 9JS (Alan Fraser): Three distinct small to medium gardens in one. Two large ponds have been created allowing water lilies, frogs, fish and wildlife to thrive.

Open: Saturday 5 May, 10am - 5pm, admission £5.00, children free. Any questions about the gardens should be directed to Keir Allen (01738 850676)

Directions: Seven miles south of Perth. Leave the M90 at Junction 9 and follow signs for *Abernethy, Newburgh* and *Cupar* on the A912 for approximately five miles. Go left (straight on) at the mini roundabout. The church hall, for teas and tickets, and carpark will be signposted on the day.

· *Scotland's Charity Air Ambulance & Abernethy in Bloom*

4

ARDVORLICH
Lochearnhead FK19 8QE
Mr and Mrs Sandy Stewart
T: 01567 830218

Beautiful hill garden featuring over 170 different varieties of rhododendrons and many hybrids, grown in a glorious setting of oaks and birches on either side of the Ardvorlich Burn. Beautiful rhododendron glen.

Open: 1 May - 3 June, 9am - Dusk, admission £4.00, children free. The ground is quite steep in places and boots are advisable.

Directions: On South Loch Earn Road three miles from Lochearnhead, five miles from St Fillans.

· *The Gurkha Welfare Trust*

Perth & Kinross

The large lawn at 7 Drum gate

5 BLAIR CASTLE GARDENS
Blair Atholl PH18 5TL
Blair Charitable Trust
T: 01796 481207 E: office@blair-castle.co.uk
W: www.blair-castle.co.uk

Blair Castle stands as the focal point in a designed landscape of some 2,500 acres within a large and traditional estate.   Hercules Garden is a walled enclosure of about nine acres recently restored to its original 18th century form with landscaped ponds, a Chinese bridge, plantings, vegetables and an orchard of more than 100 fruit trees. The glory of this garden in summer is the herbaceous border which runs along the 275 metre south facing wall. A delightful sculpture trail incorporates contemporary and 18th century sculpture as well as eight new works, letter-carving on stone from the *Memorial Arts Charity's Art and Memory Collection*. Diana's Grove is a magnificent stand of tall trees including grand fir, Douglas fir, larch and wellingtonia in just two acres.

Open: Saturday 23 June, 9:30am - 5pm, admission details can be found on the garden's website.

Directions: Off A9, follow signs to *Blair Castle*, Blair Atholl.

· *All proceeds to SGS Beneficiaries*

6 BOLFRACKS
Aberfeldy PH15 2EX
The Douglas Hutchison Trust
T: 01887 820344 E: athel@bolfracks.com

Special three acre garden with wonderful views overlooking the Tay Valley. Burn garden with rhododendrons, azaleas, primulas and meconopsis in a woodland garden setting. Walled garden with shrubs, herbaceous borders and rose rooms with old fashioned roses. There is also a beautiful rose and clematis walk. Peony beds are under planted with tulips and Japanese anemone. The garden has a great selection of bulbs in spring and good autumn colour.

Open: 1 April - 31 October, 10am - 6pm, admission £4.50, children free.

Directions: Two miles west of Aberfeldy on A827. White gates and Lodge are on the left. Look out for the brown tourist signs.

· *All proceeds to SGS Beneficiaries*

Perth & Kinross

7 ## BONHARD HOUSE
Perth PH2 7PQ
Stephen and Charlotte Hay
T: 01738552471

A traditional 19th century garden of five acres approached through an avenue of magnificent oaks. Mature trees, six classified by the *National Tree Register* as 'remarkable', including a handsome monkey puzzle tree, sequoias, Douglas Fir and a wide variety of hollies. Grassy paths wind around ponds, rockeries, flowering shrubs and smaller trees, providing some splendid perspectives. Rhododendron and azalea beds, and a productive kitchen garden. There is a Pinetum on a knoll behind the house containing 25 species. Possible sighting of pine marten, red squirrels, and green and greater-spotted woodpeckers.

Open: Sunday 27 May, 10am - 4pm, admission £4.00, children free.

Directions: A94 one and a half kilometres north of Perth take right turn, signed *Murrayshall Hotel*. After approxiamately one mile take entrance right marked *Bonhard House* at a sharp left turn. From Balbeggie turn left, signposted for *Bonhard*, one mile north of Scone. Turn right in a half a mile, pass any sign for Bonhard Nursery, and enter drive at sharp right turn.

· *Freedom from Fistula Foundation*

8 ## BRACO CASTLE
Braco FK15 9LA
Mr and Mrs M van Ballegooijen
T: 01786 880437

A 19th century landscaped garden with a plethora of wonderful and interesting trees, shrubs, bulbs and plants. An old garden for all seasons that has been extensively expanded over the last 26 years. The partly walled garden is approached on a rhododendron and tree lined path featuring an ornamental pond. Spectacular spring bulbs, exuberant shrub and herbaceous borders, and many ornamental trees are all enhanced by the spectacular views across the park to the Ochils. From snowdrops through to vibrant autumn colour this garden is a gem. Look out for the embothrium in June, hoheria in August, eucryphia in September and an interesting collection of rhododendrons and azaleas with long flowering season.

Open: 28 January - 31 October, 10am - 5pm for the Snowdrop Festival, admission £4.00, children free.

Directions: Take a 1½ mile drive from the gates at the north end of Braco Village, just west of the bridge on the A822. Parking at the castle is welcome.

· *The Woodland Trust Scotland*

9 ## BRADYSTONE HOUSE
Murthly PH1 4EW
Mrs James Lumsden
T: 01738 710308 E: pclumsden@me.com

This perfect cottage garden was converted 25 years ago from a derelict farm steading to create a unique courtyard garden that will take your breath away. It has been imaginatively planted by Patricia Lumsden and her expert gardener Scott Henderson. Between them they have managed to have a long lasting changing picture of plants that complement each other in wonderful combinations. Grass walks guide you through the surrounding woodland where you can walk under mature and interesting trees, around shrubs, by a pond and discover the free roaming ducks and hens on your way. There is now a new kitchen garden adding extra interest. This is a gem of a garden and visitors who are fortunate enough to meet Patricia or Scott will be impressed by their enthusiasm and knowledge. Quite often there are plants for sale.

Perth & Kinross

Open: 31 May - 26 July (Thursdays only), 11am - 4pm, admission £5.00, children free.

Directions: From south/north follow A9 to Bankfoot, then sign to *Murthly*. At crossroads in Murthly take private road to Bradystone.

· **Donation to SGS Beneficiaries**

10 BRANKLYN GARDEN
116 Dundee Road, Perth PH2 7BB
The National Trust for Scotland
T: 01738 625535 E: jjermyn@nts.org.uk
W: www.nts.org.uk/Property/Branklyn-Garden/

This attractive garden in Perth was once described as 'the finest two acres of private garden in the country'. Originally designed and planted by the Rentons in the early 1920s, it continues to attract gardeners and botanists from all over the world. Enjoy an outstanding collection of plants, ranging from stately trees, a rare collection of rhododendron, an array of alpines planted in the original rock gardens, terraces and troughs, herbaceous and peat-loving plants, and new introductions of snowdrop varieties, plus a unique national collection of meconopsis and autumn-flowering gentians. So much to enjoy in all seasons in a peaceful setting, accompanied by a popular Tea Room.
National Plant Collection: *Cassiope, Meconopsis* (large flowered blue spp. & cvs.) and *Rhododendron* (subsect. *Taliense*).
Champion Trees: *Pinus sylvestris* 'Globosa'.

Open: Sunday 11 February, 10am - 5pm. Also open Sunday 13 May, 10am - 5pm. Admission details can be found on the garden's website.

Directions: On A85 Perth/Dundee road.

· **Donation to SGS Beneficiaries**

**Support a plant stall:
grow plants or sell
the wares!**

11 BRIGLANDS HOUSE
Rumbling Bridge KY13 0PS
Mrs Briony Multon
T: 01577 840205 E: briony@briglands.com

Lovingly restored by the current owners over the past 37 years, the nine acre garden, originally designed by Sir Robert Lorimer and then remodelled by him in 1898, surrounds the house. There are glorious displays of rhododendrons and spring bulbs, young trees and shrubs, an historic lime walk, peony garden, topiary and rockery.

Open: Open by arrangement 1 April - 10 June, admission £4.00, children free.

Directions: On A977 Kinross to Kincardine Bridge road, on the left just beyond Crook of Devon.

· **Local Animal Rescue Charities**

Perth & Kinross

12

CARIG DHUBH
Bonskeid PH16 5NP
Jane and Niall Graham-Campbell
T: 01796 473469 E: niallgc@btinternet.com

I don't know how Niall and Jane manage to grow their splendid meconopsis on the sand and rock of their garden but they do, most successfully. In this stunning situation, when not admiring the views, you will find wonderful primulas, cardiocrinum, meconopsis all interspersed between beautiful shrubs and other herbaceous plants. Look up and in July you will see roses flowering forty feet up in the tree. This is a gem of a garden and you will be welcomed by Niall and Jane Graham-Campbell with all their expert knowledge.

Open: Open by arrangement 1 May - 30 September, admission £5.00, children free. Prepare for steep slopes.

Directions: Take the old A9 between Pitlochry and Killiecrankie, turn west on the Tummel Bridge Road B8019, ¾ mile on north side of the road.

· *Earl Haig Fund Poppy Scotland*

13

DOWHILL
Cleish KY4 0HZ
Mrs Colin Maitland Dougall
T: 01577 850207 E: pippamd@icloud.com

A peaceful garden with ponds, poppies and primulas that has matured over the past 25 years like its octogenarian creators.

Open: Open by arrangement 1 May - 31 May (Wednesdays only), admission £5.00, children free.

Directions: Three quarters of a mile off M90, exit 5, towards Crook of Devon on the B9097 in the trees.

· *MND Scotland*

14

DRUMMOND CASTLE GARDENS
Crieff PH7 4HZ
Grimsthorpe & Drummond Castle Trust Ltd
W: www.drummondcastlegardens.co.uk

Activities and events for a great family day out. The gardens of Drummond Castle were originally laid out in 1630 by John Drummond, second Earl of Perth. In 1830 the parterre was changed to an Italian style. One of the most interesting features is the multi-faceted sundial designed by John Mylne, Master Mason to Charles I. The formal garden is said to be one of the finest in Europe and is the largest of its type in Scotland.

Open: Sunday 5 August, 1pm - 5pm, admission details can be found on the garden's website.

Directions: Entrance two miles south of Crieff on Muthill road (A822).

· *BLESMA*

Perth & Kinross

15 ## EASTBANK COTTAGE
Perth Road, Abernethy PH2 9LR
Mike Thompson

Traditional Scottish cottage, a third of an acre garden, walled and bounded by a small burn to the East. Erythroniums, varieties of wood anemones, trillium, a fine display of clematis, rhododendrons and azaleas. Altogether a little haven in the country.

Open: 1 February - 30 June, 2pm - 5pm, admission by donation.

Directions: When coming from Perth, drive past Abernethy *30 mile* sign. Layby on the left. Gate has property name on it. Bus 36 stops very close.

· All proceeds to SGS Beneficiaries

16 ## ERROL PARK
Errol PH2 7RA
Jamie Herriot-Maitland
E: enquiries@errolpark.co.uk
W: www.errolpark.co.uk

Errol Park dates from 1747 and is hidden behind ancient boundary walls. A romantic place which is one of Scotland's secret treasures. The garden still has the remains of a maze of yews from that date, and in 1815 the Wellingtonia Avenue was planted. There are vast walled gardens, glasshouses, superb specimen trees, ancient yew avenue, a quirky summerhouse, folly tower where couples can wed, stunning views over the Tay, gracious parkland with mighty oaks, herbaceous borders, vegetable garden and commercial flower picking garden. The walled gardens are a work progress (having been put down to grass in 1990).
Champion Trees: Seven trees including *Chamaecyparis obtusa* 'Aurea'.

Open: Wednesday 11 July, Wednesday 18 July & Wednesday 25 July, 11am - 4:30pm, admission £5.00, children free. Bunches of fresh flowers for sale on open days.

Directions: Enter by the main gate in the village of Errol, east of Perth.

· Carse of Gowrie Sustainability Group

17 ## EXPLORERS GARDEN
Pitlochry PH16 5DR
Pitlochry Festival Theatre
W: www.explorersgarden.com

This six acre woodland garden celebrates the Scottish Plant Hunters who risked their lives in search of new plants. The Explorers Garden is divided into geographic areas, each containing examples of the plants collected from that corner of the globe. Set in beautiful Highland Perthshire countryside, the garden is known for its meconopsis collection, stunning vistas and interesting sculptures and structures. Each year a photographic exhibition is held in the David Douglas Pavilion.
National Plant Collection: *Meconopsis* (large blue flowered spp. & cvs.).

Open: Sunday 3 June, 2pm - 5pm, admission £4.50, children free.

Directions: Take the A9 to Pitlochry town, then follow signs to *Pitlochry Festival Theatre*.

· Acting for Others

Perth & Kinross

18
FINGASK CASTLE
Rait PH2 7SA
Mr and Mrs Andrew Murray Threipland
T: 01821 670777 E: andrew@fingaskcastle.com
W: www.fingaskcastle.com

The garden with a sense of humour: Alice in Wonderland topiary staggers across the lawn, bumping into stone globes, marble balls and statues from three centuries. Historical and literary figures are scattered among pleasure gardens first laid out in the 18th century. Both Bonnie Prince Charlie and his father are said to have approached the castle from the longer yew parade, the Kings Walk. There is a marked 15 minute walk down the steep dell to a medieval wishing well (St. Peter's), over a Chinese Bridge crossing the Fingask burn via the Iron Age Fort to Fingask Loch and Sir Stuart's House, back along another path to the orchard car park (wellies recommended). There are large drifts of snowdrops, daffodils and flowering shrubs depending on the season. Champion Trees: Bhutan Pine.

Open: Open by arrangement 29 January - 8 March (Mondays & Thursdays) for the Snowdrop Festival, admission £3.00, children free. Also open Sunday 6 May, 12pm - 5pm, admission £4.00, children free.

Directions: Half way between Perth and Dundee. From the A90 follow signs to Rait until small crossroad, turn right and follow signs to *Fingask*.

· *Fingask Follies & All Saints Church, Glencarse*

19
GLENDOICK
by Perth PH2 7NS
Kenneth Cox
T: 01738 860260 E: manager@glendoick.com
W: www.glendoick.com

Glendoick is the ideal spring day out with a visit to both the gardens and garden centre in April and May. Glendoick was included in the *Independent on Sunday* survey of Europe's top 50 gardens with a unique collection of plants from Cox plant-hunting expeditions in China & the Himalaya. Glendoick's five acres includes spectacular rhododendrons, magnolias and meconopsis, grown in the woodland garden with its burn and waterfalls, the walled garden and the gardens surrounding the house. Many Glendoick plants have been bred by the Cox family, and new unnamed hybrids are in the walled garden. The award-winning Glendoick Garden Centre has one of Scotland's best selections of plants including their world-famous rhododendrons and azaleas.
National Plant Collection: *Rhododendron* (sect. *Pogonanthum*, subsect. *Uniflora*, subsect. *Campylogyna* & subsect. *Glauca* and Cox hybrids).

Open: 1 April - 31 May, 10am - 4pm, admission £5.00, children free.

Directions: Follow brown signs to *Glendoick Garden Centre* off A90 Perth - Dundee road. Drive up driveway and park on gravel, gardens are a short walk up a slope. Bus X8 is hourly except on Sunday. Stops by garden centre, ½ mile from garden.

· *Donation to SGS Beneficiaries*

Many of our gardens offer fantastic homemade teas!

Perth & Kinross

20

GLENERICHT HOUSE ARBORETUM
Blairgowrie PH10 7JD
Mrs William McCosh
T: 01250 872092

Spectacular collection of Victorian planted trees and shrubs which are centred around a Grade 'A' listed suspension bridge (1846). Ninety-two tree varieties, mostly conifers including a top Douglas fir which is 171 feet and still growing, also a collection of younger trees. In May you will be able to view the wonderful daffodils and the rhododendrons in flower.

Open: Open by arrangement, admission £4.00, children free. Drive is single track and steep in places. The bridge marks the border of the arboretum and the private garden.

Directions: Off A93, the Lodge House is five miles north of Blairgowrie on the right hand side A93 from Blairgowrie. Follow the avenue to the bridge.

· *Sands*

21

GLENLYON HOUSE
Fortingall PH15 2LN
Mr and Mrs Iain Wotherspoon
T: 07974 350533

Interesting garden framed by hedges, with colourful herbaceous borders and fruit trees underplanted with perennials and annuals. There is a kitchen and cutting garden as well as a wildlife pond.

Open: Open by arrangement, admission £5.00, children free.

Directions: Take the A827 Aberfeldy, B846 Coshieville then turn off for Fortingall and Glen Lyon.

· *Fortingall Parish Church*

22

HOLLYTREE LODGE
Muckhart, Dollar FK14 7JW
Liz and Peter Wyatt
T: 0797 337 4687 E: elizwyatt @aol.com

A tranquil garden, divided by internal hedges into smaller areas. These include a small Japanese garden, spring bulbs naturalised in grass, a mini orchard and wildflowers, a rill, a wildlife pond, mixed herbaceous borders, all within an acre plot. An interesting variety of unusual trees and shrubs, a good collection of rhododendrons and deciduous azaleas, a snow gum, a *Metasequoia glyptostroboides* and a Persian ironwood which colours beautifully in autumn, as do the acers. Plus a Tree Trail. The garden featured in *Country Homes* and *Interiors* January 2015 edition. Our aim is to garden with nature, and organically, complementing our beekeeping interests; the best planting scheme often seems to happen by accident!

Open: Open by arrangement 1 April - 31 October, admission £4.00, children free. Family friendly pond dipping and nature hunt available for children, sensory garden plants. Groups up to 25 most welcome, short notice no problem.

Directions: Approxiamately 100m off the A91 (between Dollar and Milnathort) down the small lane directly opposite the entrance to the Inn at Muckhart.

· *Coronation Hall, Muckhart*

Perth & Kinross

23

KILGRASTON SCHOOL
Bridge of Earn PH2 9BQ
Kilgraston School
T: 01738 815517 E: marketing@kilgraston.com
W: www.kilgraston.com

Enjoy the carpet of snowdrops, admire the ancient yews, towering wellingtonias, and the resident red squirrels, whilst exploring the pathways and woodlands within the extensive ground of this 19th centurwy house. Formerly home to the Grant family, it has been a girls' boarding school since 1930. Statues and sculptures, some by renowned architect Hew Lorimer, dot the landscape. There is a ruined chapel to visit in the grounds, a good children's play area and an excellent display of artwork within the school.

Open: Sunday 25 February, 1:30pm - 4pm for the Snowdrop Festival, admission £4.00, children free.

Directions: Bridge of Earn is three miles south of Perth on the A912. *Kilgraston School* is well signposted from the main road. Maps are available at http://www.kilgraston.com/contact.

· *The Mission to Seafarers Scotland Limited*

24

MACHANY HOUSE
Auchterarder PH3 1NW
Mr and Mrs J Robertson
E: jcr@machany.com

An informal garden within an arboriculturalist's heaven. The open lawns allow visual space to appreciate the splendour of mature trees. In particular, giants of the American Pacific coast; majestic specimens of wellingtonia and Douglas fir and many hardwoods. A magnificent array of rhododendrons, azaleas, bamboos and much more.   A developing collection of herbaceous and a comprehensive display of bulbs feature throughout the garden. Visitors will wander through a variety of settings, ranging from the informal woodland dell leading to a tranquil burn, to the more formal around the house.

Open: Sunday 13 May, 2pm - 5pm, admission £5.00, children free.

Directions: Machany is five miles from Crieff (turn left in Muthill), four miles from Auchterarder (Castleton Road via Tullibardine towards Strathallan Airfield) and three miles from the Gleneagles Hotel. Route from the north and south: A9 to Gleneagles, signposted to *Crieff* A823. Follow road approximately two miles and look for *SGS* signs.

· *St Kessog's Episcopal Church - Auchterarder*

**Creating an inspiring,
rewarding and enjoyable
experience for volunteers and
visitors alike**

Perth & Kinross

25 ## MILL OF FORNETH
Forneth, Blairgowrie PH10 6SP
Mr and Mrs Graham Wood
E: gaw@gwpc.demon.co.uk

Built on the site of a watermill on the Lunan Burn, originally laid out in the 1970s by James Aitken, the Scottish landscape designer and naturalist. The sheltered four acre garden has a range of mature trees, including a Himalayan blue cedar, large rhododendrons, azaleas and a wide range of shrubs. The former mill lade feeds rocky waterfalls and a lily pond. Planting includes established perennials with seasonal colours, many bulbs, primulas and heathers, plus a vegetable garden on the site of an old tennis court.

Open: Sunday 3 June, 2pm - 5pm, admission £4.50, children free.

Directions: Take the A923 Dunkeld to Blairgowrie road. Six miles east of Dunkeld turn south onto a minor road signposted *Snaigow* and *Clunie*. Mill of Forneth is the first gate on the left hand side.

· Blairgowrie Black Watch Army Cadet Force & Perth and Kinross District Nurses

26 ## MUCKHART VILLAGE
Dollar FK14 7JN
The Gardeners of Muckhart Village

Hollytree Lodge Muckhart, FK14 7JW (Liz and Peter Wyatt): A tranquil garden, with unusual trees and shrubs, azaleas and rhododendrons.
Mount Stuart House Glendevon, FK14 7JZ (Gordon Smith): Large rural garden with drystone wall terraces, mature trees, and a new wetland under construction.
5 Golf View Pool of Muckhart FK14 7JP (Joy Scott): This is a wildlife friendly cottage style garden with vegetables and fruit growing alongside the flowers.
Moss Park Coach House Rumbling Bridge KY13 0QE (Meriel Cairns): A small new garden created from a paddock with shrubs and herbaceous flowers, and an attractive pond.
The Willows Muckhart, FK14 7JH (Sheena Anderson): Mixed herbaceous garden with edible plants, patio feature, fruit trees, azaleas and rhododendrons.
17 Cairns Place Pool of Muckhart, FK14 7LH (Marilyn Smith): The open aspect at the front of the garden borders a small stream, a lovely village garden which has a bit of everything.
Balliliesk House Yetts O'Muckhart, FK14 7JT (Alison Peden): Large mature garden with impressive Japanese maples, rhododendrons and azaleas.
The Steading Yetts O'Muckhart, FK14 7JT (Fiona Chapman): Paths meander through terraced beds and ponds planted with seasonal plants and species trees.

Open: Sunday 10 June, 12pm - 5pm, admission £6.00, children free. Group ticket and map will be available from the village hall, known locally as *Coronation Hall* where refreshments will be available.

Directions: The adjacent village of The Pool and Yetts O'Muchhart are situated on the A91, approximately four miles east of Dollar. Parking is available at Mount Stuart House and Moss Park Coach House. A shuttle car will be available for those who want it. There is also some parking at various gardens.

· Coronation Hall, Muckhart

Perth & Kinross

27

PARKHEAD HOUSE
Parkhead Gardens, Burghmuir Road, Perth PH1 1RB
Mr & Mrs M.S. Tinson
T: 01738 625983 M:07748186815 E: maddy.tinson@gmail.com
W: www.parkheadgardens.com

Parkhead is an old farmhouse sited within an acre of beautiful gardens. Mature trees include an outstanding 300 year old Spanish chestnut. This hidden gem is a garden for all seasons. Gentle terracing and meandering paths lead you past a large variety of unusual and interesting plants and shrubs. If you seek colour and inspiration come and see this garden.
National Plant Collection: *Lilium* (Mylnefield lilies).

Open: Open by arrangement 1 May - 30 September, admission £5.00, children free. We can accept short notice bookings.

Directions: Parkhead Gardens is a small lane off the west end of Burghmuir Road in Perth. More detailed directions on request.

· *Plant Heritage*

28

PITCURRAN HOUSE
Abernethy PH2 9LH
The Hon Ranald and Mrs Noel-Paton
T: 01738 850933 E: patricianp@pitcurran.com

The garden was created 14 years ago. It includes an interesting combination of trees, rare shrubs and herbaceous plants including azaleas, rhododendrons, tree peonies, trillums and *Smilacena racemosa* and also a rose pergola, eucryphias and a large west-facing hydrangea border for the later summer. Above the pond there is a good collection of pink and white barked birches.

Open: Open by arrangement 1 April - 30 September, admission £5.00, children free.

Directions: South East of Perth. From M90 (exit 9) take A912 towards Glenfarg, go left at roundabout onto A913 to Abernethy. Pitcurran House is at the far eastern end of the village.

· *Juvenile Diabetes Research Foundation Limited*

29

ROSSIE HOUSE
Forgandenny PH2 9EH
Mr and Mrs David B Nichol
T: 01738 812265 E: judynichol@rossiehouse.co.uk
W: www.rossiegardens.com

This romantic garden has been establishing itself since 1657. It is a magical mystery tour of endless paths meandering under magnificent trees, unusual shrubs with a plethora of woodland bulbs and plants at your feet. Lift the branches of a *Hamamelis mollis* to find the startled heron take off from the pond and look up to the massive trunk of the *Abies alba* 100 feet up. From snowdrops to hellebores then trillium and bluebells, flowering shrubs and roses, the interest of the garden continues until the wonderful autumn colours. The sculptures by David Annand and Nigel Ross. Look out for the ten foot tea pot and the yew table ready for the Mad Hatters' tea party! The garden is at its best in May.

Open: Open by arrangement, admission £5.00, children free.

Perth & Kinross

Directions: Forgandenny is on the B935 between Bridge of Earn and Dunning.

· Donation to SGS Beneficiaries

Aconites and snowdrops at Rossie House

30 SGS PLANT SALE AT PITCURRAN HOUSE

Abernethy PH2 9LH
The Hon Ranald and Mrs Noel-Paton
T: 01738 850933 E: patricianp@pitcurran.com

Extensive, interesting and unusual plant sale, mostly sourced from private gardens. The garden which was created 14 years ago is also open. Leslie Bisset (ex Curator of the Dundee Botanic Gardens) will be available to answer any horticultural questions.

Open: Sunday 20 May, 12pm - 5pm, admission by donation.

Directions: South East of Perth. From M90 (exit 9) take A912 towards Glenfarg, go left at roundabout onto A913 to Abernethy. Pitcurran House is at the far eastern end of the village.

· Juvenile Diabetes Research Foundation Limited

31 STORYTELLING AT FINGASK

Rait PH2 7SA
Mr and Mrs Andrew Murray Threipland
T: 01821 670777 E: andrew@fingaskcastle.co,
W: www.fingaskcastle.com

Once upon a time...

There is many a tale to be told at Fingask. Alice in Wonderland topiary staggers across the lawn, bumping into stone globes and statues from three centuries. Historical and literary figures, steel shapes, black torsos, and belvederes are scattered among pleasure gardens first laid out in the 18th century. Three jolly drinkers: Burns, Tam O'Shanter and Souter Johnnie dominate the short yew walk above the castle. Both Bonnie Prince Charlie and his father are said to have approached the castle from the longer yew parade aptly named the King's Walk.

Join Scotland's Gardens Scheme and The Scottish International Storytelling Festival in "Growing Stories". A fun packed way to explore some of Scotland's gardens. See gardens with new eyes once you hear stories, from local Storytellers, about their creation, history and interaction with the environment.

Open: Thursday 11 October, 2pm - 5pm, admission £5.00, children free.

Directions: Half way between Perth and Dundee. From the A90 follow signs to Rait until small crossroad, turn right and follow signs to *Fingask*.

· Fingask Follies

Perth & Kinross

32 THE BIELD AT BLACKRUTHVEN

Blackruthven House, Tibbermore PH1 1PY
The Bield Christian Co Ltd
T: 01738 583238 E: info@bieldatblackruthven.org.uk

The Bield is set in extensive grounds comprising well maintained lawns and clipped hedges, a flower meadow and a large collection of specimen trees. Visitors are encouraged to stroll around the grounds and explore the labyrinth cut into the grass of the old orchard. The main garden is a traditional walled garden containing extensive herbaceous borders, manicured lawns and an organic vegetable plot. The walled garden also contains a wide variety of trained fruit trees, a fruit cage, a glasshouse and a healing garden.

Open: Saturday 30 June, 1pm - 5pm, admission £5.00, children free.

Directions: From Dundee or Edinburgh, follow signs for *Glasgow, Stirling* and *Crianlarich* which lead onto the Perth bypass. Head west on the A85 signed to *Crieff/Crianlarich* to West Huntingtower. Turn left at the crossroads to Madderty/Tibbermore. Entrance left after ½ mile passing the gate lodge on your right. Parking signed to right at the steading.

· Southton Smallholding

33 THE GARDEN AT CRAIGOWAN

Ballinluig PH9 0NE
Ian and Christine Jones
T: 01796 482244 E: i.q.jones@btinternet.com

"I am just bowled over! I have never ever seen so many and such a variety of species rhododendrons growing in a private garden in this country!" - the reaction of an eminent gardener from Ireland. Craigowan is a hidden gem overlooking the Tay and Tummel valleys at an elevation of 600 feet. The garden of five acres has woodland, lawns and beautiful herbaceous and planted areas. The plant collection is mainly rhododendrons, magnolias, lilies and traditional companion plants as well as a wonderful show of meconopsis, and giant Himalayan lilies in June.

Open: Open by arrangement 15 April - 31 July, admission £6.00, children free.

Directions: From north or south A9 to Ballinluig junction. Follow sign for *Tulliemet* and *Dalcapon*. Pass the filling station and Red Brolly Cafe. Turn right following the *Tulliemet/ Dalcapo* sign. This is a steep narrow road so take care. About ½ mile up the road take a left turning with fields on either side and Craigowan is the first house on the left about ½ mile along. Park on paviours adjoining house.

· LUPUS UK

60% of a garden opening's proceeds can be donated to the Garden Owner's nominated charity

Perth & Kinross

34

THE STEADING AT CLUNIE

Newmill of Kinloch, Clunie, Blairgowrie PH10 6SG
Jean and Dave Trudgill
T: 01250 884263

....

The Steading at Newmill is situated on The Lunan Burn midway between Lochs Clunie and Marlee. There is a small cottage garden with a fish pond that leads on to the wild flower meadow that, hopefully, will be carpeted with cowslips. A bridge over the tail-race of the old mill is the start of the woodland walk around two ponds and for more than 0.5km along the Lunan Burn with displays of wood anemones, lady's smock and primoses. The area is a haven for wildlife with beavers burrowing into the banks of the mill race.

Open: Sunday 29 April, 2pm - 5pm, admission £4.50, children free. Narrow paths, bridges and flowing water. Friendly hens - hence no dogs.

Directions: Three miles west of Blairgowrie on the A923. About 600 metres after the Kinloch Hotel in the direction of Dunkeld take the track on the left, just after a mobile phone mast and a breeze block wall. There is parking for ten vehicles on a paved area, and ample parking in a neighbour's field, provided the ground is not soft.

· Save the Children UK

Cowslips at The Steading at Clunie

35

WESTER CLOQUHAT

Bridge of Cally PH10 7JP
Brigadier and Mrs Christopher Dunphie

....

Terraced garden, water garden, lawns, mixed borders with a wide range of shrubs, roses and hebaceous plants. Splendid situation with fine view to the River Ericht.

Open: Sunday 1 July, 2pm - 5pm, admission £5.00, children free.

Directions: Turn off A93 just north of Bridge of Cally and follow signs for ½ mile.

· ABF The Soldiers' Charity

RENFREWSHIRE

Scotland's Gardens Scheme 2018 Guidebook is sponsored by INVESTEC WEALTH & INVESTMENT

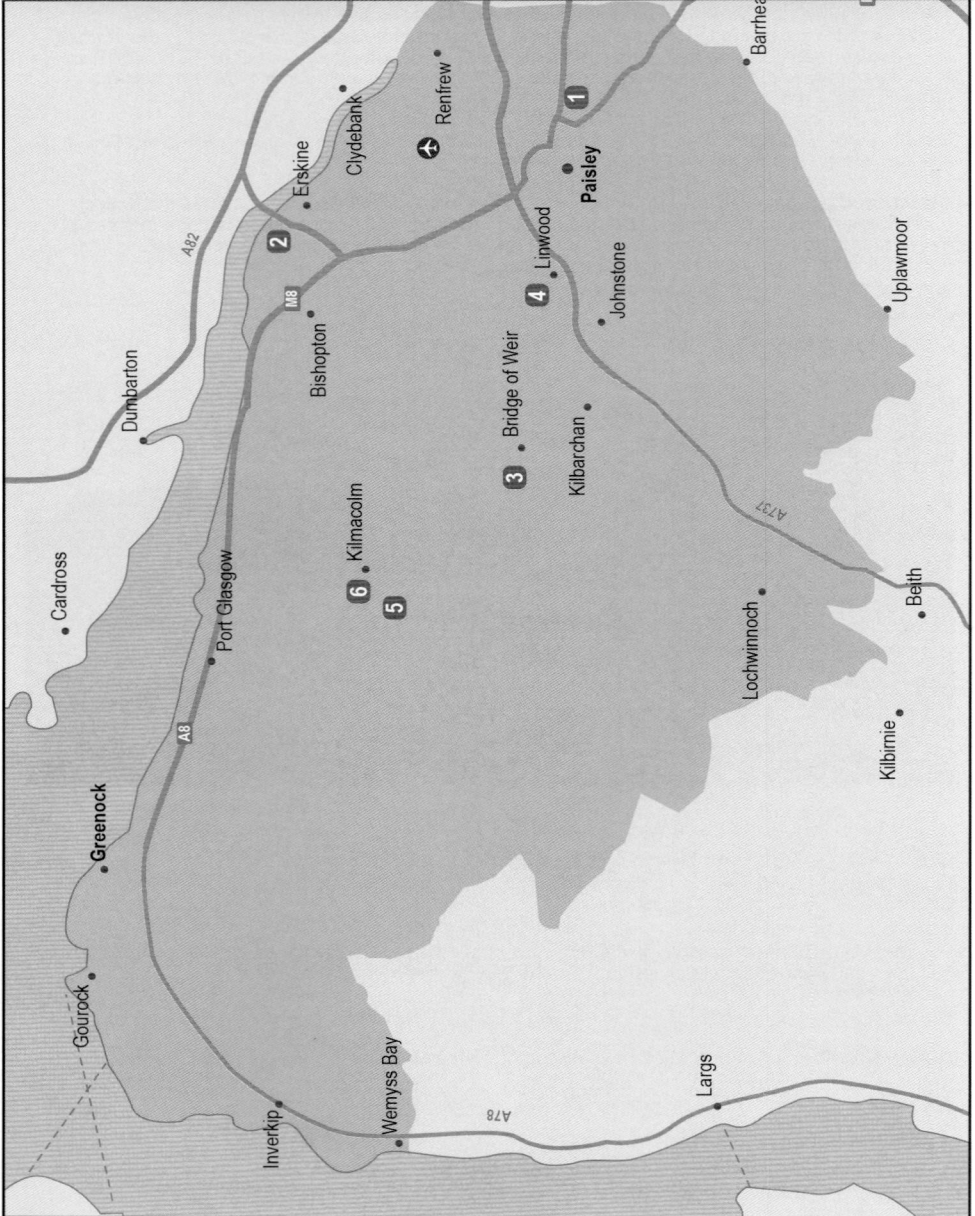

RENFREWSHIRE

OUR VOLUNTEER ORGANISERS

District Organisers:	Rosemary Leslie	High Mathernock Farm, Auchentiber Road, Kilmacolm, PA13 4SP T: 01505 874032
	Alexandra MacMillan	Langside Farm, Kilmacolm PA13 4SA T:01475 540423 E: renfrewshire@scotlandsgardens.org
Area Organisers:	Helen Hunter	2 Bay Street, Fairlie, North Ayrshire, KA29 0AL
	Barbara McLean	49 Middlepenny Road, Langbank, PA14 6XE
Treasurer:	Jean Gillan	Bogriggs Cottage, Carlung, West Kilbride, KA23 9PS

GARDENS OPEN ON A SPECIFIC DATE

Kilmacolm Plant Sale, Library, Lochwinnoch Road, Kilmacolm	Saturday, 28 April
Highwood, off Lochwinnoch Road, Kilmacolm	Sunday, 13 May
Barshaw Park Walled Garden, 176A Glasgow Road, Paisley	Saturday, 19 May
Carruth, Bridge of Weir	Sunday, 27 May
Craig Hepburn Memorial Garden, Linwood High School	Saturday, 9 June
Bravehound - Erskine Hospital, Old Garden Centre, Bishopton	Sunday, 26 August

KEY TO SYMBOLS

NEW New garden	Full wheelchair access	Dogs on leads
Basic teas	Partial wheelchair access	NPC National plant collection
Homemade teas	Plants for sale	Champion trees
Cream teas	Children's activities	Designed landscape
Refreshments	Accessible by public transport	Snowdrop opening

All our gardens open to raise money for charity. Each opening may nominate a charity(s) to receive up to 60% of the takings and these are included with each listing. The net remaining raised supports our core beneficiaries. Information about our core beneficiaries can be found in the front section of the book. More information about our charity scheme and our symbols can be found in the back foldout section of the book under 'Tips for Using Your Guidebook'.

Renfrewshire

1 **BARSHAW PARK WALLED GARDEN**
176A Glasgow Road, Paisley PA1 3LT
Friends of Barshaw Park

The old walled garden, a haven in a busy world and one of Paisley's forgotten treasures, has been adopted by 'Friends of Barshaw', volunteers, who are working to bring it back to its formal glory. Designated a Peace Garden, it contains borders of colour and interest all year round, from bulbs to perennials and glorious bushes. The rest of the park with a boating pond and children's play area, can be enjoyed at leisure. Teas are available to buy in the teashop in the park.

Open: Saturday 19 May, 2pm - 4pm, admission £3.00, children free. The park has a pond for sailing model boats, miniature railway and cafe.

Directions: From Paisley town centre along the Glasgow road (A737) pass Barshaw Park and take first left into Oldhall Road and then first left again into walled garden car park. Pedestrian visitors can also approach from Barshaw Park by mid gate in Glasgow Road. Accessible by McGill's buses.

· *FOBP: The Friends of Barshaw Park*

2 **BRAVEHOUND - ERSKINE HOSPITAL**
Old Garden Centre, Bishopton PA7 5PU
Glen Art Volunteers
E: bravehound@glenart.co.uk
W: bravehead.co.uk

A quirky enclosed tarmac garden, run by the charity Glen Art, features an assortment of outdoor raised planters, covered growing areas, shady/quiet garden and other features embracing the upcycling ethos. Glen Art helps those from a military background return to civilian life through a variety of creative ventures and this garden can testify to the therapeutic benefits of gardens and dogs. Being the 'Bravehound' site, this new project looks to provide companion dogs to veterans to support their transition to civilian life.

Open: Sunday 26 August, 1pm - 4pm, admission £3.50, children free.   The opening will include doggy displays in an enclosed part of the garden, check website for more details.

Directions: From M8, take exit for Erskine Bridge and turn off to Bishopton. From the North, go over Erskine Bridge, take turning to Bishopton. Located on the south side of the Erskine Bridge, enter the Erskine Home Estate and follow signs for *Bravehound*.

· *Glen Art : Bravehound*

3 **CARRUTH**
Bridge of Weir PA11 3SG
Mr and Mrs Charles Maclean

Over 20 acres of long established rhododendrons, woodland with good bluebells, young arboretum and lawn gardens in lovely landscaped setting.

Open: Sunday 27 May, 2pm - 5pm, admission £4.00, children free.

Directions: Access from B786 Kilmacolm/Lochwinnoch road. From Bridge of Weir take Torr Road until you get to the B786. Turn right and after approximately 100 yards the garden entrance is on the right. About 3½ miles from Kilmacolm and 5½ miles from Lochwinnoch on B786.

· *Marie Curie: Renfrewshire*

Renfrewshire

4

CRAIG HEPBURN MEMORIAL GARDEN
Stirling Drive, Linwood PA3 3NB
Linwood High School
T: 01505 336146 E: craighepburnmemorialgarden@yahoo.co.uk
W: facebook.com/welovegardening14/
....

The Craig Hepburn Memorial Garden and Outdoor Learning Centre is located in Linwood High School. Our original garden with an outdoor classroom has been expanded to include community raised beds, an orchard, greenhouse, and presentation area. We work with all years in the school reconnecting them to the natural world whether it is through growing in our organic garden, encouraging biodiversity or learning about sustainability.

Open: Saturday 9 June, 2pm - 5pm, admission £3.50, children free. Face painting, bouncy castle, "how-to" classes and planting seeds.

Directions: Exit M8 at St James Interchange and take A737. Take exit for Linwood onto A761, follow to Clippens Road and then Stirling Drive. Accessible by McGill buses.

· *Accord Hospice*

5

HIGHWOOD
off Lochwinnoch Road, Kilmacolm PA13 4TA
Jill Morgan
....

Woodland walk around 50 acres of beautiful native bluebells in a delightful setting bordering the Green Water river with tumbling waterfalls. Stout waterproof footwear is essential as paths can be muddy. Dogs welcome on a lead. Fantastic opportunities for lovers of wild flowers and photography.

Open: Sunday 13 May, 2pm - 5pm, admission £5.00 per car. Duck races on the day, weather permitting.

Directions: Take B786 Lochwinnoch Road out of Kilmacolm and continue for approximately two miles. From Lochwinnoch take B786 Kilmacolm road for approximately six miles. Then follow SGS signs.

· *Orkidstudio*

6

KILMACOLM PLANT SALE
outside Kilmacolm Library, Lochwinnoch Road, Kilmacolm PA13 4EL
Scotland's Gardens Scheme - Renfrewshire
....

Spring plant sale in the centre of Kilmacolm.

Open: Saturday 28 April, 10am - 12pm, admission by donation.

Directions: The plant sale will be held at the Cross outside the Library and Cargill Centre. Accessible by McGill Buses.

· *Parklea Branching Out*

**Are you snap happy?
Send us your garden
photographs**

ROXBURGHSHIRE

Scotland's Gardens Scheme 2018 Guidebook is sponsored by INVESTEC WEALTH & INVESTMENT

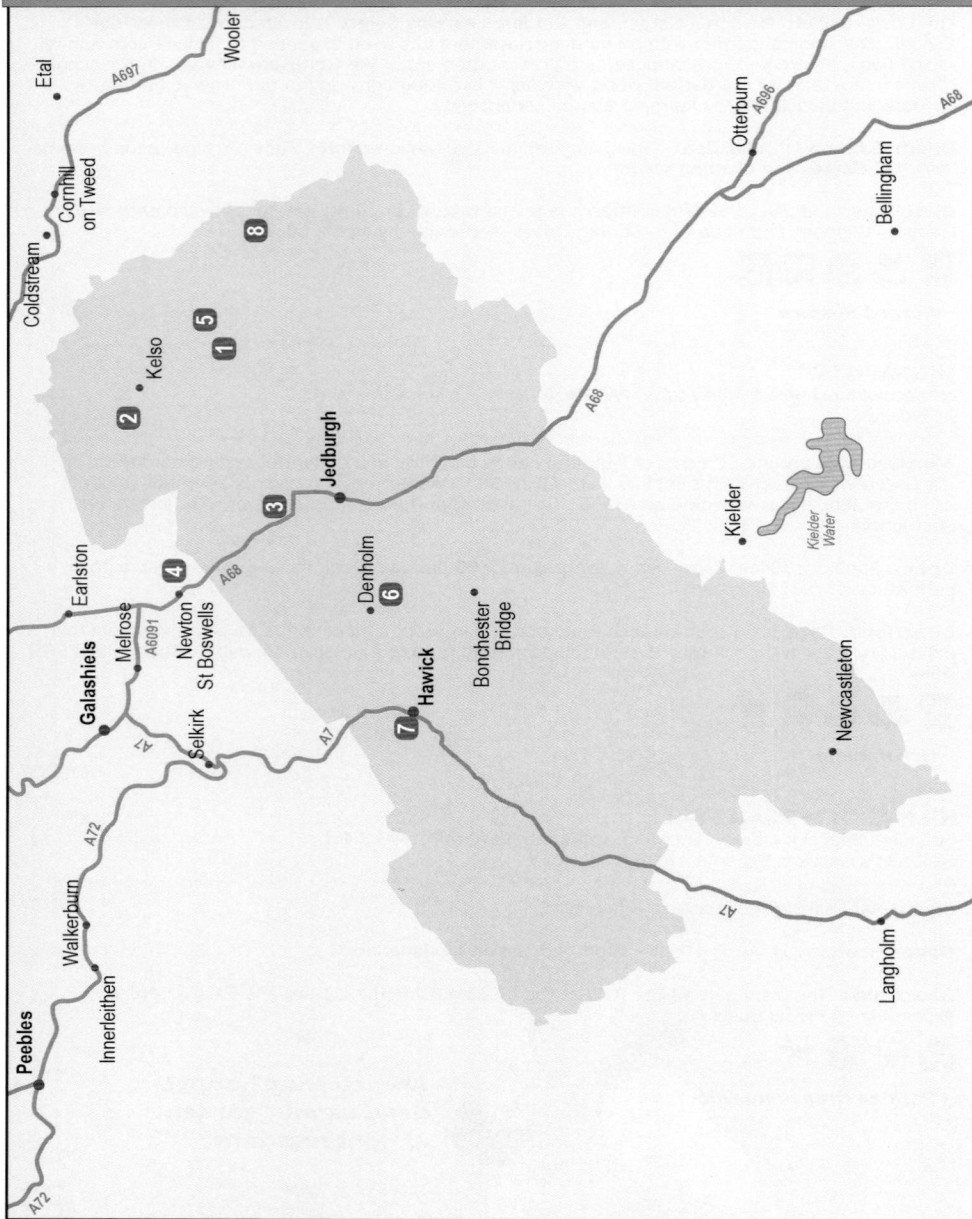

ROXBURGHSHIRE

OUR VOLUNTEER ORGANISERS

District Organiser:	Sally Yonge	Newtonlees House, Kelso, TD5 7SZ E: roxburghshire@scotlandsgardens.org
Area Organiser:	Marion Livingston	Bewlie House, Lilliesleaf, Melrose, TD6 9ER
Treasurer:	Peter Jeary	Kalemouth House, Eckford, Kelso, TD5 8LE

GARDENS OPEN ON A SPECIFIC DATE

Thirlestane, Kelso	Saturday, 2 June
West Leas, Bonchester Bridge	Sunday, 3 June
Corbet Tower, Morebattle, Near Kelso	Saturday, 30 June
Yetholm Village Gardens, Town Yetholm	Sunday, 8 July
West Summerfield, Rosalee Brae, Hawick	Sunday, 22 July
West Leas, Bonchester Bridge	Sunday, 29 July

GARDENS OPEN REGULARLY

Floors Castle, Kelso	Daily
Monteviot, Jedburgh	1 April - 31 October

GARDENS OPEN BY ARRANGEMENT

West Leas, Bonchester Bridge	On request
Thirlestane, Kelso	31 March - 31 October
Stable House, Maxton, St Boswells, Melrose	1 May - 1 October

Roxburghshire

KEY TO SYMBOLS

NEW	New garden		Full wheelchair access		Dogs on leads
	Basic teas		Partial wheelchair access	NPC	National plant collection
H	Homemade teas		Plants for sale		Champion trees
C	Cream teas		Children's activities		Designed landscape
	Refreshments		Accessible by public transport		Snowdrop opening

All our gardens open to raise money for charity. Each opening may nominate a charity(s) to receive up to 60% of the takings and these are included with each listing. The net remaining raised supports our core beneficiaries. Information about our core beneficiaries can be found in the front section of the book. More information about our charity scheme and our symbols can be found in the back foldout section of the book under 'Tips for Using Your Guidebook'.

Encouraging, promoting and supporting garden opening since 1931

Roxburghshire

1

CORBET TOWER
Morebattle, Near Kelso TD5 8AQ
Simon and Bridget Fraser

Charming Scottish Victorian garden set in parklands in the foothills of the Cheviots. The established garden includes a formal box parterred rose garden with old fashioned roses, a well stocked traditional, walled, vegetable and cutting garden, terraced lawns around the Victorian house and medieval peel tower. The gardens are approached via an attractive woodland walk with lime avenue.

Open: Saturday 30 June, 2pm - 5pm, admission £5.00, children free.

Directions: From A68 north of Jedburgh take A698 for Kelso. At Kalemouth (Teviot Smokery) follow B6401 to Morebattle, then road marked Hownam to Corbet Tower.

· *Cheviot Churches: Church of Scotland: Morebattle Church & The Children's Society*

2

FLOORS CASTLE
Kelso TD5 7SF
The Duke of Roxburghe
T: 01573 223333
W: www.floorscastle.com

The gardens are situated within the grounds of Floors Castle. Meander through to the formal Millennium Parterre and soak up the spectacular visions of colour, texture and the most delicious scents around the four herbaceous borders in one of the finest Victorian kitchen gardens in Scotland. New perennial gardens, fruit cage, Tapestry Garden & glasshouse access. Terrace Cafe, Castle Kitchen deli shop and play area. Explore the grounds which offer woodland and riverside walks from Easter to October.

Open: Daily, 11am - 5pm, admission details can be found on the garden's website. See website for details on the snowdrop, Easter and daffodil weekends, and Winter and Summer opening hours. Please note last admission is 30 minutes before closing time.

Directions: Floors Castle can be reached by following the A6089 from Edinburgh; the B6397 from Earlston or the A698 from Coldstream. Go through Kelso, up Roxburgh Street to the Golden Gates.

· *Donation to SGS Beneficiaries*

**Creating an inspiring,
rewarding and enjoyable
experience for volunteers
and visitors alike**

Roxburghshire

3

MONTEVIOT

Jedburgh TD8 6UQ
Marquis & Marchioness of Lothian
T: 01835 830380
W: www.monteviot.com

A series of differing gardens including a herb garden, rose garden, water garden linked by bridges, and river garden with herbaceous shrub borders of foliage plants. The Garden of Persistent Imagination has been recently created and planted with rose and clematis avenues leading to a Moonstone Gate.

Open: 1 April - 31 October, 12pm - 5pm, admission details can be found on the garden's website. Last entry to the garden is 4pm.

Directions: Turn off A68, three miles north of Jedburgh on to B6400. After one mile turn right.

· *Donation to SGS Beneficiaries*

View of the River Teviot from Monteviot

4

STABLE HOUSE

Maxton, St Boswells, Melrose TD6 0EX
Ian Dalziel
T: 01835 824262 E: imd4@mac.com

An enclosed private garden built around converted stables with a sunny courtyard. The garden extends to over half an acre and includes mixed borders in sun and shade, a wildflower meadow, a plant house and a new (under construction) hot border.

Open: Open by arrangement 1 May - 1 October, admission £4.00, children free.

Directions: Two minutes from A68 on A699 to Kelso.

· *Royal Blind: School, Edinburgh*

Roxburghshire

5

THIRLESTANE
Kelso TD5 8PD
Catherine Ross and John Wylie
T: 01573 420487

Thirlestane is a large, informal garden, with some rough ground and long grass. It previously opened as one of the Yetholm gardens, but since then a nine acre wood has been planted. This young woodland has a wide mix of trees, including some specimen trees. A spiral mount gives views of the Cheviot hills. There are two ponds and a burn. An orchard has about fifty varieties of apples and other fruit trees. Beech hedges enclose prairie planting in a formal setting. There is an enclosed flower garden, raised beds for vegetables and colour themed planting.

Open: Saturday 2 June, 12pm - 5pm. Also open by arrangement 31 March - 31 October. Admission £4.00, children free.

Directions: Thirlestane is near Yetholm, not to be confused with Thirlestane, Lauder. Do not follow SatNav, it will try to take you to Lochside. From Kelso, take the B6352 towards Yetholm for about six miles. Continue past a cottage on the edge of the road. Thirlestane is next on the left, opposite the road to Lochside. From Yetholm, take the road to Kelso for about two miles. After a very sharp corner, Thirlestane is on the right.

· *Macmillan Cancer Support*

Prairie planting at Thirlestane

Roxborghshire

6

WEST LEAS
Bonchester Bridge TD9 8TD
Mr and Mrs Robert Laidlaw
T: 01450 860711 E: ann.laidlaw@btconnect.com

The visitor to West Leas can share in the exciting and dramatic project on a grand scale still in the making. At its core is a passion for plants allied to a love and understanding of the land in which they are set. Collections of perennials and shrubs, many in temporary holding quarters, lighten up the landscape to magical effect. New dams and water features and woodland planting are ongoing for 2018.

Open: Sunday 3 June, 1pm - 5pm. Also open Sunday 29 July, 1pm - 5pm. And open by arrangement 1 January - 31 December. Admission £4.00, children free. Teas in Bedrule Village Hall (Sunday 3 June & Sunday 29 July).

Directions: Signposted off the Jedburgh/Bonchester Bridge Road.

· *Macmillan Cancer Support: Borders Appeal*

7

WEST SUMMERFIELD
Rosalee Brae, Hawick TD9 7HH
Eddie and Sandra Anderson

West Summerfield is a small private walled garden which has been developed over the past 14 years by the current owners. Formal planting to the front of the house leads to less formal planting at the boundaries. A particular feature is the herbaceous border, which was previously a driveway and which involved many months of gardening with a pickaxe. The garden is an inspiration to anyone who worries that they don't have the time to garden while bringing up a young family and working full time.

Open: Sunday 22 July, 2pm - 5pm, admission £4.00, children free.

Directions: Travelling south from Edinburgh on the A7, continue to drive through Hawick then take a right turn on to Princes Street (if you pass Teviotdate Leisure Centre on the left you have missed Princes Street). Look out for the 'Bamboo Box' takeaway and take a right on to Langlands Road. When you see the *No Entry* sign ahead, take a sharp right up Rosalee Brae. West Summerfield is the third entrance on the right immediately past East Summerfield.

NEW

· *NSPCC*

60% of a garden openings proceeds can be donated to the Garden Owner's choice of charity

Roxburghshire

8

YETHOLM VILLAGE GARDENS
Town Yetholm TD5 8RL
The Gardeners of Yetholm Village

The villages of Town and Kirk Yetholm are situated at the north end of the Pennine Way and lie close to the Bowmont Water in the dramatic setting of the foothills of the Cheviots. A variety of gardens with their own unique features and reflecting distinctive horticultural interests will be open. The Yew Tree Allotments running along the High Street will open again, providing an ever popular feature with their unique water collection and distribution system. The short walking distance between the majority of the gardens provides magnificent views of the surrounding landscape to include Staerough and The Curr which straddle both the Bowmont and Halterburn Valleys where evidence of ancient settlements remains.

Open: Sunday 8 July, 1pm - 5:30pm, admission £5.00, children free. Attractions include the ever popular music, local wood-turning products at Almond Cottage, home baking and produce stall. An excellent plant stall supported by Woodside Walled Garden Centre is also planned for the afternoon. Additional new events include 'The Newest of Books' fair and a craft stall. Tickets are available in the local village hall.

Directions: Equidistant between Edinburgh and Newcastle. South of Kelso in the Scottish Borders take the B6352 to Yetholm Village. Ample parking is available along the High Street.

· *RDA: Border Group*

Formal planting at West Summerfield

STIRLINGSHIRE

Scotland's Gardens Scheme 2018 Guidebook is sponsored by INVESTEC WEALTH & INVESTMENT

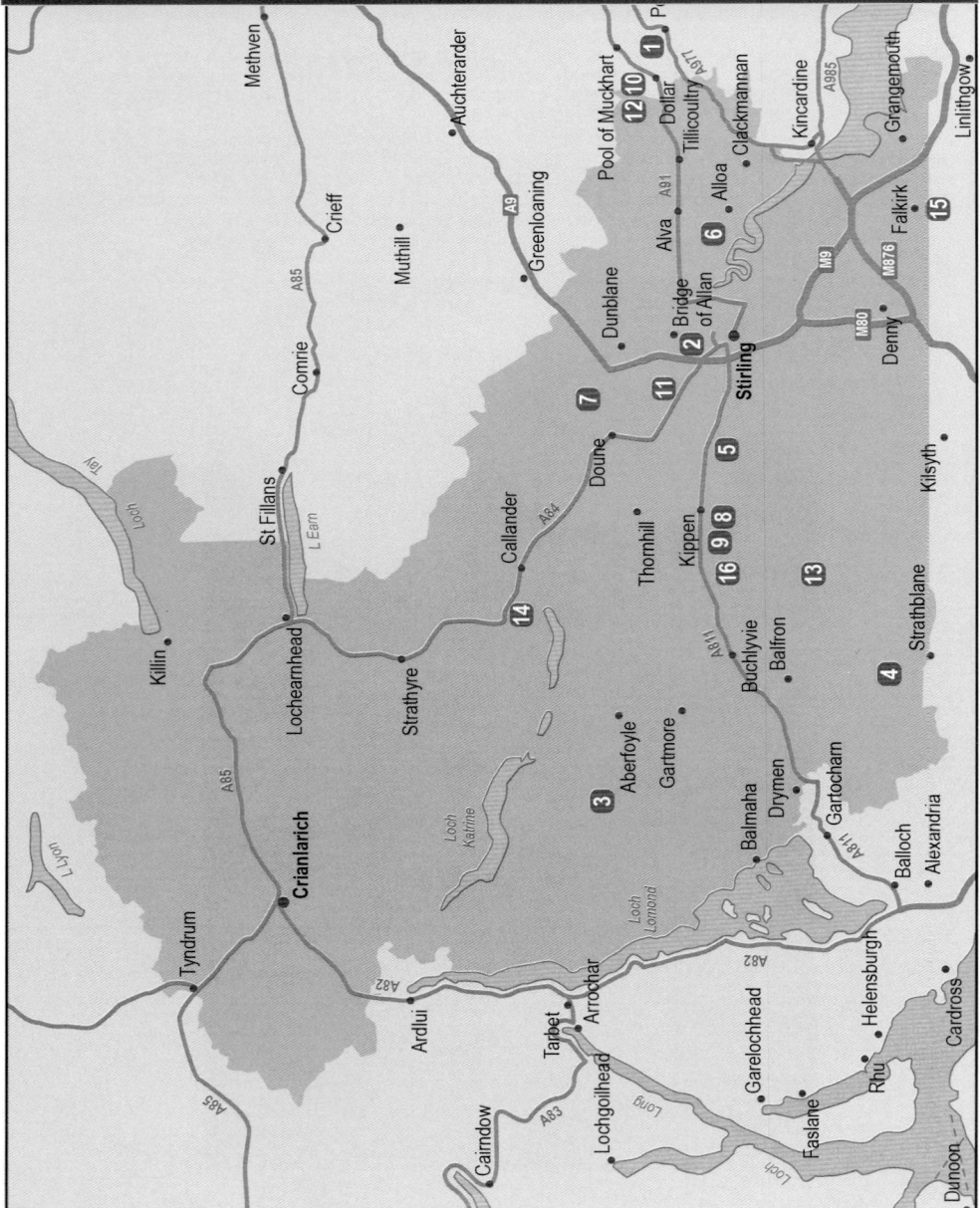

STIRLINGSHIRE

OUR VOLUNTEER ORGANISERS

District Organiser:	Mandy Readman	Hutchison Farm, Auchinlay Road, Dunblane, FK15 9JS E: stirlingshire@scotlandsgardens.org
Area Organisers:	Gillie Drapper	Kilewnan Cottage, Main Street, Fintry, G63 0YH
	Maurie Jessett	The Walled Garden, Lanrick, Doune, FK16 6HJ
	Miranda Jones	122 High Street, Dunblane, FK15 0ER
	Rosemary Leckie	Auchengarroch, 16 Chalton Road, FK9 4DX
	Ian Lumsden	The Myretoun, Menstrie, FK11 7EB
	Iain Morrison	Clifford House, Balkerach Street, Doune, FK16 6DE
	Gillie Welstead	Ballingrew, Thornhill, FK8 3QD
Treasurer:	David Ashton	Moon Cottage, Greenyards, Dunblane, FK15 9NX

GARDENS OPEN ON A SPECIFIC DATE

The Pass House, Kilmahog, Callander	Sunday, 29 April
Little Broich, Kippen	Sunday, 6 May
Dun Dubh, Kinlochard Road, Aberfoyle	Sunday, 13 May
Bridge of Allan Gardens , Bridge of Allan	Sunday, 20 May
Shrubhill, Dunblane, Perthshire	Sunday, 27 May
The Japanese Garden at Cowden, Dollar, Clackmannanshire	Sunday, 3 June
The Mill House, Kippen Road, Fintry, Stirlingshire	Saturday - Sunday, 9-17 June
Kippen Village, West Stirlingshire	Sunday, 17 June
Gean House , Tullibody Road, Alloa	Tuesday, 19 June
Thorntree, Arnprior	Sunday, 24 June
The Tors, 2 Slamannan Road, Falkirk	Sunday, 29 July
Rowberrow, 18 Castle Road, Dollar	Sunday, 2 September
Kilbryde Castle, Dunblane	Sunday, 16 September

GARDENS OPEN REGULARLY

Gargunnock House Garden, Gargunnock	27 January - 11 March
Gargunnock House Garden, Gargunnock	14 March - 28 September (not Saturdays & Sundays)

GARDENS OPEN BY ARRANGEMENT

Duntreath Castle, Blanefield	1 February - 30 November
Rowberrow, 18 Castle Road, Dollar	1 February - 31 December
Kilbryde Castle, Dunblane	1 March - 30 September
Thorntree, Arnprior	1 April - 15 October
The Tors, 2 Slamannan Road, Falkirk	1 May - 30 September
Arndean, by Dollar	14 May - 17 June

Stirlingshire

KEY TO SYMBOLS

NEW	New garden	♿	Full wheelchair access	🐕	Dogs on leads
☕	Basic teas	♿	Partial wheelchair access	NPC	National plant collection
H	Homemade teas	🌷	Plants for sale	🌳	Champion trees
C	Cream teas	👪	Children's activities		Designed landscape
🍽	Refreshments	🚌	Accessible by public transport		Snowdrop opening

All our gardens open to raise money for charity. Each opening may nominate a charity(s) to receive up to 60% of the takings and these are included with each listing. The net remaining raised supports our core beneficiaries. Information about our core beneficiaries can be found in the front section of the book. More information about our charity scheme and our symbols can be found in the back foldout section of the book under 'Tips for Using Your Guidebook'.

The Mill House

Stirlingshire

1

ARNDEAN
by Dollar FK14 7NH
Johnny and Katie Stewart
T: 01259 743525 E: johnny@arndean.co.uk
....

Opening for 40 years, this is a beautiful mature garden extending to 15 acres including the woodland walk.   There is a formal herbaceous part, a small vegetable garden and orchard.   In addition, there are flowering shrubs, abundant and striking rhododendrons and azaleas as well as many fine specimen trees.   There is a tree house for children.

Open: Open by arrangement 14 May - 17 June, admission £5.00, children free.

Directions: Arndean is well signposted off the A977.

· *Marie Curie*

2

BRIDGE OF ALLAN GARDENS
Bridge of Allan FK9
The Bridge of Allan Gardeners
E: r.leckie44@btinternet.com
....

A variety of both large and small gardens, with specimen trees, shrubs and rhododendron, perennials, water features, vegetables and a Japanese garden.

Open: Sunday 20 May, 1pm - 5pm, admission £5.00, children free. Tickets and maps from all gardens. Teas and plant stall at St. Saviour's Church Hall, Keir Street from 1.30-5.00pm.

Directions: Signposted from village.

· *St Saviours Episcopal Church: Bridge Of Allan & Artlink Central Ltd*

3

DUN DUBH
Kinlochard Road, Aberfoyle FK8 3TJ
Callum Pirnie, Head Gardener
T: 01877 382698 E: callumpirnie@gmail.com
....

A late Victorian garden of six acres undergoing restoration and development. It is set on a series of terraces and slopes which run down to the shores of Loch Ard with superb views west to Ben Lomond framed by stands of mature conifers. There is an enclosed, colour themed formal garden laid out on three terraces and a new Victorian style glasshouse overlooking a terraced kitchen and fruit garden. The formal paved terrace at the front of the house overlooks a newly developed rock garden and crag while the lower walk running from the boat house to the main lawn gives views across the Loch. A developing woodland garden leads on to a formal late summer herbaceous border and terraced heather garden.

Open: Sunday 13 May, 2pm - 5pm, admission £5.00, children free. Car parking limited to disabled badge holders. Do not park on road outside Dun Dubh. There is free transport to and from Aberfoyle car park during opening.

Directions: Follow the signs to the car park in the centre of Aberfoyle. The minibus will leave from the bus stop beside the Tourist Office, which is next to the car park. Turn around time about 15 minutes.

· *Help for Heroes*

Stirlingshire

4

DUNTREATH CASTLE
Blanefield G63 9AJ
Sir Archibald & Lady Edmonstone
T: 01360 770215 E: juliet@edmonstone.com
W: www.duntreathcastle.co.uk

Extensive gardens with mature and new plantings. Ornamental landscaped lake and bog garden.
Sweeping lawns below formal fountain and rose parterre with herbaceous border leading up to an
attractive waterfall garden with shrubs and spring plantings. Stunning display of snowdrops along
the side of former drive. There is a woodland walk and a 15th century keep and chapel.

Open: Open by arrangement 1 February - 30 November for the Snowdrop Festival, admission
£4.00, children free.

Directions: A81 north of Glasgow between Blanefield and Killearn.

· All proceeds to SGS Beneficiaries

5

GARGUNNOCK HOUSE GARDEN
Gargunnock FK8 3AZ
The Gargunnock Trustees
T: 01786 860392 E: gargunnockgardens@btinternet.com

Large mature garden five miles from Stirling, with a walled garden, well established house garden,
woodland walks with species and hybrid rhododendrons, massed plantings of azaleas and wonderful
specimen trees. Snowdrops in February/March, over 40 varieties of daffodils in bloom in April and
the glorious display of azaleas and rhododendrons in May. In Autumn, stunning colours from the
many wonderful trees along the drive to the house. The three acre walled garden contains perennial
borders, cut flower beds, greenhouses, fruit orchard and newly planted arboretum of specimen trees.

Open: 27 January - 11 March, 11am - 3:30pm for the Snowdrop Festival. Also open 14 March -
28 September (not Saturdays & Sundays), 11am - 3:30pm. Admission £4.00, children free.

Directions: Five miles west of Stirling on A811, follow the *Scotland's Gardens Scheme* signs. Car
parking at entrance by lodge. Honesty box in car park.

· Gargunnock Community Trust & Scotland's Charity Air Ambulance

6

GEAN HOUSE
Tullibody Road, Alloa FK10 2EL
Ceteris (Scotland)
E: ebowie@geanhouse.co.uk
W: www.geanhouse.co.uk

Gean House is an early 20th century Arts and Crafts style mansion. On arrival, the sweeping
driveway from the main road takes you through beautiful parkland lined with trees to the mansion
set on top of the hill facing northeast. The gardens surrounding the house were originally 40
acres and included a Japanese garden in the woods. All that remain now are seven acres on the
southern and eastern aspects of the house.

Open: Tuesday 19 June, 2pm - 5pm, admission £4.00, children free.

Directions: Gean House is located on the Tullibody Road, Alloa.

· Scottish Autism

Stirlingshire

7

KILBRYDE CASTLE
Dunblane FK15 9NF
Sir James and Lady Campbell
T: 01786 824897 E: kilbryde1@aol.com
W: www.kilbrydecastle.com

The Kilbryde Castle gardens cover some twelve acres and are situated above the Ardoch Burn and below the castle. The gardens are split into three parts: formal, woodland and wild. Natural planting (azaleas, rhododendrons, camellias and magnolias) is found in the woodland garden. There are glorious spring bulbs and autumn colour provided by clematis and acers. There will be some new plantings for additional late summer/autumn colour for 2017. Featured in *Scotland on Sunday* in September 2016.

Open: Sunday 16 September, 2pm - 5pm. Also open by arrangement 1 March - 30 September. Admission £5.00, children free (Sunday 16 September) and £4.00, children free (1 March - 30 September).

Directions: Three miles from Dunblane and Doune, off the A820 between Dunblane and Doune. On *Scotland's Gardens Scheme* open days the garden is signposted from A820.

· *Leighton Library Trust*

8

KIPPEN VILLAGE
West Stirlingshire FK8 3DN
The Gardeners of Kippen Village

Kippen is a village with views! At least six gardens will be open with a variety of design and horticultural interest, ranging from well established to more recent.

Arnmoulin Cauldhame, Kippen FK8 3JB (Joanie Littlejohn): At the top of the village with more amazing views towards the Trossachs. A variety of interesting shrubs and perennials, vegetable garden and small orchard area.
Dun Eaglais Station Brae, Kippen FK8 3DY (Martin Sales and Barry Topping): The historic home of the artist D.Y.Cameron, built in stages between 1902-1924 and finished in the Scottish Renaissance and Arts and Crafts manner. It is thought that the terraced gardens were influenced by landscape designer, T.H.Mawson. Wonderful specimen trees, rhododendrons and perennials, full of twists and turns revealing more around every corner.
Farringford Fore Road, Kippen FK8 3DT (Val and Alan Beaton): This garden has yet more stunning views and good disabled access. Beautiful variety of planting includes a 'dry' garden, an Acer garden and a big collection of hostas.
Glentirran Station Brae, Kippen FK8 3DY (Sir Michael and Lady Hirst): A sweeping driveway leads up to the house passing grass terraces surrounded by rhododendrons and perennial borders, mixed planting and climbers including wisteria. Wonderful views across the Carse of Stirling.
Woodstone House Cauldhame, Kippen FK8 3JB (Roddy and Mary Lawson): Bounded to the south by the old Kippen Vinery Wall, this is a relatively new garden of about one acre, with some species trees (including a mulberry), shrubs, rockeries and vegetables.   Wonderful views to the Trossachs.

Open: Sunday 17 June, 1:30pm - 5:30pm, admission £5.00, children free. Teas in the Reading Room with Kippen Community Garden and the garden at Stonelea behind. Maps and tickets available from all gardens. Only disabled parking at the gardens please.

Directions: Kippen is off the A811, gardens will be signed from the village.

· *Alzheimer Scotland & Start-Up Stirling*

Stirlingshire

9
LITTLE BROICH
Kippen FK8 3DT
John Smith
T: 01786 870275

A tree lover's heaven! An opportunity to see this hidden arboretum in it's spring colours, vibrant greens, blossom and a wonderful display of daffodils, camassia and bluebells. Slightly sloping grass paths which can be slippery when wet. Stunning views across the Carse of Stirling and the autumn colours should be outstanding. The garden featured in an October 2014 issue of *Scotland on Sunday* and on the *Beechgrove Garden*.

Open: Sunday 6 May, 2pm - 5pm, admission £4.00, children free.

Directions: Will be signposted off the B8037. Parking on the road, disabled badge holders can park at the bottom of the lane.

· *Strathcarron Hospice*

10
ROWBERROW
18 Castle Road, Dollar FK14 7BE
Bill and Rosemary Jarvis
T: 01259 742584 E: rjarvis1000@hotmail.com

On the way up to Castle Campbell overlooking Dollar Glen, this colourful garden has several mixed shrub and herbaceous borders, a wildlife pond, two rockeries, alpine troughs, fruit and vegetable gardens, and a mini-orchard. The owner is a plantaholic and likes to collect unusual specimens. Rowberrow was featured on the *Beechgrove Garden* in summer 2011.

Open: Sunday 2 September, 2pm - 5pm. Also open by arrangement 1 February - 31 December. Admission £4.00, children free.

Directions: Pass along the burn side in Dollar, turn right at T junction, follow signs for Castle Campbell and Dollar Glen. Park at the bottom of Castle Road or in the Quarry car park just up from the house.

· *Hillfoot Harmony Barbershop Singers*

11
SHRUBHILL
Dunblane, Perthshire FK15 9PA
Tiff and Michaela Wright
E: wrightrascals@btinternet.com

Two acres of mixed, informal planting of some unusual rhododendrons, azaleas, specimen trees and other shrubs. Beautiful all round views particularly over the Carse of Stirling and towards Ben Ledi and Ben Lomond. Herbaceous borders, meconopsis, late spring bulbs, water feature with a wide variety of primulas. Small walled garden predominantly for fruit and greenhouse with well established vine.

Open: Sunday 27 May, 2pm - 5pm, admission £5.00, children free.

Directions: Two miles from Keir roundabout on the B824 on the left, just after the David Stirling Memorial, follow the signs and parking advice.   One mile from A820 and on right.

· *Crossroads Scotland Caring For Carers: West of Scotland Branch*

Stirlingshire

12

THE JAPANESE GARDEN AT COWDEN
Dollar, Clackmannanshire FK14 7PJ
Cowden Castle SCIO
E: info@cowdengarden.com
W: www.cowdengarden.com

Created in 1908, The Japanese Garden at Cowden is a remarkable early example of its type in Western Europe. Nestled beneath the Ochil Hills the five acre garden wraps around a large pond. Enjoy the meandering perimeter walk, taking in the changing scenes created by sculpted landforms, carefully placed stones, clipped shrubs and original stone lanterns. Restoration of this historic garden is ongoing, so this is an opportunity to see the project in its early stages.

Open: Sunday 3 June, 12pm - 6pm, admission £6.00, children free. There is a large body of open water so children must be supervised at all times.

Directions: The entrance is from the Upper Hillfoots Road, approximately one kilometre west from the junction with the A91. Bus 23 Stirling - St Andrews runs four times daily. Stop is called *Cowden Farm Road End*, at the east end of the Upper Hillfood Road, just before the pools of Muckhart. There is a one kilometre walk (no pavement) to the entrance.

· Cowden Castle SCIO & St. James the Great Scottish Episcopal Church, Dollar

The large pond at The Japanese Garden at Cowden

Stirlingshire

13 THE MILL HOUSE
Kippen Road, Fintry, Stirlingshire G63 0YD
Mrs Katherine Cowtan
T: 01360 860009 E: cowtan@weefoot.com

Delightful small country garden with interesting planting at the front of the house. Plants are chosen for their resistance to both deer and rabbits.   Late spring bulbs, geraniums, poppies and other colourful herbaceous plants and shrubs.

Open: Open Saturday 9th - Sunday 17th June, 10 - 5pm (except Monday 11th June, 12 - 5pm) admission by donation. Opening during Forth Valley Art Beat (Open Studios) week, there will be an opportunity to see the other artists' studios as well as the garden which provides a lot of inspiration. There may be other artists, country crafts and interesting activities on offer.

Directions: Signed from the Kippen Road. Disabled parking only at the house, but there is parking at the Fintry Sports Club or on the road in the village nearby. Buses run Monday - Friday only.

· *All proceeds to SGS Beneficiaries*

14 THE PASS HOUSE
Kilmahog, Callander FK17 8HD
Dr and Mrs D Carfrae

Well planted, medium sized garden with steep banks down to a swift river. The garden paths are not steep. There are lovely displays of camellias, magnolias, rhododendrons, azaleas, alpines and shrubs. The *Scotland's Gardens Scheme* plaque awarded for 25 years of opening is on display.

Open: Sunday 29 April, 2pm - 5pm, admission £4.00, children free. Tea/coffee and a biscuit for a donation if the weather is fine.

Directions: Two miles from Callander on the A84 to Lochearnhead.

· *Crossroads Scotland Caring For Carers: West of Scotland Branch*

15 THE TORS
2 Slamannan Road, Falkirk FK1 5LG
Dr and Mrs D M Ramsay
T: 01324 620877 E: dmramsay28@yahoo.co.uk
W: www.torsgarden.co.uk

An award winning Victorian garden of just over one acre with a secret woodland garden to the side and an orchard leading off to a wild area at the rear of the house. Many unusual maple trees, hydrangeas and rhododendrons are the main interest of this garden and two fine avenues of Chinese paperbark maples are especially noteworthy. Featured on the *Beechgrove Garden* for autumn colour in September 2010, but the best time to see this garden is at the end of July or the beginning of August. The *Scotland on Sunday* featured the house and garden in an article with many lovely photographs in September 2015.

Open: Sunday 29 July, 2pm - 5:30pm. Also open by arrangement 1 May - 30 September. Admission £4.00, children free.

Stirlingshire

Directions: The B803 to the south of Falkirk leads to Glenbrae Road. Turn right at the traffic lights into Slamannan Road and The Tors is a Victorian building immediately on the left. The house is within 200 yards of Falkirk High Station.

· *Strathcarron Hospice*

16

THORNTREE
Arnprior FK8 3EY
Mark and Carol Seymour
T: 01786 870710 E: info@thorntreebarn.co.uk
W: www.thorntreebarn.co.uk

The amazing views from Ben Lomond to Ben Ledi and on to Stirling sold Thorntree to Carol and Mark 25 years ago.   The garden evolved while trying to keep a "cottage" feel.   Carol sold old silver, which had not been used in years, to build the dry stone wall. An apple arch was given to Mark to encourage him into the garden.   The lawns are mown like a bowling green (or to a millimetre) by Mark. The courtyard includes flower beds.   The saltire bed was designed in 2002 when Carol stopped growing dried flowers in a 20x20 metre square. The slightly sunken bed, all that they inherited on arrival, now holds Meconopsis.   And so it evolves, Carol is now making a wooded area filled with primroses and Martagon lilies.   Do come and see!

Open: Sunday 24 June, 2pm - 5pm. Also open by arrangement 1 April - 15 October. Admission £4.00, children free. There may be coffee/teas and a biscuit on the 24th June, if the weather is fine. Plants for sale throughout the year.

Directions: A811. In Arnprior take Fintry Road, Thorntree is second on the right.

· *Forth Driving Group RDA SCIO*

WIGTOWNSHIRE

Scotland's Gardens Scheme 2018 Guidebook is sponsored by INVESTEC WEALTH & INVESTMENT

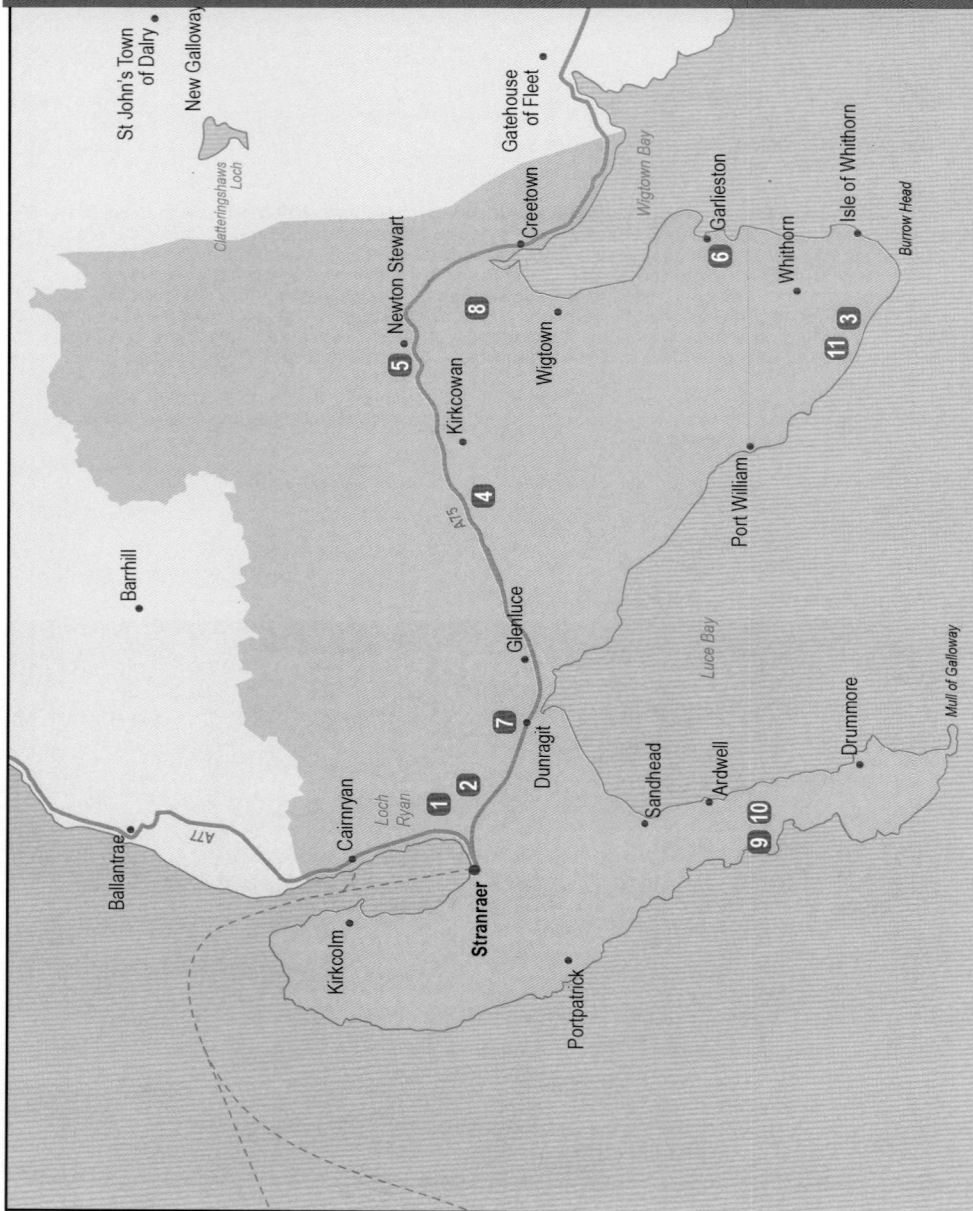

St John's Town of Dalry

New Galloway

Clatteringshaws Loch

Gatehouse of Fleet

Creetown

Wigtown Bay

Garlieston

6

Isle of Whithorn

Burrow Head

Whithorn

5 Newton Stewart

Kirkcowan

8

Wigtown

11 **3**

4

A75

Port William

Kirkcowan

Barrhill

Glenluce

Luce Bay

Mull of Galloway

7

Dunragit

Sandhead

Ardwell

Drummore

Cairnryan

Loch Ryan

1 **2**

9 **10**

A77

Ballantrae

Stranraer

Kirkcolm

Portpatrick

Wigtownshire
WIGTOWNSHIRE

OUR VOLUNTEER ORGANISERS

District Organiser:	Ann Watson	Doonholm, Cairnryan Road, Stranraer, DG9 8AT
		E: wigtownshire@scotlandsgardens.org
Area Organisers:	Eileen Davie	Whitehills House, Minnigaff, Newton Stewart, DG8 6SL
	Andrew Gladstone	Craichlaw, Kirkcowan, Newton Stewart, DG8 0DQ
	Shona Greenhorn	Burbainie, Westwood Avenue, Stranraer, DG9 8BT
	Janet Hannay	Cuddyfield, Wigtownshire, DG8 7DS
	Enid Innes	Crinan, Creetown, Newton Stewart, DG8 7EP
	Annmaree Mitchell	Cottage 2, Little Float, Sandhead, Stranraer, DG9 9LD
	Vicky Roberts	Logan House Gdns, Port Logan, by Stranraer, DG9 9ND
Treasurer:	George Fleming	Ardgour, Stoneykirk, Stranraer, DG9 9DL

GARDENS OPEN ON A SPECIFIC DATE

Claymoddie Garden, Whithorn, Newton Stewart	Sunday, 29 April
Logan House Gardens, Port Logan, by Stranraer	Sunday, 6 May
Logan Botanic Garden, Port Logan, by Stranraer	Sunday, 20 May
Galloway House Gardens, Garlieston, Newton Stewart	Sunday, 27 May
Castle Kennedy and Gardens, Stranraer	Sunday, 10 June
Balker Farmhouse, Stranraer	Saturday, 16 June
Woodfall Gardens, Glasserton	Sunday, 17 June
Woodfall Gardens, Glasserton	Sunday, 8 July
Fernlea Garden, Newton Stewart	Sunday, 22 July

GARDENS OPEN REGULARLY

Glenwhan Gardens, Dunragit, by Stranraer	Daily
Castle Kennedy and Gardens, Stranraer	3 February - 31 March (Sats & Suns)

GARDENS OPEN BY ARRANGEMENT

Craichlaw, Kirkcowan, Newton Stewart	On request
Liggat Cheek Cottage, Baltersan, Newton Stewart	1 April - 31 October

Wigtownshire

KEY TO SYMBOLS

NEW	New garden	♿	Full wheelchair access	🐕	Dogs on leads
☕	Basic teas	♿	Partial wheelchair access	**NPC**	National plant collection
H	Homemade teas	🌷	Plants for sale	🌳	Champion trees
C	Cream teas	👥	Children's activities	🌿	Designed landscape
🍴	Refreshments	🚌	Accessible by public transport	🌱	Snowdrop opening

All our gardens open to raise money for charity. Each opening may nominate a charity(s) to receive up to 60% of the takings and these are included with each listing. The net remaining raised supports our core beneficiaries. Information about our core beneficiaries can be found in the front section of the book. More information about our charity scheme and our symbols can be found in the back foldout section of the book under 'Tips for Using Your Guidebook'.

Rhododendrons at Logan House Gardens

Wigtownshire

1

BALKER FARMHOUSE
Stranraer DG9 8RS
Davina, Countess of Stair
T: 01581400225/01776 702024

Balker Farm House was restored in 2002 and the garden, formerly a ploughed field was started in 2003-4 by Davina, Dowager Countess of Stair and Anne-Marie Mitchell. It is now full of wonderful shrubs, and plants for all seasons, and is being opened especially in honour of Davina, who sadly died in late 2017.

Open: Saturday 16 June, 2pm - 5pm, admission £4.00, children free.

Directions: One and a half miles off the A75, three miles from Stranraer. Go through the farmyard to the blue gate.

· *Inch Parish Church*

Balker Farmhouse © Andrea Jones

Wigtownshire

2

CASTLE KENNEDY AND GARDENS
Stranraer DG9 8SL
The Earl and Countess of Stair
T: 01581 400225
W: www.castlekennedygardens.com

Romantically situated, these famous 75 acres of landscaped gardens are located on an isthmus surrounded by two large natural lochs. At one end the ruined Castle Kennedy overlooks a beautiful herbaceous walled garden with Lochinch Castle at the other end. With over 300 years of planting there is an impressive collection of rare trees, rhododendrons, exotic shrubs, and featuring many spectacular Champion Trees (tallest or largest of their type). The stunning snowdrop walks, daffodils, spring flowers, rhododendron and magnolia displays, and herbaceous borders make this a 'must visit' garden throughout the year.
Champion Trees: 6 British, 11 Scottish and 25 for Dumfries and Galloway.

Open: 3 February - 31 March (Saturdays & Sundays), 10am - 5pm for the Snowdrop Festival. Also open Sunday 10 June, 10am - 5pm. Admission details can be found on the garden's website. Also see website for further information on wildlife ranger events, Head Gardener guided walks, tree and family trails, bird hides, open air theatre and cinema, tea room, plant centre, gift shops and holiday cottages. Open daily 31st March – 31st October.

Directions: On the A75, five miles east of Stranraer. The nearest train station is in Stranraer. On a local bus route.

· *Home-Start Wigtownshire*

3

CLAYMODDIE GARDEN
Whithorn, Newton Stewart DG8 8LX
Mrs Mary Nicholson
T: 01988 500422 E: mary.claymoddie@aol.co.uk
W: www.claymoddiegarden.com

This romantic five acre garden, designed and developed by the owner, an avid landscaper and plantsman, reflects half a century of dedicated work. It provides a range of timeless, intimate settings, both shady and sunny, for a vast range of plants from both hemispheres, all helped by the proximity of the Gulf Stream. Running through the lower part of the garden is the burn feeding a large pond which, along with the variety of plants and their backdrop of mature woodland, provides the perfect habitat for wildlife, in particular birds. There are changes in levels, but most of the garden is accessible to wheelchairs.

Open: Sunday 29 April, 11am - 5pm, admission £5.00, children free.

Directions: From Whithorn take the A746 south for two miles to Glasserton crossroads, turn left onto the B7004. After 300 yards turn right up farm road signed *Claymoddie*.

· *The Whithorn Trust*

4

CRAICHLAW
Kirkcowan, Newton Stewart DG8 0DQ
Mr and Mrs A Gladstone
T: 01671 830208 E: craichlaw@aol.com

Formal garden with herbaceous borders around the house. Set in extensive grounds with lawns, lochs and woodland. A path around the main loch leads to a water garden returning past a recently planted arboretum in the old walled garden. The best times to visit the garden are early February for snowdrops, May to mid-June for the water garden and rhododendrons and mid-June to August for herbaceous borders.

Wigtownshire

Open: Sunday 20 May, 10am - 5pm, admission details and other open dates can be found on the garden's website.

Directions: Ten miles south of Stranraer on the A716 then 2½ miles from Ardwell village.

· **Board Of Trustees Of The Royal Botanic Garden Edinburgh**

LOGAN HOUSE GARDENS
Port Logan, by Stranraer DG9 9ND
Mr and Mrs Andrew Roberts

The Queen Anne house is surrounded by sweeping lawns and a truly spectacular woodland garden. Rare and exotic plants together with champion trees and fine species of rhododendrons provide an excellent habitat for an interesting variety of wildlife.
Champion Trees: 7 UK and 11 Scottish.

Open: Sunday 6 May, 2pm - 4:30pm, admission £4.00, children free. Ice-cream.

Directions: On the A716, 13 miles south of Stranraer, 2½ miles from Ardwell village.

· **Port Logan Hall**

WOODFALL GARDENS
Glasserton DG8 8LY
Ross and Liz Muir
E: woodfallgardens@btinternet.com
W: www.woodfall-gardens.co.uk

This lovely three acre 18th century triple walled garden has been thoughtfully restored to provide year round interest. Many mature trees and shrubs including some less common species; herbaceous borders and shrub roses surround the foundations of original greenhouses; grass borders; a parterre; extensive beds of fruit and vegetables; a herb garden and a small woodland walk. This unusual garden is well worth a visit.

Open: Sunday 17 June, 10:30am - 4:30pm. Also open Sunday 8 July, 10:30am - 4:30pm. Admission £5.00, children free. Admission includes self-service tea/coffee and scones. Gardens are also open by arrangement.

Directions: Two miles south-west of Whithorn at junction of A746 and A747 (directly behind Glasserton Church).

· **Glasserton Church & Macmillan Cancer Support**

Creating an inspiring, rewarding and enjoyable experience for volunteers and visitors alike

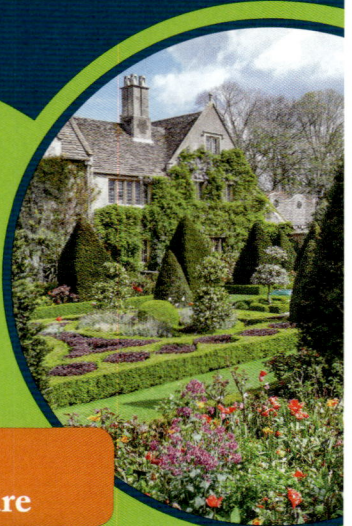

"The Most Outstanding
Continuous Care Retirement
Community in the UK."

UK OVER 50'S HOUSING AWARDS

An integral part of our Retirement Village is Inchmarlo House Care Home which is highly rated by the Care Commission. Inchmarlo's Care policy gives confidence to our Home Owners and their families as our nursing, care and security staff are on site 24 hours a day and assistance can be there in minutes.

We also reserve a room in Inchmarlo House for Home Owners who require respite care for short periods. If longer stays are required Home Owners have priority admission.

Our overall policy is to provide social, physical or nursing care to enable Home Owners to continue to live in their own homes longer than might be the case elsewhere.

To find out more call
+44 (0) 1330 826242 or email
dawn.ronaldson@
inchmarlo-retirement.co.uk

Then come and see why Inchmarlo is the ideal spot to put down some roots.

INCHMARLO
RETIREMENT VILLAGE

**Where Gracious Living
Comes naturally**

THE MILL GARDEN CENTRE

Bloomin' good plants

- Japanese Maples
- Conifers
- Shrubs
- Bedding
- Herbaceous
- Grafted Pines
- Roses
- Trees
- Pots
- Compost

The Mill Garden Centre is an independent, family owned and run business where you can be assured the emphasis is firmly on the plants.

When visiting us you can be sure that you are buying plants from people who have been growing for generations and are qualified horticulturalists.

Our main strength is our constantly evolving range of unusual plants held in stock throughout the year and backed up by our own wide selection of plants grown on our adjacent nursery.

Whether you are a beginner, serious gardener, plant collector or would just like an alternative to the 'lifestyle chains', you are sure to find something to suit.

The Mill Garden Centre

Barbauchlaw Mill, Mill Road

Armadale, West Lothian, EH48 3AP

Visit four Botanic Gardens to see one of the richest plant collections on Earth.

Royal Botanic Garden Edinburgh

Arboretum Place and Inverleith Row,
Edinburgh EH3 5LR
Tel 0131 248 2909 | www.rbge.org.uk
Open every day from 10 am (except 1 January
and 25 December) | Garden is free | Entry
charges apply to Glasshouses

Royal Botanic Garden Edinburgh at Logan

Port Logan, Stranraer,
Dumfries and Galloway DG9 9ND
Tel 01776 860231 | www.rbge.org.uk/logan
Open daily 1 March to 15 November
Admission charge applies

Royal Botanic Garden Edinburgh at Benmore

Dunoon, Argyll PA23 8QU
Tel 01369 706261 | www.rbge.org.uk/benmore
Open daily 1 March to 31 October
Admission charge applies

Royal Botanic Garden Edinburgh at Dawyck

Stobo, Scottish Borders EH45 9JU
Tel 01721 760254 | www.rbge.org.uk/dawyck
Open daily 1 February to 30 November
Admission charge applies

The Royal Botanic Garden Edinburgh is a Charity registered in Scotland (number SC007983) and is a Non Departmental Public Body (NDPB) sponsored and supported through Grant-in-Aid by the Scottish Government's Environment and Forestry Directorate (ENFOR).

James Byatt BSc (Hons) MLD

Garden & Estate Cartography

www.jamesbyatt.com
07796 591197
enquiries@jamesbyatt.com

Lochview Cottage Scarffbanks
Pitgaveny, Elgin
Moray IV30 5PQ

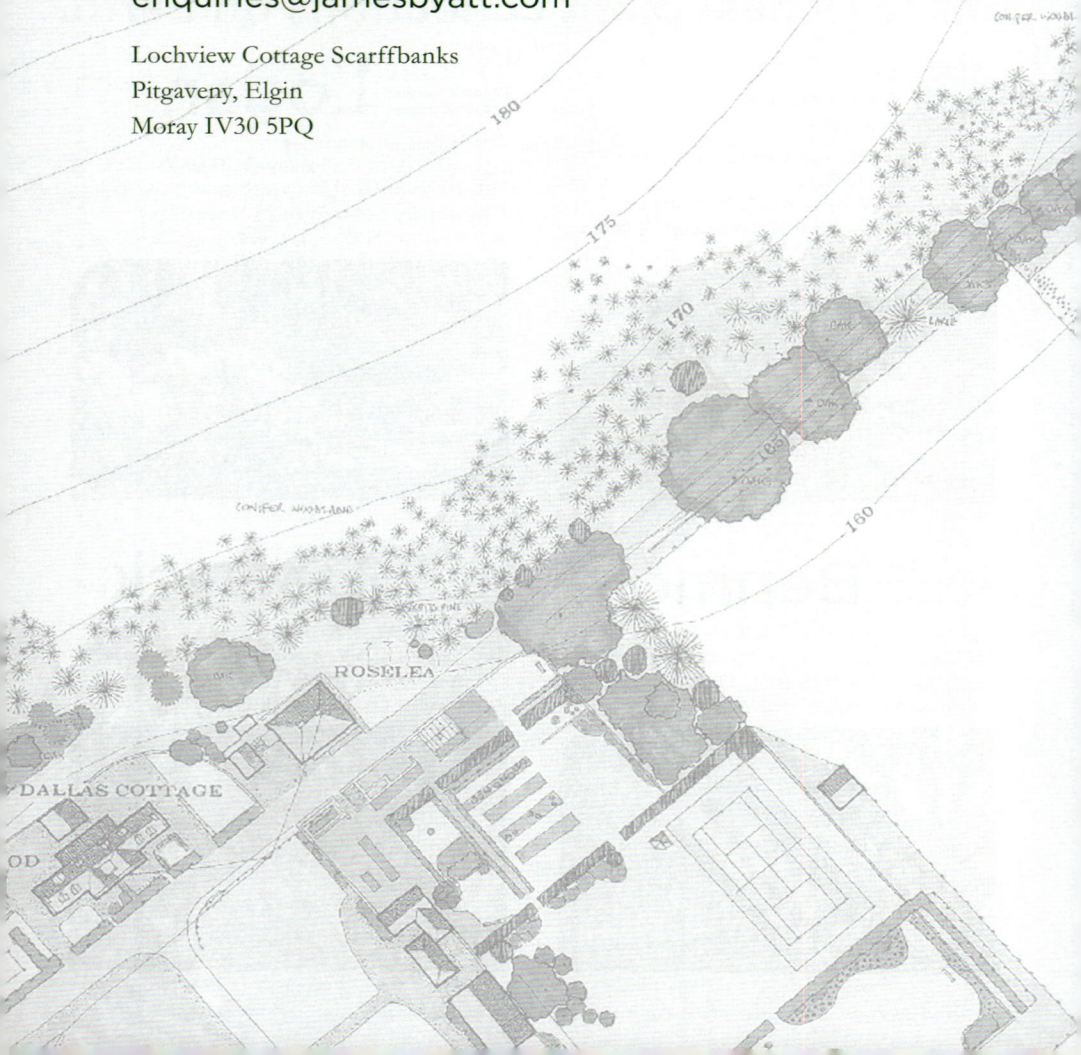

RHS CAMPAIGN FOR
SCHOOL GARDENING

Grow the next
generation
of **gardeners**

© RHS/Georgi Mabee

Royal
Horticultural
Society

Sharing the best in Gardening

RHS in Scotland

Community Outreach Team
scotland@rhs.org.uk

rhs.org.uk /communities
Charity no: 222879/SCO38262

282

DEVENICK DESIGNS

GARDEN ART AND ACCESSORIES

Garden Art
Beautiful Products with elegant lines. All art work is designed and made by us in Scotland.
These unique and eye catching designs are unlike any other products on the market.
All items are easily positioned and transferrable enabling the art work to provide interest within different locations as the seasons change.

Garden Accessories
Give your plants support from the wind and rain with these fully welded steel frames that will literally last a lifetime. Manufactured in Scotland from 8mm and 10mm solid steel rod, they provide a robust solution to damage from the elements.

Contact : Jenny Corrigan Tel : 07478 672853
e mail : sales@devenickdesigns.co.uk
Website : www.devenickdesigns.co.uk

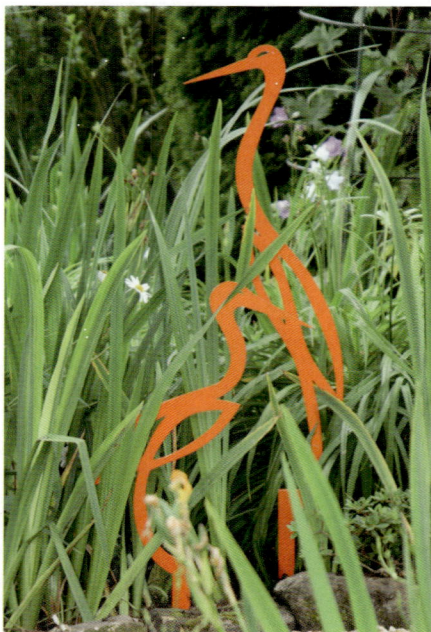

NEW HOPETOUN GARDENS

...so much more than just a garden centre

The perfect place for a relaxed visit at any time of year. Set in six acres of woodland with 20 small themed gardens to explore and probably the biggest range of garden plants for sale in Scotland. The Scottish Home of Miniature and Fairy Gardening.

The Orangery tearoom will revive you and the gift shop will tempt you with the most exciting range of presents for everyone.

Art in the garden runs during July and August and features original works of art by artists working in Scotland installed in the gardens.

(Entry is always free to our gardens.)

Welcome to Dougal Philip's
NEW HOPETOUN GARDENS

OPEN EVERY DAY 10.00AM – 5.30PM
New Hopetoun Gardens, by Winchburgh
West Lothian EH52 6QZ   01506 834433
www.newhopetoungardens.co.uk

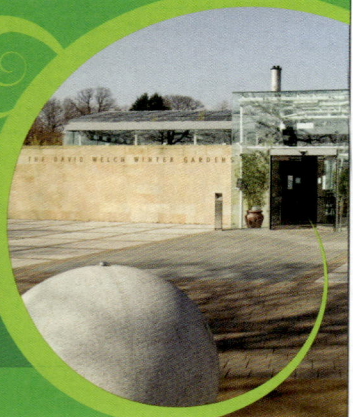

![Corney & Barrow logo] CORNEY & BARROW
INDEPENDENT WINE MERCHANTS 1780

THE A-Z OF PLANTS & WINE

ALBIZIA
Or Persian silk tree – match with a smooth, delicate classic Claret

BAOBAB
The tree of life – match with all giving Sauternes

CALLUNA
Heather originating in Azores – match with Ruby Port

DAISY
A wild flower – match with busty Malbec

EVERGREEN
Timeless appeal – match with reliable Sloe Gin

FEATHERED MAIDEN
A one year old tree – match with up and coming English Sparkling wine

GINKGO BILOBA
One of the oldest living tree species – match with an ageing Cabernet Sauvignon

HONEYSUCKLE
Opulent smelling flower – match with a flavoursome Chenin Blanc

IRIS
Graceful flower – match with an elegant Viognier

JASMINE
Deeply scented flower – match with an aromatic Muscat

KALMIA
Native to North America – match with sophisticated Canadian Ice Wine

LILIES
Symbolic and spiritual – match with organic Torrontes

MIMOSA
A beautiful yellow blossoming tree – match with a Mimosa Champagne cocktail

NUTMEG
Spicy fruit – match with a powerful Peruvian Syrah

ORCHID
A beautiful but temperamental flower – match with an oaky Grenache

PEONY
A pretty flower – match with an even prettier Picpoul de Pinet

QUERCUS
One of the most robust trees – match with an oaked Côte du Rhône

ROSE
The most classic and beautiful flower – match with a Provence style Rosé

SEQUOIA GIGANTEUM
Resistent to all the forces of nature – match with an ageing Châteauneuf-du-Pape

TULIP
An array of bright colours – match with an Australian Shiraz

ULEX
Common gorse, blooms all year round – match with a slender Semillon

VINE
Grows grapes which makes wine – match with fruity Pinot Noir

WISTERIA
Flowering plant originating in USA – match with a punchy Californian Zinfandel

XANTHOCERAS
Grown for its pinnate leaves and star-shaped flowers – match with a Gewurztraminer

YUCCA
Evergreen spikey shrub – match with a fortified Fino

ZZZZ
What you need after a busy day gardening – match with whatever is left in the wine rack

The Garden Conservancy's
Open Days Program

opendaysprogram.org

The Garden Conservancy has been opening America's very best, rarely seen, private gardens to the public through its Open Days program since 1995. Visit us online at opendaysprogram.org for more information.

Open Days is a program of the Garden Conservancy, a nonprofit organization dedicated to saving and sharing outstanding American gardens.

The Garden of Peter Bevacqua & Stephen King, Claverack, NY

BANKERS
Handelsbanken, 18 Charlotte Square,
Edinburgh EH2 4DF

SOLICITORS
J & H Mitchell WS, 51 Atholl Road,
Pitlochry PH16 5BU

ACCOUNTANTS
Douglas Home & Co,
47–49 The Square, Kelso TD5 7HW

Scotland's
GARDENS
Scheme
OPEN FOR CHARITY

SPECIFIC DATE GARDENS

FEBRUARY

Sunday 12 February
Perth & Kinross | Branklyn Garden 116 Dundee Road, Perth

Saturday 18 February
Ayrshire & Arran | Craufurdland Estate Nr Fenwick, Kilmarnock

Sunday 19 February
Ayrshire & Arran | Blair House, Blair Estate Dalry, Ayrshire
Dumfriesshire | Craig Langholm
Fife | Lindores House By Newburgh
Kirkcudbrightshire | Danevale Park Crossmichael

Saturday 25 February
Angus & Dundee | Dunninald Castle Montrose
East Lothian | Shepherd House Inveresk, Musselburgh

Sunday 26 February
Angus & Dundee | Dunninald Castle Montrose
Angus & Dundee | Langley Park Gardens Montrose
East Lothian | Shepherd House Inveresk, Musselburgh
Peeblesshire & Tweeddale | Kailzie Gardens Peebles
Perth & Kinross | Kilgraston School Bridge of Earn

MARCH

Saturday 4 March
Angus & Dundee | Dunninald Castle Montrose

Sunday 5 March
Angus & Dundee | Dunninald Castle Montrose
Angus & Dundee | Lawton House Inverkeilor, by Arbroath
Kincardine & Deeside | Ecclesgreig Castle St Cyrus
Lanarkshire | Cleghorn Stable House, Cleghorn Farm, Lanark

APRIL

Tuesday 11 April
Fife | NEW Fife Spring Trail Various locations across Fife

Wednesday 12 April
Fife | NEW Fife Spring Trail Various locations across Fife

Thursday 13 April
Fife | NEW Fife Spring Trail Various locations across Fife
Inverness, Ross, Cromarty & Skye | Dundonnell House Little Loch Broom, Wester Ross

Sunday 16 April
Aberdeenshire | Auchmacoy Ellon
Dunbartonshire | Kilarden Rosneath
East Lothian | Winton Castle Pencaitland
Fife | NEW Fife Spring Trail Various locations across Fife
Kirkcudbrightshire | 3 Millhall Shore Road, Kirkcudbright

Tuesday 18 April
Argyll & Lochaber   Crarae Garden Inveraray
Fife   NEW Fife Spring Trail Various locations across Fife

Wednesday 19 April
Fife   NEW Fife Spring Trail Various locations across Fife

Thursday 20 April
Fife   NEW Fife Spring Trail Various locations across Fife

Saturday 22 April
Moray & Nairn   Brodie Castle Brodie, Forres

Sunday 23 April
Aberdeenshire   Westhall Castle Oyne, Inverurie
Argyll & Lochaber   Benmore Botanic Garden Benmore, Dunoon
Argyll & Lochaber   Crarae Garden Inveraray
Moray & Nairn   Brodie Castle Brodie, Forres
Peeblesshire & Tweeddale   Bemersyde Melrose

Tuesday 25 April
Fife   NEW Fife Spring Trail Various locations across Fife

Wednesday 26 April
Fife   NEW Fife Spring Trail Various locations across Fife

Thursday 27 April
Fife   NEW Fife Spring Trail Various locations across Fife

Saturday 29 April
Renfrewshire   Kilmacolm Plant Sale outside Kilmacolm Library, Lochwinnoch Road

Sunday 30 April
Argyll & Lochaber   Arduaine Garden Oban
East Lothian   NEW Eastfield and Redcliff Gardens Whittingehame
Fife   Balcarres Colinsburgh
Perth & Kinross   The Steading at Clunie Newmill of Kinloch, Clunie, Blairgowrie
Stirlingshire   The Pass House Kilmahog, Callander
Wigtownshire   Claymoddie Garden Whithorn, Newton Stewart

MAY

Tuesday 2 May
Fife   NEW Fife Spring Trail Various locations across Fife

Wednesday 3 May
Ayrshire & Arran   Brodick Castle & Country Park Brodick, Isle of Arran

Thursday 4 May
Fife   NEW Fife Spring Trail Various locations across Fife

Friday 5 May
Fife   NEW Fife Spring Trail Various locations across Fife

Saturday 6 May
Aberdeenshire   Castle Fraser Garden Sauchen, Inverurie
Angus & Dundee   3 Balfour Cottages Menmuir
East Lothian   Shepherd House Inveresk, Musselburgh
Edinburgh, Midlothian & West Lothian   Dr Neil's Garden Duddingston Village
Perth & Kinross   Abernethy Open Gardens Abernethy

Sunday 7 May

Aberdeenshire	Castle Fraser Garden Sauchen, Inverurie
Angus & Dundee	Brechin Castle Brechin
Dumfriesshire	NEW Crawick Multiverse Crawick, Sanquhar
Dumfriesshire	Portrack, The Garden of Cosmic Speculation Holywood
East Lothian	Shepherd House Inveresk, Musselburgh
Edinburgh, Midlothian & West Lothian	Dr Neil's Garden Duddingston Village
Edinburgh, Midlothian & West Lothian	Redcroft 23 Murrayfield Road, Edinburgh
Kirkcudbrightshire	Threave Garden Castle Douglas
Perth & Kinross	Fingask Castle Rait
Stirlingshire	Little Broich Kippen
Wigtownshire	Logan House Gardens Port Logan, by Stranraer

Monday 8 May

Ayrshire & Arran	NEW Storytelling at Culzean Culzean, Maybole
Edinburgh, Midlothian & West Lothian	NEW Storytelling at Dr Neil's Garden Duddingston Village

Wednesday 10 May

Moray & Nairn	Balnabual Cottage Dalcross

Thursday 11 May

Angus & Dundee	Inchmill Cottage Glenprosen, nr Kirriemuir
Fife	NEW Fife Spring Trail Various locations across Fife

Saturday 13 May

Argyll & Lochaber	NEW Inveryne Woodland Garden Kilfinan, Tighnabruaich
Argyll & Lochaber	Dalnashean Port Appin, Appin
Inverness, Ross, Cromarty & Skye	Storytelling at Inverewe Garden Poolewe, Achnasheen

Sunday 14 May

Angus & Dundee	Dalfruin Kirktonhill Road, Kirriemuir
Argyll & Lochaber	NEW Inveryne Woodland Garden Kilfinan, Tighnabruaich
Argyll & Lochaber	Dalnashean Port Appin, Appin
Dumfriesshire	Dalswinton House Dalswinton
Dunbartonshire	High Glenan with Westburn Helensburgh
East Lothian	Tyninghame House and The Walled Garden Dunbar
Edinburgh, Midlothian & West Lothian	Moray Place and Bank Gardens Edinburgh
Fife	Willowhill, Tayfield and St Fort Woodland Garden Newport-on-Tay
Lanarkshire	NEW 5 Fergus Gardens Hamilton, South Lanarkshire
Perth & Kinross	Branklyn Garden 116 Dundee Road, Perth
Perth & Kinross	Machany House Auchterarder
Renfrewshire	Highwood off Lochwinnoch Road, Kilmacolm
Stirlingshire	Dun Dubh Kinlochard Road, Aberfoyle

Wednesday 17 May

Fife	NEW Fife Spring Trail Various locations across Fife
Inverness, Ross, Cromarty & Skye	Inverewe Garden and Estate Poolewe, Achnasheen
Moray & Nairn	Balnabual Cottage Dalcross

Saturday 20 May

Argyll & Lochaber	Maolachy's Garden Lochavich, by Taynuilt
Argyll & Lochaber	Strachur House Flower & Woodland Gardens Strachur
Ayrshire & Arran	The Wildings Bankwood, Galston
Renfrewshire	Barshaw Park Walled Garden 176A Glasgow Road, Paisley

Sunday 21 May

Argyll & Lochaber	Maolachy's Garden Lochavich, by Taynuilt
Argyll & Lochaber	Strachur House Flower & Woodland Gardens Strachur
Ayrshire & Arran	Craigengillan Estate and Scottish Dark Sky Observatory Dalmellington
Dunbartonshire	Ross Priory Gartocharn
Edinburgh, Midlothian & West Lothian	101 Greenbank Crescent Edinburgh
Fife	Earlshall Castle Leuchars
Fife	Kirklands Saline
Glasgow & District	Kilsyth Gardens Allanfauld Road, Kilsyth
Kincardine & Deeside	Inchmarlo House Garden Inchmarlo, Banchory
Perth & Kinross	NEW SGS Plant Sale at Pitcurran House Abernethy
Stirlingshire	Bridge of Allan Gardens Bridge of Allan
Wigtownshire	Logan Botanic Garden Port Logan, by Stranraer

Wednesday 24 May

Fife	NEW Fife Spring Trail Various locations across Fife
Moray & Nairn	Balnabual Cottage Dalcross
Peeblesshire & Tweeddale	Laidlawstiel House Clovenfords, Galashiels

Thursday 25 May

Angus & Dundee	Inchmill Cottage Glenprosen, nr Kirriemuir

Friday 26 May

Aberdeenshire	Airdlin Croft Ythanbank, Ellon

Saturday 27 May

Aberdeenshire	Airdlin Croft Ythanbank, Ellon
Aberdeenshire	Leith Hall Garden Huntly
Angus & Dundee	Gallery Walled Garden Gallery, by Montrose
Edinburgh, Midlothian & West Lothian	Balerno Lodge 36 Johnsburn Road, Balerno
Inverness, Ross, Cromarty & Skye	Old Allangrange Munlochy

Sunday 28 May

Angus & Dundee	Gallery Walled Garden Gallery, by Montrose
Argyll & Lochaber	Ardverikie with Aberarder Kinlochlaggan
Dumfriesshire	Cowhill Tower Holywood
Fife	46 South Street St Andrews
Fife	Lindores House By Newburgh
Inverness, Ross, Cromarty & Skye	Hugh Miller's Birthplace Cottage & Museum Church Street, Cromarty
Inverness, Ross, Cromarty & Skye	Novar Evanton
Kirkcudbrightshire	Corsock House Corsock, Castle Douglas
Peeblesshire & Tweeddale	Haystoun Peebles
Perth & Kinross	Bonhard House Perth
Renfrewshire	Carruth Bridge of Weir
Stirlingshire	Shrubhill Dunblane, Perthshire
Wigtownshire	Galloway House Gardens Garlieston, Newton Stewart

Thursday 1 June

Inverness, Ross, Cromarty & Skye	Dundonnell House Little Loch Broom, Wester Ross

JUNE

....

Friday 2 June

Inverness, Ross, Cromarty & Skye	Gorthleck House Garden Stratherrick

Saturday 3 June

Inverness, Ross, Cromarty & Skye	Gorthleck House Garden Stratherrick
Roxburghshire	NEW Thirlestane Kelso

Sunday 4 June

Aberdeenshire	Kildrummy Castle Gardens Alford
Ayrshire & Arran	1 Burnside Cottages Sundrum, Coylton
Dumfriesshire	Capenoch Penpont, Thornhill
East Lothian	Stenton Village East Lothian
Fife	Earlshall Castle Leuchars
Glasgow & District	Whittingehame Drive Gardens Glasgow
Kirkcudbrightshire	Barmagachan House Borgue, Kirkcudbright
Perth & Kinross	Explorers Garden Pitlochry
Perth & Kinross	Mill of Forneth Forneth, Blairgowrie
Roxburghshire	West Leas Bonchester Bridge
Stirlingshire	NEW The Japanese Garden at Cowden Dollar, Clackmannanshire

Monday 5 June

Inverness, Ross, Cromarty & Skye	Inverewe Garden and Estate Poolewe, Achnasheen

Thursday 8 June

Angus & Dundee	Inchmill Cottage Glenprosen, nr Kirriemuir
Kirkcudbrightshire	Broughton House Garden 12 High Street, Kirkcudbright

Saturday 10 June

Ayrshire & Arran	Holmes Farm Drybridge, by Irvine
Caithness, Sutherland, Orkney & Shetland	Amat Ardgay
East Lothian	Dirleton Village North Berwick
Fife	Newton Mains and Newton Barns Auchtermuchty
Fife	Old Inzievar House Oakley, Dunfermline
Glasgow & District	Greenbank Garden Flenders Road, Clarkston
Glasgow & District	Kirklee Circus 14 Kirklee Circus
Renfrewshire	Craig Hepburn Memorial Garden Stirling Drive, Linwood
Stirlingshire	The Mill House Kippen Road, Fintry, Stirlingshire

Sunday 11 June

Aberdeenshire	NEW Three Hidden Gardens Blairs, Westhill and Banchory-Devenick
Ayrshire & Arran	Holmes Farm Drybridge, by Irvine
Caithness, Sutherland, Orkney & Shetland	Amat Ardgay
Dumfriesshire	Glenae Amisfield
Dunbartonshire	Geilston Garden Main Road, Cardross
East Lothian	Dirleton Village North Berwick
Edinburgh, Midlothian & West Lothian	Temple Village Gardens Temple
Edinburgh, Midlothian & West Lothian	The Glasshouses at Royal Botanic Garden Edinburgh 20A Inverleith Row
Fife	Newton Mains and Newton Barns Auchtermuchty
Fife	Old Inzievar House Oakley, Dunfermline
Glasgow & District	Greenbank Garden Flenders Road, Clarkston
Inverness, Ross, Cromarty & Skye	Field House Belladrum, Beauly
Kincardine & Deeside	Kincardine Castle Kincardine O'Neil
Kirkcudbrightshire	NEW Linden Lea Islesteps, Dumfries
Lanarkshire	20 Smithycroft Hamilton
Moray & Nairn	10 Stuart Avenue Ardersier, Inverness
Peeblesshire & Tweeddale	NEW SGS Plant Sale at Halmyre Mains West Linton
Perth & Kinross	Muckhart Village Dollar
Stirlingshire	The Mill House Kippen Road, Fintry, Stirlingshire
Wigtownshire	Castle Kennedy and Gardens Stranraer

Monday 12 June

Stirlingshire	The Mill House Kippen Road, Fintry, Stirlingshire

Tuesday 13 June

Stirlingshire	The Mill House Kippen Road, Fintry, Stirlingshire

Wednesday 14 June

Peeblesshire & Tweeddale	Laidlawstiel House Clovenfords, Galashiels
Stirlingshire	The Mill House Kippen Road, Fintry, Stirlingshire

Thursday 15 June

Stirlingshire	The Mill House Kippen Road, Fintry, Stirlingshire

Friday 16 June

Stirlingshire	The Mill House Kippen Road, Fintry, Stirlingshire

Saturday 17 June

Argyll & Lochaber	The Shore Villages by Dunoon
Stirlingshire	The Mill House Kippen Road, Fintry, Stirlingshire
Wigtownshire	Balker Farmhouse Stranraer

Sunday 18 June

Aberdeenshire	Birken Cottage Burnhervie, Inverurie
Argyll & Lochaber	The Shore Villages by Dunoon
Ayrshire & Arran	Barnweil Garden Craigie, Nr Kilmarnock
East Lothian	Inveresk Village Musselburgh
Edinburgh, Midlothian & West Lothian	Dean Gardens Edinburgh
Fife	NEW Hidden Gardens of Newburgh Newburgh, Fife
Inverness, Ross, Cromarty & Skye	Glenkyllachy Tomatin
Kincardine & Deeside	Ecclesgreig Castle St Cyrus
Kincardine & Deeside	Finzean House Finzean, Banchory
Kirkcudbrightshire	Glenlivet Kirkcudbright
Kirkcudbrightshire	The Limes Kirkcudbright
Lanarkshire	Dippoolbank Cottage Carnwath
Stirlingshire	NEW Kippen Village West Stirlingshire
Stirlingshire	The Mill House Kippen Road, Fintry, Stirlingshire
Wigtownshire	Woodfall Gardens Glasserton

Tuesday 20 June

Stirlingshire	Gean House Tullibody Road, Alloa

Thursday 22 June

Angus & Dundee	Inchmill Cottage Glenprosen, nr Kirriemuir

Friday 23 June

Aberdeenshire	Airdlin Croft Ythanbank, Ellon
Dumfriesshire	NEW Kirkcaldy House Kirkcaldy, Burnsands, Thornhill

Saturday 24 June

Aberdeenshire	Airdlin Croft Ythanbank, Ellon
Angus & Dundee	Arbroath Collection of Gardens Locations across Arbroath
Ayrshire & Arran	Gardens of West Kilbride and Seamill West Kilbride
Edinburgh, Midlothian & West Lothian	NEW Open Gardens of the Lower New Town 24 Fettes Row
Perth & Kinross	Blair Castle Gardens Blair Atholl

Sunday 25 June

Aberdeenshire	Bruckhills Croft Rothienorman, Inverurie
Ayrshire & Arran	Blair House, Blair Estate Dalry, Ayrshire
Berwickshire	East Gordon Smiddy Gordon
Dumfriesshire	Newtonairds Lodge Newtonairds
East Lothian	Tyninghame House and The Walled Garden Dunbar
Edinburgh, Midlothian & West Lothian	14 East Brighton Crescent Portobello, Edinburgh
Edinburgh, Midlothian & West Lothian	Merchiston Cottage 16 Colinton Road, Edinburgh
Fife	Culross Palace Garden Culross
Fife	Strathmiglo Village Gardens Fife
Inverness, Ross, Cromarty & Skye	House of Aigas and Field Centre By Beauly
Kincardine & Deeside	Clayfolds Bridge of Muchalls, Stonehaven
Kirkcudbrightshire	Drumstinchall Cottage Drumstinchall, Dalbeattie
Kirkcudbrightshire	Drumstinchall House Drumstinchall, Dalbeattie
Stirlingshire	Thorntree Arnprior

Monday 26 June

Aberdeenshire	Bruckhills Croft Rothienorman, Inverurie

Tuesday 27 June

Aberdeenshire	Bruckhills Croft Rothienorman, Inverurie

Wednesday 28 June

Aberdeenshire	Bruckhills Croft Rothienorman, Inverurie

Thursday 29 June

Aberdeenshire	Bruckhills Croft Rothienorman, Inverurie
Aberdeenshire	Leith Hall Garden Huntly
Kirkcudbrightshire	Broughton House Garden 12 High Street, Kirkcudbright

Friday 30 June

Aberdeenshire	Bruckhills Croft Rothienorman, Inverurie
Dumfriesshire	NEW Kirkcaldy House Kirkcaldy, Burnsands, Thornhill

Saturday 1 July

Aberdeenshire	NEW Parkvilla 47 Schoolhill, Ellon
Ayrshire & Arran nock	Netherthird Community Garden Craigens Road, Netherthird, Cum-
Perth & Kinross	The Bield at Blackruthven Blackruthven House, Tibbermore
Roxburghshire	Corbet Tower Morebattle, Near Kelso

JULY

Sunday 2 July

Aberdeenshire	NEW Parkvilla 47 Schoolhill, Ellon
Ayrshire & Arran	NEW Glendoune House Walled Garden Coalpots Road, Girvan
Berwickshire	Lennel Bank Coldstream
Fife	Backhouse at Rossie Estate By Collessie
Glasgow & District	Strathbungo Garden March Street
Kirkcudbrightshire	Southwick House Southwick
Peeblesshire & Tweeddale	Glen House Glen Estate, Innerleithen
Perth & Kinross	Wester Cloquhat Bridge of Cally

Tuesday 4 July

Ayrshire & Arran	Dougarie Isle of Arran

Wednesday 5 July

Kincardine & Deeside	Drum Castle Garden Drumoak, by Banchory

Thursday 6 July

Angus & Dundee — Inchmill Cottage Glenprosen, nr Kirriemuir

Friday 7 July

Dumfriesshire — NEW Kirkcaldy House Kirkcaldy, Burnsands, Thornhill

Saturday 8 July

Angus & Dundee — Hospitalfield Gardens Hospitalfield House, Westway, Arbroath
Inverness, Ross, Cromarty & Skye — Torcroft Balnain, Glenurquhart

Sunday 9 July

Berwickshire — NEW Coldstream Open Gardens Coldstream Community Centre,
High Street, Coldstream
Dumfriesshire — Whiteside Dunscore
East Lothian — Gifford Village and Broadwoodside Gifford
Fife — NEW Lathrisk Gardens Lathrisk
Inverness, Ross, Cromarty & Skye — Torcroft Balnain, Glenurquhart
Kirkcudbrightshire — Seabank The Merse, Rockcliffe
Lanarkshire — NEW Symington House By Biggar
Moray & Nairn — 10 Pilmuir Road West Forres
Peeblesshire & Tweeddale — West Linton Village Gardens West Linton
Roxburghshire — Yetholm Village Gardens Town Yetholm
Wigtownshire — Woodfall Gardens Glasserton

Wednesday 12 July

Aberdeenshire — Cruickshank Botanic Gardens 23 St Machar Drive, Aberdeen
Kincardine & Deeside — Drum Castle Garden Drumoak, by Banchory
Perth & Kinross — NEW Errol Park Errol

Saturday 15 July

Fife — Crail: Small Gardens in the Burgh Crail
Inverness, Ross, Cromarty & Skye — Malin Glenaldie, Tain
Moray & Nairn — NEW Gordon Castle Walled Garden Fochabers, Moray

Sunday 16 July

Aberdeenshire — Drumrossie Mansion House Insch
Angus & Dundee — NEW Melgund Castle Melgund, Aberlemno, Brechin
Ayrshire & Arran — NEW Clover Park Langdyke, Waterside, Kilmarnock
Dumfriesshire — Amisfield Tower Amisfield
Fife — Crail: Small Gardens in the Burgh Crail
Fife — Falkland Palace and Garden Falkland, Cupar
Inverness, Ross, Cromarty & Skye — Malin Glenaldie, Tain
Kincardine & Deeside — Douneside House Tarland

Wednesday 19 July

Kincardine & Deeside — Drum Castle Garden Drumoak, by Banchory
Perth & Kinross — NEW Errol Park Errol

Thursday 20 July

Angus & Dundee — Inchmill Cottage Glenprosen, nr Kirriemuir

Saturday 22 July

Aberdeenshire — Middle Cairncake Cuminestown, Turriff
Angus & Dundee — Gallery Walled Garden Gallery, by Montrose
Ayrshire & Arran — Whitewin House Golf Course Road, Girvan
Caithness, Sutherland, Orkney & Shetland — NEW The Gardens of Dornoch Dornoch
Edinburgh, Midlothian & West Lothian — Rivaldsgreen House 48 Friars Brae, Linlithgow.
Peeblesshire & Tweeddale — Harmony and Priorwood Gardens St Mary's Road, Melrose

Sunday 23 July

Aberdeenshire	Middle Cairncake Cuminestown, Turriff
Angus & Dundee	NEW The Gardens of Brechin Locations across Brechin
Angus & Dundee	Gallery Walled Garden Gallery, by Montrose
Ayrshire & Arran	Whitewin House Golf Course Road, Girvan
Berwickshire	NEW Marlfield and Ruthven Gardens Coldstream
Edinburgh, Midlothian & West Lothian	Hunter's Tryst 95 Oxgangs Road, Edinburgh
Fife	Tayport Gardens Tayport
Inverness, Ross, Cromarty & Skye	2 Durnamuck Little Loch Broom, Wester Ross
Inverness, Ross, Cromarty & Skye	NEW Kiltarlity Gardens Kiltarlity
Kincardine & Deeside	Findrack Torphins
Kirkcudbrightshire	Crofts Kirkpatrick Durham, Castle Douglas
Lanarkshire	Dippoolbank Cottage Carnwath
Peeblesshire & Tweeddale	Gattonside Village Gardens Gattonside
Peeblesshire & Tweeddale	Harmony and Priorwood Gardens St Mary's Road, Melrose
Roxburghshire	NEW West Summerfield Rosalee Brae, Hawick
Wigtownshire	Fernlea Garden Newton Stewart

Wednesday 26 July

Kincardine & Deeside	Drum Castle Garden Drumoak, by Banchory
Perth & Kinross	NEW Errol Park Errol

Thursday 27 July

Aberdeenshire	Leith Hall Garden Huntly

Saturday 29 July

Angus & Dundee	The Herbalist's Garden at Logie Logie House, Kirriemuir
Ayrshire & Arran	Whitewin House Golf Course Road, Girvan
Edinburgh, Midlothian & West Lothian	45 Northfield Crescent Longridge, Bathgate
Kincardine & Deeside	Crathes Castle Garden Banchory

Sunday 30 July

Angus & Dundee	The Herbalist's Garden at Logie Logie House, Kirriemuir
Argyll & Lochaber	Ardchattan Priory North Connel
Ayrshire & Arran	Whitewin House Golf Course Road, Girvan
Edinburgh, Midlothian & West Lothian	45 Northfield Crescent Longridge, Bathgate
Inverness, Ross, Cromarty & Skye	NEW 5 Knott Clachamish, Portree, Isle of Skye
Inverness, Ross, Cromarty & Skye	House of Aigas and Field Centre By Beauly
Lanarkshire	Wellbutts Elsrickle, by Biggar
Moray & Nairn	Glenrinnes Lodge Dufftown, Keith, Banffshire
Roxburghshire	West Leas Bonchester Bridge
Stirlingshire	The Tors 2 Slamannan Road, Falkirk

AUGUST

Saturday 5 August

Ayrshire & Arran	Whitewin House Golf Course Road, Girvan
East Lothian	Greywalls Gullane
Edinburgh, Midlothian & West Lothian	39 Nantwich Drive Edinburgh

Sunday 6 August

Aberdeenshire	Middle Cairncake Cuminestown, Turriff
Angus & Dundee	Montrose Gardens Montrose
Ayrshire & Arran	Whitewin House Golf Course Road, Girvan
Dumfriesshire	NEW Dalswinton Mill Dalswinton, Dumfries
Edinburgh, Midlothian & West Lothian	Craigentinny and Telferton Allotments Telferton Road, Edinburgh
Kincardine & Deeside	Glenbervie House Drumlithie, Stonehaven

Kirkcudbrightshire	Threave Garden Castle Douglas
Lanarkshire	NEW Viewpark Allotments and Gardens Bairds Avenue, Viewpark
Peeblesshire & Tweeddale	Peebles Gardens Peebles
Perth & Kinross	Drummond Castle Gardens Crieff

Monday 7 August

| Caithness, Sutherland, Orkney & Shetland | Langwell Berriedale |

Thursday 10 August

| Angus & Dundee | Inchmill Cottage Glenprosen, nr Kirriemuir |

Saturday 12 August

Ayrshire & Arran	Whitewin House Golf Course Road, Girvan
Fife	The Tower 1 Northview Terrace, Wormit
Lanarkshire	Old Farm Cottage The Ladywell, Nemphlar, Lanark

Sunday 13 August

Aberdeenshire	Middle Cairncake Cuminestown, Turriff
Aberdeenshire	Pitmedden Garden Ellon
Ayrshire & Arran	Whitewin House Golf Course Road, Girvan
Edinburgh, Midlothian & West Lothian	101 Greenbank Crescent Edinburgh
Kincardine & Deeside	Fasque House Fettercairn, Laurencekirk
Kirkcudbrightshire	NEW Dalbeattie Community Allotments Association Port Road, Dalbeattie
Lanarkshire	Old Farm Cottage The Ladywell, Nemphlar, Lanark

Thursday 17 August

| Inverness, Ross, Cromarty & Skye | Dundonnell House Little Loch Broom, Wester Ross |

Saturday 19 August

Angus & Dundee	12 Glamis Drive Dundee
Fife	Kellie Castle with Balcaskie Pittenweem
Inverness, Ross, Cromarty & Skye	Old Allangrange Munlochy

Sunday 20 August

Angus & Dundee	12 Glamis Drive Dundee
Edinburgh, Midlothian & West Lothian	NEW Whitburgh House Walled Garden Pathhead, Midlothian
Fife	Kellie Castle with Balcaskie Pittenweem
Inverness, Ross, Cromarty & Skye	2 Durnamuck Little Loch Broom, Wester Ross
Inverness, Ross, Cromarty & Skye	NEW Kilcoy Castle Redcastle, by Muir of Ord
Lanarkshire	Culter Allers Coulter, Biggar

Monday 21 August

| Edinburgh, Mid othian & West Lothian | NEW Whitburgh House Walled Garden Pathhead, Midlothian |

Tuesday 22 August

| Edinburgh, Midlothian & West Lothian | NEW Whitburgh House Walled Garden Pathhead, Midlothian |

Thursday 24 August

| Angus & Dundee | Inchmill Cottage Glenprosen, nr Kirriemuir |

Saturday 26 August

| Aberdeenshire | Leith Hall Garden Huntly |
| Fife | Blebo Craigs Village Gardens Cupar |

Sunday 27 August

Fife	Blebo Craigs Village Gardens Cupar
Peeblesshire & Tweeddale	8 Halmyre Mains West Linton
Renfrewshire	NEW Bravehound - Erskine Hospital Old Garden Centre, Bishopton

SEPTEMBER

Saturday 2 September

Angus & Dundee   Angus Plant Sale Logie Walled Garden, Logie

Glasgow & District   Horatio's Gardens Queen Elizabeth Hospital

Sunday 3 September

Dunbartonshire   Hill House Plant Sale Helensburgh

Edinburgh, Midlothian & West Lothian   NEW Belgrave Crescent Gardens Edinburgh

Glasgow & District   NEW The Good Life Gardens 12 & 14 Chatelherault Avenue

Kirkcudbrightshire   3 Millhall Shore Road, Kirkcudbright

Moray & Nairn   Gordonstoun Duffus, near Elgin

Stirlingshire   Rowberrow 18 Castle Road, Dollar

Thursday 7 September

Angus & Dundee   Inchmill Cottage Glenprosen, nr Kirriemuir

Saturday 9 September

Ayrshire & Arran   Netherthird Community Garden Craigens Road, Netherthird, Cumnock

Sunday 10 September

Inverness, Ross, Cromarty & Skye   2 Durnamuck Little Loch Broom, Wester Ross

Sunday 17 September

Stirlingshire   Kilbryde Castle Dunblane

Thursday 21 September

Angus & Dundee   Inchmill Cottage Glenprosen, nr Kirriemuir

Saturday 30 September

Aberdeenshire   Tarland Community Garden Aboyne

Sunday 1 October

Aberdeenshire   Kildrummy Castle Gardens Alford

Fife   Hill of Tarvit Plant Sale and Autumn Fair Hill of Tarvit, Cupar

OCTOBER

Sunday 8 October

Inverness, Ross, Cromarty & Skye   Glenkyllachy Tomatin

Peeblesshire & Tweeddale   Dawyck Botanic Garden Stobo

Thursday 12 October

Perth & Kinross   NEW Storytelling at Fingask Rait

Sunday 22 October

Dumfriesshire   NEW Storytelling at Dalswinton Dalswinton

INDEX OF GARDENS

ORDER YOUR GUIDEBOOK FOR 2019

The first Scotland's Gardens Scheme Guidebook was created in 1932, and it has become the 'go to' guide for garden visitors in Scotland ever since. So, don't co without your copy in 2019!

Order now and your copy will be posted to you on publication Fill in the form below and send to: Scotland's Gardens Scheme, 23 Castle Street, Edinburgh EH2 3DN

" **The daffodil-coloured tome of horticultural promise"**

Joanna, Edinburgh Garden Diary

"Supporting your community through local charities"

✂

Scotland's
GARDENS
Scheme
OPEN FOR CHARITY

Please send me _____ copy / copies of our Guidebook for 2019, price £5.00 plus £2.00 UK p&p, as soon as it is available.

I enclose a cheque / postal order made payable to Scotland's Gardens Scheme.

Name _____

Address _____

_____

Postcode _____

WELCOMING YOU IN 2019

Scotland's Gardens Scheme, 23 Castle Street, Edinburgh EH2 3DN
Copies of our Guidebook for 2018 may also be purchased on our website: **www.scotlandsgardens.org**

TIPS FOR USING YOUR GUIDEBOOK

NEW Gardens open for the first time, or after a long break.

Feeling a bit peckish? Enjoy a spot of tea? So do we, which is why many of our gardens give a range of refreshments, at an extra charge:

Basic teas

Cream teas

Homemade teas

Refreshments

Bring your dog (on a lead please)

Wheelchair accessibility (full or partial)

Plants will be for sale at the opening. This is a fantastic opportunity to find locally grown plants for your garden

These gardens will offer family friendly children's activities, varying from quizzes, identification exercises to hands-on projects

These gardens are participating in the Scottish Snowdrop Festival so don't miss a chance to get out for a brisk winter walk

These gardens can be accessed via public transport, details can be found either in the directions section or with a map navigation app

Gardens can also be the site of special features, including:

Champion trees, from the UK Tree Register

NPC National plant collection, from Plant Heritage

Gardens and Designed landscapes by Historic Environment Scotland

Your guidebook is packed with information about garden open days for you to visit. It's organised alphabetically by geographical district (often the county). Here at the back of the book is a fold out map which will help you to locate these districts across the map of Scotland. You'll see that we also use colour coding to highlight our regions.

Most of our Garden Openers elect to raise money for their own nominated charity(s) for up to 60% of their net takings. These nominated charities are listed within each opening description. Some Openers donate all their takings to support our beneficiaries. And a few open commercially and provide us with a donation. After the nominated charity donation, the net remainder is designated for our beneficiaries, highlighted on pages 10-17.